The Right *Not* To Remain Silent

✦

Living Morally in a Complex World

Rabbi Jack Stern

iUniverse, Inc.

New York Lincoln Shanghai

The Right *Not* To Remain Silent
Living Morally in a Complex World

iUniverse books may be ordered through booksellers or by contacting:

iUniverse
2021 Pine Lake Road, Suite 100
Lincoln, NE 68512
www.iuniverse.com
1-800-Authors (1-800-288-4677)

ISBN-13: 978-0-595-39461-6 (pbk)
ISBN-13: 978-0-595-67710-8 (cloth)
ISBN-13: 978-0-595-83859-2 (ebk)
ISBN-10: 0-595-39461-2 (pbk)
ISBN-10: 0-595-67710-X (cloth)
ISBN-10: 0-595-83859-6 (ebk)

Printed in the United States of America

To my feisty and gallant
Priscilla
of blessed memory
for our forty-three precious years
of life and love together,
and for the family
we have been blessed to share

Contents

Foreword. xv

Introduction xvii

Questions of Our Faith

What Is Faith?. 3

The Jewish Sense of Time 8

Faith, Humor and Silence. 13

Sacred Moments 17

When Bad Things Happen to Good People 22

The Secular and the Sacred 26

Spiritual Energy 31

Our Shared Humanity

On Being a Survivor 39

The Nature of Being Human 43

Voyagers 49

In the Image of God 54

Loneliness 59

Power 64

Human Power to Change the World. .68

Anger. 73

The Feeling of Guilt 78

A Gift for Creativity

Our Tradition of Creativity. 85

Creativity and the State of Israel 90

Creative Remembering 96

Gates of Opportunity 99

Reform Judaism

A New Prayer Book—A New Year. 107

This Most Amazing Day 112

Who Will Live and Who Will Die. 117

Reform and Orthodoxy Together 122

Jewish Dilemmas

The Problems of Power 129

Future Shock. 134

The Day of Remembering 140

Kurt Waldheim and Jewish Morality. 145

Beyond Auschwitz. 151

Israel

A Plea for Peace. 159

The State of Israel: Jewish Morality and Jewish Power. 164

Addendum on Israel and Beirut. 170

Anti-Semitism and Israel 172

The Jewish Sense of Family

Parent to Parent 181

Mixed Marriage. 186

The Jewish Sense of Family. 192

A Message to Our Children. 197

A Time for Renewal 203

Ethical Wills 209

A People of Conscience

Why Is a Jew? 217

Success and Failure 222

The Need to Speak of Sin 226

The Plight of a Liberal 230

Religion and Politics 236

Sacred Voting 242

I Am Seeking My Brothers 247

Living Morally in a Complex World

The Possible Meaning of Entebbe. 257

Lying and Other Moral Conflicts 262

The Uses of Power 268

Beyond the Contract. 273

The Meaning of Sacrifice 280

Obstacles. 284

Jewish Names in Public Scandals 289

Personal Jewish Morality 294

Living with Ambiguity 300

The Right Not to Remain Silent 307

The Book of Life

Remembering 313

Precious Gifts 315

The Mystery of Death 318

To Weep, to Be Silent, to Sing 322

Memory and Melody 325

Mind the Light 327

At the End of the Day 330

The Lonely Climb 332

National Leadership

Installation As CCAR President 337

President's Message, 1986 340

President's Message, 1987 349

Milestones

Caring 367

Twenty-Five Years 372

What My Teachers Have Taught Me 377

To the Next Rabbi 383

Spiritual Aging 389
Trying to Be a Mensch 395

Walk with me into the woods
Leave the edge of the forest behind—

Come deep into the green
until the shafts of
sunlight are lost.
Feel the stillness of
the center.

Walk with me to the top
Of the hill.
Leave the broad path
behind.
Up—up beyond where
the trees grow.
Hear the quiet of
the heights.

Walk with me into
this New Year—
Into its demands
Into its joys
Into the clamor of
its unfolding.

Walk alone
each on her own right
path
With the echoes of the
blasts of the *shofar*
With the stillness of the
center
With the help of our God.

—Priscilla Rudin Stern

Foreword

When Rabbi Richard Jacobs first approached me with the idea for this book, I was less than enthusiastic (an understatement). When he assured me that my only responsibility would be to make available these three decades of sermons and that a committee would do its own selecting and editing, only then did I accede to his gentle but persistent suasions.

The reason for my reluctance was neither ingratitude nor modesty; rather it had to do with the way I view myself as a person and as a rabbi. I have always thought of myself as a communicator, but not by way of the written word, rather of the spoken one. Writing has never come easily to me; I am much more comfortable speaking. Yet I realized early on that for a message to be communicated by voice, the words first had to be put down on paper. Concision was the goal, along with a discriminating vocabulary; sentences had to be crafted, paragraphs constructed. The entire process was often a painful ordeal but a necessary one. In order to communicate orally the challenging insights of our Jewish tradition, the message first had to be hammered out by hand on yellow legal pads.

And another hesitation: When a book is printed, the words are permanently stamped in black letters on white paper—a suggestion of validity for the future. For me, however, each sermon belongs to the time and circumstances immediately at hand, to be explored under the lens of what our Jewish faith and tradition are ready to teach us, what the existentialists call "the living moment." As such, it makes no claim to future validity, but if, by chance, a sermon offers some insight that extends to some future "living moment," so much the better.

My loving gratitude goes out to those who helped make it possible for these sermons to enjoy a second hearing in black and white: to my three children, Jonathan, David and Elsie, who unfailingly make me think and make me laugh; to Rabbi Richard Jacobs, former rabbinic intern and now my successor at Westchester Reform Temple; to those rabbinic colleagues who at one time or another kept the fires burning at WRT and never let my life get boring: Rabbi Deborah Zecher (now my rabbi), Rabbi Beth Singer and Rabbi Aaron Panken; to Rabbi Nancy Kasten (happily, also my daughter-in-law); and to my constant friend Steve Schnur, who assumed a major share of the responsibility in the editorial process. And, of course, none of this would have come to pass without the congregants who have lent their ears to the words and sometimes have even argued with them.

I thank my dear friend Al Vorspan, who, with his unique gift for both the written and the spoken word, has graced this book with his introduction—hyperbole and all—which I thoroughly enjoyed. Al and Shirley have been mainstays in my life.

Lastly and mostly, to my Priscilla, of blessed memory, who always recognized when a sermon was good and when it wasn't. I always valued and respected her critique, even when I didn't appreciate hearing it. Without Priscilla's love and inspiration many of the pages of this book would have remained empty.

To those who may decide to read through some of these black-and-white pages, I ask one favor: Hear the voice, join with me in conversation, even if you choose to argue with what I am trying to say. For whatever you may think or feel in response to these pages, your active engagement carries on the tradition of our Jewish give-and-take, of our people's ongoing dialogue that "has kept us alive and sustained us and brought us to this day."

Jack Stern
Great Barrington, MA
February 15, 2006

Introduction

I was honored to be asked to write a brief introduction to this volume of sermons by Rabbi Jack Stern, but I did wonder, Why me? The answer, on reflection, was obvious. Jack and I are dear friends, live near each other in the Berkshires, attend the same shul and share many interests in politics, culture and Jewish life. But more to the point, Jack and I long ago agreed to give each other's eulogies. Only one of us will have to deliver, of course, but we both have to prepare. So it is understandable that when Jack's oldest son, Jonathan, called on behalf of Jack's three children (son David and daughter Elsie), he said, "Look, this will be easier for you than anybody else. You have already done your research, and you get to try out your material." He's right. It is a great relief and a pleasure for me to be using this material for a book introduction rather than a eulogy. A book is a new birth, a baby sounding off in a new world, so we do not eulogize: We celebrate and we say mazal tov to the author and to the midwives who helped deliver the new life.

Many years ago, when I spoke at Westchester Reform Temple at Jack's invitation, I told the congregation that although I am a layperson, I probably know more about rabbis than any other Jewish layperson in the country. My job at the Union of American Hebrew Congregations (now the Union for Reform Judaism) required constant visits to synagogues all over the country. Not only are some of my best friends rabbis, all of my best friends are rabbis. Several of my humor books are about rabbis, and one was even titled *My Rabbi Doesn't Make House Calls*. So I told Rabbi Stern's congregation, in all honesty, that I believed their rabbi was one of the three best rabbis in the Reform rabbinate. Rabbi Stern had barely concluded the benediction when the late Priscilla Stern, feisty wife of the rabbi, descended upon me. "So, who are the other two?" she demanded.

In a career of more than fifty years of Jewish organizational life, I have listened to thousands of sermons, including my own. I have heard a few heart-pounding, electrifying oratorical barn burners, but they occurred mostly in an earlier generation. The age of theatrical oratory is mostly over. Jack Stern never belonged to that pyrotechnic, pulpit-pounding school of oratory. What is characteristic of a Jack Stern sermon is that it is a thoughtful conversation with fellow Jews assembled in a congregation. It is a sermon, but it is not a monologue; it honors and respects the thoughtful congregant on the receiving end. It is a dialogue of sorts. It is the distilled and carefully considered wisdom of a man who has lived a long life and learned much from its vicissitudes. It is never ad-libbed, never a frothy playback of the morning's newspaper editorials.

A Stern sermon is an expression of wisdom that derives from the joys and sufferings of his own life. Martin Luther King, Jr., once said that nobody can be fully human who has not endured a broken heart. Jack has endured more than his fair share of pain, having suffered through fifteen operations (at current count), beginning with his first at age five. A life of chronic disability did not drive him to negativism, cynicism or despair. It helped shape his character. And that character—strong, positive, loving, resilient, courageous and wise—infuses these sermons. The best sermon is a well-lived life. The best Jewish sermon is a reflection of wisdom forged by real-life experiences and infused with the ancient-modern wisdom of Jewish tradition. That is Jack Stern.

The sermons in this volume, like Jack himself, face life with courage. They do not offer simple panaceas to complex dilemmas or obscurantist escapes from political or private reality. They are grounded in sensitivity and reverence for Jewish ethical values. They have no patience for solipsistic spirituality or grandiose theologies that reduce the human voice and conscience to empty puppetry. Like their author, they are brave and funny, affectionate and sensitive. Reading the best of Jack Stern's sermons is as refreshing and stimulating and invigorating as having lunch with him. Because he is a good man, his book is a good read. My rabbi not only makes house calls, he makes sermons that are worth reading and that, like the author, wear very well indeed.

The sermons selected for this volume were delivered mostly on the High Holy Days during Rabbi Stern's twenty-nine years as rabbi of Westchester Reform Temple in Scarsdale, New York, and they range from the meaning of God to the secrets of Jewish survival, the essence of Reform Judaism, and the evolving relationship between American Jewry and Israel, but they also zero in on such timely subjects as the need for pluralism in an Orthodox-monopolized Israel and such live issues in America today as racial injustice, church-state separation and abuses of power by government and corporation. If there is a motif that gleams through most of these sermons, it is the imperative of ethical accountability in every institution. When he was president of the Central Conference of American Rabbis, this was one of Rabbi Stern's major themes, and it resulted in a system that dealt with ethical issues in the rabbinate and within congregations (including decent conditions for custodial help and health benefits for all synagogue employees) as well as in a society stained by repeated business and political scandal. For Rabbi

Stern, Judaism is much more than an ethical imperative, but a Judaism that neglects the ethical commandments is an empty vessel. Also included, happily, in this volume, is one of Rabbi Stern's presidential addresses, which, like his High Holy Day sermons to his own congregants, brims with challenges that do not seem to come down from lofty, prophetic heights, standing ten feet above contradiction, but from a good and wise man conversing with his peers about serious matters that he takes seriously while, remarkably, never taking himself too seriously.

Someone once said that it doesn't matter which denomination you belong to as long as you are properly ashamed of it. Jack Stern respects all denominations of Judaism—he glories in the creativity of the Jewish people—but he is especially proud to be a Reform Jew. He is proud of the major institutions of Reform Judaism and has played a vital role in the Central Conference of American Rabbis, the Hebrew Union College—Jewish Institute of Religion and the Union for Reform Judaism—the rabbinic, educational and congregational arms of American Reform Judaism. He is not only a strong voice of the Reform Movement but has played and continues to play a significant role in the shaping of Liberal Judaism worldwide.

Priscilla Stern, had she lived, would have written this introduction, for she was Jack's best and most loving critic. But Jack Stern is a rabbi who has earned the love and respect of not only a doting family but hundreds of rabbinic colleagues and thousands of former congregants. Young Reform rabbis, contemporaries of his son, Rabbi David Stern, see Jack as the link between generations. The qualities of mind and heart that have gained him such widespread respect and admiration are embedded in these sermons as well. A caring committee selected these sermons from among the hundreds he delivered during his more than fifty years in the rabbinate, including scathing sermons demanding civil rights for all Americans drawn from his own experiences fighting segregation in Mississippi, impassioned probings into the mysteries of death, the ambiguities of religious and political policies in Israel, the directions of the Reform Jewish Movement, the blessing and the curse in the hunt for spirituality, and Jewish contributions to America and to the civilized world.

The sermons that follow are often challenging, but they are always fair. They are not self-righteous and do not offer facile answers. They are thoughtful, reflective, sensitive, often funny, proudly Jewish and deeply human. In the end, the only sermon worth listening to, much less rereading, is one that reflects a good life. What good is oratorical lightning if it comes from an empty vessel? Jack Stern's sermons are rooted in his character. They are crafted with infinite care.

And they reveal not only a love for the life of the mind but also a profound respect for Jewish values and, strikingly, for his congregants, fellow Jews with whom he is linked in community and dialogue. So read them already!

Al Vorspan

Questions of Our Faith

What Is Faith?

On an evening like this one, hundreds of years ago, congregations would assemble for *Kol Nidrei* in darkened basements, away from the watchful eye of the Inquisitor and the police. And in each of these clusters of worshipers, there were usually a few who had deserted the faith of their fathers, for reasons of safety and for reasons of opportunity. But as the Holy Days approached, the power of *Kol Nidrei* was strong enough to draw them back. They walked into the synagogue for these few hours, they took off their masks, they owned up to who they were. For these few hours, they felt impelled to tell the truth.

And thus it has ever been, something about the pleading urgency of a melody that calls the Jew back from wherever he is and from whatever he is doing to stand with his congregation, to stand with his people, to stand on trial before God and tell the truth.

But we Jews are a strange paradox, which may be part of our charm. At *Kol Nidrei*, we are ready to stand on trial in the synagogue. The rest of the year, we put the synagogue on trial, or Judaism on trial, or God on trial.

It can be seen in the sprouting up of *chavurot*, small groups of young people who are eager to engage seriously in the Jewish quest, but who have been unable to discover within the synagogue the kind of quest that is suited to their needs and their interests.

It can be seen in the proliferation of research studies on the role of the synagogue in the life of its members, or in a cutting question that was asked in *Commentary* magazine by Milton Himmelfarb: "How can I be a good Jew despite the obstacles put in my way by the synagogue?" It can be seen in the criticisms of the service, the prayer book, the rabbi. One group demanded that the rabbi doff his clerical robe and conduct the service from floor level, in the midst of the congregation.

One complaint seems to course through all of the criticism: that the faith of Judaism is not modern enough, that it does not speak to the Jew of today, that it does not capture his imagination nor grip his feelings nor stoke the furnace of his intellect.

3

What are the critics really saying? Are they speaking of form? Or is it content? On this evening of self-searching and truth, let me share with you what I have gleaned from members of this congregation, including some younger ones, and what I have learned from some colleagues in the rabbinate, including some younger ones.

Partly it *is* form. The language of many passages in the *Union Prayer Book* is borrowed from the Jewish Publication Society version of the Bible, which is borrowed from the King James Version of the Bible, which was written in England in 1611. In the opinion of some, if we could alter the form, change "hath" to "has" and "brethren" to "brothers" and "Thou" to "You"—then we would be taking the first step with which every long journey must begin.

There are others who argue that changes in word style are not enough. Modern man has become so conditioned by the multitude of media that the written and spoken word have lost some of their power to evoke a response. Modern man needs stronger stimuli than mere verbiage. If, they say, aside from updating the words, some of those words and some of those sentences could be converted into pictures and sounds—then we would be that much closer to a religious experience.

I share that hope, but with one caveat: that while so-called religious experiences may be recognized as part of a religious faith, they are not *tantamount* to a religious faith. The observant Jew worships faithfully three times a day, and you can be sure that each time is not a stirring religious experience. It may be that one of the tests of faith is its ability to withstand the absence of a stirring religious experience.

A member of a former congregation once said to me; "Whenever I go to temple, I want to be *sent*"—and I suggested that she join some other congregation.

Modernize the words, update the form, but there is still the content to consider. Even after we prepare the special readings to gear a portion of the service to this contemporary moment in history, there is still the idea of God to consider. Abraham Heschel contends that the problem for the modern Jew is not prayer but God.

There are some who feel that the personal God of the *Union Prayer Book* is not for them: a God who is said to hear prayer and answer it, who revives our drooping spirits, who upholds the sorrowing and heals the sick, the Father who forgives—such a paternalistic concept is not for them. Their God is a force moving through the panoply of nature, coursing through the events of history: a natural force and a moral force, who directs no attention to me individually; not personal God to personal man, but a force who is accessible to me as power, as strength, to the degree that I reach out for that strength and power. And if I do and become strong enough to acknowledge my misdeeds, to stand in judgment before this highest level of morality, and strive for that level—*thus* do I return to God and *thus* do I perceive the power of forgiveness.

Teach that kind of God, they say, modernize the theology, they say, and then there would be a modern faith for modern man.

The fact is that Judaism has always been receptive to different ideas of God. The rationalist Maimonides is in the same prayer book as the mystical song of *L'chah Dodi*. The truth is that nobody knows the truth. God *is*, says Judaism, but no one knows what He is like. The truth is that traditionalist or modernist, both are potentially men of faith. And both are potentially men without faith—for there is still the question of faith to consider.

What is faith, according to the Jewish definition? Faith is a hypothesis that all of the jumbled pieces of life, all of the sunlight and all of the storm clouds, the living and the dying, all that we understand and all of which we are ignorant—all are of one piece, joined together by a thread of meaning, by a Presence that calls us to live our lives with meaning, with justice, with mercy, with feeling.

It cannot be absolutely proven. It is admittedly a postulate based upon evidence, but not conclusively. It may be the most daring hunch in all of human history, and no one can force anyone else to accept it. A Jew can be an atheist and not be read out of the religion. But this also must be said for the record: that the atheist is no less a gambler than the believer, except that the atheist is betting the other side, that the events of life and history are all chance, or are driven by some mechanical causation, with no moral connection, with no moral purpose, other than what we as human beings create.

The believer *and* the atheist are both taking a chance. The story is told of the pious Chasidic rabbi who was accosted by a skeptic. Almost brashly, the young skeptic burst into the rabbi's room while the rabbi was deep in meditation. "What makes you so sure there is a God?" blurted out the young man. And the rabbi looked into the depths of his eyes and said to the young man, "And what makes you so sure there isn't?"

If a human being should decide to take the chance and say "*Adonai*! Lord," the only authentic decision can be with his whole being, because only a total human being can listen to the drumbeat of history, of life and death. Only a total human being can perceive himself to be standing in the presence of his God.

If a man's faith would be modern and that man is a Jew, let him change the words and show the pictures and prepare the extra readings, but mostly let him stand face front to life, to the beauty and ugliness. Let him reckon with the street and the battlefield, the human loneliness and the human hope, and let him stand in awe and wonder before the Mystery, and let the Mystery and the Presence speak to him of *his* life, *his* tomorrow, *his* task in the world.

The prayer in the prayer book begins: "Our God and God of our fathers." Why both? was the question. Because, went the answer, a man's faith is from two sources: from his own encounter, his own experience, and thus our God, whom we discover, each man for himself; but also "God of our fathers," as Abraham heard His command, as Moses stood before the Burning Bush, as Jeremiah was inflamed by the fire in his bones, as the Baal Shem Tov danced in the streets, as the concentration camp inmate on his way to the gas chamber recited *Ani maamin*—"I believe"—as the Israelis marched into Jerusalem in 1967 and went straight to the Wall.

To be modern is not to begin today, but to follow the faith from all of the yesterdays to the place and time where we are.

The writer Sholem Asch tells of the terrible massacre of Jews in seventeenth-century Lublin. One of the few survivors of the tragedy learned of the death of his family, as Asch writes:

> *And he roamed about through the fair of Lublin among the refugees, among the husbands separated from their wives and the wives separated from their husbands, among the widows and the orphans. He heard the sighs and moans of his people, which rose up over the fair. And he pondered deeply on the matter. He sought to understand the meaning of it all. For one minute the meaning escaped him—he could not understand, and he fell into a state of melancholy. And this caused him deep grief, for it is a matter of common knowledge that melancholy is only one degree removed from doubting.*
>
> *And one day he walked in a narrow street in Lublin where the merchants' stalls were located. And he saw standing before an empty booth an old man who was calling buyers into his booth. And he marveled greatly, for the booth was empty, there was nothing in it to sell. And he walked into the booth and asked the old man: "What do you sell here? Your booth is void and empty, and there is no merchandise at all."*
>
> *And the old man answered: "I sell faith."*
>
> *And he looked intently at the old man, and the old man appeared to him familiar, as though he had seen him before....*

"The booth was empty"—for each of us to fill it with his own encounter, his own personal decision, his own faith.

"He looked intently at the old man"—at Abraham, at Moses, at the Baal Shem Tov, at the Jew on his way to the gas chamber, at the Israeli on his way to the Wall. He looked at the old man as though he had seen him before.

Our God and God of our fathers.

Amen.

Yom Kippur 1970/5731

The Jewish Sense of Time

An article recently appeared in an Athens newspaper that condemned the United States for not preventing the crushing defeat of Greece by Turkish forces on the island of Cyprus. The most bristling indictment was directed against Secretary of State Kissinger, to whom the article repeatedly referred as "the German Jew Kissinger."

In Italy, which is being battered by its own share of political and economic turbulence, leaders in the Jewish community have expressed fear of an underground revival of anti-Semitism.

And in the United States, some 126 radio stations, including one near our own community here in Westchester County, New York, carry a program entitled *Liberty Lobby*, which makes repeated reference to the State of Israel as a "bastard State," and in its depiction of the American Jewish community makes use of words like "subversive" and "disloyal"—scattered, isolated references to be sure, in no way calling for the panic button, and yet each one a suggestive echo of that old refrain that was heard already in Spain in the days of the Inquisition, that was heard in seventeenth-century Poland during the Cossack revolt, that was heard in Germany during the 1930s, the old refrain that when a country is beset with internal turmoil, when competing forces are vying with each other for power and control, then let the Jew beware: Because at that moment, the Jew becomes the chosen candidate by all sides, by the right and the left, to be offered to the beleaguered populace as the simplistic solution to all their troubles and all their ills. The slogan in Germany in the '30s was *Die Juden sind unser Unglück*—"The Jews are our misfortune." And especially when we had achieved some measure of success, as we did in Spain and Poland and Germany, especially then we were forced into our all-too-familiar role while the politicians scrambled for power. It is reported that when a Japanese mission visited Germany in 1932 to study the workings of the Nazi Party, one member of the delegation was asked his opinion of the movement, and he answered: "It is magnificent. I wish we could have something like it in Japan. Our problem is that we don't have any Jews."

The echo of that refrain helps us better understand those charming stories about Jewish grandparents, newly immigrated to this country. When their children or grandchildren would come home with reports of the latest happenings, be they political, economic or technological, the response of the Jewish grandparents was invariably the same: "Is it good for the Jews?" Such a response, which to us may sound so naive and parochial, was in fact their own intuitive awareness shaped by years of experience and years of misery that the Jew can get caught in the maelstrom of forces not of his own making, that he can be forced into the role of *kaparah*, as "atonement" for sins he did not commit. The pages of history are stained with the blood of Jewish scapegoats.

So thank God for America, which gives to bigotry no sanction, which empowers the Jew to search out individual instances of anti-Semitism and to seek official redress. Yet even in America the Jew gets caught: We were caught in the New York teachers' strike; we were caught in the Forest Hills housing crisis; we were caught in the Affirmative Action Program; we are inevitably caught in the advance of the emerging minority groups because we are where they want to be, and Jews are not about to surrender the gains for which they have struggled and worked so hard.

The echo of that old refrain, in some measure, has come from our immigrant grandparents down to us. We may view social and political changes with a more sophisticated eye than they did, but the question of whether it's good for the Jews has, of late, become a question for us, too. When Gerald Ford became vice president and later president, *The Jewish Press* ferreted out every statement that he had ever made, every vote that he had ever submitted about Israel, about the Middle East, about the Jews in Russia. And when Henry Kissinger became the "shuttle diplomat" of the Middle East, the Jewish community debated and still debates whether Kissinger is good for the Jews; or whether, perhaps, his even-handedness might not bend backward in favor of the Arabs if only to prove how impartial a Jew can be. And while Duddy Kravitz wheels and deals his way across the movie screen, there is concern by some about the kind of Jewish image he is projecting to the community-at-large. *Mah yom'ru haGoyim*—"What will the gentiles say?"—and is it good for the Jews?

So what does it all say about us? What does it say about the Jew in America as we walk that line between realistic vigilance on the one side and a touch of paranoia on the other? Does it say that America has shortchanged us on its promises, that the Lady in the Harbor who once held her lamp aloft has now pulled her arm down to her side? Does it say that the doors of opportunity that were once declared wide open have now been partly shut?

I can answer only as one Jew, and each one in this sanctuary must answer for himself. I answer as one, I believe, who is not unaware of the pockets of anti-

Semitism in America. I answer as one, I hope, who tries to feel the crunch when the Jew is caught in the middle by forces not of his own making. But I believe, as one Jew, that America has not reneged on its promise to the Jew. Whatever promises have been broken have been broken not just for the Jew but for all America: the black, the white, the Christian, the Jew. And the pieces of a broken dream that lie about our feet are America's dream and not specifically the Jewish dream.

As one Jew, I believe that America has been good to the Jews, even as the Jew has been good to this country. And yet, that irritating, persistent feeling of less-than-total acceptance; of belonging but not quite; of being in the front office but not quite making it to the executive suite. I once reported to the congregation about a meeting that several of us had with Governor Rockefeller, an unofficial meeting on the issues of the Middle East. At the end of the session, he made a statement that was intended as a high compliment: that as far as the State of Israel's intelligence system was concerned, "there is no doubt that you people have the best intelligence system in the whole world." There we were, about ten in the room, everyone of us a citizen of the United States of America, everyone of us a voting citizen of New York State, and yet to our governor, we were still "you people."

It was not an anti-Semitic remark, but it was his perception of the fact. We may have been his constituents, we may have been among his most loyal public servants, but, in fact, we had come to champion the cause of fellow Jews in the State of Israel, and at that moment (as at all moments), we belonged, but not quite. We are the "you people" of the world.

I once asked a question of a close minister friend during the time that we were trying to mobilize the community-at-large during the Six-Day War: "Tell me the truth, what do the members of your congregation think about Jews? What do they really feel about Jews?" And he answered in total candor: "They don't know quite what to do with you. They don't know quite how to fit Jews into their order of things." And I told my minister friend not to feel too bad because we Jews don't know quite what to do with ourselves either, or how to fit ourselves into the established and structured order of things. Wherever we are, we belong, but not completely; we always live a little bit toward the edge; we are, I believe, the marginal people of the world.

Now some people have sought relief from their state of marginality in the State of Israel. From 1967 to the present, some 17,000 Jews have made *aliyah* and have settled permanently in *Eretz Yisrael*, and whoever of us has made a visit to that blessed place can attest to that mysterious feeling of security, as a Jew, that he never felt before.

But as strengthening and transcending as that experience can be, as reassuring as it is to know that all the policemen are Jewish, as comforting as it is to know the waiters can insult you and you will not be insulted because they are fellow Jews, with all the ways my heart sings when I stand upon its soil, I, as one Jew, do not believe that even the State of Israel is the answer to Jewish marginality. It is surely the haven for the oppressed. It is surely the resting place for battered Jewish souls and tired Jewish feet. It is surely the witness to thousands of years of Jewish history and the closest we have ever come to having a home. It is surely a well-spring of Jewish culture and creative expression, and surely the focus of Jewish attention and Jewish concern. But to assert that in Israel a Jew can shed his marginality and finally achieve a total sense of belonging is for me to belie the truth of the Jew.

Because the truth of the Jew, I believe, is that by nature we are not creatures of place, of any place. But we are instead creatures of time. When we came into peoplehood at Sinai, the God with whom we became partners was not, like the gods of other peoples, the God of any one place who needed a people to build Him a shrine and to nurture His soil. But ours was the God of time, the God of history, who needed a people to shape time and to direct history toward a future day when "superstition would no longer enslave the mind or idolatry blind the eye, when corruption and evil would give way to purity and goodness."

Even when we created the tapestry of our holidays, we started out the way the other people did: Pesach was the festival of the place, the land, the barley harvest. Shavuot was the festival of the wheat, for which we dug our hands into the soil. Sukkot was the festival of the final, beautiful harvest that the land yielded. But little time elapsed before we superimposed our own personality, our own philosophy of life, on those festivals, and Pesach became *the moment in time* of the Exodus from Egypt; and Shavuot became *the moment in time* of the Ten Commandments at Sinai; and Sukkot became *the years of time* we spent in the desert.

We understood full well, because we are pragmatists, that a human being cannot live without land, without space. We need it to live, to work, to accumulate, to fight over, to race in, but we Jews insisted that space was only the stage, only the backdrop, because the real drama belonged to time and to the events of history.

Some months ago, when we were on a congregational trip to Israel, several of us were excited about the prospect of climbing the mountain that has been identified as Sinai, Mount Sinai, to which our guide responded with something of a snicker: "You want it to be Sinai, all right, it's Sinai." Because he understood what we had ignored—that it was the moment of Sinai, the moment of the Commandment and the moment of the encounter and not the geographical location that was the essence of the drama—and we never climbed the mountain.

Space is for things; time is for visions of the future and memories of the past. "Space is that which we conquer; time is that to which we link ourselves." Dr. Heschel has said: "There is a realm of time where the goal is not to have but to be, not to own but to give, not to control but to share, not to subdue but to be in accord."

How do we live in time? By recognizing, I think, that the ultimate is not the piece of land beneath my feet, not the thing in my hand, not the race I am out to win, but the ultimate is this very moment that is passing through my life, waiting for me to link myself to it, waiting for me to shape it with a bit of human love, a bit of human justice, a bit of human compassion, even at the very moment that we are caught in the maelstrom.

How do we live in time? With the understanding, I think, that no moment is by itself, that it inherits a past that is for me to discover, that it moves toward a future that in some mysterious way is being shaped by me and by you at this very instant. Time is my parents and my parents' parents; time is my children and my children's children.

How do we live in time? By understanding, I think, that our very marginality, our very nonestablishment is linked to the very truth of our beings, to those elemental Jewish qualities we prize: the Jewish quality of personal independence and the Jewish right of every individual to exercise his own critical judgment. The political party to which I never completely belong cannot tell me what to think. The society to which I never completely belong cannot tell me what my values should be, completely. I am eternally on the border, not only because they won't let me in but because I don't want in, because I am a creature of time with a vision of the future, a partner of God in history with the power to shape this very moment.

May God grant that we never trade in time. May we never surrender our yesterdays and tomorrows. And when we cherish the vision of those tomorrows, of our children and our children's children, when we cherish the partnership with our God and the God-given independence of our souls, may we cherish them as the most precious possessions of our lives.

Amen.

Rosh HaShanah 1974/5735

Faith, Humor and Silence

Many ancient peoples, including the Jews, arranged their calendars according to their own personal involvement with the life of nature. When we Jews lived as nomads caring for our sheep, we arranged for the year to begin in spring when the flock gave birth to their young. Later, when we took up farming, we connected our calendar and our festivals to the seasons of the field. And still later, when we became a people conscious of our own destiny in history, our year was marked out according to the events of that history, like our escape from Egypt, our covenant at Sinai and all those other events that Abraham Heschel describes as "the sacred moments," when mortal human beings encounter the eternal God.

In every instance, the Jewish calendar that we begin tonight became an intimate personal experience. Time itself was personal because it allowed interaction between human beings and their world. It allowed words of love and acts of love—human beings with each other and human beings with their God who made their world possible. Time was personal continuity, from parents to children and then to their children, from generation to generation. It was very personal.

And then onto the stage of history walked the Greeks, with their declaration that human beings could separate themselves from nature and the world, that they could depersonalize, that they could step back and see it for what it was, as an orderly mechanical operation, once set in motion by a Prime Mover, by God, but now able to proceed on its own. And the Greeks incorporated their view of time into their calendar, which later became the Roman calendar, which later became the secular calendar of our Western world. Mechanical and mathematical, no personal ties, not with the world and not with God.

It's the difference between the mood of tonight in this sanctuary and the mood that sometimes comes through at those New Year's Eve parties on December 31, when the people there sometimes seem to suspect that their lives will not be nearly as tidy as those neat divisions of times and hours. Sometimes the people there seem uneasy about beginning a year that recognizes no Someone or Something that's outside of their little worlds, except perhaps some Prime Mover Emeritus. And that uneasiness may call for a drink, and yet another drink, as a kind of pathetic gesture of defiance against the sobering prospect of those 365 impersonal days ahead. And those who make a point of staying up all night on December 31, some of them seem to be doing it not just for fun but to declare themselves on guard, awake and on guard, and thus perhaps less vulnerable to uncertain fate and fortune, and thus perhaps more powerful to conquer each day ahead in what they're afraid will be a losing battle. New Year's Eve on December 31 could be fun—except for all the times that it's sad.

Compare it with tonight in this sanctuary, in any sanctuary where Jews gather in numbers as large as this, including those Jews for whom these High Holy Days may be their once-a-year pilgrimage to the synagogue. But why do they pick these days? Why not Pesach or Shavuot or Sukkot, which are also pilgrimage festivals to the Temple? Because, I believe, that with everything that many Jews have traded off to belong to the secular world, what they refuse to trade is the first of Tishrei for the first of January. What they refuse to trade is Jewish time for Greek time.

Surely the difference between the two is not in the uncertainty of the days ahead, because our Rosh HaShanah makes no better promises than January 1. All we need do is think back to Rosh HaShanah a year ago and think of all that has happened since then that we did not expect and had not bargained for—both the good days and the bad days—and then surely not one of us here would claim certainty for the days and nights that lie ahead of us now.

The certainty of which Rosh HaShanah *does* speak is that there will be both kinds of days, all kinds of days, days to be born and days to die, days to laugh and days to weep, days to seek and days to lose. The reason I love the Jewish wedding is that it has both the wine cup full of joy and also the shattered pieces of glass with the rough edges, and it presents both of them to that starry-eyed young couple with the truth of what life is all about. We are a people who, in that beautiful phrase of Alfred Kazin, "holds no umbrella against the sky," whether that sky be brilliant with sunlight or dismal with clouds. We are a people who dance at weddings and weep at funerals and keep quiet at the graveside, because in the presence of that final mystery we have nothing to say.

And the other certainty of which Rosh HaShanah speaks is that we do not take this journey alone. There is a Someone, there is a Something, even though our theological beliefs may differ one from the other. Some may believe in a God that directs the destiny of each of His children through all the days of the year: who will live and who will die, who will stay sick and who will get better—a God who hears each prayer individually and responds to each prayer individually. A very personal God. And there are others who may believe in God as a Force, moving through the panoply of nature and coursing through the events of history and the daily struggles of human beings. They believe in a natural and moral Force, not necessarily answering each prayer individually, but still a Force that is available to each one of our prayers as we pray it—that we might draw from that Force the strength we need to help us confront what each day may bring.

Different beliefs, but they express the same Jewish faith: that all the jumbled pieces, all the wine-filled cups and the rough edges, all the good days and the days clouded over, all of the living and the dying, all that we understand and all that is shrouded in mystery, all of the pieces are overarched by a single Presence, a single Someone, a single Something. Surely it is not a faith that promises all problems will be resolved or that the wilderness will be made to flower. It's not that kind of faith because Pollyanna, to my knowledge, was not Jewish. It is not a naive faith but rather a belief that when we walk through that wilderness, we do not walk alone, because Moses was Jewish, and he made it through forty years in the desert through more problems than any human being has ever imagined.

But even more, the Hebrew word for faith is *emunah*, from the word *uman*, which means a "craftsman," a "creative artist." *Emunah* is not only to survive (although some days we would settle for that) but to move *beyond* survival, not only to endure life but to affirm that life creatively, as the unique person that each one of us is, to do what each of us alone can do, to deliver the message that each of us alone can deliver, to create, each of us to create, his own sacred moments between himself and the other humans, between himself and the Eternal.

Some political analysts will call me naive, but I believe that what we saw on television two weeks ago tonight was itself a sacred moment, that what emerged out of those days at Camp David was itself an act of creative faith. I believe that it is not mere coincidence that each of those three men claims an abiding religious belief, that very belief that made many of us wary when each of those men came into office. I believe that with all the political maneuvering and some of the vague wording, what came out of Camp David may never have come if each of those three men, in addition to his own political interests, had not been a man of creative faith, had not been willing to stretch himself and to take risks because of his religious belief in the one universal God and because of his religious vision of peace in the world. John Stuart Mill once wrote that "one person with a belief is a social power equal to ninety-nine who have only interests."

So it's that kind of personal *emunah* that is needed for tonight's journey into time, each of us willing to take risks of the soul, willing to stretch our spirits to the limits of our being, to sally forth where even angels would have second thoughts, even to convert an enemy to a friend, even to forgive grudges that have been forever, even to heal wounds that are still open, even to barge into the dark places of our world and splash them with the colors of the rainbow, even to create shalom in places we thought shalom could never be, even in the beleaguered places of our own lives.

And there was yet another moment in that happening of two weeks ago that could help us to prepare for our journey tonight, the moment when Menachem Begin caused the room to fill with laughter when he said that Jimmy Carter worked harder at Camp David than did his own Jewish ancestors at the pyramids of Egypt. That was a very Jewish moment because it expressed what someone once wrote: that just as we Jews find strength in our faith, so we find relief in our sense of humor. How many times in our peripatetic history have we consciously chosen to laugh because we knew that the only other alternative was to cry? And how many tensions that we know of, instead of getting tenser, could instead be eased by a sense of humor? How many problems that we so overdiscuss and so overanalyze that their seriousness becomes totally stifling—how many such problems could be solved, at least in part, by the ability to laugh at our own deadly seriousness? And how many human relationships, strained to the breaking point, could have been rescued, can still be rescued, if only those humans would themselves decide to laugh? The most important advice we can give to any young couple ready for marriage is that they should laugh a lot, about each other, about themselves, even about their marriage.

And so we stand at the gate of the New Year. And what is absolutely certain as we embark upon our journey into time is that:

—moments will come that will cry out for a sense of humor, and may we fill those moments with laughter;

—moments will come that will cry out for faith, and may we create such faith, not only to survive those moments but to make them sacred;

—and there will be moments that will cry out for only silence, and may we be content with nothing to say.

As we begin our journey toward such moments of humor and faith and silence, may God go with us, and may He give us the wisdom to know one from the other.

Amen.

Rosh HaShanah 1978/5739

Sacred Moments

A parable from the midrash for these High Holy Days:

> *A king's son was at a distance of a hundred days' journey from his father's home. His friends said to him: "Return to your father."*
> *He said to them: "I am unable."*
> *Whereupon his father sent word to him and said: "Go as far as you are able, and I shall come the rest of the way to you."*

Thus the theme of these High Holy Days: alienation from God, however differently we may perceive Him, and the hoped-for return and reconciliation. "Return unto Me," God says through the mouth of the prophet, "and I shall return unto you."

What is striking about that story is its noticeable absence of detail: things that we would like to know that we are not told. For example: Why was the son at such a distance in the first place? Had his father turned him out of the house for conduct unbecoming the son of a king? Or had the son left of his own volition, to take a year off, and then stayed away? And what came through from the son to his friends that prompted them to suggest that he return? Was he upset? Was he depressed? What was he?

So many omissions that we suspect they were on purpose, that all the storyteller intended to do was to provide that broad theme of alienation and return so that each Jew could then compose his own version together with all the details of his own alienation and his own return.

The version that many of our ancestors rendered, and which still holds true for a small company of Jews today, would have been in terms that are intensely personal and warmly intimate. Their religion enfolded their lives, and with every *Baruch Atah Adonai*, which they could utter a hundred times a day, the bond with their God was being reinforced. He was their Friend, *Atah*—"You"—with whom they were in constant touch and not only when they were in need of something. And now, on Yom Kippur, they were pleading for forgiveness, and the prayer book was stained with their tears, and they hoped and prayed that the final call of the shofar would signal not only a dutiful return but a personal reunion between the Jew and his Eternal Thou: "Return unto Me," says God, "and I shall return unto you."

But most of us, and the people we know, and our sons and daughters (happily, many of them with us here) have grown up with a version of that old parable that is considerably different. We would label ours "A Modern Version" because it has evolved over the past two hundred years in the world of modern science and modern technology and modern rationalism and modern psychology and modern nationalism and modern everything else.

In our modern version, the prince leaves the palace for primarily one reason: that under no circumstances is he willing to miss out on all the activity and all the excitement that has enlivened the atmosphere of that modern world. He refuses to be excluded from that magnificent parade of human progress: what could be invented in the laboratory, what could be produced on the machine, what could be performed in the symphony hall, what could be designed in the fashion salon, what nations could do to improve the well-being of their citizens. The air was astir with jubilant confidence in what human effort would be able to accomplish. And out there with the best of them were the Jewish princes and princesses of our parable, trumpeting their faith in humanity—and some of them even denying the existence of the Divine King because He could not be proven in the laboratory.

So there were Jewish atheists and Jewish agnostics, just as there were Jewish believers. But by far the largest group consisted of those Jews who never denied their King, who never denied their own identity as children of that King. They even belonged to synagogues, but so busy were they with the researching and the producing and the symphony going and the getting and the spending and the organizing and the socializing and the parading that when it was suggested to them that the King might be calling to them and commanding them, they felt particularly free to respond: "Not now, God. I'm too busy. I'll keep in touch, but don't call me. I'll call you."

An example, slightly toward the extreme: Many years ago in another congregation (all my stories are from another congregation), I was pleased to see at several Shabbat services a family whose son was scheduled to have a bar mitzvah in the near future. They were people whose lives in the world and whose social lives were very busy, and I was especially pleased to see that they were undertaking this spiritual orientation for the bar mitzvah of their son. When I shared my feeling with them, one of the two parents responded with the slightest embarrassment: "To tell you the truth, we're planning an outdoor party after the bar mitzvah and we've been coming every Friday night to pray that the weather might be in our favor." And now that they had brought me in on their project, they asked if there was anything I could do to help them out. When I answered that the weather prayer with which I was most familiar was *T'filat Geshem*, which is the Prayer for Rain, they no longer sought my participation in the entire enterprise. They had their bar mitzvah, the weather was beautiful, and I never saw them again until the next High Holy Days, when they did not stain their prayer book with their tears. Don't call us God, we'll call you.

But now in our own day, yet another version of that old story, reflected, I believe, in the lives of many members of our congregation, including its young people. It is a version told by those who had also been far away from the King, who had also joined the ranks of the human forward march. But what each of them eventually discovered, to his pain and to his disillusionment, was that this humanity in which he had stored all his faith, which in the name of science could invent cures for diseases, could also, under the banner of that same science, invent Zyklon B gas, which could murder 12,000 Jews a day in the chambers of Auschwitz. What our storyteller discovered, to his pain and disillusionment, was that this same humanity, which in the name of democratic freedom could rescue a child from the urban ghetto and give him hope, could also splatter the blood of children in Vietnam in the name of that same democratic freedom.

Human progress had let him down. It deserved his participation but not his absolute faith. It could goad him toward accomplishment but could not guide him toward values. It totally ignored his human yearning to reach outside of himself, to discover a meaning that would call him to the task of his own life, that would offer him a system of unphony values by which he could assess the days and deeds of that life. When 8,000 college students on some forty-eight campuses were asked: "What do you consider the primary goal of your life?" 78 percent gave as the first goal "to find a purpose and meaning to my life," which is what humanity on the march had ignored and neglected. It is what Viktor Frankl calls "the will to meaning," which humanity on the march had ignored and neglected.

It is that yearning that seeks strength and support on those days when the ground seems to be giving way beneath us.

It is the yearning that calls out on the lonely days and nights of our lives.

It is the yearning for clarity when our vision is dim.

It is the yearning that in Hebrew is called the *neshamah*, the soul at the center of our being, which has as its goal "not to get something, but to be with Someone," with the Eternal Thou of one's life.

It is the yearning that may not yet have defined itself but that may ache all the same.

Such is the story, I believe, that many of our congregation have to tell: many have been victims of spiritual neglect. Some of their children cried out because of that neglect and are now ready to search for their own spiritual selves. Many so long absent from the palace are now ready at least to pray the words of return: *Avinu Malkeinu*—"Our Father, our King."

We wish there could be a neat packaged formula, but the truth is that Judaism itself is the formula. It structured a ladder from earth to heaven by which the *neshamah* could try its upward climb. It fashioned a structure of Shabbat and prayer and diet and study and humanitarian deeds, and they were all directed to that same purpose: to allow the Jew, in concert with other Jews, to express the yearning of his human spirit to make that upward climb, to be with the Eternal Thou.

We may not have the neat little package, but what we have is the big package of Jewish tradition. And some of those modern Jews, including the Jews in this congregation, are beginning to come back to take another look at that package so long ignored. They are coming back not only on the popular wave of ethnic identity and ethnic belonging but also with the unfulfilled and sometimes undefined yearning of their own souls.

We rabbis make a mistake, I believe, and so does our Religious Services Committee, and so do the members of our congregation, when we talk about ritual and adult study only in terms of ethnic belonging, only in terms of whether it makes someone feel more Jewish or not. The question that is rarely asked and that needs to be asked is whether it also makes us feel more spiritual or not, whether it allows what Abraham Heschel says is the goal of all spiritual experience inside temple or out: the goal of "sacred moments" in our lives.

We have all known such moments and many of them we have shared together, those moments when, as the Chasidim speak of them, "heaven and earth touch each other":

—the moment on this bimah when the Torah is handed from the arms of one generation into the arms of the next;

—the moment when we stand by the side of the dying and hold their hand;

—the moment when we behold a son or daughter standing at the altar of marriage;

—the moment when a child is born into the world;

—the moment in a classroom when a student's eyes brighten with the discovery of his own new truth, or his brow is wrinkled with the burden of his own new question;

—the moment to which many of us can attest when after sickness there can be health again, after anguish, hope again, after death, life again;

—the moment between two people who love each other when, in the words of the Kabbalah, "two lights merge and generate one light," a moment soon past, forever remembered.

Thus do we pave the road of our own return with our own soul's awareness of such moments and of their awesome power.

But we also know of other moments: Thirty years ago, I was a counselor at a summer camp and a particular five-year-old evidenced a complex of behavior problems. One night the boy and I were returning to the cabin after a walk, and he asked if we could stop at the meadow where the cows were grazing. We stayed for a little while, and then I looked at my watch because I was impatient to get back. As I turned to leave, the boy took my hand and held it tightly and did not move, and the two of us stood there in perfect silence.

The mystics believe that the world is filled with God's radiance, that the ordinary world is filled with His light, but we, by putting our hands in front of our own eyes, block out that light. But that extra moment of perfect stillness, with that child's hand holding mine to keep it away from my eyes, that radiant moment was one of the most sacred moments of my life.

The road of return is paved with those extra moments when we are willing to surrender our own agenda, when we stop long enough to stand in awe and feel the wonder, to discover the sacred within the ordinary, an ordinary meadow or an ordinary human being.

A modern parable for these Holy Days:

A king's son was at a distance from the palace, which he had left for better things. There came a day when he decided to return because the better things were not that good and because his soul was yearning for a meaning to his life and for a task in his world. He remembered his sacred moments, and he made a road of them. And he took the ordinary rocks from the field and added them to the road. And thus he made his journey, stone by stone, step by step.

And in the midst of that journey, there was a moment of meeting with his Father, the King, and heaven and earth touched each other.

Amen.

Yom Kippur 1980/5741

When Bad Things Happen to Good People

In the spirit of these days, so totally global and so totally personal, I would share with you one of the most personal journeys any human being can travel. Most of us have walked this road one way or another. We have spoken of it in family living rooms, in Bible class, in adult bar/bat mitzvah class, in confirmation class, but never in the sanctuary on the Holy Days.

What determined it as my theme for this Yom Kippur is the recently published book *When Bad Things Happen to Good People* by Rabbi Harold Kushner, following the death of his child at age fourteen. The child's condition, present from birth, was diagnosed as progeria, rapid aging. The condition meant that the child would never grow to a height of more than three feet, would never develop hair on his head or his body, would have the face of a little old man and would die in his early teens. What made the book so compelling was the author's ability to universalize his own family's experience, to connect the child Aaron's life and death with a whole gamut of bad things that happen to good people in the course of their lives and with the possible ways in which they might respond to them.

What I, in reading this book, did not anticipate, and what I understand Rabbi Kushner did not anticipate, was the extent of the reception that would be accorded his book—now on the best-seller list for the thirty-third week—and the number of people who were ready and willing to share someone else's journey to see if they might discover some direction for their own.

Thus my intention on this Yom Kippur, not to debate a position, and surely not to intrude into anyone's personal feelings, but only to share the journey of this one traveler, myself, who has shared the journeys of many others, including those good people to whom bad things sometimes happen.

As I was reading the book this summer, a newspaper report told of a man, thirty-one years old, who was walking down Madison Avenue, and a piece of construction equipment on the roof of a newly finished building broke away from its derrick, fell on the roof of the building and dislodged a piece of granite, which plummeted to the street below and killed the man.

Ask any rabbi or minister to contemplate within the family of his or her own congregation how many good people feel cheated in their lives—because in truth they have been cheated by a lingering illness, by death that claimed the young, by prolonged dying that humiliated the old, by handicap of mind or body, by trust betrayed, by a home once intact now broken, by love once assumed now denied, by the once even keel of financial security now floundering.

And the cry you hear is the cry of pain. Sadness always hurts, but tragedy hurts more. It may spew out in anger or lament, in self-discrimination or accusation, in complaint or in self-pity or in silence, but more often than not, it is the cry of someone cheated and hurting, as if to say (in Rabbi Kushner's words): "This can't be happening. This isn't the way it is supposed to be." Even the question, Why?, is not necessarily for an answer, not for information, not for speculation, but, as Rabbi Harold Schulweis has said, "It is less why than it is woe." And with the wound still fresh, the best response to the question is not to answer the question but to share the pain.

But to some, including myself, there does come a day when you have to talk about the why. Because if that happening or that condition that, by itself, is without sense and without reason cannot admit to some slight measure of understanding, cannot be set even the slightest into some framework of meaning, then all the rest may be without sense and without reason and without meaning. If, in God's supposed good and just world, such a terrible thing can happen, then where is goodness? Where is justice? Where is God?

The old responses to the question are familiar and still valid for many: that some questions have no answer and "ours is not to reason why"; or the response that is contained in the word *beshert*—which means "determined," "decided," "written in the book"—that when it's your time it's your time, and if you have a seat reserved on an airplane that will crash and it is not yet your time, you'll miss that plane, *beshert*; or the response that only God knows and none of us is God; or the response that there is no God.

My purpose is not to debate any of the answers but only to suggest one other and the direction, which it allows.

I begin on the common ground of all Jewish believers that however we think of God, God is the moral power that sustains this universe, that God represents what is good and just and right and that ours is the power to choose what is good or reject it, to go with God or away from God. We who are believers also share the belief that God is the power that sustains the physical universe and all the laws of its operation that scientists explore and interpret so that we can use them to our best advantage.

But here is where some of us part company, because some of us believe—even contrary to teachings of the Bible, even contrary to the prayer book—that God does not operate the physical universe for or against specific individuals, afflicting one, sparing another. Some of us do not believe in *beshert* (except on those rare occasions when we do). Some of us do not accept the literal meaning of the prayer that we shall read tomorrow, that God decides in advance who will live and who will die, and who will succeed and who will fail. But we interpret that prayer as simply a catalog of human experiences to which we are subject. Some of us believe that the suffering we see in the world is not the work of a God who doles out plagues and plane crashes, but rather the workings of God's imperfect world and the imperfect people in it, and secrets of nature yet undiscovered, and nature's randomness, and nature's pockets of chaos. Good people get just as sick as bad people, not because of their goodness or badness, but because of what is happening in their bodies, sometimes of their own doing, sometimes from their environment, sometimes from a mystery of nature yet undeciphered, because that's how God's law of nature operates. And the moral tragedy of Beirut is not from on high but from Beirut and from all the chain of circumstances before, because that's how God's moral law operates—that a sin produces its own tragedy, just as a good and decent deed produces its own nobility. That's how the moral law operates, and bad things can sometimes happen to good people because even good people can hurt each other, and bad things sometimes happen to good people because sometimes we do the best we know how and it comes out wrong—but God didn't do it!

If I may be personal, a few years ago I was struck by an automobile as I was crossing 65th Street between the House of Living Judaism and Temple Emanu-El, and there could be no more sacred route than that. A member of the congregation came to visit and was so distressed by my discomfort and condition that she said: "How could God have let this happen to you?" As I think of it now, it was probably her question of woe, but since I construed it then as a question of why I presumed to answer it: "God had nothing to do with it," I said. "Some damned fool jumped the light!" To which someone later added, "And maybe there was another fool who wasn't looking carefully enough when he was crossing." The man was killed by the falling chunk of granite because perhaps the building code regulations in New York City allowed the overhead protective bridge to be removed before the construction machinery was removed from that building.

Thus I am not among those who agonize over unanswered whys. Rather do I look to where the shattered pieces of my world are lying and bend down to pick them up again. My question, in Rabbi Kushner's words, is: "If this has happened to me, what do I do now, and who is there to help me do it? From where will come my strength?"

Rabbi Jacob Rudin told of the Greek writer Xenophon, who recorded the 2,000-mile march back to Greece by the Greek army following its campaign in Persia. And in the diary account of that terrible ordeal, one phrase kept repeating itself: "From there we went on." And thus do believers believe: that God, however differently we may conceive of God, is the source of our strength that allows us to go on. Ask any doctor about patients, or social worker about clients, or clergymen about congregants, and they will tell you the difference between a person in whom the spirit is weak and the person in whom the spirit is strong, because the strong go on from there. They are the ones who struggle to survive. Those doctors and social workers and clergymen will tell you how people somehow find the strength to do what they never thought they had the strength to do—to go on from there.

So when bad things happen to good people, we turn to God not only for answers, but for strength to pick up the pieces, to find a way out of our darkness, and then to carry that light to someone else's darkness, like the rabbi who wrote a helpful book on bad things that happen to good people.

And when bad things happen to good people, we come together on Yom Kippur, on the day of forgiveness, and we forgive God for not being as powerful as we would like Him to be. We forgive each other for not being as perfect as we would like each other to be. And we forgive ourselves for all the times we thought that what we were doing was right and it came out wrong.

And may God grant that this will be the day of which it will be said of us, and of the Jewish people, and of the Arab people: "From there we went on."

Amen.

Yom Kippur 1982/5743

The Secular and the Sacred

What many of us are inclined to do at the turn of the year is review the old and look forward with hope to the new. Every year there are the peaks and the valleys and the level day-to-day terrain in between. For me, as a rabbi of this congregation, this year's claim to distinction has been that in all my years as a rabbi, I never officiated at so many weddings in the span of one year, thirty by count. And with at least another half dozen weddings of our congregants at which other rabbis officiated, including one a few weeks ago in Jerusalem, this has been a banner year for chuppahs at Westchester Reform Temple. In Jewish tradition, when you talk about something like thirty-six weddings in one year, you add the words *Kein yir'bu*—"May they continue to increase!"

I love the meetings I have with the couples in advance of their big day. What I discover is that many of them already know about the wine and the rings and the breaking of the glass. What is often new to them, and often intrigues them, is that part of the ceremony called the *Sheva B'rachot*—"the Seven Blessings"—and especially how those blessings move from one to the next, from praising God for creating the world and then for creating God's human children, and then for ordaining the Jewish institution of marriage, and then for this bride and this groom who are about to make their promises of a lifetime of love. What often intrigues the couple, and surprises them even, is how their ceremony and their marriage, which they have looked upon in very personal and private terms, involving themselves and their friends and their families—how that ceremony is now, by those blessings, given a place not only in the generations of Jewish marriages but also in the vast order of divine creation. For that reason is a marriage called *kiddushin*, from *kadosh*—"holy, sacred"—having to do with God. Until the couple and I talk about those Seven Blessings, they usually do not realize that they are inviting their friends and family to an event that is historic and cosmic.

In that spirit, the year 5749 is about to begin, and I share a hope for these Holy Days. When we walked in here tonight, like that bride and groom, most likely we came with the personal and private soundings of our own hearts: with the cups that brim over with our joys and, for some, the vessels that are choked with their tears; with the badges of our achievement that we wear with quiet pride

26

and also with the smudges that give us quiet embarrassment. We walked in here with our hopes for what the New Year could bring and with uneasiness for what the New Year might bring. All very personal and private.

And thus the hope: that by the time we walk out of here a week from Wednesday, when the last *t'kiah g'dolah* will call out from the shofar, that we will be like that bride and groom when they walk out of the chuppah; that what we brought here tonight privately and personally from our day-to-day lives in our day-to-day world will no longer remain only private and only personal; but instead that our voices and our silences will join in chorus, that besides being alone we will be together, with each other and with the Holy One, however differently we may conceive of the Holy One. The hope is that by a week from Wednesday this big room (and that's all it is, a big room) will have been transformed by us into a sanctuary, which in Hebrew is called *mikdash*—from that same word *kadosh*—holy, sacred, having to do with God.

So my theme for these Holy Days will be the secular and the sacred and ourselves. For purposes of definition, "secular" is from the Latin word *secular*, which means "world," our day-to-day world. Secular is the political system that governs our society but must also include the corruption in high places. Secular is the economic life that strives for our material well-being but must also include Black Monday a year ago, and the most recent inside trading scandals a week ago. Secular includes our technological breakthroughs that with their cures for disease give hope for life, and with their atomic mushroom clouds give fear of death. Secular is who's who and what's what in the world of humanity: It is art, it is music, it is VCRs, and it is AIDS. It is tennis matches, and it is Olympic games. For better or for worse, secular is our day-to-day lives in our day-to-day world.

And then this other word, *kadosh*, which we usually translate as "holy" and "sacred." But *kadosh* in its most original meaning is "to be separate," "to be set apart," beyond the everyday. What made us Jews different from other peoples in ancient times was that their *kadosh* was an assortment of spirits and gods who would fight with each other and make love with each other. Our *Kadosh* was this one God, this *Adonai*, who represented compassion and fairness and justice. What was different between our religion and theirs was that ours taught us that this God created not only the cosmos but also created us *b'tzelem Elohim*—"in the image of God." And that means that every one of us in this room, aside from our human powers to think and create and make money and play golf and vote in the election, aside from all those things we do in our secular world, we have this *kadosh* part of us. It means that when we feel weak, we are able to reach out to that Other, that *Kadosh*, for strength; and when we feel thankful, we are able to reach out to that Other, that *Kadosh*, with a blessing of thanks. It is the part of us that can reach out to the God of compassion and fairness and justice and then be moved to act more compassionately and more fairly and more justly.

Thus our question for all of us for these Holy Days, including those of us who may feel more at home in the domain of the secular than we do in the domain of the sacred: How do we secular human beings energize the *kadosh* part of our-selves? How do we see to it that our spiritual selves can function and thrive with the same vigor as our secular selves?

How do we do it? First, I believe, by confronting the difference between what is secular and sacred: to know that the secular question is mostly, "Can I make it work?" and the sacred question is, "Is it right?" In the secular world the question is, "Am I a success at what I do?" In the sacred world the question is, "What is the value and what is the meaning of what I do?" The Viennese psychiatrist Viktor Frankel tells how he asked that question regarding the meaning of life of his students in medical school at Vienna University. Among his European students, 40 percent expressed despair that their lives lacked meaning and value. Of the American students, the figure was 81 percent.

To know the difference between secular and sacred is to know that in the sec-ular world, courage means to find an answer to every question. Courage in the sacred world is to ask questions that have no answers. In the secular world we stand in judgment only before ourselves and each other: What do I think of myself? What do you think of me? In the sacred world we stand before the *Kadosh*, the Other, exactly where we stand on this Holy Day. And this time the question is from the *Kadosh*: "O man, O woman, where are you?"

And surely to know the difference between the two is to know how the two can get mixed up. I once shared with you the true incident of a family whose child was having a problem in the religious school. We arranged with the child's teacher for a meeting with the parents on a Sunday morning when the teacher would be here. I called the parents, and the mother said that she would be there but that her husband could not. Why? Because every Sunday morning he played tennis. And that game, she said (and she even used that word), that game was "sacred." Or the time I was in the supermarket and I overheard one Jewish lady say to another, "My husband and I play bridge every Friday night—religiously." By no stretch of the imagination and by no acrobatics of definition can a tennis game on Sunday morning be called sacred or a regular bridge game on Friday night qualify as religious. (They have the right night, only the wrong activity.)

And once we do know the difference, and once we have stoked up our own powers for the sacred and the spiritual (which is what we shall talk about on Yom

Kippur), then we will be ready for what has always been the Jewish mission, to which the shofar will call us tomorrow morning: to go back to that secular world and to infuse it, or at least our own corner of it, with so much compassion and caring, so much fairness and justice, so much meaning and value that because of our personal touch, some of those places that were once only secular will now have a touch of *kadosh* and a touch of the sacred.

So how do we do it? The Jewish mystics gave us a clue. They tell us that scattered throughout the world are a vast number of shells, and beneath each of those shells is a spark, a divine spark of the *Kadosh*. And when a Jew performs a mitzvah, the shell is lifted and a spark is released, and a sacred divine light shines into our lives and into the world.

The clue is those shells. And the key is to go out and look for them in all the places of our motley world, to go to our jobs and charge them with enough value and enough meaning that our jobs are able to become our calling. The key is how we relate to our clients, our patients, our customers, our congregants with enough compassion and fairness that the relationships are touched with the quality of the sacred. The key to *kadosh* is how to turn to those who are in the autumn or winter of their lives and, even though they have lost their agility and perhaps even their mobility, to let them know that they are still persons of value. The key to *kadosh* is to turn to you, our high school students and junior high school students who are here tonight, to turn to you and let you know that being "high" on liquor or drugs is not assertion of the self or fulfillment of the self but treason to the self. The key to *kadosh* is to let you, our college students, know that your education should not be just to make a lot of money but to repair God's shabby world, the way some of you do when you report to a soup kitchen at six o'clock in the morning before you go to your job at nine. The key to *kadosh* is how you, our Jewish grandparents, communicate to your grandchildren that a good doctrine has been given to them and they should not forsake it. The key is how we teach our little ones that the God who brought the Jewish people out of Egypt, which is what we teach them all the time in religious school, is also the God that belongs to their lives every day. The key to *kadosh* is what you who are in the Torah study group and the Tuesday Bible class have already come to know—and perhaps you can persuade some of the others—that every time a Jew sits down with the sacred texts of our people, the sparks begin to fly. The key to *kadosh* is what you who have celebrated a bar or bat mitzvah or a wedding or any other *simchah* in your life and then have contributed three percent to MAZON, the Jewish Response to Hunger, already know—and perhaps you can persuade some of the others—that by the simple act of sharing a joy, that joy becomes more joyful and becomes sacred.

And finally, as we seek to find those shells and release those sparks, let me share with you a personal experience of many years ago that I shared with our colleagues at the Central Conference of American Rabbis.

It was an ordinary day in my study, which for most rabbis is never that ordinary. There was a telephone call from a young man who identified himself from Great Neck days when I was first ordained and was assistant to Rabbi Jacob Rudin, of blessed memory. I had served there as youth director of the congregation, and the young man, now in his late twenties, all these years later, was calling me to ask if I would officiate at his wedding. Why? I asked. Because, he said, when he was a teenager, everyone, including his family, had given up on him, academically and personally. But as his rabbi, he said, I was the only one who had conveyed to him the sense of his own worth, the only one, he said, that had reminded him that with all of his crazy behavior, he was still a valuable human being.

I tell you that story because the truth is that I was totally unaware that I had performed the mitzvah when I did it. I tell you that story because I believe that from day to day everybody in this big room is performing mitzvahs and yet may be unaware of their sanctity.

So part of the key to *kadosh*, besides finding the shells and releasing the sparks, is to recognize when we are doing it that we are doing it, that it's not just a good deed but a sacred deed in an everyday hour on earth, in a corner of our secular world.

Jacob in the Bible had a dream of a ladder that went from earth to heaven, from secular to sacred. Ascending and descending that ladder were *malachim*, which we usually translate as angels but also means messengers.

Jacob awakened from that dream and knew what he had never known before, that he himself was a messenger. And so may we be. Jacob awakened from that dream and exclaimed, "The Lord God is in this place, but until now I did not know it."

And so may we.

Amen.

Rosh HaShanah 1988/5749

Spiritual Energy

Kol Nidrei is the melody of the Jewish soul. No one knows who composed it. We only know that someone sang it, and all who heard it knew that it was right and claimed it as their own.

Several years ago, after undergoing cardiac surgery, I was told by my surgeon how, during the procedure, he had cupped my heart in the palm of his hand. Amazing! *Kol Nidrei* is like that. Gently it holds us in its sway and sings to the heart of our being: of crisis and survival, of suffering and redemption, of offending hurts and then of forgiving love, of disappointment and then of hope. *Kol Nidrei* sheds our tears and then wipes them away.

On Rosh HaShanah, I tried to make the distinction between the world of the secular and the world of the sacred. We defined *kadosh* as the sacred and the spiritual inside of us, which reaches out to the *Kadosh* beyond us, however differently we may conceive of that *Kadosh*. But when *Kol Nidrei* sings, no definitions are necessary, because even as we listen, we are already hearing the still, small voice of our own spiritual selves.

But when today is over, when we go back to the secular world we just left, we will hardly ever hear the word "spiritual" or the word "spirituality." They are temple words rarely ever uttered on the train or downtown or at cocktail parties or even at our dinner tables. The subjects that once were rarely mentioned, like sex and like death, have now become fair game. But this one subject, which has just as much to do with who, in truth, we are, this one subject of our spiritual selves (in the words of a member of our congregation) is not "very cool."

If the secular world to which we shall return stays the same as when we left it this afternoon, the likelihood is that the still small voice that we heard in here will get drowned out in the din and the noise out there. I drive up Mamaroneck Road in the morning, and I see runners on their daily rounds; and when I see a Walkman plugged into their ears, I wonder why they are shutting out the very silence in which they could be listening to their own still small voice. And since Yom Kippur is a time when you are allowed to present grievances and seek relief, let me present one of mine. When I call people at their offices and am asked to wait and am put on hold, I cherish the prospect of those few seconds of silence. Why

31

then am I forced to listen to recorded announcements I did not solicit and music I don't want to hear? It's not so serious; it's only that the trouble with the secular world is that it never shuts up.

Thus the hope for these next moments on the most spiritual day of the Jewish year, the day when we strip down to our very souls. I ask you to brave with me the question that is not very "cool." How can we sustain or store up the energy of *Kol Nidrei* and Yom Kippur so that when we go back to our secular worlds, we can live lives that are more complete and more whole than they were before, still small voice and all? How can we activate and energize the spiritual force in ourselves so that the sound of our own still voices will be heard in all the places where we live and work and love and play?

All of us who turn to that undertaking will do so not as strangers, because everyone in this big room has his or her own spiritual stories to tell, even aside from *Kol Nidrei*. It could be a story told by parents when they stood in front of the ark with their newborn in their arms for a name and a blessing. It could be when a child or a grandchild was called as bar or bat mitzvah to take the Torah in arms and to take a place in the chain of Jewish generations. Or it could be when a confirmand, older now and more understanding, stood for a private moment before the open ark.

Through all of those moments I have watched the experience, the expressions on the parents' faces and grandparents' faces, and even on the faces of the nervous kids themselves. And what I have often detected there, besides the glow of pride and joy, is the soul's whisper that this moment is bursting into the beyond, into the flow of timeless time, into all the Jewish generations, those who are here and those who are not here—that this moment is touched with the Holy. And some of you have even spoken the words *shehecheyanu v'kiy'manu v'higi-anu laz'man hazeh*": O Lord, our God, "who has kept us alive and sustained us and brought us to this day." A holy moment. A spiritual story.

And there are some of those other moments we have shared by the side of the dying and at the side of the grave. And what I often detect there, among the very ones who grieve, is not only the crushing power of grief and loss, but also the soul's whisper of the mystery itself: life and death, love and loss, grief and hope. And we even have the words for the mystery: "The Lord has given, the Lord has taken away; blessed be the name of the Lord." A holy moment of mystery. A spiritual story.

And not only in the cemetery and in the sanctuary. Rabbi Samuel Karff tells of asking his confirmation class to write down occasions when they felt especially close to God. One confirmand wrote:

The time I felt nearest to God was when my family and I were having difficulties communicating with each other. I was going through a lot of problems and really had trouble dealing with them. And I really felt like my life was falling apart. Then I became strong enough to put the pieces together, and I felt that God was with me through that.

Can you tell the stories of such moments? Rare perhaps, precious for sure, moments when there was a gleam of light even against our own darkened sky; or moments when our own mountaintop seemed to tower over the world; or when holding the hand of someone we love made us feel safe.

Last week a rabbi friend of mine visited a friend of his who is stricken with leukemia. "What are you going to talk about on Yom Kippur?" the patient asked.

"I want to say something about spiritual things," the rabbi answered, "but I don't yet know what it should be."

"I do," said the patient. "Tell them about the preciousness of life. Tell them what a day is like. Tell them what a life is like."

We all have our spiritual stories to tell: how the still, small voice is not mute; how when life says, "Yes," we can say, "Amen"; how when the God of life calls, we can say, "Here I am."

Once we know that, once we can acknowledge that we have heard the whispers of our own soul in our own mountain-peak moments, then we are ready for the undertaking that I ask you to share with me beginning tonight: to search out all the ways in which the whispers and the voice can be heard down the mountain, on ground level, on the plain road, in an everyday hour on earth.

When Priscilla and I first came to Scarsdale twenty-six years ago, we were invited to a series of "coffees" immediately after the High Holy Days, in order to meet members of the congregation. We would go around the room and everyone would tell something about himself or herself. And this one lovely lady told how much she and her husband had enjoyed the High Holy Days and how spiritually uplifting she had found them. Then she said: "And we're looking forward to next September, when we can come back to the temple again."

The truth is that they didn't have to wait that long. Because if there are only the peak experiences, then as inspiring as *Kol Nidrei* may be, as spiritual as the wedding or the funeral may have been, it's a moment that comes and a moment that goes, and it's nothing but a memory until the next time. If there are for us only the spiritual highs, then however successful we otherwise are in our secular worlds, in this world of our spiritual selves, we belong to the ranks of underachievers.

The Jewish test of spirituality is all those other times down the mountain: how in the course of an ordinary day, we open our ears to a cry for help even when it may sound like a scream of anger; how in the course of an ordinary day, we behold the wondrous beauty of God's world on Mamaroneck Road. All those times down the mountain, because the Jewish test of spirituality is not only what happens to us but what we cause to happen, not only the reaching in but the reaching out. Doing the mitzvah, doing the deed. Every spiritual act, every mitzvah, is the self giving to the other; no strings attached and no scorecard to be kept.

I have a request to make. Find the most recent issue of *Reform Judaism* and read the piece entitled "A Call to Commitment" (and if your copy is not at hand, we shall be glad to send you one). Get a beginning idea of what we as Reform Jews can do to raise the spiritual level of our homes and ourselves and our lives and our world. Consider what mitzvot, what Jewish acts, you can perform that you have never performed before: what ritual acts, what ethical acts, what books to study, what spiritual fuel to fire up in order to bring this other warmth, this other brightness into our homes and our lives.

There may be some of you who are perfectly content with your lives as they are, with your own present balance of sacred and secular, and for you the undertaking that hopefully will begin tonight will have little appeal. Your situation is like that of the Boy Scout who was asked by his father: "And what good deed did you do today?" The boy answered, "Four other Boy Scouts and I took an old lady across the street." "That's nice," said the father, "but why did it take five of you?" "Because she didn't want to go," said the Boy Scout.

Some of you may decline the journey of this undertaking, and we have no choice but to respect your decision and your privacy. But I know of others who will make a different decision because they have said so. I know of men and women who meet in New York offices in the middle of a regular day not to work out the next deal but to work through a Jewish text, a Jewish value, and what effect it might have on their lives. I know that there are young Jews on college campuses who are taking more religion courses than ever before, who are doing charity work more than ever before, who are studying again to be social workers and to be teachers and not just to be millionaires. I know that there are young people, including young Jews, in cities like New York who have had enough of the secular craziness. With Boesky and Levine, unbridled greed is going out of style. With AIDS, casual sex is going out of style. After October 19 a year ago, to want something is no longer necessarily to get it. And not to get it all can keep one from wanting it all.

More and more young people are expressing, in Arthur Schlesinger's words, "a pent-up idealism," and they are talking about the spiritual stuff of meaning and value in their lives. I love what one twenty-four-year-old said in an interview: "I'm still twenty-four, and I don't need God yet. When I'm thirty-five and it's time to find meaning in my life outside work, then I'll struggle." It was only a few years ago that a twenty-four-year-old would have laughed off the question, but now all he wants to do is wait until he is thirty-five, for which we shall gladly settle.

People are ready, people of all ages, people who have concluded that the goodies out there are not all that great. And that there is this other part that has been missing and they are ready.

And thus my Yom Kippur appeal: that you, the members of this congregation, will say "yes" to the spiritual search for the sake of your families and yourselves, and for the sake of God's world. And for those of you who are even braver, I ask that you join with me and a cadre of others to ask this question: How can we, not only as individuals but as Westchester Reform Temple, do more than we are already doing to help it all to happen; to offer guidance for each one's personal search; to provide the resources for all of us spiritual underachievers to raise the level of our achievement? How can we see to it that Westchester Reform Temple becomes a more spiritual place than it is?

If you, the members of our congregation, will say "yes" to the journey, and if brave ones will let themselves be known, then we can begin our shared journey with this statement of its purpose from an incident of many years ago.

In the town of Berditchev, there lived the saintly Levi Yitzchak. One day he ordered the *shammas* of the shul to go to every store and every shop in the marketplace and say: "Close your business and come to the town square because Levi Yitzchak has a very important announcement to make."

"But Rabbi," the *shammas* said, "today is a market day. Everybody is selling and buying, and this is the busiest time of the day. Can't you postpone the announcement for another day or at least for later today?"

"No," said Levi Yitzchak. "Tell them that I have an important announcement to make that will not wait another day or another hour. Now!"

The *shammas* proceeded reluctantly to his task. The shopkeepers and customers grumbled and complained. But with their concern for the urgency, they did as they were told.

When they were all assembled, Reb Levi mounted a box, signaled for silence and began to speak: "I have asked you to come on this busy day and this busy hour because I have news that is of great importance to you, and this is my announcement. 'I, Levi Yitzchak, son of Sara of Berditchev, I announce and pro-claim to you: There is a God in the world!'" And then he dismissed the assem-blage.

May that declaration become the goal of our shared journey, however differ-ently we may conceive of the presence of God in the world.

May that declaration come to pass not only on the mountaintops but on the plain roads.

May that declaration come true for our strength and our blessing.

And if it does, then this big room, in which *Kol Nidrei* was sung and in which the journey began, then this big room may yet become a *mikdash*, a holy and sacred place, which it was always meant to be.

Amen.

Yom Kippur 1988/5749

Our Shared Humanity

.

On Being a Survivor

The theme that I hope to share with you through these High Holy Days was chosen already last spring. Like everyone else, I was feeling the troubled mood of our times and our world. People I knew had been hit hard by the falling economy. Homes I knew were being fractured by family conflict. America was trading its self-respect for the petrol dollar. The State of Israel was being pressured and threatened by its enemies, and also by its friends.

Spring was stifling this year, and the theme for the High Holy Days suggested itself in one word: "Survival," a universal word and a deeply Jewish word, so deeply connected with the Jewish affirmation of life on this earth and in this world, so deeply engraved, and so often with blood, in the Jewish life story of three thousand years.

The word was "Survival," and after the theme was decided upon, it seemed that wherever I turned, in newspapers, in magazines, in public speeches, the word was there, insisting that it be read, demanding that it be heard: *Will Capitalism Survive? The Survival of the Family, The Food Shortage and Human Survival, Will America Survive Détente?* A host of books explored the theme, and among them two volumes that promised content that would be especially appropriate. One was called *Alive* and recorded the experience of the sixteen survivors of an airplane crash in the Andes who managed to stay alive until their rescue two months later, and who attracted world attention when it became known that they had resorted to the consumption of the human flesh of fellow passengers already dead.

The other book was entitled *The War Against the Jews* by Lucy Davidowicz and has been acclaimed the definitive work on the Nazi Holocaust.

My theme was chosen, some material was at hand, and I was ready to discover where the reading and thinking would take me. I was all prepared, except for what actually happened. Before I tell you of it, a word of explanation: Under most circumstances, a rabbi in the pulpit exercises special caution not to impose his own personal experiences upon his captive congregation. In this instance, however, I have set the caution aside because, hopefully, my personal experience has something to say about the theme.

During the first week of vacation, early in the summer, I was feeling less than myself. As the symptoms heightened, I was admitted to the hospital, and two days later a lumbar puncture revealed evidence of viral meningoencephalitis, a virus of the brain. In my lowered state of consciousness, I was but vaguely aware of what was happening around me, including the eight or ten hours following the diagnosis, when the doctors harbored some question as to whether the outcome would be life or death and informed my family accordingly.

There was one moment during those eight or ten hours, while I was still in the limbo of deep sleep, that I perceived myself as standing quietly in a beautiful outdoor garden. A clear blue sky was above, and the garden itself was surrounded by walls covered with ivy. Set into one of the walls I saw a door, and I knew as I stood there that it was the door leading to death and that I was about to walk through.

In a book called *Living Your Dying*, the author Stanley Keleman asserts that in our culture, the very subject of dying is so often overloaded with terror and panic that it is difficult to get at what the pure feeling of dying might be. Because our exposure to death is so often linked with violence and assault, be it in the streets or on the battlefields, or with the diseases that attack the human body, we have trouble moving beyond our own anxiety about violence to the experience of death itself.

So for whatever it is worth, I would share with you that the pure experience of dying, for one person at least, was without terror or panic, without fear or anxiety. There was simply a garden and a clear blue sky and a door.

There have been occasions through the years where, like many of you, I have pragmatically considered the contingency of death, and foremost in that consideration was concern for the well-being of my family and distress at the thought of being separated from them. But the actual moment itself, the moment in the garden, was totally solitary and completely alone, without connection to any other human being. Someone once wrote that we are born alone and we die alone. And that's the way it was, just the garden and the door. And then the moment ended, and the imagery faded, and I did not walk through the door.

Later in the course of those eight or ten hours, there was a second moment, this one immediately upon my return to consciousness. Unbeknown to me, corrective treatment had begun, and the pressure on the brain had begun to subside. And as I awakened to the real world, without the need for anyone to tell me, I knew that I was better and that I had survived the crisis. I was still the living person that I had been, and I knew, consciously knew, that I was a survivor.

I believe that, in a very real sense, we are all survivors, though personally we may have never stood before the garden door. There is no human being who has not had his own dark hours, his own time of crisis through which he has struggled and which he has survived as his own person, with the conscious awareness that he has survived. I have seen mourners shattered by grief at the loss of their beloved, but there eventually comes a day or a moment when they consciously know that they have emerged from the dark valley and they consciously know that they have survived their own grief. I have seen marriages survive a veritable mountain of obstacles, and I have seen marriages that did not survive, but the former partners do survive, each on his own, each as his and her own person.

In one way or another, all of us have known the crisis of failure, whether financial failure or professional failure or personal failure. We have all lost something in our lives, even if it was the innocence of our childhood, or the idealism of our youth, or the closeness with our children once they grew up and flew the nest. At every turning point in life, writes Stanley Keleman, we do a little dying, and every one of us has seen something die that we wanted to live. But we have survived our little dyings, and we have survived our losses, and we have survived our failures, sometimes even better than we survive our successes.

And in the course of that process, we discover the truth of what the psychiatrist Robert Lifton has said: that every survivor is a Creator, that we move from each crisis to a more creative quest for our own authentic being. In the course of that process, we cannot help but discover the simple, profound wisdom of the Jewish saying that "a man has to swim upstream or he never knows who he is." No human being who survives a crisis is ever exactly the same as he was before.

We are all survivors, but surely very different one from the other. The one who survives an illness, with doctors and nurses and family and friends pooling their talents and their prayers for his recovery, is a very different kind of survivor than the one who has come out of Auschwitz, where everyone conspired toward his destruction. Someone who loses an elderly parent is a different kind of survivor than a parent who has lost a child. And while, according to Lifton, everyone who has survived the crisis of actual physical death feels a measure of guilt—Why him and not me?—the guilt differs from survivor to survivor, from crisis to crisis.

But we are still all survivors, whether of little dyings or big dying, and we are all here to tell the tale that, according to Elie Wiesel, is what survivors often feel impelled to do. We can here to testify that however severe or however moderate the blow, there is that human drive, there are those human resources, there is the power of that human spirit that God has given to us and to the allies that stand at our side that enable us to respond to the blow. It is the response of the old Jewish grandfather to his young grandson when they noticed a rock on the ground cracked ever so slightly, and through the crack a flower was growing, and the child asked how such a thing could be, and the old man answered; *Es will leben, mein kind, es will leben!*—"It wants to live, my child, it wants to live!"

It was something of what I felt when I awakened in that hospital room. Only a few hours earlier there had been a resignation about dying, and now there was a conscious, excited affirmation about living, the will to live asserting itself that all survivors experience when they consciously know they have returned to life and self and then celebrate, silently giving thanks.

Only a few hours earlier there was a passive acceptance of the future beyond the door, but now in that hospital room I was making plans for the future, however unrealistic, for the summer days that lay ahead, like all survivors who turn from yesterday to tomorrow, who, in the word invented by Stanley Kellerman, begin to "futurize" their lives.

And only a few hours earlier, I had stood solitary and alone before the garden door, and now all I wanted to do was call my family and connect with the human beings who were closest to me and tell them that they had no more reason to worry. I was like all survivors who begin to turn outside of themselves and back to the people they love.

And these, I believe, are God's gifts to us through every crisis, through every day of our lives: the human power to affirm our own will to live, the human power to futurize our own lives, and the human power to turn outward from ourselves to the ones we love and to the God who gives us strength to survive.

Thus does the New Year summon us, and thus does the New Year reassure us that we have survived the old year, that we have moved forward in the quest, with the allies who stand at our side.

In the words that are deeply Jewish and remarkably human: *Baruch Atah Adonai Eloheinu Melech ha-olam, shehecheyanu, v'kiy'manu, v'higi-anu laz'man hazeh.*

Blessed art Thou, O Lord our God, King of the universe, who has kept us alive and sustained us and allowed us to reach this day.

Amen.

Rosh HaShanah 1975/5736

The Nature of Being Human

It was the eve of *Kol Nidrei* in the year 1913. A young man of twenty-six walked into a little Orthodox synagogue in Berlin, Germany, with a particular purpose in mind. He was a student of philosophy, he prided himself on being a searcher after the truth, and he had come to the conclusion that the Judaism he knew, in which he had grown up, failed to offer him a philosophy of truth by which he could live in his world and at his moment of history. As it happened, one of his teachers was a former Jew who had sought relief for his own restlessness of spirit by converting to Christianity. And now, on this *Kol Nidrei* eve, the twenty-six-year-old Franz Rosenzweig was about to follow in his teacher's footsteps. As a person of integrity, however, he would not allow himself simply to steal away but insisted that his departure from Judaism be taken with dignity—and this *Kol Nidrei* and this Yom Kippur in this Orthodox synagogue was to be his farewell to the faith of his fathers.

But something happened to Franz Rosenzweig in the course of that *Kol Nidrei* and during the prayers and songs of the next day, because when the day was over, after the last call of the shofar, he left the synagogue fully determined that he was a Jew, would always be a Jew, and it was inconceivable that he could be anything else. And Franz Rosenzweig spent his few remaining years, prior to his premature death, in creating literary and philosophical works that became major additions to the mainstream of modern Jewish thought.

My intent is not to romanticize a piece of music or to idolize the melody of a song, but there is something in the pathos of *Kol Nidrei* that so authentically sings from the Jewish soul that anyone who has the slightest vestige of a Jewish soul left in him cannot usually help but respond. It is a song of tears but as much tears of endurance as they are tears of sadness. And it happened again and again: with the Marrano in Spain who had divested himself of all the outward and even some of the inward signs of his Jewishness, but on this very night he would steal away to some darkened basement where a service was being conducted secretly, away from the watchful eye of the Inquisitor, and he would listen to the melody of *Kol Nidrei* and he would be home again. It happened with the children of newly arrived immigrants to this country around the turn of the century, young people who thought that in order to free themselves from the old-world ways of their parents they also had to liberate themselves from the religion of their parents, but on *Kol Nidrei* they could not stay away. And it happened with Franz Rosenzweig. And it should only happen with some young Jews of our own day who seek the truth of their lives in Hari Krishna or in Reverend Moon's Unification Church or in Jews for Jesus. It should only happen that they should hear and respond to the melody of *Kol Nidrei*.

My intent is not to romanticize a song, but there are Jews everywhere, walking into synagogues tonight, who are not Marranos, not renegades, indeed have never denied what they Jewishly are. Not on the basis of any principle but for reasons that are not always clear to themselves, they have absented themselves from the ranks of active duty. They are our passive resisters, our non-conscientious objectors. But then *Kol Nidrei* sings and there is amnesty and they come back home with their Jewish souls.

And then we recognize that the Jewish part of us, which we thought we had pigeonholed or compartmentalized in some peripheral cubby of our busy lives, is in fact much closer to the center of our being, of our very selves, than we had ever intended or realized. Sigmund Freud, who rejected the religious aspects of Judaism and the ethnic aspects of Judaism, said it about himself—that his passion for knowledge and his willingness to stand in opposition to the majority, which were at the center of his being, were properties of his Jewish soul. Surely many Jews discovered it in 1967 when their own visceral Jewish response to the threatened destruction of the State of Israel was a matter of surprise and astonishment to them. Jean-Paul Sartre once wrote that a Jew's Jewishness is part of his primary being, whether he intends it or not, and that any attempt to negate or reject his Judaism becomes a negation and rejection of his own self.

Kol Nidrei, then, is the primary Jewish melody that sings not into a little Jewish cubby but into the primary center of our beings. It puts to rest that tired, old and naive question that never stops being asked: whether one is a Jew first or a human being first. The truth of *Kol Nidrei* is that the two are not separable. The Jew that I am and the human being that I am are inextricably bound together, because to be a Jew is not only to belong to a particular group but to a group that in its own particular way takes up the task of becoming a human person and of living in a human world—and all of our beliefs, and all of our rituals and all of our messianic hopes are unswervingly and inevitably directed toward that end.

It is not to say that other religions do not have their own program of humanization, and it is only a waste of time to debate which one is better. The truth is that they are different, that each one shapes its teaching about humanity through the idiom of its own tradition and beliefs and rituals and messianic hopes. Other religions or philosophies may very likely teach human compassion for the under- dog, but the taste of the *maror*, the bitter herb, at the Passover seder, the bitter reminder of what it feels like to be a slave, teaches me sympathy for the underdog in a particular kind of way. The question is not whether I am a Jew first or a human being first. The truth is that I am a Jewish human being or a human Jew, and it makes no difference which is the adjective and which is the noun. Judaism and humanity come together in the center of my being and together they help me to characterize the person that I am.

My Jewish and my human name is Adam, because, as we have mentioned at other times, Adam by Jewish perception is not simply the first man but every man. Adam is not only the beginning of humanity, he *is* humanity, the Jewish view of our own primary human nature.

Adam is born into a world of starry skies and green things and living creatures of field and sea, but with all the multiplicity that surrounds him, Adam is born alone, a unique being of incomparable singularity, the like of which there would never be in the world again. And even when the human population would increase to 372 billion, each child newly born would be an individual Adam, like no one else in the world. There is an old Yiddish proverb: "If I keep trying to be like someone else, or like everyone else, who will be like me?" There is only one *I* in the world, and only I can be like me, which delineates the sacred task of every parent to help his own child to grow into the unique individual Adam that he was born to be.

It was Adam alone, confronting his world—life, death, beauty, ugliness, the world—and when the day would come that there would be 372 billion Adams on the face of the planet, there would still be moments that could be only between Adam alone and the world. We are born alone, we die alone, and there are moments along the way, primary moments, when the only way to be is to be alone. There are moments in our lives when only the experience of aloneness, even without the people we love the most, can put us in touch with our own unique primary beings.

And then a new note is added, that it was not good for man to be alone all of the time, because there were other moments in Adam's life when his aloneness only made him feel lonely, when the starry skies and green fields and creatures of field and sea, even the God who created him were not antidote to his empty feel- ing of loneliness. What Adam needed was a human companion with whom he could face the world, with whom he could establish communication in words and a myriad of other ways, whom he could search out and touch physically and a myriad of other ways. He needed another person unique like himself, and, for that very reason, different from himself. The Hebrew word in the Bible is *k'neg'do,* which means both "similar to" and also "in contrast to," which is exactly what Adam needed.

So God created Eve, similar to, in contrast to, and Eve, by Jewish perception, was not only Adam's wife but also the second human being in the world. Eve is the beginning of human society, of community. And every Adam and every Eve in this world is an answer to someone else's loneliness, to communicate with, to touch, to be with, to take on the world.

And so we are, this delicate balance between Adam alone who is singular, self-sufficient, independent and individualistic, and Adam who is lonely, who needs another person, who needs Eve not only to ease the pain of his loneliness but to help him by the very experience of communicating and touching and being with, to help him become the unique person he was born to be. As Martin Buber keeps saying, the I, by the nature of its being, cannot become a complete I without a relationship with the Thou.

And when this delicate balance is upset, when the weight is shifted disproportionately to one side or the other, then our own humanity is in danger, and our own *Kol Nidrei* urgently calls us back to the center of our being.

It is that danger to which Philip Slater calls attention in his book *The Pursuit of Loneliness,* where he contends that much of the sense of frustration and despair in America today, much of the undefined ache of things not being right, can be traced to our unreserved overloading of the scale on the side of Adam alone, Adam self-sufficient, Adam independent with a fearsome independence.

We take our own children and push them toward a position of independence at a rate far accelerated beyond that of other societies. We try to guide them toward social relationships, we tell them to make dates, but most of the prizes and most of the promises are for doing things on their own. Our ideal housing arrangement is a separate room for each child; our ideal community is a homogeneous one so that our children can be with duplicates of themselves; our ideal family arrangements are ones in which grandparents are independent (which usually means far away), parents are independent and children are independent. The technology that we have created, for all its advantages, has made of our children's world and ours one big supermarket: You take, you pay, you go, without people, without relationships.

We call it individualism, says Harold Schulweis, but in reality, it verges on solitary confinement. We call it self-reliance, but in reality, it is an inhuman and unrealistic expectation.

And with the result, as many of us have seen, that some young people are burdened with deep concerns about the prospect of their own marriage, of making a commitment to another person, for fear that they might relinquish one iota of that idealized independence, even for the sake of a new relationship with a strength and beauty all its own.

And with the result, as I have seen in this very place, that some intelligent young people and some intelligent grown-ups have blocked and stymied themselves in their own personal search of their own lives. It is one matter for a person to read the books, to explore the ideas, and then to reach the conclusion that for him there is no Supreme Power in the world. It is something quite different when a person rejects out-of-hand the idea of a Supreme Power because it implies a dependence that he is unable to tolerate in himself: To him it is an affront to the self-sufficiency that his parents and society have taught him. I am always suspicious when someone describes religion as a crutch. My instinctive response is: "Why are you so intimidated by a crutch?"

With motives that were noble, with love for their children, in the best traditions of Emerson and rugged individualism, we loaded down the scale on the side of Adam alone. We missed the mark, we sinned against our own humanity and the humanity of our children. *Kol Nidrei* calls us back to the center of our being, to say that of all the problems that are beyond our reach, this is not one of them. Beginning this night, we could begin to shift the balance. Beginning this night, we could transfer part of the weight from selfness to otherness, from fierce independence to a mutual I-Thou relationship. We could begin with our children, with our marriages, with our offices by opening up our own closed existence, by stepping out of ourselves to communicate, to reach out and to touch.

The most I-Thou person I ever knew was Leo Baeck, the rabbi of the concentration camp, who spent the adult years of his life in the shadow of death and refused every offer of rescue for himself because he wanted to be with his people. And it was this man who said before and after that in Judaism, *hope is not only a privilege, it is a commandment.*

As we restore the balance of our own humanity, what awaits us is the commandment of hope and the commandment of courage that goes with it—the courage to be, to love, to laugh, to communicate, to touch, the courage to believe and to bring children into the world and to send them out into the world.

As we return to our own primary beings, what awaits us are the words of the commandment: *Chazak v'ematz*—"Be strong and of good courage"—and the hopeful, courageous, enduring melody is *Kol Nidrei*.

Amen.

Yom Kippur 1974/5735

Voyagers

One day I was working in my study at the temple and received a telephone call from a member of the congregation. In a quavering voice, she told me that her father had just died and that she was calling to make arrangements for the funeral. Soon after our conversation ended, another phone call, someone else, voice quavering with joy, to say that his wife had just given birth to a son and that he was calling to make arrangements for the *b'ris*.

In many respects, it was a usual day at the temple. But somehow the timing of those two phone calls, one right after the other, delivered an impact that thrust that particular day out of the realm of the ordinary. It was somehow saying that however we may live our lives from day to day, that whatever happens to us or we cause to happen, with all that we've learned and all that we've loved and all that we reject, with all of our medals of accomplishment and all of our battle scars, somehow they are all connected with the human reality of those two phone calls: that we're born and someday we die, and that in between we manage the voyage as best we can. With all of our philosophical discussions about whether Judaism is a religion or a culture, whether its emphasis should be on ethics or on ritual, what sometimes gets overlooked is that from its very inception, the special concern of our religion has been to chart that voyage between those two shores and those two phone calls.

And every year the High Holy Days arrive, and whatever they may or may not mean to each of us individually, to all of us they direct one common question: Voyager, where are you?

And if we keep nothing back, there are some modern voyagers who would have to tell of the little gods that they themselves have made and that they take along for the journey. It's no different from Isaiah's day 2,500 years ago, when he tells of the man who cuts down a tree and uses half of the wood for a fire to warm himself and cook his food. And from the other half, he carves an idol and bows down to it and calls out, "Deliver me, for thou art my god!"

That is no different from some of our modern voyagers who fortunately have managed to achieve a certain lifestyle with its leisure time activities, its sports, its music, its vacations and all the rest, a lifestyle that gives legitimate warmth and comfort to themselves and the members of their families. But then they will sometimes take that lifestyle and they will make it into a god, or at least they let it become a god, and they will even sacrifice to their little god that they have made.

I was once in a congregation where we were having a serious problem with a youngster in one of the classes, and we were able to arrange a conference on a Sunday morning that would include all of the staff who were involved with this child, all of whom were eager to help him as much as they could. And then I called the home, only to be told by the mother that the father could not possibly come to such a conference on a Sunday morning because that was his time on the golf course or the tennis court, or whatever it was. And then she added—and she even used the word—she said that her husband's Sunday morning game was "sacred." And he did not come.

Or a person will resign from the temple sometimes and he'll say, "It's too expensive to belong," and I'll say that no one is ever excluded from our temple for reasons of financial hardship, and he'll answer that it's not exactly hardship but that he has to cut down somewhere. And then we'll talk further only to discover that the rest of his lifestyle has not been cut down one bit, including the season tickets to the football games or the subscription to the opera or the vacation or anything—everything had been kept intact. Everything was sacred except his religion.

We have all known human beings who downtown have pushed themselves beyond their own endurance because up here the lifestyle had to be maintained exactly as it was.

We have all known (and we see in public life) perfectly decent human beings who will compromise themselves and their own principles of integrity because their lifestyle up here was their little god, to be preserved at any sacrifice, even of themselves.

All of us make sacrifices, but every sacrifice is not genuinely sacred. Some sacrifices are simply stupid, and some are pathetic, including those to the little gods who are not gods at all.

Voyager, where are you?

There are other modern voyagers who have no use for such idols. They have embarked on a more complex course. In their own words, they will say that they are searching for life's meaning or for their own true selves or for the one true God. Some of them are to be found among the followers of Reverend Moon or Hari Krishna or the Maharaji, each with its own promise of spiritual quest and absolute truth. It is estimated that the Jewish and Christian followers in such movements may number up to one million.

On a totally different course are some voyagers who are to be found in all kinds of encounter groups, or perhaps in the offices of rabbis and ministers, as they speak of their authentic attempt to find some meaning in the routine of their lives or as they speak of their dissatisfaction with the emptiness that pervades their lives.

And there are yet other voyagers on psychoanalysts' couches in their authentic attempt to deepen awareness of their own selves and to try to live by that awareness. And when we put all of the voyagers together, different as they are from each other, we are, as one observer described it, in the midst of a "Consciousness Revolution." Or as Theodore Rozack said a bit more pungently: "America in the mid-70's is launched on the biggest introspective binge any society in history has undergone."

To suggest Judaism's response to such voyagers, there is a Chasidic story told by Martin Buber:

> *Rabbi Chayim of Zans had married his son to the daughter of Rabbi Eliezer. The day after the wedding, he visited the father of the bride and said: "Look, my hair and beard have already grown white. I'm an old man and I have not yet atoned for my shortcomings!"*
>
> *"Oh, my friend," answered Rabbi Eliezer, "why are you thinking so much of yourself? How about forgetting about yourself, including your shortcomings, and think about the world?"*

And then Buber adds: "We should begin with ourselves but not aim at ourselves. We should try to understand ourselves, but not be preoccupied with ourselves."

And such is the risk of those voyagers who quest for final answers and ultimate meanings and total self-understanding: the risk that the purpose of their quest is not for the *value* of those answers that would help them reach out to the world or at least to their little corner of the world, but for the very triumph of *possessing* those answers. They want God or the meaning of life or self-understanding the way Lancelot wanted the Holy Grail and the way happiness hunters want the bluebird, so that they can cup it in their hands and claim it as their own, dead or alive. The risk is that some will want the opposite of what their psychoanalysis is intended to achieve, which is to help them creatively and productively find a place in the world. The risk is that they will not only begin with themselves but aim at themselves, because what some of them want, as Irving Kristol describes it, is a "patent medicine of the soul."

Judaism surely has no argument with the introspective search for self or the meaning of one's life. They are, in fact, the very reason for these High Holy Days. What Judaism does take difference with is *stretching it out,* because tomorrow, with the last blast of the shofar at *Ne'ilah,* an end will be put to the High Holy Days and their self-searchings and then we shall be called upon to take the results of our search and go back to the waiting world. And then, if we take the advice of the rabbis of old, throughout the year we shall take an hour a day to look at ourselves and see where we are—but the rest of the day is to look at the world and other human beings and see where *they* are and what *they* need and what gives *them* pain. Begin with ourselves but not aim at ourselves.

And when a Jew quests for God, it is not a God whom I can possess because that would make Him less than a God, but rather the God beyond, the totally Other, before whom I stand but cannot hope to understand. And all those responsive readings in the prayer book that sing praises to God and that are boring to so many modern Jews may have been included on purpose to divert us from ourselves to the outside, to God and God's world. And if we are bored, it may be that we are so inclined to self-involvement and personal relevance that we have trouble and boredom with anything that does not relate directly to ourselves.

But that same God for whom we quest, who by His essence is beyond understanding, farther than the furthermost star, is also, by Jewish belief, as close to us as breathing—to be sensed, to be encountered, to be experienced. Those other voyagers seek God in the Himalayas or in an ashram, but we look for Him, as Buber says it, "in our everyday hour on earth, in a streak of sunshine on a maple twig." For those other voyagers, God is a product; for us, He is a presence.

Those other voyagers are seeking a completeness of self and of life that by Jewish perception was never intended to be complete, except for those occasional moments that come to most of us as a by-product of our daily labors and everyday loves, those precious moments of completeness when, in the words of the Talmud, "heaven and earth kiss each other."

Those other voyagers speak of a search for what lies somewhere beyond. We speak of a now that extends into the Beyond.

They speak of a light at the end of the tunnel that will resolve all conflicts and solve all problems. We speak of a light that now and again shines through the cracks in the tunnel as we go on coping with our conflicts and our problems from day to day.

They center on themselves, which can make them so deadly serious. We center on life, for which a sense of humor is absolutely essential.

I told earlier this year of my visit to Macon, Georgia, on the occasion of the ninety-fifth birthday of Julian Morgenstern, president emeritus of Hebrew Union College and my Bible professor of many years ago. At ninety-five, he was slow of gait and blind in one eye; he spoke like a sickly man.

But when I asked him what he was doing and he told me of his unfinished book, numbering 1,600 pages, on the relationship between the practices of ancient Judaism and the origins of Christianity, his voice strengthened, his good eye brightened, his face shone.

In our brief voyage from shore to shore, all of the seekers after the grails and the bluebirds and the total self-fulfillment and the patent medicines of the soul are doomed to failure because they concentrate on their own ailments, because their failure to reach their unrealistic goals will simply deepen the emptiness that their unrealistic quest was intended to fill in the first place. Voyager, where are you?

My Jewish Bible professor, however close to the other shore, reaching out to his unfinished book and his unfinished world: his voice was strong, and his face shone.

Amen.

Yom Kippur 1976/5737

In the Image of God

Some of you who are here tonight shared in the inception of this sermon. It happened when we were together for one of those discussions that explored the middle years of life (which we decided could be anywhere from the age of thirty-five on.)

Among the women in that discussion were some whose children had grown up and were out of the house, women who had been through and had flourished in the whole experience of nurturing and caretaking. And now that their children were grown, they were looking for some new direction in their lives. There were others in the group whose children were not grown, not out of the house, but they, too, felt the need for something else besides childrearing and caretaking—some new direction in their lives.

Among the men in the group were some who had set goals for themselves when they were young and now, while they were still striving for those goals, had begun to question some of them. And there were others who had already reached the goals of their youth, but they, too, had begun to ask some questions: Was this the dream that we had dreamed? Is this the way it was supposed to be? Someone referred to George Bernard Shaw's statement that there are two tragedies in this life: One is not getting what you've always wanted; the other is getting what you've always wanted.

There was talk of aging and dying, including our own. There was talk of life's finitude, including our own. What was happening that night, just as what is happening during these High Holy Days, had all the makings of a truly Jewish religious experience, not only because we were confronting the ultimate questions of life and death, but also because we were confronting the ultimate personal question: How shall we, personally, live our lives on this earth so that we will have something to show for them, so that they will bear the stamp of our own personal value, our own personal dignity, our own personal sense of purpose? How shall we live our lives so that, when the day comes that we must take leave of this earth, we shall have left our footprints in the sand?

It was very religious and very Jewish, because Judaism has always addressed itself to that question. And Judaism's response has always begun with a premise, a

54

premise that like all premises cannot be proven but can only be declared. And this premise is declared in the very beginning of the Bible: that every human being on this earth is created *b'tzelem Elohim*—"in the image of God"—not simply a creature of earth and of instincts, of hunger and sex and all the rest, not even simply a creature of high intelligence who can win Nobel Prizes, but a creature *b'tzelem Elohim,* somewhat like God. Each creature has a God-given *neshamah*—"soul"—which, according to the mystical *Zohar*, is the mysterious light of each one's individual selfhood that shines through everything he is and everything he does.

And beginning with that premise of each one's sacred value and each one's *neshamah*, Judaism responds to the ultimate personal question: How do we live our lives and make our footsteps in the sand? By taking the light of that *neshamah* and carrying it out into the world and touching other *neshamahs*—of our wives, our husbands, our children, our parents, our friends, our job, our community, our world. Light touching light.

It was all very Jewish and very religious in that discussion of our middle years. Except for one problem—and it was a problem not only for that night and those people in that room but a problem for many people and many nights and many places—the problem of human beings like ourselves who have great difficulty in accepting that premise of *tzelem Elohim*, that premise of their own sacred value. Because when you listen closely to them, not all but some of them, they seem bent upon changing their directions, perhaps their careers, perhaps even their marriages, not only to invest the world with the value of their own souls but somehow to create that value in the first place. It seems that they're making their foray into the world not to light it up with their *neshamah* but with some fancy, fairy-tale expectation that they will kindle out there what they were unable to discover within themselves. Find someone, for example, preoccupied with his own self and you may be finding someone who has never accepted the premise of his own value and must now spend all his time trying to provide it. Or find someone who lives his life selfishly, always demanding and rarely giving, and you will find someone whose demands are an attempt, a vain attempt, to substitute for the value he never found in the first place.

It is the problem of the missing premise. It is the problem that Martin Buber conveys in the story of Rabbi Bunam, who instructed his students in the following parable:

It is said of Rabbi Isaac, son of Rabbi Yekel of Cracow, that after many years of great poverty that had never shaken his faith in God, he dreamed that someone told him to look for a treasure in Prague, under the bridge that leads to the king's palace. The rabbi set out for Prague, and every day he would walk around the bridge, which unfortunately was guarded by the captain of the guards, who one day asked him whether he was looking for something or somebody. Rabbi Isaac told his story, which caused the captain only to laugh: "And to please your dream you walked out your shoes to come here? If I believed in dreams, a long time ago I would have gone to Cracow, because I had a dream that in Cracow, under the stove of Rabbi Isaac, son of Rabbi Yekel, a treasure is buried. If I believed in dreams, I would have gone from house to house looking for Reb Yekel or Reb Isaac, and every house would have had a Reb Isaac and a Reb Yekel." Reb Isaac heard the story and bowed silently; he then returned home to Cracow and dug up the treasure from under his own stove.

And according to Buber, Rabbi Bunam added these words: "Take this story to heart and make what it says your own. There is something you cannot find anywhere in the world, even with your tzaddik, your leader, and yet there is a place where you can find it."

Whoever there is that has trouble with the premise, the project at hand is not to go out to prove what cannot be proven, not to demand from the outside what can only come from within. The treasure is where we are, beneath all the debris under which it has been buried. The project at hand is not to go out and buy a *neshamah* the way we buy everything else, but to reckon with all the obstructions that have kept our own *neshamah* from our own view. We have to reckon with all the wars we have lived through in our lifetime: how every casualty list and every *Kaddish* for every one of the 6 million, how every wanton and needless destruction of a human self could not help but do something to our own sense of self. We have to reckon with all the ways in which a technological computerized society has not only made our lives more efficient and more comfortable but also less personal, and how that depersonalization could not avoid doing something to our sense of self. It's a trivial instance, I know, and not very serious, but however helpful and efficient those automatic telephone devices can be, there is still for me a strange feeling about what's happening to my sense of self when I begin to talk after the beep and when I finish my conversation by telling the machine to have a good day.

We have to reckon with the society that tries to keep telling us that personal value at home, at school, at work is measured almost solely by external performance and not by inner worth, by external performance that is then given a grade and that, according to the grade, labels us either as a success or as a failure. Almost every week I try to tell the bar or bat mitzvah who stands on this pulpit that he or she doesn't have to worry about making a mistake because a bar or bat mitzvah is not a performance but the time when a young Jew takes the Torah, and yet I know how hard it is for that message to come through. Herbert Hendin reports from his research among college students that a large number of young men on the campus are haunted by feelings of being humiliated if they fail and by feelings of being murderous fighters if they succeed. Women students show a vulnerable need to fulfill unreasonably high expectations, to perform at unreasonably high levels, because otherwise they feel they will not be noticed, they will not be treated as persons.

What does that pressure do to a sense of self? Because in addition to everything else, we have to reckon with a society that places such an exorbitantly high premium on the approval that others give that we fall into the trap of measuring our own value by the price tag that others put on us. If some instance or other did not win "their" approval (whoever "they" may be), then we sense our failure not simply in that one instance but in our very selves. And we end up so vulnerable and so fragile that even a constructive criticism is perceived as an assault on our total fragile selves, and then we rise to our own defense, most often in anger, without even looking to see whether or not the criticism was valid. And when a possible flaw is perceived as a major total failure, what does this do to our sense of self? How does that pile up the debris over our buried treasure?

Many years ago, a group of rabbis was working with a group of psychiatrists to explore ways in which religion and psychiatry might work hand in hand. I remember one patient whose life was a shambles. She had been deprived all her life—materially, emotionally, physically—and now she was having problems with her husband and her children. She had the lowest self-image of any human being I have ever known. The psychiatrist had worked many hours with her in helping to clear away some of the crippling debris that had piled up through her life. And then one day, after he had done his work, I was able to say to her: "Don't you realize that you are created in the image of God, that nobody can take that away from you, not your unsympathetic husband or your rebellious children? No one can take that away from you despite what all the others and what you yourself say about yourself." And for the first time, that lady was able to brighten up, and her voice became stronger, and her eyes sparkled the slightest bit. Perhaps for the first time, she had caught a glimpse of her own *neshamah*.

If there be those whose view of their own selfhood has been blocked by the particular circumstances of their own lives, then that's what psychiatrists are for, and that's what other doctors of humanity are for, to help clear the obstruction so that the light can come into view. And for all the rest of us, for all who have lived together through the years of war and technology and verdicts of success and failure, to all the rest of us there comes this Day of Days to dig through all the debris, to call it for what it is, to reestablish the contact with our very selves that still are and that have always been in the image of God and therefore of value and dignity and therefore sacred. It is still a premise without proof, but we have to take Yom Kippur's word for it that the human soul, which can approach the throne of divine forgiveness, is more than human. We have to take three thousand years of Jewish history's word for it—that what is really of value is not what can be measured or weighed or showed on a profit-and-loss sheet or performed or approved of by the rest of the world, but what is in the heart of hearts of a human being.

We have to take the word of those inmates in the concentration camp who consciously decided that their own human dignity would not succumb to every attempt of their oppressor to break that dignity. In the words of one of them, Viktor Frankl, "A person's inner strength could raise him even above his outward fate." And if we can say that, if we can say "Amen" to the premise, then we're ready to go back to the world. Then whatever we choose to do in that world, whether it be a new direction or a new career or a new anything, our choice will be based not on an attempt to prove what cannot be proven but rather on an attempt to bring to that world the *neshamah* that has been there all the time and share it with that world and bless the world with it. And if we decide to stay closer to our homes and our communities and let that be our careers, then we shall know that these, too, are places for the light of our selfhood to shine. These, too, are places where our sacred value can be expressed and shared.

We have to take Yom Kippur's word for it and go back to the world no longer preoccupied with the need to find ourselves because now we know we were there all the time, no longer demanding so much because now we have discovered what our demands could never have produced. Now we can go out to the world to celebrate its joy and its beauty without wearing out our shoes and our psyches traveling to Prague, because the treasure is right here in Cracow in the place where we are.

Now we can go back to the world where tomorrow the debris is bound to start piling up again, but at least we shall go back with the truth that this day has tried to teach us, the truth expressed in words that are very Jewish: "Blessed is man and blessed is woman that they were created in the image of God." Especially blessed are they when they *know* that they were created in the image of God.

Amen.

Yom Kippur 1977/5738

Loneliness

Many years ago, in another congregation, a group of men were away for a weekend retreat sponsored by the Men's Club. I do not recall the exact topic for that Shabbat afternoon and for good reason: because in the course of the discussion, one of the men veered off the topic that had been programmed and made mention of a feeling of loneliness in his own life. He could not define it; he could not specify what caused it; he only knew that there were times when he felt it and felt it most keenly.

And then it happened: Almost everyone in that room—men in the professions, men in the world of business, many of them well established and well along the road of achievement, almost everyone in that room—proceeded to talk about his own feelings of loneliness.

What made the experience so rare and so unforgettable was that the subject is hardly ever discussed, hardly ever among friends, hardly ever at the family dinner table, surely not downtown, and hardly ever even among doctors and teachers and clergymen who will always discuss a gamut of professional concerns but rarely include the concern of their own human loneliness.

The way we usually approach the subject of loneliness is the way we used to approach death and dying before it was almost forced into the public arena: mostly by avoiding it, because we have all seen lonely people sitting next to other lonely people on lonely park benches, and they are the people that we would least like to be. So we shy away from the subject altogether, because in our idealized, packaged version of healthy adjustment, there is no room for loneliness, not even a little bit.

What made that Saturday afternoon so rare and so welcome was that here almost no one was shying away, with the exception of one man in the room, and I suspect that he was the loneliest one in the crowd. But otherwise, in this small sampling of humanity, there was proof of what Thomas Wolfe once wrote in his essay entitled "Loneliness," "that far from being a rare and curious phenomenon," loneliness "is the central and inevitable fact of human existence."

In these next few moments, in the spirit of not shying away, we turn to the subject of loneliness. First, a distinction between "lonely" and "alone." Both are usually used to mean "by oneself," but alone is voluntary; alone is by oneself and liking it. Alone is time for books and music and trees and walking on the beach. Alone is for spending time with one's thoughts, for discovering one's resources, for praying one's prayers. Alone is what Thoreau experienced at Walden Pond when he said that solitude was his best companion. Alone is what Rabbi Nachman of Bratzlav advised when he said that everyone should spend at least one hour a day by himself or herself, for only thus can we achieve union with God. Alone is usually without other people, but even when they are there, even in a sanctuary with people in it, everyone can be alone as the unique, singular, alone human being that our Creator intended us to be.

The other word, the other feeling, is lonely, also being by oneself but *not* out of choice and *not* with our own consent. It speaks of those times when the need is for contact with other human beings, when, in the words of Martin Buber, the I needs his Thou, when there is need for what Buber calls "a meeting," in which each one acknowledges the personal value and God-given worth of the other. And when I am deprived of that meeting that I so badly want, when the Thou is not there to recognize my value and my worth, it is then that I feel less than a total person, and it is then that I suffer the pain of loneliness. It is then that I may avoid all time by myself for fear that it may become lonely time. It is then that I know what the person must have meant who described his loneliness as standing by himself on an island with the shore in view and all the other people on shore in view, everything in view, nothing in reach. And sometimes it can happen even in a crowded room.

There can be the loneliness in growing up: the child we have all seen or been who stands longingly outside the circle where others are friends with each other and they make no room for this one person, perhaps because this one sees the world from a different mountaintop, perhaps simply because they have no need for this person. And this one person stands outside, even at times when the others are members of the family, but still there's no room, except on the outside.

There can be the loneliness in growing old, as Suzanne Gordon speaks of it in her book *Lonely in America*, the feeling of being shut out not because of *who* one is but because of *what* one is; the feeling of being treated by those closest not as a person who happens to be old but just simply as old. I knew an old man in the bombed-out Hunts Point section of the Bronx who many years ago showed me a letter he had received from his son. He received such letters twice a year, he said, although he and his son hardly ever saw each other. I looked at the return address on the envelope to discover that the son lived on Long Island.

And there can be the loneliness of the single life as so many have described it: people looking for partners but without partnership, looking for lovers but without love. It has made the singles industry a multibillion-dollar operation. It has made the singles bars in New York among the loneliest places in the world.

And there can be loneliness in marriage, in some marriages a far-reaching loneliness of two people who once reached out to each other in love but no more. Or there can be, as there is in most marriages, a little bit of loneliness with two people still in love, still reaching out to each other, but not always at exactly the same time.

And there is the universal loneliness of those who have loved and lost, whom separation or death has dealt "the most unkindest cut of all." At such moments we may have been surrounded by friends, and the friends helped, and surely the family helped, but they could not ease the pain of standing alone on the island unable to reach across, unable to touch, unable to love. The loneliness of grief is the most lonely of all.

So a little bit or a lot, we are all lonely. Farther or closer to the shore, we are all on the island. And if we do not shy away, if we are willing to confront the distance between island and shore, then we ready ourselves for the journey, a journey in two parts.

One is to find the way out of our own loneliness. If it was caused by grief, then our journey out begins when we begin to taper our own grief, to channel toward the outside all the emotion we had poured into our own plight and our own selves. What is so wonderful about the Jewish laws of grief and mourning is that they are a guidebook that begins with self-concern and self-pity and then moves us away toward the world, away from ourselves toward the others who need our help and toward the world that needs all the help it can get.

Many years ago a woman who had suffered the grief of a marital breakup called me. She was very lonely even two years after the separation, and it all came through in her voice. At one point I interrupted and said, "You know, if you don't stop whining, no one will ever want to be around you." I worried later that my response was not very rabbinic, but now I can tell you that it worked. We cannot confront our loneliness without confronting our self-pity.

And then, if our loneliness comes from being rejected by other human beings, then we ask: How much of it is of our own doing? How much rejecting comes from us to them? How critical are we? How judgmental? How self-righteous? How much of the distance begins with our own resistance to getting close? How much are we like that youngster in the short story by the Yiddish writer Peretz, who one day came home from school very irritable and entered into a squabble with his brother and sisters. When they reported him to the mother, she dealt harsh judgment upon the son, whereupon he ran out of the house angry and distressed, went down the hill into the valley between the mountains and sat on a rock and yelled, "I hate you." Whereupon the echoes all around him resounded with a chorus of replies. And he ran home and sobbingly complained to his mother that everybody in the world hated him. Whereupon the mother placed her hand on his head with a maternal pat and said, "Why don't you go back and sit on that same rock and call out 'I love you' and see what happens?" As we take our journey from island to shore, we must reckon with the echoes that we elicit from other human beings.

And for those little bits of loneliness in every marriage, in every family, between parents and children, whatever the ages, the journey out of that loneliness begins simply by smoothing the rough spots from island to shore, by listening to what the other is saying even when the other is not speaking, by feeling each other's pain even when there are no tears, by reaching out not for a keeper but for a partner.

No matter what age, no matter what the cards have dealt out, there is no one in this sanctuary who cannot reach out to another as partner and not as keeper, as person to be valued and not as case to be handled. And thus the journey out of our own loneliness.

And then the second journey, this one the journey to someone else's loneliness.

Let me describe a scene that happens in the social hall on some Friday nights during the *Oneg Shabbat*. Friends and acquaintances cluster in little groups of friendship. But then there is someone or some couple awkwardly balancing the coffee cup because there is no one to talk to, lonely at that moment, lonely because they are strangers to everyone else, on an island not of their own making. And what could happen at a sacred moment is that someone could walk over and make room in the circle and thus begin the journey to someone else's loneliness.

There are lonely human beings in every community and every congregation. There are lonely human beings where we work and where we go to school and where we live. There are lonely human beings wherever we are, and of them the Chasidic teacher said: "There are those who feel deep distress and are unable even to tell what they feel in their hearts. But if they meet one person with a joyful face, he can revive them with his joy. And to revive a person is no slight thing."

May we not shy away from the journey—the journey to overcome, with God's help, our own loneliness, to know the joy of the meeting, to know again the joy of being alone without the fear of being lonely.

And with God's strength and help to take the second journey, to rescue another human being from his isle of loneliness, to counter another person's sadness with whatever joy we have, because it is written: "To revive another human being is no slight thing."

Amen.

Yom Kippur 1978/5739

Power

The journey of Yom Kippur may well have been the first guided tour in Jewish history, and it has been repeated every year until this very day. The tour begins at the gate, at the Gate of Repentance, and to the melody of *Kol Nidrei* we walk inside the gate into the courtyard for a twenty-four-hour stay.

It may, in fact, be the only organized Jewish tour in history that included no meals, not even Israeli breakfast. It was decided long ago that this journey would be one of the spirit, to match the truth of our very selves against the Supreme Truth that some of us call God, to locate the trails on which we have wandered away, which some of us call sin, and then to find our way back, which some of us call repentance.

As the guidebook for this unusual journey, we look again to the book of our people's prayers. Aside from the private time that we need within the gate to do our own personal exploring without a book and without someone else's words, our people also felt the need for some signposts to help us locate and identify those paths onto which we had blundered throughout the year. Thus do we find in our prayer book that catalog of *Al Cheit*s, each beginning with "For the sin that we have sinned against Thee," and each followed by some category of misconduct for which each of us is asked to fill in privately the details of our own meandering.

And should it happen that one or another of those *Al Cheit*s has no application for one or another of us, there is no reason for anyone in this congregation to feel unjustly accused. For that very reason, the commentators tell us, the declaration is worded in the first-person plural: "For the sin that *we* have sinned against Thee," because in any congregation with its minimum of ten or as large as this one, the chances are good that every one of the *Al Cheit*s applies to someone.

The *Al Cheit* to which I ask you to turn tonight could easily be one of those that get glossed over: *Al cheit shechatanu l'fanecha b'chozek yad*: "For the sin that we have sinned against Thee by abuse of power."

It could get glossed over because as a people who have walked our own rocky road through history, we may have experienced the abuse of power but much more as its victims than as its perpetrators. Some may recall many years ago when Richard Rubenstein, the author of *After Auschwitz*, told us that even when Jews do achieve a position of privilege in a society, it has never been a position of power, never a position with the final say on the turn of events or on the lives of people. It was always a position not of power but of influence, a secondary position that would provide advice and direction to the people who would wield the power, and Henry Kissinger may be cited as the most recent example of a Jew of influence and not of power.

And on a personal level, there may be some among us who are business magnates or molders of public opinion or powerful figures in politics and thus are would-be candidates for the abuse of power, but for the great majority of us, it seems that we have enough trouble gaining control over our own lives without even thinking about interfering in the life of anyone else. We own up to our share of sins, but abuse of power is not one of them.

I ask you to consider it with me tonight because it sometimes happens that "what the builders reject may be the chief cornerstone." And it may happen that the problem of power that we are inclined to gloss over may be the chief cornerstone of the very religion that brings us to this place on this day.

So here is one Jew's version of the problem of power. According to divine plan, as we read it in the Bible, every human being in the world, like Adam, is endowed with a unique combination of talents and abilities, and these constitute the source of his own personal power, which in Hebrew is referred to as *koach*. *Koach*—the power to make it through a day, to forge ahead, to work, to create, to live. *Koach* is physical ability and mental ability and artistic creativity and business astuteness and professional expertise and political sophistication.

The divine plan, according to the Bible, was that Adam and Eve and all the other human beings in the world would pool their respective *koach*s. With each one fulfilling his own potential, they would not only affect and influence each other but would come to depend on each other for what each one uniquely had to offer, in a very happy arrangement.

And according to that original plan in the Bible, the one arena where Adam and his confreres would exert dominant control was in the things of nature, regarding the beasts of the earth and the fish of the sea and the fowl of the air and the things that grow out of the earth—with the exception, of course, of those two trees in the garden that God told Adam were off limits.

Where the plan goes awry is that no sooner does Adam sense the full vigor of his *koach*, than he has no concern for limits, and he eats from the forbidden tree, which is one of the problems of power. Where the plan goes awry is that some members of that human family, early on, began to ignore the boundary line between the world of nature and the world of people and began to use their *koach* not to share with other human beings but to dominate and control and manipulate and exploit as though they were things and not people, to relate to them in the manner that Martin Buber labels as "I-It"—a person as a thing, which is the problem of power until this very day. In *The Culture of Narcissism*, Christopher Lash describes what he perceives as the new pattern of corporate life, where the primary objective of an executive is not to win the loyalty of his subordinates (even to himself) and surely not to the task at hand but rather to learn their weaknesses and locate their areas of vulnerability, which will then assure him a position of supremacy over them. He quotes the boss in Joseph Heller's book *Something Happened*, who contends that what he wants from his subordinates is "not good work but spastic colitis and nervous exhaustion."

We all have our moments of "I-It," says Buber—husbands and wives, parents and children, friend and friend. There are times when we all use each other a little; we manipulate each other a little. But if those times are only now and then, we are still for each other persons and not things. But when we reach the point where a parent sees the child only as a clone of himself, or when a growing-up child sees his parent only as a caretaker or a giver of attention, or when a doctor perceives a patient only as a diseased part of a body, or when a teacher perceives a student only as a passive receptacle for that which that teacher wants to teach, or when a clergyman expects his congregation to say "yes" to everything he says, or when a congregation expects a clergyman to say only what they want to hear—then we have entered the realm of "I-It," of people turned to things, of power running amok.

The classic Jewish example of power run wild is Pharaoh in Egypt, because by reducing human beings to slavery, Pharaoh resorts to the ultimate in "thinghood," next to murder itself. And when the Jewish people is born out of that slavery, then the very birth and existence of the people become a protest against the abuse of power. And then that people makes a covenant to amend the carte blanche that Adam and all of the pagans took away with them from the Garden of Eden. Now there are specifics, set limits. As a person develops his *koach*, as he expresses his talents and abilities, he is told: You shall not kill! You shall not steal! You shall not commit adultery! You shall not embarrass another human being in public! You shall not oppress the poor! You shall not manipulate! You shall not take advantage of another human being's area of vulnerability! You shall not do any of those things that turn another human being into a second-hand thing!

The one question that Adam had when he left Eden was "Can I?" The two questions the Jew had when he left Sinai were "Can I?" and then "Should I?" And as he asks those questions, he stands, as we do tonight, in the very presence of his God.

Adam came out of Eden with his sense of *koach,* the power of his mind and his body. The Jew came out of Sinai with a sense of what my teacher, Rabbi Soloveitchik, referred to as *g'vurah*—the strength of his spirit, the power sometimes *not to* do even when he could—*g'vurah,* which in Hebrew also means "heroism."

G'vurah is for people who love each other and who, in a moment of conflict, do not use their power to attack the other's weakness even though they have the *koach* to do so.

G'vurah is for parents whose children must deal with their problems every day, and we, their parents, have the *koach* to intercede every day, to protect them from the harshness of the world, to have a class changed because they don't get along so well, to make their problems go away. We have the *koach,* but then we use the *g'vurah* and we hold back, so that the child can learn for himself to deal with life.

G'vurah is what we try to instill in our children when they grow older and become aware of their own *koach* to hurt other children.

And I believe that *g'vurah* was what God Himself practiced at the very moment when Abraham placed his son as sacrifice upon the altar, that moment when God's will was about to reign supreme in proving the loyalty of His servant. And at that moment, even God retreated from His position of absolute power, never to know whether Abraham would have completed the deed or not. God gave up the *koach* of His own knowing so that a human being should not become a lifeless thing on the altar.

Al cheit shechatanu, "For the sin that we have sinned against Thee" by abuse of power, by people turned into things, forgive us. As we stand before Thee and as the gates will soon close and a New Year begins, give us, O God, the *koach,* the power to live each day, to do what we can and to share what we can. Give us, we pray, the *g'vurah,* the power, sometimes *not* to do. Give us the *g'vurah* to live, at least a little bit, like heroes.

Amen.

Yom Kippur 1979/5740

Human Power to Change the World

It is a curious happening that we, the members of Westchester Reform Temple, together in this place on this night, should be welcoming a new year that we designate in the traditional mode as 5743, which suggests that it was precisely 5,743 years ago that God, the Creator, caused the light to break through the darkness and that a world came into being. And the sky of that world was studded with stars, and the earth of that world was garbed with trees and flowers, with an astonishing assortment of creatures romping around. And a man and a woman were taking it all in.

The curiosity is that Reform Judaism, which claims to combine the teachings of Jewish tradition with the teachings of science and reason, should cling to a tradition that flies so fiercely in the face of scientific theory with its millions and billions of years. And while a recent Gallup poll reported that 44 percent of those interviewed (and the number included a sizable number of college graduates) subscribed to the position that God created the human being within the last 10,000 years, we would hardly expect an enlightened Reform Judaism to count itself in the rank of those old-time believers.

So why 5743? Because such a tradition, I believe, despite the detail of its numbers, is telling us that our being here together tonight for these High Holy Days is somehow connected with the totality and the majesty of the world *whenever* it was created. It was expressed by one of our own members when she said to me that somehow Rosh HaShanah and Yom Kippur are missing some of the cozy intimacy of a regular Friday night in temple, and she was absolutely right. The congregation on a regular Friday night is smaller, much smaller. The mood on a regular Friday night, the prayers and the music are more homey, more *haimish*.

The mood and the prayers and the music of these days are what their title suggests: Yamim Noraim, "Awesome Days," cosmic days, with the blast of the shofar piercing the heavens and proclaiming that far-off day when the Lord shall be one and His name shall be one in all the world.

And of all the Jewish holidays, the music and the prayers and the mood of these Holy Days are the least ethnic, the least to do with the glories and struggles of our Jewish people descended from Abraham, and the most to do with our personal selves descended from that first man and woman. Each year we come back as descendants of those first ones, those human beings in the raw, to stand before our God a year older, our resumés updated, carrying our good days and bad days and the days in between, and what makes us feel proud and grateful and strong and what gives us ache and makes the ground shaky underfoot. We're here with the people we love, and we miss some of the people we love.

And thus our being here together, totally cosmic and totally personal, how the world is and how each of us is in it, what a person does and how that doing ripples outward to the world. It is what the ancient proverb said: that if in a person's life there is shalom—well-being, put-togetherness, peace—then there will be shalom in that person's family; and if there is shalom in that person's family, then it can be in his community; and if in his community, then in his nation; and if in his nation, then there is hope for shalom in the world.

An example of the ripple effect: In June of this year, the United States Senate passed legislation to extend the Voting Rights Act, which prevents discrimination in the voting booth and thus strengthens the democratic fabric of our country. What was not recorded in those press announcements is what some of us remember from almost twenty years ago: how young people, then of college age, many of them Jewish, traveled to Mississippi at risk of life and limb to organize the members of the black community to claim their rights as voting citizens, despite opposition and intimidation and harassment. I spoke then to many of those young people in their headquarters in Jackson, Mississippi, and they talked about their work and why they were there and what their conscience told them to do. They said not a word about changing the world, but twenty years later the verdict of history is that they did.

Another ripple effect: how what a person does moves out into the concentric circles of his world. There are many college students here tonight who, at no small inconvenience, decided to take their belongings to school and then to come home to be with their families for these High Holy Days. And there are other young people from our congregation who are away tonight but let it be known to their parents that they are seeking out a service for Rosh HaShanah. And what we can attest to is how their decision to be here, or wherever, ripples with strength of spirit into the world of their families and the world of this congregation and the world of their Jewish people. And even though they did not set out to shape the world, they do.

And on and on: when one human being tutors another in that person's struggle to learn, when one human being visits a nursing home to preserve human contact, when members of this congregation give a lease on life to two brothers from Vietnam and then a mother and daughter, when members of this congregation send lifelines and "hopelines" to fellow Jews in the State of Israel, when the seder tables are set in that room for elderly Jews from the Bronx (however they may disrupt the proceeding) who live from year to year for that night, and on and on—with all of these mitzvot, with all the deeds that we here could collectively compile, with all those divine sparks that the Chasidim say are encased in shells and that we liberate when we do a mitzvah, without ever intending to shape the world, yet we do.

Then we ask: With all of our power to release the sparks, why do community causes go begging for volunteers? Why have we become such a litigious society with someone always ready to sue someone? Why is there so much of what someone dubbed as the "spirit of meanness in the land"? Why do able-bodied people take parking spaces clearly reserved for the handicapped? Why is narcissism so popular a word?

In part, I believe, because we have lost that conviction of our own power to shape the world. For some it can only be the paycheck that proves the worth of the work they do, and they do not volunteer. We concentrate on taking because we are no longer convinced of the power of giving. We control because we are not convinced of the power of sharing. We clutch because we are not convinced of the power of embracing. And doubting our power to release the sparks, we step on the shells.

For the sin that we have sinned against Thee by abuse of power.

I shared the following experience from this bimah on the High Holy Days about fifteen years ago. The experience had taken place years before when I was assistant rabbi at Temple Beth El in Great Neck. One day I was walking down the hall of the religious school and overheard a bar mitzvah boy calling his mother on the hall telephone and asking her to drive to the temple and take him home. It would have been a fifteen-minute walk. And because I knew that there was an infant at home and what a production it would be for the mother, I said to the youngster: "It's such a beautiful day. Why don't you walk for those fifteen minutes and let your mother be?" And his answer became a major influence on my entire rabbinic career. He said: "Because I'm selfish, but at least I know it." And I said: "But that's not the way you should be. You should change." And the reason that my preachy plea accomplished nothing was because as far as he was concerned, knowing that he was selfish took care of everything. "That's the way I am" was not only a statement of fact but a statement of self-vindication.

But now, after a lot of years and a lot of life and a lot of watching the likes of that boy grow up, I would offer a different answer. Now when he would tell me that he's selfish but he knows it, I would not tell him to change. Rather I would say to him: "But that's not the only way you are."

Because what I have come to believe is that no one really changes. We are what we are—the children of our parents, the repository of our life experiences, what our bodies are, our minds are, our psyches are, our souls are. What some people call the "new me" (even if the grammar were correct) cannot ignore or dismiss the "old me" and the old values and the old relationships, because if I do dismiss them, I am no longer I but inauthentically someone else.

People do not change. What people do is discover their own other possibilities, their own alternative resources, their own untapped powers, their own unliberated sparks. They discover, we discover, that besides the pettiness in us, there is also the power to be generous and to be significant; that besides the grudges that practically all of us hold, there is also in us the power to let go of those grudges (some of which we had so long that we forgot why we had them in the first place). We discover that besides the bluntness that has the power to hurt (which we pass off as "honesty," and may God spare us from such "honest" people), we also have the power to keep our mouths shut. And besides the part of us that lashes out in anger, there is the part of us that regrets the fallout of that anger. And besides everything that gets in the way of people who care for each other and allows them to drift apart, there is another resource in those very people that wants them to stay close and to stay loving. And besides the power of that boy at the telephone to get what he wanted and have his mother come and get him, there was also in that boy the power to care for the plight of his mother and to walk those fifteen minutes home.

Thus do we begin 5743, with thanks to God that we have reached this day, with thanks for children and parents and friends that are close at hand, and even if they are not, still they are.

May God give all of us of God's strength to release the sparks. May we be strong and find shalom for ourselves, and thus for each other, and thus for our families, and thus for our community, and thus for our world.

And God looked upon all that He had created, and He saw that it could be good again.

Amen.

Rosh HaShanah 1982/5743

Anger

We are speaking this Yom Kippur of that moment when Moses, on his way down the mountain, saw his people dancing round a calf of gold, whereupon he hurled down and shattered the tablets of the Commandments that he had been cradling in his arm. We are speaking on this Yom Kippur of that moment when King Lear furiously ordered his daughter Cordelia out of the kingdom because the words she had spoken displeased her father. We are speaking of that human emotion that the ancient writer Horace described as *furor brevis*—"the brief madness"—that Aristotle defined as "the desire for retaliation," that John Locke characterized as "the desire to injure others." It is the human emotion that never tires of research, whether by psychologists or biologists or anthropologists or political scientists and most recently by a social psychologist, Carol Tavris, in her much-discussed book entitled *Anger: The Misunderstood Emotion*.

Most of us, although we may not claim expertise on the subject of anger, at least can claim a measure of direct personal experience. Parents get angry at children and vice versa. Husbands and wives, ex-husbands and ex-wives, employers and employees, widowers, widows—none of us escapes the stormy assault. The anger may be at each other, at us, at God, at life.

This sermon for Yom Kippur with its thoughts on anger is intended for people who sometimes get angry, and not for angry people. Angry people are continually that way: They expect to be wronged and cheated at every turn, just as they feel that life has wronged and cheated them until now. Most minor annoyances become major grievances, and they insist on telling you exactly how they feel, which is usually furious. They say that they are simply being honest, but they do not say or do not recognize that their honesty is fired in the furnace of their own anger.

Sometimes we feel sorry for them, for in the words of an anonymous writer of the fifteen century: "Whoever is habitually angry, his life is no life at all." We feel sorry for them, even become angry at them for they usually manage to provoke our anger. For them is needed not some sermon thoughts or a book but a search in depth, monitored by doctors of the soul, to discover where the bad seed was planted, how it grew to be so overgrown, and how to plant again, now with hope and trust for the days that are still to come.

So this sermon, with its thoughts about anger, is not for them but for all the rest of us who live our lives from day to day, some days better than others, some days spectacularly good and some woefully bad. From day to day we steer the course as best we can, and then something happens, sometimes major, sometimes minor, and depending on the day and depending on the mood and depending on what else is happening in our lives, that something can ignite the explosive of our anger.

It is one of those emotions that we share with all the other animals in the kingdom. An animal becomes angry when it feels threatened or thwarted or insulted, and so do we. The anger of an animal sets off bodily changes that gird it for defense or attack, and so does ours. The anger of an animal can persist beyond the time and place and cause that provoked it; so let everyone else beware after a bad day in the jungle or a bad day at the office. Let everyone beware, especially at home, because home is not only where members of a family, living and loving so close, are bound to provoke in each other a normal family quota of anger, but home is also where the members of that family, feeling so safe with each other, will sometimes bring their unexploded anger all ready to be set off.

Animal anger and human anger: But what marks the difference between the two? As in any other emotion or instinct, what marks the difference is that human trait called *seichel*—a Hebrew word whose meaning finds no exact English equivalent. *Seichel* is intelligence, but more than that. *Seichel* is insight, but other than that. *Seichel* is *seichel*, that extraordinary human power to assess a moment or a situation or a crisis, to set it within perspective and then to act on the basis of that assessment so that it will produce a maximum of benefit and a minimum of hurt.

What *seichel* does to anger is give that intermediate step of assessment and perspective, that middle step between the angry feeling of fret and thwart and insult and the moment of taking action. That middle step is not to squelch our anger, not to bury it so that it will force up the pressure of our blood or feed our silence. The purpose of the middle step is that once having felt the anger in all of its intensity, then with our *seichel* we decide, we consciously decide, what to do with our own anger. And it can no longer be assumed, reports Dr. Tavris, that the soundest decision is to give our rage full expression, to ventilate it all the way in order to be rid of it. The problem with that decision, she writes, is how often that talking out our anger doesn't reduce it but simply rehearses it, all those times that coming out with the anger simply gets us more angry, firing us up instead of cooling us down. And even more, the problem with letting it all out even those times when it may make us feel better is all the other people that it makes feel worse, which is why Dr. Willard Gaylin describes this freewheeling ventilation of our anger as "a form of public littering." And even for the person who has ventilated, there is the feeling afterward sometimes of embarrassment, sometimes of shame. There is an old proverb: "When the kettle boils over, it overflows on its own sides."

In place of letting loose, then, that step in between, not only for the proverbial counting to ten but during that counting time, to ask some questions with our own God-given *seichel*.

The question for when a person gets angry: Does what just happened or what was just said that is provoking me call for *all* the anger I am feeling? Is it significant or is it trivial? Is it a matter of true principle or simply someone else's different way of doing things that calls for a little tolerance and perhaps a little silent suffering?

And if our *seichel* tells us that the answer to all of those questions is that indeed we have been offended, indeed we have a grievance, then these words from Maimonides in the twelfth century: "When one person wrongs another, the aggrieved must not hate the offender while keeping silent. Rather he ought to inform the offender by saying, "Why did you do this to me? Why did you wrong me in this instance to make me so angry?"

Not to get even, because the Torah commands: "Thou shall not take vengeance." Not to get even, not to attack and not to hurt, except maybe just a little. Not "This is what you always do!" but "Why did you do this in this instance?" Not to revisit a collective list of grievances but to put this grievance in context, which someone described as a "loving rebuke." And only when that loving rebuke is ignored, then are we entitled to that display of our strong anger, to goad the other to listen, to put the other on the way to correcting the grievance; but now we are in control of our anger and not propelled by it. Now we are directing it and not consumed by it. In the words of a Chasidic rabbi of former generations: "Long ago I conquered my anger and placed it in my pocket. When I have need of it, I take it out."

The strongest, most fiery anger in the years of our Jewish story is from the mouth of the prophets. They cried out God's grievances, not only that the poor were suffering, not only that the rich were exploiting the poor, but that the rest of the people were not angry enough to correct the grievance "because they were not grieved for the hurt of my people," cried the prophet Amos. And so with us and so with our children: As they diligently pursue the opportunities of their lives and their careers that give us so much love and so much pride, how do we stir up in those very children some anger at Anatole Scharansky's wasting in prison, at millions of humans walking day to day hungry, at old people who have abandoned hope because there is no hope left and because they are indeed abandoned? How do we stir up our anger and the anger of our children? How do we transform their intellectual acuteness of poverty and suffering in this world into a feeling of personal grievance that needs to be corrected in a voting booth or in a petition or by joining the ranks of protesters or simply by feeling the grief?

A suggestion: I was privileged to have the friendship of Arthur Morse, of blessed memory, who wrote the book *While Six Million Died*, which exposed the unwillingness of our government to obstruct Hitler's plan of total Jewish extermination. From discussion with Arthur Morse, I know that the writing of that book was an expression, in part, of his anger, his righteous anger, for a woeful grievance in this world. Once when I was with him in his study, I noticed over his desk a photograph, now famous, of Jewish passengers ready to board the train, their transport to death: the foreboding in the eyes of the parents and the bewilderment in the eyes of the children. Arthur Morse told me that he kept the picture there in front of him so that the factual exercise of his research and the intellectual formulation of his thesis would never cool off the passion of his anger at such insult to human existence, at such grievance that even in retrospect cried out to be corrected.

Or close to home: Many years ago, members of our congregation, some of them here today, had been informed of the plight of the Jewish poor in the South Bronx. Then came the day when we had the opportunity to assist that little synagogue on Intervale Avenue. The neighborhood was a jungle and the roof of that one-story synagogue was piled with garbage that had been thrown from the windows of buildings on either side, and only then for us (or at least for me) did the abstract word "plight" and the abstract word "problem" become transformed into the feeling of anger for the anguish of such existence.

Thus the suggestion of a "hands-on" approach, coming close, becoming angry, to correct the grievances in God's world: Scharansky in prison, old people hopelessly old, poor people hopelessly poor.

And thus does Yom Kippur speak of anger. Forgive us, O God, on this day of forgiveness, for all the times in our lives when we rushed in with anger and should have kept our distance with a loving rebuke or a silence or a funny remark. Forgive us even as we seek forgiveness from those we love.

And forgive us, too, O God, for all those other times when we kept too much our distance from Your world, when we should have come close to Your suffering children and their bewildered eyes and the garbage on their roof, all those times when we should have become angry.

And so do we pray for the year now begun. Guide and strengthen us when our anger is too much. Guide and strengthen us when our anger is too little. And help us, O God, to know the difference.

Amen.

Yom Kippur 1983/5744

The Feeling of Guilt

When we spoke last week about choosing sermon topics for the High Holy Days, I was waiting until this week to tell you that the choice for Yom Kippur is always the most taxing. The themes that logically suggest themselves as the most likely possibilities are expressed in words like *cheit*, which means "sin," and *t'shuvah*, which means "repentance." But since rabbis, like everyone else in the field of communication, are looking for words that are familiar enough to open up and not close off the channels of communication, a rabbi's concern is that words like "sin" and "repentance" do not fall into the familiar category. You who are home from college (and we never tire of telling you how glad we are that you're here, or if not here, in a synagogue somewhere): When was the last time in a dormitory rap session that your subjects were "sin" and "repentance"? I have never heard the words in the village, and I suspect that they are rarely uttered downtown. Even in our homes, you would hardly ever hear the word "sin," except perhaps in reference to a piece of rich, fattening chocolate cake. All of which would suggest that the logical words may not be the most promising candidates.

But that leaves one gaping question still unanswered, especially for those of us who are fascinated by what motivates people to do what they do: Why is the Eve of Yom Kippur, when we keep saying "sin" and keep saying "repentance" in the prayer book, why is this the one time in the year that we can predict that empty seats will be a rare commodity? Our ancestors in ancient Jerusalem must have had the same problem because they, too, ask in the Talmud: "What do you do with overcrowding at the Temple on Yom Kippur?" And they answered that when the atmosphere is permeated with peace and friendship, there is always room, which only suggests that there were no fire regulations in the ancient Temple in Jerusalem.

But why Yom Kippur, even more than Rosh HaShanah? Rosh HaShanah we can understand: the beginning of a New Year, the hopes and prayers for what the year should be. Sukkot I can understand even better, because Sukkot is the holiday of thanksgiving for the abundant harvest with which most of us are happily blessed and which deserves a little gratitude to God. But you would never have a problem finding a seat on Sukkot.

Why Yom Kippur? Is it simply habit from that time of the ancient Temple in Jerusalem? But consider then all the other Jewish habits that we have no trouble discarding. Why not this one? Is it the melody of *Kol Nidrei*? What then is the staying power of that melody?

What now follows is but one Jew's attempt to respond to the question of why such a full sanctuary on Yom Kippur: that even if words like "sin" and "repentance" may be alien to our daily vocabulary, their meaning is not alien at all. Whether at home or at college or even downtown, we do talk about cheating and lying and not caring and not responding, even if the word "sin" never is uttered. And even if the word *t'shuvah*—"repentance"—hardly ever comes tripping off our tongues, we do talk about making amends and getting back on course and forgiving and reconciling. Out there in the world, it is between us and our friends and our families, between myself and myself. In here, it is also between myself and my God, however I conceive of my God. But out there or in here, whether wrongdoing and amends or sin and repentance, it is that same human condition of our human selves. Whether out there or in here, it is our willingness (or perhaps, more accurately, our need) to confront that human condition of our human selves, and that's why it's hard to find an empty seat on *Kol Nidrei*.

Yet there is one word, germane to the human condition, that bridges the world out there and the one in here. It is spoken exactly the same way in both worlds. We said it in here tonight—*Asham'nu*, "We feel guilty"—and out there we say it all the time—children, adults, everybody.

Tonight, of course, I make no attempt to explore that vast domain of human guilt feelings, many of which are beyond the limits of my understanding. We shall not tonight probe the question of guilt for the Holocaust and the degree to which the pope of the Catholic Church and the president of the United States and the Christians in Europe and the Jews in America may have been implicated in that guilt. We shall not even approach the feelings of guilt that are expressed by so many survivors of the Holocaust—that they remained alive to enjoy life that was denied to the rest—because those feelings are in the private territory of human hearts that I dare not presume to enter. I shall not address the crippling feelings of guilt that still lurk in some adult human beings out of the dark corners of their childhood, because those feelings are the proper discourse between those suffering persons and the doctors who can help them conquer the darkness with the light of understanding. And there are always, of course, those who feel guilty more than they should about matters beyond their control, beyond anyone's control. They make themselves responsible for everything that goes wrong and for what they did not do to prevent it. They feel continually guilty, and they run the risk of becoming what someone aptly described as "moral hypochondriacs." Or those others who purposely produce guilt in other human beings, who use guilt as a ploy to get their way or as their own little way of striking out in the tug and tussle of making it through a day, who become the tour directors of the guilt trips that they force the rest of us to take, who begin their remarks with "It's alright" or "Don't worry" or "It's what you always do."

Such are not our subjects for tonight, but rather all those times when we feel guilty and very well should, or didn't feel guilty and very well should have. It is what Martin Buber calls "authentic guilt," because we have violated the well-being of God's world and the creatures in it, and we have violated the moral integrity of our own selves. Rabbi Joseph Soloveichik describes that guilt as the "feeling of being marooned," of being isolated from the mainland of our central being. It is the feeling that we have violated those standards of right and wrong that we learned from our parents and that then passed the test of our own learning and experience. And when we violate them, we feel the guilt in the pit of our stomachs. To this day I never lock my automobile when there are groceries in the car because as a child I learned from my mother that if a person is hungry enough to steal food, you should let him.

We break a promise, and we feel guilty. We are unfaithful to someone who is faithful, and we feel guilty. We have a bad day at the office or at school and we lash out at home, and we feel guilty. We forget a birthday, and we feel guilty. And in case we miss any of the possibilities, we come to temple on Yom Kippur, and there is that long list of *Al Cheit*s in the prayer book to refresh our memory.

Jacob in the Bible is one of the guiltiest people that ever lived. He manipulated his brother, Esau, out of a birthright. He deceived his father, Isaac, to receive a blessing. He out-tricked his tricky uncle Laban. Each time he comes up with a rationale that is convincing enough to convince himself. But now, at this juncture in our story, Jacob is on his way home, and in the darkness he engages in combat with an unknown assailant, who turns out to be a messenger of God. In the course of that combat, the divine messenger, the still, small voice that every human being has the power to hear, that voice confronts Jacob: "*Ya-akov* (which in Hebrew means, "a cheater," "a trickster," "a con artist"), Jacob, you are what your name is! You are that kind of person!" And Jacob, confronted with the voice of that truth, struggles with the angel and protests the verdict: "All those things are what I *did*, not what I *am*!" And Jacob becomes Israel—"The one who struggles with God."

And thus does Yom Kippur confront us with the inescapable truth: that whatever we do, including what makes us feel guilty (or should), not only does hurt to

God's world and the creatures in it but is on its way to determining the kind of persons that we may become. Just as someone who performs repeated acts of caring is on his way to becoming a caring person, so the one who tells lies is on his way to becoming a liar, and the one who won't let go of grudges is on his way to becoming a disagreeable misanthrope, and the one who fails to express gratitude is on his way to becoming ungracious and ungrateful, and the person who complains about that and then about this is on the way to becoming a kvetch. Every sin in the prayer book, whatever gratification it may bring at first for the one who does it, eventually becomes habit-forming.

"What is the difference," the teacher asked, "between a hot bath and a sin?" And the teacher answered his own question: "When you get into a hot bath, right away you say 'Oy!' but eventually you say 'Ah!' A sin is exactly the opposite: First it's 'Ah!' but as the habit develops and you become that kind of person, it becomes 'Oy!'"

So welcome to Yom Kippur. Welcome to our tradition's *ladder of repentance*, which we begin to climb, each one with his or her own baggage of guilty feelings.

The first rung: in the spirit of full disclosure, we reveal the truth before God, lay bare the feeling of our guilt. And if we have not yet made redress to those whom we have hurt, if we have not yet sought forgiveness from them, there is precious little time to do it.

The next rung: to make a promise not to repeat that *cheit* even should the same opportunity arise, lest it become a habit.

Then the next rung: my plea for forgiveness as the decent person I am. I have left my guilt baggage down below, because I am guilty no more. I am a *baal t'shuvah*—"an expert in repentance"—the title of highest honor our religion can bestow on the sacred climb of Yom Kippur. I am what the doctors say about one who has recovered from an illness: "I am weller than well," almost ready for the world, to take up the struggle again.

But before we do—in that same spirit of full disclosure—there is certain baggage of guilt that we did not bring along tonight. I speak of all those times when we do something or neglect to do something and we say to ourselves or someone else that we feel guilty. And yet, if we were to be confronted with the same prospect all over again, we would act in exactly the same way and would be willing to feel guilty all over again. We could call it "the luxury of guilt." Not a sickness in the pit of the stomach but a little twinge that goes away and even makes us feel better for having had it.

All those days when there's so much to do and not enough hours to do it all, and that twinge of guilt for that decent thing that didn't get done—such guilt is the "guardian of our goodness," our moral survival mechanism, letting us know that we still *care*, even if we don't *do*. The luxury of guilt—and You understand, don't You, God?

And then those other days, more trying, more disturbing, when life demands a choice between alternatives: Do I fire a perfectly decent human being who lacks what it takes to do the job? Do I place my parent in a nursing home? Do I move upward in my business or profession even if it means less time with my family? With every decision, however I decide, a twinge of guilt. And if we had to do it all over again, we would do it the same way, guilt and all, because that's the way life is in God's world. It is the struggle to make decisions and the guilt that goes away. It's only when the struggle stops, only when the choice becomes automatic, only when it's always "what's best for me" and not for someone else, only when my question is always "Will it work?" and not "Is it right?"—only then does my guilt become a luxury that I cannot afford. Only then does my guilt become baggage I bring to Yom Kippur.

Tomorrow night when the shofar calls its last piercing call, may all of us have reached the highest rung of the ladder. May we be blessed with forgiveness and free of guilt. As we are soon to return to the struggling world, may each of us resume the journey as a *baal t'shuvah*, as one who has returned or is at least on the way back to the God-given truth of who we are.

Amen.

Yom Kippur 1984/5745

A Gift for Creativity

Our Tradition of Creativity

We share our sense of shock and loss at the death of Anwar Sadat. He demonstrated to the world the extraordinary power of human creativity because when he made the historic journey to Jerusalem in 1977, it was a new turn in an old road that had been leading toward a dead and destructive end. As he and Menachem Begin pursued the process of peace, something new was brought into the world that we pray will not be abandoned and not be destroyed by people and forces who seek to destroy it. When Anwar Sadat made the journey to Jerusalem, it was a turning like the turning of Yom Kippur.

So this day of our turning, away from the dead ends of our lives back to the road on which we know we belong. Tomorrow morning when we read from the Torah, we shall turn back to that place and that time at which the road began.

It was a meeting that Moses called to order in which he set before the people the terms of their covenant with God: that they should impress upon the rest of humanity, beginning with themselves, that this God whose banner they carry is the Giver of life and that life is, therefore, of infinite value. They were to impress upon the rest of humanity, beginning with themselves, that the God whose banner they carry imparts a spark of His divinity to every human being and that every human being is, therefore, sacred, not to be destroyed by bombs of war or ravages of hunger or the assassin's bullet. We were to impress upon the rest of humanity, beginning with ourselves, that only when a community of people, be it nation or neighborhood or congregation, only when a community infuses its existence with the value of that life and the sanctity of those human beings, only then would that community deserve to hold the banner high and to claim the pursuit of life and not death, the blessing and not the curse.

It was that stunning event and that manifesto of life's value and a person's sanctity and a community's responsibility that sent us on our way into history. It was our flash of inspiration, and if we use the language of the creative process we talked about on Rosh HaShanah, it was the first line of the Jewish poem, because then we entered the hard race with much sweat and much toil and even much blood, generation after generation, to continue the poem and turn it into an epic, yet unfinished to this day.

There are many theories and explanations for the mystique of Jewish survival. There are those who contend that God Himself preserved us. And those who say that our faith in God sustained us. There are those who cite the economic factor: that when we were driven from one country, there was always another country at the particular stage of economic development that welcomed the function that we could perform and welcomed us, and thus did we survive. There are those who cite the persecution from the outside that made us more cohesive on the inside.

To all of these explanations for our continuing epic, I would add one more: that from the time we entered the covenant with the God of history, we, as a people, consciously and deliberately cultivated our talent for creativity, from the first line of our inspiration through the hard labor of the creative product that brought something new into the world. Because whatever the reality that we confronted or that confronted us during that hard race, whether we liked it or not, we were willing to take on that reality as it was, as God's partners on behalf of the infinite worth of human life and the sanctity of human beings and the responsibility of communities.

Rome tried to bully us, and 1,900 years ago when the Jewish defenders of Jerusalem were no match for the battering rams of General Vespasian, when the power of resistance was giving way to the certainty of defeat, the story in our tradition is that Rabbi Yochanan ben Zakkai had his students circulate a false rumor about his own death, and then he had himself carried in a coffin outside the city walls so that he could present himself before Vespasian because had he tried to walk out on his own, his fellow countrymen would have stopped him and branded him a traitor. According to the story, he secured from Vespasian the permission that when Jerusalem would fall and Vespasian would become emperor, he, Yochanan, could join the Sages in the village of Yavneh and there continue his study and his interpretation of the Torah. Now regardless of whether that story is factual or not, the Jewish tradition saw fit to preserve that story and did not brand Yochanan a traitor but praised him with high praise for the way that he responded with such creativity to the new reality, even the reality of a falling Jerusalem, the way he carried the banner forward and made a new life at Yavneh.

With Greece a few centuries earlier, it had been a different reality because Greece did not bully us as much as it tried to tempt us with its scientific curiosity and its rational philosophy, all of which held strong appeal and still do for Jewish minds. Had we embraced that culture of Greece, it would have meant the end of Judaism. Had we totally rejected it, we would have lost a lot of Jews. So the way we responded with our ingenious talent for creativity was to borrow a little Plato, to help ourselves to a little Aristotle, and take over some Euclidean mathematics and lace them into the fabric of our own tradition and our own Talmud and our own philosophy. It is what the writer Achad Ha'am referred to as "healthy Jewish imitation," for which we Jews, he said, have not only a tendency but a genius. We borrow architecture that is Greek or Gothic or Byzantine or contemporary; we borrow whatever technology has to offer to make a sanctuary warm or a sanctuary cold (which does not always work), or microphones to amplify voices (which do not always work), but the building is still, with all of its borrowings, a synagogue. We borrow a catchy tune that was probably either a German marching song or one that was sung in the church and we put it to the words of "Ma'oz Tzur"—"Rock of Ages"—and it becomes a Jewish song for Chanukah. Because the one condition of our borrowing was that we never surrender the first line of the poem, and the one risk that we guarded against was the risk of overstepping the line, that with Plato and Aristotle we might end up with the pagan gods, that with all the benefit of technology, we might end up with the computer that is deemed more precious than a person.

And thus our creative talents through the years: sometimes to resist, sometimes to borrow, sometimes to find ourselves another way, but always that willingness to confront a new reality in our lives and then to ask the questions and then to search for the answers. Some of you have already begun to be familiar with that body of Jewish literature called responsa. It incorporates the questions and answers over these past 1,200 years when Jews had questions for which they themselves had no answers, and they would submit them to renowned rabbis whose reputations for learning qualified them to give answers that would be accepted authoritatively. The number of responsa is now estimated to number close to 500,000 and still continuing, of which 100,000 are presently being programmed in a computer arrangement that operates by satellite between Yeshiva University in New York and Bar-Ilan University in Israel. Thus, Jewish creativity.

Included in those questions and answers is this one from the living moments of our own century, from a collection of responsa issued by rabbis in concentration camps during the dark night of those Holocaust years, and they make their own poignant statement about Jewish creativity.

The question was posed by a fifteen-year-old boy at Auschwitz who wanted to change places with a twenty-year-old brilliant yeshivah student whose name was on the death list. The younger boy asked permission to volunteer himself for that death list because the exchange might be considered an act of suicide, which is theoretically forbidden in Jewish law. The rabbi to whom he submitted the question refused to grant permission, perhaps on the basis of the rabbinic principle that no human being has the right to decide that one life is more valuable than another, and the exchange did not take place.

And from our own living moments of history and our own new realities, these are the subjects of some contemporary responsa:

When a patient is dying, what measures are appropriate for sustaining life?

Are test-tube babies in accord with Jewish tradition?

When medical resources such as kidney dialysis machines are in scarce supply, what shall be the criteria for determining their allocation?

Or this question directed to Dr. Freehof, who is the dean of Reform Jewish responsa and who has already published seven volumes of responsa: Is an unmarried couple living together eligible for family membership in a synagogue?

They are all living questions with answers that require more than a simple yes or no because the value of human life and the sanctity of the individual require more than a yes or no. They are answers that come from the Jewish tradition, which for Orthodoxy is the word of God and, therefore, binding even though a question such as the one on artificial insemination received exactly opposite answers from two different Orthodox rabbis.

For Reform Jews there is, of course, the freedom to choose from that tradition without being bound by it. But that very freedom requires us to know what the tradition has to say. That very freedom calls us individually to a personal encounter with the values of that tradition and of connecting the events and the realities of our lives with those values. Because as we shall read in tomorrow's Torah portion, those values are not in the heavens and not beyond the sea and not beyond our grasp but within our very reach, in our very hearts that we may do them.

So I have a plan for our congregation: that we shall create within our ranks a systematic program for our own encounter with the tradition. We would search out some of the materials and we would bring in some of the experts and we would conduct the exchange of our own ideas. We would proceed subject by subject, vocation by vocation to cull from the tradition, perhaps to add to it and then to take it with us into the living moments of our lives and to the functions that we perform in the world of humanity.

Because for those in this congregation who by profession and commitment are dedicated to the healing of body and mind, and for the rest of us as well, it is a tradition that has always confronted and struggled with matters of life and death, of living and dying and coping.

And for those of us who are practitioners in the conduct of law, and for all the rest of us, it is the most long-standing, continuous legal tradition of any people or nation in the world with a profound respect for the legal process.

And for those who are teachers of students and those who are students of teachers, and for all the rest of us, it is a tradition that connects knowledge to living, that perceives achievement in learning not only as a way to the best college or the most lucrative job but to the most decent and most ethical and most productive life.

And for those in the congregation in the world of business and finance and industry, and for all the rest of us, it is a tradition concerned with the rights of the producer and the rights of the consumer, to live and let live, and in the words of Eugene Borowitz, it is a tradition that holds high regard for the human and social consequences of our own profit making.

And for those whose vocation is in the home, and for all the rest of us, it is a tradition that was itself preserved in that home and the values we transmitted from generation to generation were in that home more than anyplace else, more than in school and more than in synagogue.

For all of us who are citizens of a nation or members of a community, it is a tradition that never denied the well-being of that community, that never surrendered its concern for the poor of that community. And at this moment, we of that tradition have no choice but to confront the reality, the new reality of the poor, as we shall do on a Friday night in the near future, to respond creatively to the new reality of the poor, including the 74,000 elderly Jewish poor around New York, including the budget cutbacks that will deprive them of social services and senior citizens programs and hot lunches, which we in this congregation, who have worked with those poor heart to heart and hand to hand, can attest are life-giving supports to the loneliness and poverty of their lives.

So this is my Yom Kippur appeal: not for money, which is contrary to the tradition of this congregation at *Kol Nidrei*, but on this night when we mourn the death of a creative human being, on this night when we pray for a creative response to the place he has left empty, on this night this is my appeal for a personal decision to share in the creative encounter, to explore the creative tradition, and then each of us to add to the first line of the Jewish poem, each of us to create something new in the world—something of life, something of blessing.

Amen.

Yom Kippur 1981/5742

Creativity and the State of Israel

In the year 1798, the Chasidic Rabbi Nachman of Bratzlav announced his intention to make a journey to the Holy Land. When family and friends tried to dissuade him because of all the hazards and obstacles that such a trip entailed, Rab Nachman persisted. He wanted to set foot in that place that he believed had been the starting site of the Creation of the world.

He made the trip, and when he returned, he rendered his report: that in many respects, *Eretz Yisrael* was like any other place in the world, with real houses and real villages and real people. And yet, he added, there is a special quality to the dust of its earth that makes it holy and that has the power to spur the spirit of the Jewish people to be strong and to create and to fulfill the dream of a holy place, where justice will be set right and peace will reign and light will shine forth to the world.

A hundred years after Rabbi Nachman, when the Zionist Movement was already underway, the call was not only Theodor Herzl's plea for a political Zion where the Jewish people could establish its own national home and determine its own national destiny away from the constant shadow of anti-Semitism. The Zionist call was also Achad Ha'am's vision of a cultural and spiritual homeland, where this people, who had always refused to remain in lockstep with the rest of the world, could take root on its own soil and cultivate its own moral philosophy and develop its own creative center of science and scholarship and art and literature.

Four months ago I stood on the Givat Ram campus of the Hebrew University, and I was surrounded by the emerging reality of Rabbi Nachman's "holy dust" and Theodor Herzl's dream and Achad Ha'am's vision. Within a few minutes in any direction, I could be at the Israel Museum or Hadassah Hospital or Shaare Zadek Hospital or Binyanei HaOoma, which is Jerusalem's center for the performing arts. Across the way I could be at the Knesset, which, with all of its problems and all of its foibles, still represents a democracy of people still walking its rocky road toward a society of peace.

Standing on that hilltop campus, I turned into the university bookstore, and the title that caught my eye was a that of a book entitled *Creativity*, and at that moment my theme for these High Holy Days was conceived.

A few days later we heard President Yitzhak Navon, who told us how in 1956 he was in Argentina and how then President Juan Peron offered to buy anything Israel had to export. The only three items that Navon could offer in 1956 were citrus fruits and false teeth and the tops of gasoline stoves—not the stoves, just the tops. And now, twenty-five years later, included in Israel's ever-growing list of exports would be CAT scan machines for American hospitals that produce three-dimensional color plates of all parts of the body. Included in the list would be one of the world's most sophisticated dialysis machines that is the size of a medium-sized suitcase and is being produced on a kibbutz in the Negev. Included in the list would be solar energy projects that are already being used in Israel's heavy industry to provide alternative sources of energy.

The prolific creativity that confronted us is what all Jews should see for themselves on the soil of that Land, because hearing it secondhand is usually hearing it as part of a UJA fund-raiser, which usually puts Jews on guard and makes them suspect (like the UJA worker who made his first trip to Israel and came back astonished because, he said, "I found out that all those lies I've been telling are true"). What we were witnessing in every direction is what we were talking about last night as the indispensable prerequisite to creativity, what Professor David Hartman of the Hebrew University designated as the "courage of a people to begin again," including the people who had come with tattoos on their arms and including the people who came directly from the primitive ghettos of North Africa and Yemen.

One more example of Jewish creativity in Israel. The day before we left, we spent the afternoon at Kibbutz Negba, where our daughter was working for the summer. As we toured the kibbutz, we learned about its agricultural products and its plastic bag factory. Then we approached a medium-sized building and were told that this was the retail shop for the sale of children's clothing, to which Israelis came from a radius of many miles to make their purchases. The clothing is manufactured by the senior citizens of the kibbutz who were no longer able to work in the fields or even in the plastic bag factory. But there was also no way in which they were about to stop working and stop fulfilling some useful function and thus become candidates for the *malben*, the old age home.

As those kibbutzniks confronted that reality of their lives, someone asked the creative question: What then can we do? And someone offered the creative suggestion that we can design and make children's clothing, which has now become, in addition to agriculture and plastic bags, a substantial source of income for the kibbutz, because of the will and the courage to begin again.

When Rabbi Nachman returned from that trip about 200 years ago and submitted his report about the creative potential of the holy dust of the Land, he added a somber note: that another kind of dust is mixed in with the holiness, this kind anti-creative, this kind anti-holy. There are both kinds of dust, he said, the holy dust and this "dust from the other side." The two sometimes even look the same, he said, "because in this world everything gets mixed up and confused."

The day that we left Israel was June 30, and there was unholy dust sticking to our shoes because June 30 was the day of national elections. The dust had been gathering all through the election campaign with slur tactics and cars crowded off roads (because they had a bumper sticker of an opposing party) and unruly mobs. But what was about to emerge after the election, and what everyone in Israel predicted, was the State of Israel knee-deep in its most unholy dust.

When the ballots were counted, the Orthodox political parties had received approximately 11 percent of the popular vote and had won 13 out of the 120 seats in the Israeli Knesset. Because of the particular structure of Israel's coalition government, Menachem Begin and the Likud Party needed those 13 seats to give it a majority in the Knesset and make it the viable party in power. In return for this support of the Orthodox religious parties, Mr. Begin guaranteed the Orthodox parties billions of shekels of government money for the Orthodox religious schools, even though most of those schools allow no government supervision of their educational functions and standards. In return for their 13 seats, Mr. Begin guaranteed strict enforcement of Shabbat restrictions, including departures and arrivals of El Al airplanes. In return for their 13 seats, Mr. Begin assured the recall of married women from the army, which is perceived in Israel as a major setback for women's rights. In return for their 13 seats, Prime Minister Begin pledged exemption of military service not only for yeshivah students from Orthodox homes, which has always been the case, but also for *Chozrei T'shuvah*, those who have recently returned to Orthodoxy, on the one condition they enroll in a yeshivah. Such a proposal is perceived by many Israelis as a tempting opportunity for draft evasion.

How is it that a minority is able to impose its will on the majority? How is it that the Chief Rabbinate is so politically powerful that it felt entitled to halt the archaeological dig that is under state auspices at the City of David? How is it that the Orthodox power structure, which has its own share of infighting, can make sure that no Reform rabbi or Conservative rabbi can officiate at a marriage or a funeral in the State of Israel? How is it that those Orthodox in Israel who are genuinely committed to the study and pursuit of Jewish values are overshadowed by the political antics of their coreligionists?

Because, I believe, in a country that bristles with creativity and that devises creative solutions to water shortages and immigrant influxes, in this one respect, in this system of government and religion, none has had the courage to ask the creative questions and none has sought the creative answer, and thus the unholy, uncreative dust has been allowed to gather.

The system is as old as Muslim rule over Palestine 1,500 years ago and is called the millet system. It provided that each religious grouping under Muslim control, each non-Muslim religious grouping, was given the authority to conduct its own internal religious affairs and to designate its own religious officials to be in charge. This system was taken over by the Turks when they controlled Palestine, and then by the British during the mandate. The British added yet another ingredient: Because the Christian and Muslim communities had an ecclesiastical head who represented that community to the British mandate government, the same system was instituted for the Jews, and the Chief Rabbinate was established with an Ashkenazic and Sephardic rabbi at the head. And thus it is that the Chief Rabbinate in Israel today is the invention of the British government.

If the State of Israel had been as creative in this matter as it was in so many others, the problem would have been resolved in 1948 because David Ben-Gurion and his colleagues would have acknowledged that now, with a corporate nation to govern the internal affairs of the community and to be its own liaison to the community, the millet system and the Chief Rabbinate deserved to be abolished. Then, perhaps, all of those Israelis who today stay away from religion altogether because Orthodoxy is not for them might have discovered other Jewish ways to engage in their spiritual quest, and Jewish religious life in Israel would have been allowed to develop on its own. But for whatever reason, perhaps because there were too many other problems to resolve or perhaps because Rav Kook, who at that time was the Chief Rabbi, was such a wonderfully spiritual man, the old system remained in force and became more and more political and less and less spiritual, and even to this day, seats in the Knesset are horse traded for concessions granted.

And thus, this one particular concession for which the Orthodox have been pressing that affects all of us, including members of this congregation. I refer to the Law of Return, which was enacted during the 1950s when Jews were pouring into Israel, and this Law of Return, as a creative response to that new reality, decreed that every Jew had the right to become a citizen of the State of Israel without any process of naturalization. Nobody thought to ask the question:

What is a Jew? because there was no question about concentration camp survivors and ghetto dwellers from North Africa and Yemen. Only years later when test cases were brought before the Supreme Court in Israel did the term have to be defined in its traditional technical way: A Jew is someone born of a Jewish mother or who has converted to Judaism. The amendment to that law for which the Orthodox have been pressing seeks the addition of one word "halachah," according to "halachah," according to traditional Jewish law, which means not only circumcision for males and the ritual bath and the acceptance of the mitzvot, but also that the entire procedure must be conducted under Orthodox auspices, with the result that anyone who has converted to Judaism anywhere in the world under non-Orthodox auspices would not be considered a Jew when he or she arrives at Ben Gurion Airport.

Rabbi Weintraub and I have worked with scores of prospective converts who, after instruction and discussion, joined the Jewish community and pledged themselves to preserve the continuity of the Jewish people within their own families and through their own children, and at the instant of their pledge they were no longer converts but full-fledged Jews. Those Jews-by-choice are very dear to us. I am saddened if an Orthodox rabbi here in America would deny the validity of the conversion, just as I am saddened if a colleague denies that I am a "real" rabbi or that this is a Jewish congregation. And yet, I know that one of the facts of life in a pluralistic religious society is that one religious group can declare another invalid; it goes on all the time between the Satmar and Lubavitch Chasidim.

It is something quite different, however, for the government of the State of Israel officially to endorse that verdict, to say to all of the non-Orthodox Jews in the Diaspora, including Reform and Conservative Jews who constitute two-thirds of those who belong to synagogues in the Diaspora, to say to them: "Your converts are not converts; your rabbis are not rabbis; your Judaism is not Jewish because whoever was converted under your auspices is not considered a Jew by the government of Israel when he comes to the State of Israel," which is what an amendment to the Law of Return would mean.

What Prime Minister Begin or any other aspiring political leader must be made to understand is that however many seats he would get, the price would be too high, because the price would be the unity of the Jewish people, inside and outside of Israel. It would be sheer tragedy for such a price to be exacted by the very State of Israel that has been so powerful in welding that unity, the very State of Israel that is supported and sustained by that unity. The price is not worth it, which is what the leaders of our Movement in Israel and here communicated to

Prime Minister Begin in July when the Orthodox approached him for the deal. And although no deal was made, the issue was left open.

What Mr. Begin and the government of Israel must continue to hear is the voice of the Jewish people from all over the world on behalf of the unity of the Jewish people. While we protest to our own government about the sale of AWACs to Saudi Arabia for the sake of the Jewish people, we also protest to Mr. Begin and the government of Israel for the sake of the Jewish people. They must hear from us, from members of our congregation who are leaders in the UJA and other projects in Israel, that we, to whom these causes are very dear, are Reform Jews, not to be excluded by fellow Jews, even if it does mean seats in the Knesset. They must hear from us not by our withholding our gifts to the UJA or our purchase of bonds, because while we are trying to heal we must not also hurt, but by our letting it be known that the contribution is being made by a Reform Jew who has learned from his Reform Judaism to be an *ohev Yisrael*—a "lover of Israel"—and that love is not worth selling for a few seats in the Knesset.

We should let the government of Israel hear our voices through our membership in an organization like ARZA, the Association of Reform Zionists of America, so that our voices can be heard in chorus by the State of Israel. We should let them know that the time has come, in this specific respect, to be creative, to do away with the relics that date from 1,500 years ago. With our voices in a rising chorus, we should make the plea that the State of Israel clean up its dust and make it holy again so that, as Rabbi Nachman envisaged, it would spur the spirit of our people to be strong and to create and to fulfill the dream.

Amen.

Rosh HaShanah 1981/5742

Creative Remembering

We turn backward in the Book of Life as we approach this service of *Yizkor* to the pages that were before—to pages inscribed with a name and a date of birth and the story of a life and a date of death.

Some pages too scant, a story that was ended before it could blossom into full telling. When the Angel of Death comes too soon, there are too many unlived years. The story is incomplete and the ink on the page is smudged with our tears.

Some pages are ripely full, a harvest complete with years and love. But on those pages, too, there is the watermark of our tears. Because whether the Angel of Death comes sooner or later, it can still be too soon. Someone was asked, "How long would you like to live?" and the person answered, "To the ripest age possible, just short of senility." Because even in the autumn time of a person's years, there is still the task unfinished, the brush stroke unpainted, the song unsung. There is still another grandchild's bar mitzvah or bat mitzvah to attend. But the Angel of Death does not wait.

John O'Hara has penned the story of a merchant in Baghdad who sent his servant to the marketplace to buy provisions. The servant returned white and trembling:

> *"Master, just now when I was in the marketplace, I was jostled by a woman in the crowd. When I turned, I saw that it was Death that jostled me. She looked at me and made a threatening gesture. Now Master, lend me your horse and I will ride away from this city and divert my fate. I will go to Samarra and Death will not find me."*
>
> *Then the merchant himself went to the marketplace and saw Death standing in the crowd. He came to her and said: "Why did you make a threatening gesture to my servant when you saw him this morning?" "That was no threatening gesture," answered Death. "It was only a start of surprise. I was so astonished to see him in Baghdad for, you see, I have an appointment with him tonight in Samarra.*

Death has its own schedule, and all we can do is say good-bye by the side of the grave, at the boundary between the land and the infinite sea. And then we

96

learn the loneliness of an empty chair, half-expecting them to answer, half-forgetting that they are not there. We mourn for them but we also mourn for ourselves, for what we have lost.

There are three ways to mourn, said the Baal Shem Tov. The first is to weep with our love and our loneliness. But only if we do not weep too long, only if we do not, as one person said, indulge ourselves in the luxury of grief because that luxury deprives us of courage and cripples us for the journey out of the shadow.

For there is a second way to mourn, said the Bat Shem Tov, and that is to be silent; to behold the mystery of the infinite sea and *not* to say a word; to recapture the mystery of love; to recall a moment shared; to remember what someone said and to smile with the remembering; or simply at some unexpected moment to miss someone very much and wish that he or she could be there. The twinge is but for a moment and passes in perfect silence.

To weep, to be silent, and then the third way to mourn: to sing a hymn of praise to life, to sing *L'chayim*, the song that was cut off when death came for its appointment in Samarra.

The Chasidic spiritual leader of an East European community known as the Klausenberger Rebbe lost his entire family, his wife and eleven children, in Hitler's gas chambers. He himself was rescued and came to the United States, where he was recognized as a person of deep faith and learning and creativity. He then proceeded to build a network of religious and educational institutions for impoverished children in the United States and Israel. He named each institution after one of his children.

The service of *Yizkor* arrives during this journey of the spirit. Thus to let us know that there is weeping and there is silence and there is also song, to let us know that even memory can be creative and enable our beloved to live beyond their own death. Even memory can be creative when we take up their song and join it to our own on the other page with our name and our date of birth and whatever else is already there.

The gates are about to close and the day is soon to end, and in the book that lies open from cover to cover and page to page there is one word from page to page and cover to cover: There is the name of the Holy One who gave us life and who takes it back to Himself, who is our trusted guide on the homeward journey.

Adonai natan, Adonai lakach.

"The Lord has given. The Lord has taken back to Himself." In the Book of Life, blessed be the name of the Lord.

Amen.

Yom Kippur 1981/5742

Gates of Opportunity

This year marks the fiftieth anniversary of the voyage of the ship *St. Louis*, which set sail from Germany on May 13, 1939. It was bound for Cuba with 936 passengers on board, 930 of them Jewish refugees from Germany, among the last to escape from the jaws of Nazi terror. As Arthur Morse describes that voyage in his book *While Six Million Died*, on each of those passports was a *J* marked in red.

All of the 930 held landing certificates signed by Cuban immigration officials, but for 734 of them, Cuba would only be a temporary stopping place to await their turn on the immigration quota system to enter the United States.

As they sailed across the sea, they were still stinging with the memories of *Kristallnacht*, of burning synagogues, of brown-shirted mobs. There had to be trepidation in their hearts, but mostly there was glowing hope for the new life, the new opportunity, the new land of freedom.

And then came the message as the ship was crossing the sea that the president of Cuba had signed an order that invalidated all of the landing certificates, that no passenger would be permitted to leave ship without a Cuban visa, which all except twenty-two of them did not have.

Despite the heroic efforts and pleas of the ship's non-Jewish German captain and despite the extraordinary efforts by representatives of the Joint Distribution Committee (who came to Cuba and arranged within twenty-four hours the payment of the exorbitant amount of money that the Cuban government demanded, only to be told that the time limit had expired), the ship was ordered out of Cuban waters.

Their only hope was the United States, but our State Department refused to deviate one iota from our country's restrictive policy of immigration, not even for those who had already moved through the immigration process and were simply waiting their turn. As the ship cruised off Miami, a Coast Guard cutter shadowed along its side to make sure that none of the refugees jumped overboard and tried to swim ashore. The answer was no from the United States and from every other country in the Western Hemisphere. And the *St. Louis* set its course back to Europe.

But from there came a different answer, because Belgium and England and Holland and France said yes. And the passengers from the *St. Louis* wired from the ship these words: "Our gratitude is as immense as the ocean on which we are now floating since May 13."

The boat landed in Antwerp, Belgium, on June 17. But the voyage did not end there because the only one of those four countries to avoid Hitler's clutches was, of course, Great Britain. We do not know exactly how many ultimately survived the years of destruction, but we do know that the door of opportunity to rescue 908 human lives was as close as the shoreline of Miami, Florida. And that door was closed, the opportunity forever lost.

We shall read tomorrow: "I set before you life and death. Choose life that you may live." The choice that was made fifty years ago was death, somebody else's death. A lot of somebody else's deaths.

A question: Fifty years from now, in a place like this, on a Yom Kippur like this, what will some rabbi say about us? What will they say about the one billion people who are starving on the face of the earth in 1989, forty thousand of them dying every day? Will they say that the civilized world of humanity in 1989 let them die? Or will they be able to say that there were countries of the world that opened their larders and that there were people in the world who opened their hearts and their pocketbooks? When a rabbi fifty years from tonight stands in the place where I now stand, will that rabbi be able to say that in 1989 the members of this congregation went home and made out a check to MAZON, the Jewish response to hunger, in the amount that would have been spent on food on our fast day? I have no idea fifty years hence what bar mitzvah and bat mitzvah celebrations are going to be like. I don't know what wedding receptions are going to be like. But will that rabbi who stands here be able to say then, "We continue in the tradition of this congregation from fifty years ago of contributing three percent of the cost of every celebration so that every *simchah* will become a double blessing"?

I can tell you that the rabbi fifty years from now will read the same Torah portion that we shall read tomorrow because that doesn't change. But will the rabbi be able to say: "As it is written, 'Choose life,' and in 1989 they chose life, somebody else's life, a lot of somebody else's lives"?

A question: Fifty years hence, when they recall the modern miracle of the Red Sea in 1989 about an unprecedented forty thousand Jews who were allowed to leave the Soviet Union in that year, will history be able to record that the Jews of America and the Jews of Israel and the Jews of the world stood side by side with those passengers on their passage to freedom, that we strengthened their hand, that we opened the doors of opportunity to live in a place and to work at a job and to connect with the community, that we helped them discover the roots of their faith that so long have been denied them?

Fifty years from now, will our fellow Jews in the State of Israel be able to say: "We and our Arab neighbors have learned to live and even thrive together in peace because fifty years ago in 1989, when the doors of peacemaking opportunity were opened, our forebears took the first cautious steps in walking through. They took a chance because they preferred the risk of that chance to the risk of this beautiful Land being continuously soaked in blood, of these people being continuously stalked by violence and war. They took a chance and they chose life through the opening door."

All of those global opportunities, all of those human decisions on an ordinary day that can change the face of the world and can change an ordinary day into a holy one. But as our prayer book keeps telling us, Yom Kippur is not only about the big world of humanity but about our own personal worlds where all of us live and work and love.

So what of the opportunities in those worlds? As most of us go on our daily rounds, we do our best to search out every door that can be opened. And whatever individually we may have achieved with our lives and our work and our families declares our success in finding those open doors and walking through.

And sometimes when a door of opportunity is shut right in our faces and we are unable to pry the door open, we do what Jews have always done throughout our history: We look for another door. Someone once said that failure is not in falling down but in staying down. The failure is not looking for another door.

But what of those other times that come to all of us when a door of opportunity lies wide open and all we do is walk right by it?

This summer, Priscilla and I were walking, and nearby were a mother and her toddler son. When the mother became aware that the child was trailing behind, she turned around and there was this child entranced by the sight of a caterpillar winding its way across the leaf of a bush. The mother was annoyed by his dawdling and she scolded him for not keeping up, whereupon the child broke out of his gaze and toddled to his mother's side.

We saw it all—a mother in a hurry and a child standing in silent awe at the miracle of God's creation. And you can only ask: What destination of hers could have been so important that made her snatch this opportunity from her child? What reason was good enough for closing that door through which she could have beheld the wonder of her own child wide-eyed at the wonder of the universe?

The Psalmist lamented: "They have eyes but do not see."

To stand next to a child and not see the wonder on his face. To stand next to any other human being and not see that person's joy. To stand next to another human being and not see that person's pain or fears or loneliness or struggle. *P'tach lanu*, "Open for us," the doors of opportunity, O God, that we may see.

And then those opportunities we miss with the hearing of our ears.

I once spoke of the episode that Martin Buber tells about himself. He was busy at work when he was visited by a young man. Buber heard the young man out and responded with friendly, polite conversation, and all the time he was eager for the session to end so that he could get back to what he was doing. Later Buber learned that the young man had been in deep despair and that, in Buber's words; he had come "not for a chat but for a decision." Buber said that he had failed to listen to the questions the young man did not ask.

The Psalmist cried: "Ears they have but they do not listen," and so with us. We hear the words but we do not listen to the heart sounds, to the questions not being asked. We hear the complaining but we do not listen to the cry for help. We hear the anger but we do not listen to the sob of pain.

A mother once complained to me about her daughter who was away at college. The problem, she said, was that her daughter spent so much time in the dormitory listening to her friend's problems that she was only pulling down B's instead of the A's, of which she was perfectly capable. My answer to that mother was that God must be blessing the B's of her daughter. *P'tach lanu*, "Open for us," the doors of opportunity, O God, that we may listen.

And, of course, there are always the opportunities we miss with the words of our mouths and the silence of our mouths.

A man was standing at the graveside of his wife as the funeral service concluded. He just stood there refusing to leave. The rabbi walked over and put his hand on the man's shoulder to guide him away.

"But you don't understand, Rabbi. I loved my wife."

"I know you did," said the rabbi, "but you can't just stand there."

"You don't understand," the husband said. "I loved my wife."

"We all know you did. We know what you meant to each other."

"But you don't understand. I loved my wife…and once I almost told her."

For the opportunities we miss of saying words of love to those we love, of saying what we feel in our hearts for fear of sounding weak in our strength, of showing cracks in our armor.

The opportunity we miss when we keep silent and expect the other to decipher our silence.

The opportunity we miss in this sanctuary on Shabbat from week to week when the names of our beloved are recalled and the ones who love them and cherish their memory are not here to say the words of *Kaddish* in love and memory.

And because today is the day that it is, the opportunity we sometimes miss of saying "I am sorry for the hurt"; or the words "I was wrong"; or the words "Forgive me"; or the words "I forgive you."

If the outcome of this day would be to reach out to another human being, once close, now distant; friend to friend once; sibling to sibling; even parent to child and child to parent—if the words could be said and the reconciling could begin, then already today would be the holiest day of the year.

P'tach lanu, "Open for us," the doors that we may say the words and listen and see.

And I have one more prayer about opportunity. The words of this prayer are not in the prayer book, but the prayer book is filled with what these words have to say.

The prayer is *S'gar lanu*, "Close for us," O God, the gates of opportunity.

When that door is open, temptingly open, to say words that will hurt or embarrass another human being, *S'gar lanu*, may those gates be closed. The Talmud teaches that to humiliate another human being in public and cause his blood to rush to his face and make it red is to violate the commandment that you should not shed blood. Even when the hurting words may simply be clever and not intended to hurt, if they run the risk of hurting, *S'gar lanu*, close the gates, because it's better to be nice than to be clever.

And when the tempting opportunity presents itself to circulate a choice bit of gossip, *S'gar lanu*, because according to the rabbis there are three victims of gossip: the one who is talked about, the who says it and the one who listens. "God does not love gossips," said the philosopher, "even when they are right."

And when the door of opportunity opens in some moment of weakness and unreason for some act of betrayal against wife or husband or family or trusting friend, *S'gar lanu*, keep us from betraying our own decent selves.

And all those Jewish men who are doing time in jail because they were pushed so hard by their own greed or whatever it was that pushed them to grab at every opportunity whatever it was: They could have said no. They could have listened to the prayers they must have read on the previous Yom Kippur. They could have listened to the still, small voice of their own souls. They could have closed the door of opportunity.

According to an old Chasidic legend, a Jew traveled from Palestine to Rome. On the way, he had a dream that in the marketplace was a man dressed like a beggar who was, in actuality, the Messiah. The Jew awakened and made his way to the designated place to the man in beggar's clothes.

"Are you the Messiah?" he asked.

"I am," the man answered.

The Jew said, "With so much misery and pain and callousness and stupidity in the world and in the lives of people, what are you waiting for?"

To which the Messiah responded, "With so much misery and pain and callousness and stupidity in the world, what are *you* waiting for?"

Strengthen us to decide, O God, when to close the doors and when to open them wide. And may we choose life.

And what are we waiting for?

Amen.

Yom Kippur 1989/5750

Reform Judaism

A New Prayer Book—A New Year

On this special day when we have shared, for the first time in the life of our congregation, "In the beginning" of a new prayer book for the High Holy Days, some words about the prayer book.

We begin with the very fact that being together at a service like this is a remarkable declaration: that a partnership that began thirty-two hundred years ago between a people and its God somewhere on a mountain in a desert, that partnership is still in existence in Scarsdale, New York, and in congregations wherever people have come to pray on this Holy Day. There have been times when that relationship has been strained. There were attempts to break it up, both from without and from within, but if survival is the test, then we who are here this day can testify that we have made it so far.

As in any partnership, what surely helped was the constant flow of communication from the people to its God and the people to each other. Whatever the circumstance—joy, grief, confusion, anger, guilt—a person would let the words come out and let the spirit soar and thus a prayer would come into being. And whenever other members of the community would hear that prayer and it would express the meditations of their hearts, then it would happen that that prayer would gain entrance into the siddur, into the prayer book of our people.

One example: Almost two thousand years ago, a severe drought ravaged the land of Palestine, and the community was in severe distress. Rabbi Akiva stood before the ark, and in a spontaneous outburst he cried, *"Avinu Malkeinu, sh'ma koleinu*—"Our Father, our King, hear our prayer!"—and then he repeated *Avinu Malkeinu* and added yet another plea and yet another. And to the outpouring of his heart there was such universal response that *Avinu Malkeinu* entered the siddur, the prayer book of our people.

We are told that Rabbi Akiva had five lines in his *Avinu Malkeinu*. By the time, centuries later, that the Sephardic Jews had adopted it for their prayer book, they had increased the number to twenty-nine lines; and by the time the Ashkenazim, the German Jews, had finished with it, the number had reached thirty-eight lines, and the Polish-Jewish community worked it up to forty-four lines. And this morning, even in Scarsdale, New York, we called out *Avinu Malkeinu, sh'ma koleinu.*

What this prayer book became was the link between a Jew and his God and his people. What this book became was a diary of that people because each generation would make its own entries from its own mountaintop, with its own experience, with the dreams that it dreamed.

And so in our instance, more than a hundred years ago, a group of Jews gathered together because they believed that the Orthodoxy of their day was too shackled to the past. They believed that what was needed was a version of Judaism that would speak to their experience and their dreams and to their world. What they started more than a hundred years ago came to be known as Reform Judaism, and the prayer book that they created came to be known as the *Union Prayer Book*, the first edition of which was published in 1894. That prayer book exuded the spirit of that time, a spirit that abounded with optimism, a spirit convinced that the discoveries of science and the insights of human reason and the political enlightenment of nations would join forces and before very long would usher in the golden age of humanity, united in service to the one ethical God and escorted in by the Jewish people.

Those early reformers believed that by shedding some of the old Jewish traditions, not all but some, that by playing down the difference between one group and another (especially between Jews and Christians), we would come closer to that universal day of human brotherhood that was part of the divine plan. It all came out through that *Union Prayer Book* of 1894, almost as if to the accompaniment of Beethoven's Ninth Symphony, with its vision of a united humanity. And at the same time, that same prayer book turned to the life of the spirit of each individual Jew, and many of the passages in that prayer book attained to uncommon heights of spiritual beauty. Many of us grew up religiously on that *Union Prayer Book* with all its revisions, and it served us very well.

But in recent years, voices of dissatisfaction came to be heard that the *Union Prayer Book* with all of its revisions, even with its passages of eloquent beauty, no longer spoke on the mountain where we were, no longer addressed itself to the place and the dreams of the Jew in Reform Judaism in the third quarter of the twentieth century. It did not, for example, show the scars of the Holocaust; it did not, for example, sing the songs of our people in their own Land of Israel; it did not, for example, give recognition to the heightened consciousness of women and women's role and women's rights in the modern world.

Something else was needed, something to fill all the gaps, and something to remedy what may have been the mistake of our Reform elders. Because if human reason and human technology and human nationalism deserved so much confidence, there could not have been an Auschwitz. Our Reform forebears had celebrated humanity's boundless potential for good, but we, after Auschwitz, had to come to terms with humanity's boundless potential for evil.

And especially what was needed in this third quarter of the twentieth century was a way to search, the way that all peoples were searching for the authentic sources and roots of their own existence. And I can tell you of people in this congregation who grew up as Reform Jews, away from the tradition, who over these past years have searched not only in Bible but in Talmud and mystical Kabbalah and fervent Chasidism.

What was needed in this third quarter of the twentieth century was an anthology of prayer for the Reform Jew with more of the tradition than there was in that original *Union Prayer Book*, not because that tradition is the word of God, which would make us Orthodox, and not because that tradition is binding simply because it is tradition, which would make us Conservative, but because that tradition, which includes Bible and Talmud and Kabbalah and Chasidism and Rabbi Akiva's prayer, that tradition is the rich reservoir of our people's experience. We are not told to take this book and choose everything, and there will be prayers in this book and in the *Gates of Prayer,* which we use on Shabbat, that may have more or less meaning to some than to others. Not to choose everything but to explore everything, at least to experience its meaning, to try to understand, to try to feel, to try to connect, perchance to try to pray. Not to reject the old simply because it is old, and not to dismiss the new simply because it is new.

For some, understandably, the change from prayer book to prayer book may not be totally welcome. A prayer book, like any familiar friend, is hard to part with, and we would only mention that for old time's sake, we shall be pleased to make any member of our congregation a present of one of the old *Union Prayer Books*. We have eleven hundred on hand. Someone said to me that she was unhappy about giving up the old prayer book "because it's so…" and she was looking for the word, "because it's so traditional," which is sometimes simply a synonym for "familiar." And I answered her that the hope of the new prayer book was to expand that tradition.

I love the history of our prayer book because through all the revisions and all the new prayers and all the new prayer books, there runs the Jewish formula. The secret of that formula is the way Jews respond to change, the way Jews respond when their world changes or their lives change and they find that the familiar paths on which they have been walking take them only to dead ends and to nowhere in the world of reality. We are no different from other peoples in the world who once found themselves at dead ends. The difference is that some of them stayed on their dead-end road and they died. But when we reached our dead end, we dug out new roads: the road that went from the burning ashes of a Temple in Jerusalem to a new academia of learning in Babylonia; the road that went from the decaying communities of Eastern Europe to the vitality of the new America; the road that went from the death of the concentration camp to the orange groves of the kibbutz in Israel; the road that went from one prayer book to another prayer book.

Our secret formula was that we always found alternatives, that we always expanded our options, some created anew, some revived from the old—but another road that would allow us to continue our journey from that mountain somewhere in the desert to a still unredeemed future, still partners with God and partners with each other.

Thus do we cross the threshold of this New Year. For hardly any of us is the world exactly the same as last year. Children grow up, and their world gets bigger. Children move out, and our world gets quieter. Loved ones grow feeble, and the world gets sadder. Illness strikes, and the world gets scary. A beloved dies, and the world gets empty. A child is born, and the world sings.

And should we find ourselves at dead ends, we listen to the story of the prayer book; we turn to the reservoir of our own beings, to the full range of our options; and we dig out a new road for a New Year.

Jacob in the Bible had spent his whole life in contest with others, always trying to do them one better. And in a lonely night, Jacob struggles with an angel, and out of that struggle he emerges as *Yisrael*, the man of sensitivity and the man of compassion.

Jacob, as a person, did not change during that dark night because no one ever changes from being one person to being another. What happened during that night was that Jacob discovered the alternatives within himself. What Jacob did was discover a new truth.

Thus does the shofar call to us as we take the new prayer book in our hands, to explore the alternatives, to seek another truth. If there is bitterness in our hearts, another truth. If there is anger, another truth. If there is smugness, another truth. If there are only things, another truth. To move away from the dead ends, to continue our journey from the mountain into a still unredeemed future, partners with God, partners with each other.

May God give us strength for that journey.
Amen.

Rosh HaShanah 1979/5740

This Most Amazing Day

We are present together at the annual meeting of the Jewish people. According to our tradition, the first such meeting was held at a mountain in the Sinai Desert and was called to order by the blowing of the shofar, which, in the words of the Torah, waxed "louder and louder." It was at that first meeting that the Jewish people—men, women and children—entered the covenant with the one ethical God.

The Hebrew word for that covenant is *b'rit* or *b'ris*, which means an agreement, a contract between two parties. And this *b'rit* was between a God who could not be seen yet who commanded and the people who took on those commandments. It was between an ethical God who represented what was decent and right and humane and a people who accepted decency and rightness and humaneness as the behavior norms of its community. The *b'rit* was between the God of the world, although the world didn't know it, and this people who promised to get the word around. It was between a God who wanted the world to get better and a people who took on the assignment to make it that way.

That was the condition under which we Jews entered the stream of history—that we would deliver that message to the world, and centuries later, when a businessman would ask only whether something would sell or a scientist would ask only whether something would work or a politician would ask only whether something would get votes, we Jews would come with our message and ask our question: It may sell, it may work, it may get votes but before the ethical God, is it right?

As God's part of the covenant, the *b'rit*, He would be there for us, for strength when we would be less than strong, for courage when we would be less than sure, for bolstering of our spirits when our spirits would be on their way to being broken by men of power who would be irritated with our message and annoyed with our questions and fed up with our covenant.

The poet wrote: I thank You, God, for this most amazing day and the simple fact that we are here, that we have made it through all the years not only as a people who survived but as a people of the covenant, still with the message and still with the question—that fact makes this a most amazing day. And though there

112

may be Jews who never use the word *b'ris* except for a circumcision, and though there may be Jews who keep in less-than-constant touch with the God that cannot be seen, the fact is that here we are, and somewhere at this annual meeting are our growing-up children and our grownup children, and some of them are right here with us now despite all the complaints of those bygone years of how boring religious school was. The fact is that there are those of us, people of the covenant, who serve on community committees not only because of our civic responsibility but because the Jewish people promised to make the world better. The fact is that the people of the covenant are here wanting our grandchildren to be Jews. The fact is that in our own sometimes improvised ways, we are still the people of the covenant and we are here to declare that that makes this a most amazing day.

Thus the annual meeting has been called to order, and each of us is called upon to make his annual report on the condition of the covenant in our lives. And then as the shofar prepares to wax louder and louder tomorrow, we prepare to renew that covenant again for the year 5741, each of us individually in the place that we are in our own lives, our own hopes, our own dreams, our own fears, our own love—each of us with our promise to make our little place better, each of us with our prayers for the strength and courage to do it.

And besides each one's individual place, where he and she are, there is for all of us our collective place in America in the year 1980, on the eve of a bewildering election, at a time when our own people across the sea are afraid for their lives and their futures.

To share with you that time and place, I report an incident of a month ago. I was flying on the fifty-minute ride from Buffalo to LaGuardia, and in my briefcase was material for tonight's sermon on the subject of the American Jew. The man next to me, of course, began a conversation. And before long I learned that he had been born in London of an Indian father and a Portuguese mother, was Catholic by religion and was married to a Jewish woman from Milwaukee whose family, in his words, was "very Jewish." When he learned that I was a rabbi, he suggested that I might help him understand his wife a little better because as he perceived her, her being Jewish, he said, appeared more important to her than being American. "To Jews," he said, "people seem to be everything, Jewish people." And I corrected him and I said, "Not just people, but covenant." I told him about covenant, which he said might help him to understand his wife a little better.

It was not always so in America. There were Jews who came here in the early days of this country for whom or for whose children that old covenant could find no resting place suited in this new soil. And some of the descendants of those early Jewish settlers are nowhere to be found today among the Jewish people. But for most of the rest of us and our parents and our grandparents, what we love about this place was that no country on the face of this earth, through all the mountains and all of the deserts, had ever been more suited to the covenant we brought with us than this land of the free and this home of the brave. The lady in the harbor with her torch aloft was very American and very Jewish. America's concern for the poor and the hungry was out of our own book of the covenant. Even the impeachment of a president of the United States was in the spirit of the prophet Nathan as he pointed an accusing finger at King David himself. Even the travesty of a war in Vietnam could be countered by the right to protest that very war, and the right to dissent is American and Jewish. And not the least, the opportunity for an American Jew to walk the hillside of Jerusalem where Abraham walked and then return home to the land where the Pilgrims trod and to feel doubly blessed by two homes, each in its own way, is what makes the Jew feel so much at home in America.

And even more, because just as America has been good for the Jew, so the Jew, in countless ways, has enriched the life of this country. And one of the ways is what my friend on the airplane could not understand about his wife, because when our parents and grandparents came to these shores from Eastern Europe around the turn of the century, the democratic right for which they agitated and which they won and which was eventually claimed by every minority group in America was the right to press the government of the United States for its own Jewish group interests, on the one condition that those interests would not violate the free spirit of this nation. In those days, the issue was the right of Jewish labor to make its voice heard. In our day, the issue is the right of the American Jewish community to press its own government for uncowardly support of the State of Israel, both because it is our democratic ally in a sea of despotism and because the most pressing concern for the majority of Jews in America is that Israel, that beleaguered place, be given its moral right to control its own destiny on its own little piece of land. Our country, the moral United States, has no alternative but to uphold that moral right. With all the other problems to be solved, including the right of Palestinians, not one of them can compromise the moral right of Israel to exist and the moral right of the United States to insure that existence.

It is our claim and on this night, as the people of the covenant, we renew that claim. Whenever the occupant of the Oval Office will caution us that we are pressing too hard, we shall remind him how he, whoever he will be, sought us out before November 4 with more and more meetings and with more and more promises.

We make yet another claim as people of the covenant, although all Jews may not acknowledge the rightness of this claim, and that is the right of the American Jew to take difference directly with the State of Israel and the government of that state. My claim to argue with Mr. Begin's government is based not upon the citizenship in that state, which I do not hold, and not upon the taxes, which I do not pay. My claim is based upon the fact that three million of my people live within those borders, and if there are American Jews convinced that one or another policy of the State of Israel is detrimental to its right and ability to be strong and to survive, then I must speak with the fullness of that conviction.

It is absolutely correct that nothing that Mr. Begin does will change the minds of the master design of the Arab states and the PLO and the Soviet Union. But where it might make a difference is in the response of fragile Egypt, and where it might make a difference is in the response of the United States, and where it might make a difference is even in the response of the American Jewish community, which will not always agree to speak in a single voice and will not sign a single blanket endorsement for the sort of policies that it does not endorse. For the American Jew to be silenced in the name of the well-being of the Jewish people may, to some American Jews, prove in the worst interests of the people of the covenant.

And finally, at this time of renewal, we share our perplexity as we grope for clarity. As November approaches, it is easier to be against than to be for. It is easier to identify what gives us fear than what gives us hope. When our delegation from the congregation spent the Day of Jewish Concern in Washington, Rabbi David Saperstein alerted us in the approach of November to the dangers from the far right. To many of us, it was a new subject, but each day's press reports make the subject more pressing and a cause for our concern.

The far right is a coalition of most right-wing groups, diverse as they are, but they include in their ranks the moral majority, so-called, corporate wealth, fundamentalists and evangelists. Its positions on issues are consistent and predictable: anti-ERA, pro-right-to-life, anti-gun control, anti-civil rights for homosexuals, anti-welfare, pro-prayer in the public schools, pro-strong military defense, which even includes support for Israel.

The concern that we have about the far right is that no longer does it speak on street corners but provides transportation to polling booths to defeat any liberal candidate who would dare favor ERA or its ilk. Our concern about the far right is that its financial coffers have swelled from $250,000 in the election campaign of

1972 to $30 million in the election campaign of 1980. Our concern about the far right is not only its unbending stand on every social issue but its unholy alliance with the KKK and neo-Nazis and avowed anti-Semitic groups. We, the people of the covenant, can testify that any party of the extreme right that advocates repression of dissent eventually catches the Jews in the net of that repression. And though there are still those who counsel us not to yell fire, it would be ridiculous to ignore the smoke.

At such a moment in our history, at this time and place and with our people's uncertain future across the sea, I share on this night the words of Leo Baeck, who lived through the most critical moments of our people and who said: "History never provides anything ready made. All that history gives is the possibility."

On this eve of the New Year at the annual meeting of the Jewish people, may we claim the possibility. May we renew the covenant with our people and our country and our God.

And as the shofar will wax louder, may God be there for us for strength and courage even as until now He has been with us and kept us alive and brought us to this most amazing day.

Amen.

Rosh HaShanah 1980/5741

Who Will Live and Who Will Die

It was four years ago tonight that we introduced *Shaarey T'Shuvah,* the *Gates of Repentance,* as the new High Holy Day prayer book published for Reform congregations. We discussed on that Rosh HaShanah how the purpose of any prayer book is to supply a Jewish mode of expression to every generation that holds the book in its hands.

It is now four years later, and we have tried to assess periodically and informally the reactions of those members of our congregation who have been holding the book in their hands, and as all of us might have predicted, the responses have been diverse. There are some who still hanker after the old *Union Prayer Book,* not only because it served as so faithful a companion for those many years but also because of its elegant power to lift the human spirit on the wings of its words in contrast sometimes to the *Gates of Repentance,* which, in its pursuit of down-to-earth relevance, gets bogged down with words like "xenophobia," about which one congregation said to me, "When I pray from a prayer book, I shouldn't need a dictionary." There are others in our congregation who welcome the changes that the new prayer book has introduced. They welcome the changes of vocabulary because it speaks in the language of today, because it affirms the equality of men and women in the community of the Jewish people and in each Jewish congregation. They welcome the reference to the Holocaust and Israel, which are the two quintessential Jewish events of our time. They welcome the inclusion of more Hebrew and more prayers from the traditional *machzor,* because this Hebrew and these prayers join our voices to the voices of the generations, to the very voice of tradition that tended to be muffled in the old *Union Prayer Book.*

As one member of the congregation, I am among those for whom the *Gates of Repentance,* even with its imperfections, is becoming a congenial companion for these High Holy Days not, however, without a measure of struggle. And in the spirit of openness that I hope characterizes this congregation, just as its members are free to share their struggles with the leadership, so the leadership appreciates the opportunity of sharing its struggles with the members. It may even be that the struggle that I share with you tonight is not mine alone.

My struggle has to do with a particular prayer that occupies a central position in this prayer book. It is one of those prayers from our tradition that was muffled in the *Union Prayer Book*, where not only was the Hebrew abbreviated and the English rendered into pallid words, but the prayer itself was shunted out of its central position on Rosh HaShanah and Yom Kippur to the afternoon service of Yom Kippur, when very few people would be there to hear it. In the *Gates of Repentance* it has come back to its place on Rosh HaShanah and Yom Kippur, the Hebrew restored, the English translation literal and hard-hitting, word for word. The prayer is called by its first words, *Un'taneh Tokef*—"Let us declare the awesome power of this day."

Amid the vivid imagery of the heavenly court, angels and all, the power of this day is that all of us stand in judgment before the God of justice. And then the prayer moves to its second theme: that as outcome of that judgment, a verdict is issued for every human being, written on Rosh HaShanah, sealed on Yom Kippur: who shall live and who shall die; who shall see ripe age and who shall not; who shall perish by fire and who by water. And then, who shall be secure and who shall be driven; who shall be tranquil and who shall be troubled; who shall be poor and who shall be rich; who shall be humble and who shall be exalted. And then, the finale and the climax of the prayer: *U-t'shuvah u-t'filah u-tzedakah ma-avirin et ro-a hag'zerah*—"But repentance, prayer and charity change the evil decree."

Thus the prayer with which I struggle (not with the first part that summons every Jew to the bar of justice, because for most of us the power of this day is that we indeed stand in some kind of judgment): for all those times that if we had to do it again, we would do it differently; and for all those times we voiced regret for what we had done, but if we had to do it again, we would probably do it exactly the same way; for all those times we said what was better left unsaid and for all those other times we kept quiet when we should have said something; for all those times we fought to win because we refused to lose and failed to recognize that there might yet have been a third possibility. The power of this day is that we stand in judgment for our sins of the past year, and if we have trouble remembering some of them, there is that long list of *Al Cheit*s in the prayer book, and there's something for everybody, including xenophobia.

My problem is not with the Day of Judgment but with the second part of that prayer: that as a consequence of that judgment, our fate is decreed for the year now beginning. It is the old doctrine of reward and punishment that Job cried out against and that we argued with when we talked last year about the bad things that happen to good people. The problem with that doctrine is what it says about last week's plane crash and its toll of 269; what it says about people we love who die, slowly or quickly; what it says about people who are having a hard time with their marriages or their children or their jobs or their lives because it says they are paying their penalty for the misdeeds of the past year. It contradicts everything I have ever learned about the Jewish mandate of our God-given responsibility to confront the crises in our lives and in God's world, and then to assess where responsibility lies in each crisis, and then to assume whatever human responsibility we can to resolve each crisis. The problem with taking that prayer literally is that every time there's a victim, the victim is accounted responsible for his own tragedy, and I don't believe that many of our ancestors believed that. The problem with taking that prayer literally is that it robs life of its freedom and death of its mystery and human beings of their dignity—and I don't believe that.

And yet, the power of that prayer and its stirring chant that the cantor intones, its very cadence of life and death, of health and sickness, of tranquility and trouble, do not allow us to dismiss it. Somewhere in that melody and in those words is a signal about our human existence, a signal about the meaning of our lives that each of us can find for himself. And this is what I find in that prayer: That as we live our lives from day to day and we work hard, as we provide for our families, as we try to do the right thing, even though sometimes with a measure of leeway, as we celebrate our *simchah*s, as "tomorrow and tomorrow and tomorrow creeps in this petty pace from day to day," we do our best to ensure life and not death, success and not failure, tranquility and not trouble. We assume all that responsibility and we do everything within our power, but in the chant and the words of that prayer, there comes the signal that all those things can happen to a person, those good things and those shattering ones, and they are not totally in our power. We are not so totally the masters of our fate and the captains of our soul. Sometimes the crew of the other plane is; sometimes a disease is; sometimes and sometimes. How, then, shall we confront those uncertain and unpredictable possibilities of 5744? If we pray that prayer literally, then the finale has the answer: that if you do repentance, prayer and charity during these ten days, you can hope to fend off the shattering moments for the rest of the year and bribe away the days of evil before the verdict is sealed. I would tell you, however, that there is a well-known and respected observant rabbi in Brooklyn who has compiled a list of medical specialists in New York, and not only those who practice in Jewish hospitals. That rabbi, I know, prays *Un'taneh Tokef* on these Holy Days. That rabbi, I know, will exhort his people to repentance, prayer and charity. But when a member of his congregation is sick, he will also call one of those doctors on his list to arrange for an appointment. Repentance, prayer and charity—and a second opinion. You can be sure that if enough Jews really believed that doing charity during the Ten Days of Penitence would "change the evil decree," you can be sure that the UJA would switch its major fund-raising appeal from the springtime to these ten days.

And only today at twelve o'clock noon, as I was shaping the final draft of this sermon, my telephone rang. "Jack Stern?" the person said. "I am calling from…" and then he gave the name of an established brokerage house in New York. Now I quote him exactly: "Between Rosh HaShanah and Yom Kippur," he said, "we are making the offering of a high-yield stock." When I upbraided him for calling me on Rosh HaShanah, he told me it wasn't Rosh HaShanah yet and that there were observant Jews in his office who were at that moment making the same phone calls. I ended the conversation so abruptly that it took me a few minutes for its import to register: that there are enough Jews in this world, including the observant Jewish in that office, sufficiently wary of the insurance power of repentance, prayer and charity between Rosh HaShanah and Yom Kippur to fend off the uncertainties of the coming year that they saw fit to add yet the fourth option of a high-yield stock.

I don't believe that finale literally, and I don't believe that many of our ancestors believed it literally; and therefore we move beyond the literal. We ask the question: How shall we prepare for 5744, especially for that domain that is unpredictable and uncertain? In answer to our question, three roads are marked out for us, not ending on Yom Kippur but extending from now into every day of 5744. Each road aspires to the same purpose: to forge a connection between the self that is in each of us and someone or something that is beyond all of us. Repentance is my connection from my little, narrow world, my closed-in world, to the Creator and the Creator's world. Prayer is my communication: between myself thanking, asking, pleading, crying, between myself and the One beyond myself. And *tzedakah* is the glorious act of caring for someone not myself, the most exalted moment of "I and Thou." Those three roads of connection to the outside are to be marked out during these Holy Days so that whatever befalls in 5744 (whether we are responsible or someone else is responsible or no one is responsible), we shall confront those days as human beings *already connected,* because the serious threat of those uncertain days—whether the shattering ones or the stunning, good ones—is that they sever those connections between ourselves and the outside. The good ones isolate us with the thrill of our own success and put us on the mountain, and there's only room for one at the top of that mountain. The power of the shattering days is to break the connections and to isolate: Why is this happening to me, only to me? But then the signal comes from that prayer that if we get ready, if our repentance, prayer and charity forge the connection strong enough, when those straining days come, we shall be all the stronger to hold the strain. Then our isolation will have the time to which it's entitled, but that time will not drag on forever because we ourselves will call our isolation to a halt. And thus we shall avert the evil decree, whether of isolated arrogance or isolated self-pity, and we shall reconnect with the world toward health and fulfillment again, toward purpose and hope again.

Repentance. Prayer. Charity. Our own Jewish preventive therapy. As Rabbi Max Arzt has commented on this prayer, "We change the future by changing ourselves."

Un'taneh tokef, "Let us declare the awesome power of this day."
Amen.

Rosh HaShanah 1983/5744

Reform and Orthodoxy Together

The signal was to come from the blast of the shofar.

The people were to undergo a two-day period of preparation by washing their clothes, by abstaining from sex and then by waiting for the signal.

And on the third day, amid the crackle of lightning and the clapping of thunder, there came the shofar's blast, and Moses led the erstwhile slaves to the foot of the mountain. And there the commanding power of God was revealed to all of those present with the proclamation of Ten Commandments that even on this night surround us and embrace us in this sanctuary.

From that powerful moment on, a new people embarked upon a new destiny, to be a people that would shape its career by the power of those commandments, to become a people that would carry the commanding message of that one ethical God to all the world through all of history, even to this day.

Thus did our career begin like no other religion in the world. Because this one began not with a single person, not with a one-person Jesus or a Mohammed or even a one-person Moses. But this one began with the people en masse, all of them present at the divine moment, all of them present at the moment of creation of their own history, of our history.

And all of these centuries later, when the signal of that shofar is sounded in synagogues throughout the world, we are called again, as one people, to stand at the foot of the mountain.

There is a Hebrew word, also in Yiddish, *Hal'vay*—"If only it were so." If only we were one people—not necessarily of one mind because every Jew deserves the right to his and her own opinion, surely not without arguments because arguments and debates have always been part of our historic character and part of our Jewish charm, but still to be one people in history at the foot of the mountain.

Hal'vay! But instead, as one most recent example, the seventy-year-old leader of the Jewish community in Cracow—once 60,000 strong, now 600, once a center of bustling Jewish activity, now with a Jewish population the average age of which is seventy-eight years. The seventy-year-old woman who leads the community was asked by an American Jew visiting there: "What can we do to help you?" and she answered: "Send us a bar mitzvah. Send us life."

Last week a bar mitzvah from Connecticut went to Warsaw with his family and with his rabbi, Emily Korzenik, a Reconstructionist, which is an offshoot of the Conservative Movement.

What a historic moment that could have been in the destiny of the Jewish people. What a moment it could have been when that young man chanted the blessings of the Torah in the oldest synagogue in Cracow, when he could have roused the voice of the Jewish generations, when he could have brought life to that ghostly place.

Hal'vay! Because instead, a week ago Friday, official representatives of the Orthodox community in America sent a message to Cracow that it would be "a betrayal of Jewish history" if the Jews of Cracow allowed a Reform or Conservative rabbi to officiate in that synagogue. Not only was the site then changed, but some Orthodox rabbi/businessman who arranges bar mitzvah trips to Jerusalem presented himself on the bimah as the representative of the Jewish people and then unsuccessfully tried to prevent any participation by Rabbi Korzenik. (You can be sure that the rabbi/businessman will now add "Bar Mitzvah Trips to Cracow" to his brochure.)

What a glorious moment it could have been for the Jewish people at the foot of Sinai with the sound of the shofar. But what a tragic moment it turned out to be. Like a story by the Hebrew writer Bialik, which he entitled "The Ashamed Shofar."

And all the other tragic examples, including the Orthodox rabbinate in Israel that, with its political clout, has so far successfully blocked the right of Reform and Conservative rabbis to officiate at marriages; or the example of the Orthodox rabbi in Israel who in the Knesset publicly spat on the Reform prayer book; or the full-page advertisement that appeared last year in the American Jewish press that a Jew who lives too far from an Orthodox synagogue to walk there on the High Holy Days should rather remain at home than attend a Reform or Conservative synagogue that is within walking distance.

What makes it so tragic is that I know Orthodox rabbis who in no way deny my credentials as a rabbi, who would be repulsed by spitting on prayer books and full-page anti-Semitic advertisements in newspapers. I know Orthodox rabbis of the moderate wing of Orthodoxy who quietly cooperate with Conservative and Reform rabbis, but their voices are rarely heard in public because in our day the marching orders of the Orthodox movement are coming more from the far right than they are from the middle. Everyone is looking and listening over his right shoulder lest he be criticized for not being Orthodox enough. There are American Orthodox rabbis so far to the right that they refuse to recognize conversions performed by the Chief Rabbis of the State of Israel!

What makes it all so tragic is all of those pious Orthodox Jews who simply want to live an Orthodox Jewish life, who are out to condemn and undermine no one. But the beautiful accents of their faith get lost amidst the hysterical diatribes of those to their right, always accusing us who are Conservative and Reform of pushing the Jewish people into the quicksand of assimilation and intermarriage and of eventual disappearance.

If only my Orthodox fellow Jews would listen, if they would exchange diatribes for dialogue, then we would try to explain to them the fallacy in their indictments. Their mistake is assigning Reform and Conservative Judaism the responsibility for the weakening of Jewish life in the modern world. Their mistake is pointing the accusing finger at us when it should be pointed at the French Revolution and Baruch Spinoza and all the other architects of the modern secular world—all those who challenged the absolute authority of the state and religion to control the lives of their citizens. If they want to point accusing fingers, they should point them at the Statue of Liberty, which welcomed our brothers and sisters to these shores with the promise of religious freedom, which includes the promise to practice no religion at all. The problem for Judaism in America, wrote Leonard Fein, is not rape but seduction.

What we would explain to our Orthodox colleagues is that Reform Judaism came into existence for the very purpose of stemming that tide of seduction and assimilation. Reform Judaism did not lure Jews from Orthodoxy; to the contrary, it pulled them back from the precipitous plunge into the non-Jewish world. It announced to them that to live in that secular world, they did not have to stop being Jewish, that there was an alternative to the Orthodoxy they had already abandoned.

And thus did Reform Judaism, and later, Conservative Judaism, provide a way to live as Jews in the modern secular world.

And this would I declare to my Orthodox fellow Jews as a Reform Jew: Even if it were in my power, I would never want your Orthodoxy to disappear. Your political mischief I could do without, but not your authentic Orthodoxy, because what you offer, as we do, is your own Jewish option in the secular world. And that option is to keep your distance from that world, to pay its taxes and receive its services, but beyond that, to keep a safe distance from its practices and its values and its gods by safeguarding with as much zeal as you can muster your own practices and your own values and our God. It was to keep that distance, for example, that a recent Orthodox decision announced that a husband is forbidden to be present at the birth of his child, which has become an accepted procedure in modern obstetrics, because, they said, his presence would be a violation of the laws of modesty for his wife. To keep that distance from the modern secular world, strong opposition has come from Orthodox leaders to the formation of prayer groups for Orthodox women who want to come together as Orthodox Jews for study and worship because those opportunities are denied them in their Orthodox synagogue. The reason for the opposition to the prayer groups is not so much because the law forbids it, because the law could find a way to allow it, but because that request is perceived as a poisonous influence of the women's movement in modern secular society.

And I as a Reform Jew say to them: It's your world and your choice. And from families in this congregation there are some children who have made that world theirs and that choice theirs. And we say to them, *Kol hakavod*—"More power to you." More power to all of you as long as you do not impose your world on us. You are part of our *k'lal*—part of our total Jewish people.

And now, what I ask of you, my Orthodox Jewish colleagues, and am entitled to expect of you is that you will listen as openly as you are able to the choice that I and other Reform and Conservative Jews have made for ourselves. For we as Reform Jews do not reject the modern secular world. We live in it, we even embrace it, some of us carefully, some of us carelessly; we share in its achievements and try to clean up the garbage of its problems. And all of this we do with yet this other connection—this connection of our 3,000 Jewish years that began at the foot of the mountain, this connection that taught us what a Jewish family could be; and how parents should teach their children; and how human beings should treat each other; and how poverty and hunger are against the will of God; and how God wants us, the Jewish people, to clean up the garbage in the world.

As a Reform Jew, I tell you, my Orthodox colleagues, that I, too, hold the Torah closely. Not as the literal word of God, as you Orthodox do, but as the brilliant creativity of our people in love with their God and as their perception of what their God wants of them. From this Torah and from the tradition we take their ideas and we take their insights, and more and more, we are reclaiming their ways and their rituals and their practices, not all of them but some of them, even as we create new ones of our own, to draw ever closer to our people and our God. If you would witness Reform Judaism in the modern secular world, walk into our library on a Shabbat morning and watch the Reform Jews seated around a table with the portion of the week, striking sparks from the rock of the text to find new truths in old words. If you would watch Reform Judaism in the modern secular world, walk into one of our meetings where doctors from this congregation are seated around a table, sharing their own questions and their own struggles with questions of life and questions of death, seeking truth from the old words.

What I ask of you, my Orthodox fellow Jews, is not that you agree with us but that you acknowledge us, who constitute the majority of Jewish people in America, even as we acknowledge you, who are but a small minority. Acknowledge us as part of the *k'lal*—the totality of the Jewish people. Acknowledge that when it comes to rallying public support for our Jewish people in the State of Israel or for the Jewish poor of our cities, it will be more likely the Jews in the secular world (for they are at home there) who will be in the front line of action on behalf of our people.

The only hope for change, I believe, is not through debate in the public press but through private conversation that plays neither to the grandstands nor to the forces on the right.

The hope for change, I believe, is not only through rabbis talking to rabbis but Jews, members of congregations, talking to other Jews and knowing whereof they speak.

The hope for change will come from here, from Reform Jews themselves, not secular Jews who belong to Reform synagogues, not Jews who say, "I'm not religious, I'm Reform," but Reform Jews who study and learn and choose their ways to come closer to their people and God; Reform Jews who will bring the moral passion of their Torah to the garbage problems of the world; Reform Jews who will embark upon their journey of the spirit and share with others their affirmation and their doubts and their questions; Reform Jews who will be able to say to themselves and to their Orthodox friends, "I am a Reform Jew because I am very religious."

I believe that the loftiest pursuit of the Jew is the pursuit of peace. I believe it between Jew and Arab, and how much more so between Jew and Jew. I believe that my Orthodox fellow Jews, if they are as true to their faith as they claim to be, must share in this pursuit of peace. I believe that my Orthodox fellow Jews should stop spitting on prayer books in which the name of God is written and stop declaring bans on Reform and Conservative synagogues in which the God of Abraham is worshiped. Because if they are true to their faith, they will fear God more than they fear Reform and Conservative Judaism.

I believe that the time has come for the shofar not to be ashamed any longer, for a people to stand together again at the foot of the mountain.

Amen.

Rosh HaShanah 1986/5747

Jewish Dilemmas

The Problems of Power

The midrash tells of the man who had lost his way in the forest. He had been circling for days with no success when suddenly he heard the sound of human footsteps, and there before him was another human being. "My friend," he said, "I have been lost for days. Can you show me the way out of the forest?" The other man answered, "Do not follow me, my friend. I have been lost for more days than you."

Those of us who have lived through more than one war, more than one assassination, more than one blitzkrieg by Soviet Russia, more than one riot; we who have lived through six million and now must live through the starving death of thousands of children each day; we who lived through two national political conventions in a period of three weeks—we go begging from each other, from the experts and the wise men, and we walk away still lost in the forest, frightened yet more because even they, even the experts and the wise men, cannot find their way out.

In our helpless confusion, we cry out the primordial question: "O Lord, what is man?" If we could find some answer to that question, if we could learn what man is, then we might better understand what man does, what impels him to riot and to make war and to bring the world crashing down upon his own head. And then we could lead man, we could lead ourselves, out of the forest.

But here, too, the wise men and experts walk different paths. One cadre of social scientists alludes to the innate aggressiveness of the human creature. Man is a sophisticated ape, an acculturated animal, a civilized primate, and you can only expect him to behave accordingly.

I attended the meeting that considered the modest proposal of busing some Negro children into Scarsdale to attend our elementary schools. One member of the audience voiced strong opposition because the presence of Negroes in Scarsdale might depreciate the value of his property, which he had acquired through many years of labor and with hard-earned money. I shall never forget the man's face as he was ranting, and the fury in his eyes, and the crackling of his voice. He was a living illustration for Robert Ardrey's *The Territorial Imperative*, the animal guarding his territorial domain.

Then there are other experts with another theory, and they point us to primitive tribes in faraway places who live peaceably, harmoniously, nonviolently. Here, they say, is man in his original nature, peace-loving, cooperative, nonaggressive. Only when you transfer him to a teeming city, make him gasp for polluted air, make him fight for space and food and status—only then will he teach himself to act like an animal. And even worse, give him a copy of Ardrey or Lorenz with the theories of inborn aggressiveness, convince him that he is an animal, and he will begin to act like one.

This morning I would propose yet another theory. The social scientists have passed this one by because, perhaps, they have always looked upon the Bible as a religious book, a book about God. It *is* a religious book, but not so much about God, whom Jews claim to understand very dimly, as about man and his responses to God, which Jews understand very clearly.

The Bible is a book about man, and if we read the story of Creation without testing for scientific accuracy, we shall discover yet another theory of human personality.

On the sixth day, the animals and man were created. The animals and man are members of the same family, with the same biological instincts, needs, and drives—hunger, thirst, sex, power—but the man bears two marks of distinction.

First, God said to the man and the woman, "Replenish the earth and have dominion over the fish of the sea and the fowl of the air and over every living thing that creepeth upon the face of the earth." This man, like his relatives in the animal kingdom, would exert power, but with his special brain and his special creativity, he would rise to a level of power that no other animal in the kingdom could even approach. This man could break the soil and plant the seeds from which grain would grow. This man could outwit the other animals and use them to feed himself and clothe himself. Someday he would even chart his own course to the moon. Someday he would invent machines that would dispense with manual labor, and his brow would sweat no more. Behold this man, creature of power.

And second, God said to Adam: "The tree that is in the midst of the garden, you may not eat of it." Of course, Adam paid no attention to the order, but the Bible is saying that he could have. He could have restrained himself because only man, the Bible is saying, with his hallmark of the Divine, only man can listen to the voice of a higher power and a higher purpose and then impose checks and restraints upon his own power.

The criterion of a human being, by biblical definition, is how he copes with his power, his power over himself and over other people, which explains why the story of the Jew is so human. How many the times when we had no power at all!

In Egypt we were slaves and we learned what it was like, and then we went to Sinai and we promised never to shut our hearts to that feeling of human helplessness; we promised to create a society where the helpless would be helped, a society dedicated to a purpose higher than the power of those who ruled it. And when we forgot that promise, the prophet came in all his anger and proclaimed, "Thus saith the Lord!" We were a people without power on a thousand streets of Europe, and the humor and the melodies and the literature and the insights that those years produced are sensitively human. When a Jew laughs, his laughter is a little louder, and when he cries, his tears are a bit more tragic.

And those of you who have visited the Land of Israel (and when some of us take the trip at the end of February, we shall discover it together) have witnessed a state that has entered the world of power. It has a government, it has an army, and a year ago June we witnessed the dramatic impact of its power. And yet, after a few days in Israel, walking side by side with Israelis on the streets of Tel Aviv or visiting a kibbutz or talking to the young men and women in the army, you know that the humanity is still there. The Israelis do not hate the Arabs as much as they are annoyed by them. Just last week we heard the story of an incident that happened during the Six-Day War when the Israelis and Arabs were fighting from street to street, in the walled city of Jerusalem. An Israeli soldier had taken cover in the doorway of a house when he noticed an Arab child walking in the street, crying, because he was frightened by the gunfire. The Israeli soldier left his hiding place, walked into the street, picked up the Arab child, the child of his enemy, to carry him to safety. On the way back, the Israeli soldier was killed.

And after that Six-Day War there was no parade to flaunt the victory, no Israeli version of VJ Day or VE Day.

But there are other moments, like the one of a few weeks ago when an Arab terrorist planted a bomb in a Tel Aviv bus station and the bomb exploded, and the Israelis turned violently on the Arabs who happened to be there at the time and who were innocent, the very Arabs with whom the Israelis had been living at peace in Israel for the past twenty years.

In that moment the Israelis lost their humanity, for that moment they felt trapped like animals, and they responded wildly with animal power. God willing, it will never happen again.

And I weep for my America because such moments come so often, moments of violence not only by the breakers of the law but by the supposed keepers of the law, moments of riot, moments of lawlessness. America is losing its humanity.

Not because of the revolutions themselves. The revolutions were long overdue. For too long the men in power forgot what it was like, what the Jew was commanded never to forget, how it is to be powerless, how it is to be helpless. They forgot because they didn't care, because they loved their own power.

I am saddened not because of the revolutions but because of the destruction that they reap: student power vs. administrative power, without the higher purpose of what education should be; black power vs. white power, without the higher purpose of what a society should be; teacher power vs. community control, without the higher purpose of what a child in a classroom should become.

I hear demands for law and order, but their purpose is not to check the violence and then to build, it is not to create the law and order of which this Torah speaks—that a man should stretch out his hand to the poor and needy of the land, that justice should be dispensed to rich and poor alike. It is not law and order for the higher purpose of a human society but rather an angry demand to suppress power with power, to keep the Negroes "in their place," the students "in their place," the opponents to Vietnam policy "in their place," to keep everyone in his powerless, helpless place. Someone suggested that the words "law and order," as used by many, are a synonym for "nigger!" It is a law and order that could sanction the 35 percent cutback in summer programs and education for deprived children.

Their demand for law and order plays upon the animal fears of men, and those who make the demands generously promise, elected, to take us out of the forest. And they might, but they will lead us into the jungle.

By the time we reach the events of this morning's Torah portion, Abraham has come a long way in the world. With all of his flocks and all of his territory, he has become a man of power, an unbecoming posture for the founder of the people who would be God's messenger to the world.

So according to our story, God summons Abraham to surrender his power in the form of his most precious possession, his beloved son, and thus acknowledge a purpose beyond himself, beyond his own power.

Abraham accedes to the demand, but at the very moment of confrontation, God Himself, the Supreme Power of the universe, retracts His demand and thus surrenders some of His own power, while He and Abraham together discover an alternative that is mutually acceptable—a ram caught in the thicket.

What would happen if at the very moment of confrontation, we took one step backward from the line of battle—students and administration, Negroes and whites, teachers and governing boards, Arabs and Israelis—one step backward to say that otherwise men would kill each other and would destroy America, and the Middle East and the world.

One step backward from the battle line to the joint recognition of a higher purpose, of a child in the classroom, of a society that could live in peace in the world. One step backward to find an alternative and the sacrifice necessary to achieve it.

Some months ago, in an adult education program conducted in this sanctuary, we saw the motion picture *War Games*, which presumed the reality of an all-out atomic war. The impact stunned us into silence. But then the question: How much would we sacrifice to avoid the possibility? How much would we sacrifice of American power and American wealth to share them with the have-nots of the world and thus reduce the probability?

We say we are saddened by the blight of the cities. But how much would we give up, how much of our exclusiveness, how many of our zoning regulations, to relieve the pressure of the inner city, to find a viable alternative to destruction and death?

The story is told of an old man, shabbily dressed, who collapsed on the pavement. People crowded around, feeling very sorry, and afraid for the man's life. As the ambulance drove up, one man in the crowd took off his hat and extended it outward. "I'm sorry five dollars worth. How sorry are you?" And he passed the hat around.

We have lost our way in the forest, Negro and white man, student and administrator, teachers and governing board, and one says to the other," Can we find the way out?" And the other answers, "On one condition: that we go together," with God's help.

Amen.

Rosh HaShanah 1968/5729

Future Shock

Last month's hijacking by Arab terrorists provoked strong reactions from around the world, and none of them was favorable. The hijackings were one more hammer blow to a humanity already pummeled and beaten to the ground, its cities torn by riots, its universities turned into battlegrounds, and now its skyways considered fair game for political activists.

What next? is the question that plagues us. What seam in our social fabric will be the next to go, what institution of our social structure will be pegged as the next target for attack?

By coincidence, it was during this fretful time that publicity was being directed to a new book entitled *Future Shock* by Alvin Toffler. It deserves to be read by concerned, forward-looking people, but only those who have the stamina to listen to the question and probe some of the answers to the question, "What's next?"

Toffler depicts a society that is already in the throes of such rapid change that permanence and continuity are rapidly disappearing from the arena of our lives. He cites, for example, that in Washington, DC, in 1969, of the 885,000 listings in the telephone directory, one-half were different from the year before. Since 1948 and every year for the past twenty-two years, one out of every five Americans has changed his address: temporary places of residence, which mean temporary human relationships and temporary personal involvements. We live, he says, in a temporary, throwaway society, where just about everything is dispensable. And it may not be too long, predicts Toffler, that young people who fall in love will enter temporary, disposable marriages, only for a time—the first in a series of marriages and other partners yet to come.

Besides this startling rapidity of change, contends Toffler, is the startling newness of the changes themselves, thanks to science and thanks to technology. Of all the scientists who have ever lived, 90 percent are living at the present time. And with the human curiosity that goads them on, needless to say, the areas of their search are hemmed in by no boundaries.

Have you ever heard of a process called "cloning"? Thus far, it has been tried only on animals. It is the process whereby the nucleus of an adult cell is taken from one organism and used to initiate the growth of another, completely new organism that will consequently bear the same genetic characteristics as the contributor of the cell nucleus. It means, genetically, that there could be two of you and two of me. It sounds like science fiction, but according to scientific calculations, that possibility could materialize within the next fifteen years.

During that same number of years, scientists will likely perfect the process whereby a woman will be able to bring a tiny frozen embryo to her doctor, have it implanted in her uterus, carry it for nine months, and then give birth as though it had been conceived in her own body. Such is the novelty in store for us.

Rapid change, startling novelty, and third, as Mr. Toffler describes it, is the staggering number of choices—he calls it "overchoice"—that are becoming available to us in everything from commercial products to lifestyles to specialized professions. One computer operation reports that the purchase of an automobile with the number of styles, colors, gadgets and all the rest presents the prospective buyer with 25 million different choices!

The combined effect, says Toffler, of all of this speed of change, this novelty, this diversity may be so overwhelming that ordinary civilized human beings like ourselves may find it impossible to adapt as we have managed to do in the past, and we will fall victim to "future shock," a malaise of confusion and an inability to take decisive action and an urge to escape because the future has swooped in upon us too quickly, too soon.

The material and the predictions in *Future Shock* are shocking, sometimes incredible, and our first impulse is to make them go away and put down the book. But fifteen years is not a very long time, and one can only surmise that fifteen years before Dr. Christian Barnard performed his first heart transplantation, someone must have written that one of these days someone will switch a beating heart from one human being to another, and the response must have been equally incredulous.

We need not even wait the fifteen years to feel the pulse of rapid change and its consequences. We were holding a meeting at our temple a few years back for college students. A college senior had expressed an opinion on some issue or other, and a college freshman stood up and disagreed. "But, of course," he said, "the previous speaker might be expected to feel differently; he's from another generation." When I went to school, a generation was calculated at twenty-five years; now it's down to four. A cartoon in a magazine showed two rather doleful-looking men in a conversation at a bar, and one says to other: "Every time I get to where it's at, it's already where it was." Future shock is already with us.

Or walk through the streets of the East Village or Oakland, California, or Lenox, Massachusetts, or cities in Europe or villages in Israel or Vermont (why is it always Vermont?), and there you will find them, young men and women, some already victims of future shock, and others who are there, they will tell you, because they wanted to make the break before it was too late, before it happened to them. They will tell you of having felt like hostages, powerless, helpless, and the only shred of freedom left to them was to make the break. And when you ask a youngster what he's going to do with his life, sometimes he will tell you that he just wants to go to Vermont and live his days on a farm away from everything he knew during the years of his growing up.

Mr. Toffler spends the latter part of his book spelling out some possible antidotes to future shock, what he calls "shock absorbers." But on a Yom Kippur morning in the company of a congregation, in the company of that first congregation in history that Moses addressed in the Torah portion, we, the descendants of Moses, who have been subjected to more shocks, more sudden changes than any other people in history and are still here to tell the tale, we have something to say on the subject. There is a community in Argentina comprised exclusively of survivors of Hitler's concentration camps, and the name they have given their community is *Lamrot Hakol*, which means "In Spite of Everything."

One Jewish shock absorber was our sense of time. Time meant history, and history in its stretch from past to present and present to future meant change, and change meant adaptation, and adaptation meant survival. They tell the story in Israel of the building brigade that was constructing a house on a kibbutz. As one laborer handed the bricks to his fellow worker, these are the words that could be heard: *Danke schön, Herr Professor. Bitte sehr, Herr Doktor*—"Thank you, Professor." "You're welcome, Doctor." And now they were laborers on a kibbutz.

It sounds almost too elementary, but what may be missing in our educational process, what we should be teaching our children, is a sense of time and a sense of history and the reality of change. (The hard hats and the hardheads may try to deny it, but to no avail.) But even when we try, part of the difficulty, especially within the younger generation, is the sense of now-ness that fills the atmosphere. Yesterday is too long ago, tomorrow is too far away, and why do we have to learn all that history, and why can't education be more relevant, and why don't you talk about us and about our world?

This is my answer; this is the Jewish answer: "Because otherwise you would never know that problems and obstacles were always in people's way and in the world's way, and you would never know how they confronted those obstacles and sometimes even surmounted them. You would never know that the human spirit may be stronger than you in your sheltered life have been led to believe, and be able to take more than you in your sheltered life have been led to think, and be able to cope more than you in your sheltered life have been led to imagine. Maybe you don't have to move to Vermont; maybe you're not entitled to run away permanently because whose world is it? Whose problems are they? To whom does history belong? The clock of humanity is ticking away. Look at your watch and tell me what time it is. The Jewish sense of time.

And linked up with the time sense is another "shock absorber." It was a banner that Jews carried through all the changes and all the crises and all the shocks—a banner that displayed to the world and ourselves the values that were at the center of our being, the value of a God who signified justice and mercy, and the value of a human being endowed with dignity, and the value of our task to make the world better than it is.

During all those dark moments when we were held hostage by popes and kings and drunken peasants, we could look at that banner and not succumb to our powerlessness and our helplessness. Milton Steinberg once said that the secret of Jewish survival was that "we never sank to the level of our own misfortunes." We were not beaten down by the moment of time because we held on to the timeless. We were not shocked out of existence because of the values that had an existence of their own. And even when the threats were less threatening, we knew where we stood and what we believed. Jews in the Middle Ages were told not to hunt for sport the way the gentiles did because it meant taking life for fun. Jews in the Middle Ages were told not to get drunk the way the gentiles got drunk. Jews in the Middle Ages were told not to beat their wives the way the gentiles did because it was not appropriate for a Jew to beat his wife. We lived by values that were deemed valuable for their own sake, that had an existence all their own.

And the danger, the most foreboding danger in an era of future shock is what's happening to values, the loss of independence of values that by definition have an existence of their own, independent of what at this moment I may want or need or feel.

Let me suggest a minor illustration. Many years ago, one of our youngsters was to be operated on in the hospital. The shortage of space was acute, and we were told that the mother could not stay the night with the child, and we were confronted with the testimony of all of the child experts who said that the child would fare better if his or her mother were not in immediate proximity. We, with the mother's intuition, persisted, and my wife remained in the room. Several years later, articles appeared in the journals whereby a turnabout procedure was recommended—that wherever possible, a mother should remain overnight with her infant child. What had been passed off to us as a value was only a solution to a problem of space, a sanction for an existing practice.

We have taken our weaknesses and made them sound like values. We say, "Do your own thing" and make it sound like a value. A whole life of doing your own thing and avoiding social responsibility, turning your back on the world, is now made to sound like a value. But I cannot pass off my own wishes and my own desires and my own self-indulgence as values because by definition, a value must have an existence all its own.

Surely we should reexamine and surely we should reevaluate our system of values. We should examine a value like premarital chastity and struggle with it on its own merits to see if it deserves to survive as a value, but that's a far cry from giving up on it simply because the behavior of young people has changed and because we think we are impotent to stem the tide.

And if in the course of our examination we conclude, as objectively as is within our power, that the family as we know it is still the best hope for human fulfillment and social stability and cultural transmittal, then instead of accommodating ourselves to temporary marriages, we should direct our energy to the permanence of marriage, even if it means finding ways of telling young people who think they are very much in love that their marriage will probably not work.

If we enter the era of future shock without values, we shall all become its victims. We shall not survive the speed, the novelty, the diversity. We, human beings created by God and endowed with dignity, must be able to say: "This invention is beneficial to humanity and this one is not!" We must be able to say: "This pattern of behavior is destructive to human dignity and this one is not!"

Most of all, we need confidence in our own values, even if it means argument, debate, conflict, and may the best value win! I was once engaged in discussion with a young man of radical inclinations. There were many matters on which we agreed, but the moment we encountered an area of disagreement, he said: "Rabbi, that's your hang-up," and I said to him: "How do you know that you're not the one who is hung up?" We are too defensive, too apologetic, when we cling to an old value, not because it is old but because it is still valuable. And if we are called hypocrites because we do not live up to the values we profess, "the fault, dear Brutus," is not in the value "but in ourselves, that we are underlings."

As we gird ourselves for the new age, there is one difference between the shocks that the Jewish people have survived and the ones that lie in store for us. The Jewish ones came from the enemy: They made us hostages, and we rallied to the cause.

The new shocks come from ourselves, from our abundance of riches and technology. We take ourselves hostages when we fall to the level of our own prosperity.

Moses spoke to his people about what lay in store for them, a destiny of challenge and change and shock. And then he added: "See, I set before thee this day life and death, the blessing and the curse. Choose life that you may live!"

The question is not whether we can take the rudder in an era of future shock. The question is whether we will exercise the freedom of will and the blessing of dignity that God has given us. The question is not whether we can do it but whether we shall decide to do it. And if the decision be made, then we provide that one ingredient that is indispensable to a society on its way forward—the ingredient of hope.

William James once said that "the first act of freedom is to choose it."

"See, I set before thee life and death. Choose life that you may live!"

Amen.

Yom Kippur 1970/5731

The Day of Remembering

The name of the day is *Yom HaZikaron*—the Day of Remembering. I remember as a child sitting with my family in the synagogue, especially my grandmother, *aleha hashalom*, and how for her, every holiday, and especially Rosh HaShanah, was a time for remembering: how she as a child had sat with her parents in the synagogue, parents who by now had long been dead.

And then children have a way of growing up, and they begin families of their own. And somehow there comes a day when they find themselves sitting in their own synagogue, surrounded by their own families, doing their own remembering.

It is called the Day of Remembering because according to the tradition, it is the time when God Himself remembers all the deeds of human beings and judges those deeds for innocence or guilt and then waits for us, His children, to stand before Him and ask Him for forgiveness and thus become at one with Him again.

For those who may not be able to accept such a concept of a personalized God, of a God who Himself remembers, Himself judges, Himself forgives, I suspect that even for them on this particular day there is still that sense of deeds being reviewed, of deeds being judged, of behavior being revised. The vocabulary is different; the meaning is similar. Rosh HaShanah is our annual Jewish checkup, before Someone or Something or Somehow.

It is the Day of Remembering, and there's a Jewish way of doing it. Like King David who is supposed to have written his memoirs in the Book of Psalms and who left nothing out, so as we begin our remembering, we leave nothing out. We try to remember everything: our moments of glory and the moments we would just as well have never happened; how we sometimes succeeded in our failures and how we sometimes failed in our successes; how we bungled sometimes when we meant well and how we lashed out sometimes when we didn't know what we meant; all the times we said yes when no would have been better and all the times we said no when yes would have been possible.

It all gets remembered, the glory and the garbage, and if it threatens to tarnish our image, at least it keeps us honest. At least it saves us from the sin of stuffy self-righteousness, which may be the most sinful sin of all. At least it keeps us from hiding the memories we don't like, because our ancestors were very good psychologists and they understood that memories that get hidden and buried have their own way of coming back to haunt the very ones who try to hide them.

So we remember everything at the beginning, but then we do what Rollo May contends is what only human beings are able to do: We then "take a hand in our own development." We actively, consciously, decide which of all of those memories we want to hold on to, which of all those memories deserve a permanent place in our own consciousness and our own character to make us better and wiser.

The Hebrew word for remember is *zachor,* which does not simply mean to recall but means "keep in mind," to retain in my consciousness. It may be the memory of a crisis that I want to hold on to, a crisis that was surmounted, and for that very reason, I hold on to the memory in the eventuality of another crisis. It may be a remembered moment of surpassing beauty that I want to hold on to because of the way it influences my perception of the world. It may be a moment of exquisite human closeness that I want to hold on to because of the way it helped me to perceive the people in that world. It may have been one of my own moments of human weakness because I will then keep in mind my need for strength. It may be a remembered moment of sickness that always then reminds me of the blessing of health.

It is selective, conscious remembering, according to the person I am, to the person I want to be. And if, perchance, the memories I prize the most are when I won the match or pulled off the ploy or manipulated the other human being, then for truth that is the person I am, the person I want to be. May God help us to remember well.

And because I am a Jew who remembers, my Jewish remembering extends backward not only to the beginning of this year, not only to the beginning of my lifetime, but my memories are what my people culled from its own past and even may have embellished sometimes. My memories are what my people incorporated into its collective consciousness because these memories say what my people is and what my people wants to be.

Such remembering far into the past may not be the popular mood of our day. There was a series of articles in a recent issue of *The Saturday Review* that lamented the low estate of the study of history on college campuses and noted that fewer and fewer students opt for the study of the past. Mostly they turn to the social sciences because the social sciences are the "now." And we are the generation of the "now." "Ancient history," the article said, "is anything that happened before the Vietnam War." The popular word is "contemporary," and we are asked by parents to please make our Jewish teaching contemporary. But what they miss is that by Jewish definition, there is no "now" without "before." By Jewish definition, no moment, including tonight's moment, begins here and by itself. It inherits a past and moves toward a future. It is the world of our fathers and the world of our children.

Zachor, "keep in mind," for example, that your ancestors and mine were slaves in Egypt who lived below the poverty line that we have risen above, but still we shouldn't forget.

I tell you of it because on these High Holy Days, there is a little congregation that is related to us. It lives in the Intervale section of the South Bronx, and our own temple has a special relation with it through our Social Action Committee. They are isolated, elderly, impoverished Jews. One of their few contacts with the outside Jewish world is in this room at Passover time when they share in our congregational seder. I spoke to the president of the congregation a few days ago and he told me that the congregation is now down to about forty people, and this year they will not hold services on the Eve of Rosh HaShanah, tonight, but will have services all the other days because the elderly people are afraid to go out at night. But then he was quick to add that next week, on Yom Kippur, *Kol Nidrei,* they're willing to take their chances, and they will hold their service. Perhaps the Federation of Jewish Philanthropies and the United Jewish Appeal and Israel Bonds and all of the rest in which we are involved could spend their time to better advantage than looking for fund-raising strategies if only we would say to them: "We remember. We keep in mind that we were slaves in the land of Egypt below the poverty line, and we stretch out our hands to the poor and needy among our brothers."

Zachor, "keep in mind," for example, that through all the years of our Jewish history, the good times and the bad times, the most stabilizing organism was not the school and not the synagogue but the home where the family was, not only as a nest of security but as the transmitter of Jewish values that were often in conflict with the values of that world outside.

It was what Irving Howe, in his remarkable book *World of Our Fathers,* recalls about those early days when East European Jews came to this country. It was not a glorious time. There were conflicts between generations, between the values of the old world and the new. There were conflicts between parents and children. He writes of all the Jewish husbands who deserted their wives and all the Jewish daughters who walked the streets in the red-light district of the East Side of New York. He tells everything, total recall, but then he adds: "Still the ferocious loyalty of the Jews to the idea of the family as they knew it is what allowed them to survive."

And among some of the families of our time: When young people sometimes tell me that they're ready to enter a marriage with a feeling of tentativeness that says, "If it doesn't work out, we can always get a divorce"; or when marriages are sometimes perceived as two individuals each seeking his and her own individual fulfillment and satisfaction rather than both of them together struggling to build something that transcends each one's individual satisfactions and fulfillments; or when some parents see themselves as providers of room and board and mouth braces for their children and then tell the schools to give their children learning and tell the synagogues to give their children religion—at such times I counsel *zachor*, "keep in mind," the ferocious loyalty of Jews to the idea of family.

Remember poverty and relieve it. Remember family and strengthen it. *Zachor*, because only a people who remembers its past has the sense of time that allows it to hope for its future. Whoever has been to Yad Vashem in Israel and walked in that darkened room of memorial with the flickering light and then walked outside to the brightened day and the tender saplings planted along the walk will sense the Jewish linkage between memory and hope.

Yom HaZikaron, *yom hatikvah*—"Day of Remembering" and "day of hope." And day, finally, of yet something else. The legend tells that when God created the world (supposedly on this day of the New Year), God himself decided that the world would never survive unless He incorporated into it one other element, the element of *shich'chah*—the ability to forget—because there are some memories we would just as well do without. They do not inspire us but only paralyze us. They do not strengthen us but only make us suffer. They are contrary to the person I am and to the person I hope to be. I begin by remembering them along with everything else, and I place them in the full light of recognition. If they embarrass me, I do not turn away from them. If they need reparation, I make it. If they include a grudge against myself or someone else, I forgive it, but then, having done all of those things, I dispose of it. I consciously remove it from the person that I am, and good riddance.

It is the New Year:
To remember what deserves to be remembered;
To forget what deserves to be forgotten;
And to stand before our God and ourselves
With much hope for a year of blessing and of life.
Amen.

Rosh HaShanah 1976/5737

Kurt Waldheim and Jewish Morality

The meeting of September 1, 1987, will be recorded in the annals of our Jewish history. For the first time ever, a delegation from the Jewish community met in conference with the pope of the Catholic Church for the primary purpose of airing a Jewish grievance. The meeting was actually called at the initiative of the Vatican because word was circulating that several Jewish organizations were planning to boycott the projected meeting of the pope with two hundred Jewish leaders during his visit to Miami on September 11. The boycott would be a demonstration of protest against the pope for his agreement to meet officially last June with President Kurt Waldheim of Austria, who is accused of Nazi activity in World War II: Kurt Waldheim, who is accused of complicity in the deportation and eventual death of thousands of Jews, Greeks and Serbians.

The meeting on September 1 in the papal summer residence outside Rome was intended to defuse the conflict and to avoid the boycott in Miami, which it did. It was intended to allow for open and frank discussion between the Jews and the pope, which it did. Since the Vatican limited the number of Jewish delegates to nine, it became the hottest ticket in town, with no small amount of infighting and backbiting among the Jewish competitors to be part of the delegation.

Once the decision was made as to who would go, the delegates journeyed to Rome with an agenda of three issues: first, the Jewish community's sore distress with the pope's refusal to cancel the meeting with Waldheim; second, the Jewish community's renewed petition that the Vatican officially recognize the State of Israel (which until now it has not done); and third, the seeming and confusing insensitivity of the pope to the Jewish dimension of the Holocaust and its searing impact upon Jewish consciousness. Confusing because this same John Paul II, while a priest in Poland, had been responsible for the saving of countless Jewish lives from the Nazis. This same John Paul II, as a Polish priest, had advised against the baptism of a Jewish child who had been left in the care of Catholic parents. And yet, now as the pope of the Catholic Church, he could not make a visit to the Majdanek concentration camp without citing the fourteen nationali-

145

ties who had gone to their death there, yet not one mention of the Jews, for whom the ovens of death had been built in the first place.

When the meeting outside Rome was over, the assessment of its value by various sectors of the Jewish community was as diverse as anything else that is assessed in the Jewish community. As might have been predicted, no apology was forthcoming for the meeting with Waldheim, if for no other reason than that the chief vicar of the Catholic Church is not in the habit of apologizing, even to a delegation of Jews. Predictably, there was no breakthrough on the Vatican's recognition of Israel, but this time the Vatican offered an explanation: that its position on Israel was not theological but political, out of concern for Catholic minorities in Arab countries. What did emerge from the meeting was a positive and affirmative response on the third issue: the announcement of a document, to be prepared under the auspices of the Catholic Church, which would trace the history of anti-Semitism through the past nineteen centuries, including and especially the Holocaust, including and especially the involvement of the Catholic Church in those nineteen hundred years of anti-Semitic history. When the meeting was over, what had made the strongest impression upon those who participated was not only the willingness of the pope to listen and engage in frank discussion, but also the strong likelihood that this encounter might mark the beginning of an ongoing process.

To me, what was most astounding was that such a meeting took place in the first place. When Jews think historically of popes and Jews, we think of those meetings centuries ago when the Jewish representative who came to petition the pope for something or other had to kneel before the pontiff and then would receive a symbolic "kick" for the refusal of the Jewish people to acknowledge Christ as God. When we remember historically, we remember popes ordering confiscation of Jewish books, or the Vatican legislating segregation of Jews out of Christian neighborhoods where they had lived all their lives so that they could be *Judenrein*, "free of Jews." Or, even in the more generous moments, we remember the powerful pope providing some measure of protection for the powerless Jews against anti-Semitic outbursts of churchgoing Catholics.

But here, at the meeting on September 1, 1987, were the two parties, not one powerful and the other powerless but two partners in an open dialogue in the spirit of Pope John XXIII twenty years ago. Here was the chief vicar of the Catholic Church trying to conciliate the Jewish community and to respond to its upset. And there was the Jewish community, not only not bowing down but taking the pope to task for some moral sidestepping, for falling short of the divine command to do "what is right and what is good," because by no stretch of the definition could the reception that the pope tendered to Waldheim be defined as right or qualify as good. Here was the Jewish community taking a moral stand so compelling that even last June, the Catholic bishops in the United States petitioned their own pontiff not to proceed with the Waldheim audience.

But the truth be told, this time our Jewish moral position was an easy one. This was not one of those times, those many times, when "what is right and what is good" was not so readily apparent and not so crystal clear. Nor was this one of those times that have troubled so many of us Jews in these past decades when the question of whether it's "good for the Jews" might be at odds with whether it is right and good by a more universal ethical standard. This time it was both. It was good for the Jews and it was right and good by any standard. This time it was easy.

What have we learned from the Waldheim affair? That we, our Jewish community, are still capable of a strong moral voice, that we still have the moral lung power to deliver our God-given message to a world that is well-versed in fancy sidestepping, but also a world where the moral message so often is not easy because the problems so often are not simple.

For example, and here I speak for myself, in the State of Israel, which we love, the problems are not simple. In the State of Israel, decisions must be made every day: how to balance the legitimate need for national security with the legitimate moral principle of freedom and justice for all, including Israel's Arab population. That moral principle, by itself pure, insisting upon the same freedom of movement for Arabs as for Jews, would allow Arab terrorists exactly the opportunity they seek: to destroy the Jewish nation and silence the Jewish voice forever.

But then, what happens to the balance on the other side? What happens to the Jewish moral voice when it is drowned out by the gunfire of Israeli soldiers when they fire randomly in the name of national security into a crowd of Arab students demonstrating peaceably on their own campus to protest Israeli military rule? What happens to the balance and to the Jewish moral voice when, in the name of Jewish solidarity, Arab residents can be forced out of neighborhoods where they lived all their lives because the Jewish residents want it to be "Arabrein," free of Arabs? And what happens to the balance and to the Jewish moral voice when, under the guise of a system of justice, Jewish terrorists who murder Arabs are meted out a more lenient dosage of justice than Arabs who murder Jews?

And thus, to the most troubling question of all, which is at the core of all the other questions: What hope can there be for the Jewish moral voice in Israel as long as it remains a dual society with three and a half million Israelis enjoying full civil and political rights under the rule of law and one and a third million Palestinians on the West Bank and Gaza living under military rule with few civil rights and no political rights? And yet, if the Arabs had all of those rights, they might well use them to destroy the very nation that granted them. Thus the problem.

It used to be that whenever an American Jew asked such troublesome questions about the internal life of Israel, we were told that we had no right to criticize until we were ready to live there and endure the same risks to life and survival that Israelis do. As someone who has always asked those troublesome questions, I no longer respect or accept that answer. Because inside the borders of Israel is an ever-growing number of Israeli Jews, including those in the Knesset and in the Cabinet, whose lives are on the line and whose children serve in the army, Israeli Jews who are asking the same questions about the ever-growing weakness of the moral voice of the Israel they love and we love, the same questions about the chipping away of the moral bedrock on which that state was given birth almost forty years ago.

Those Israelis are seeking *d'rachim acherim*—"other ways"—other solutions to the West Bank and Gaza: solutions that would liberate the State of Israel from its unfitting role as military ruler; solutions that would provide the strength that that remarkable country so sorely needs: the strength of its security and the strength of its Jewish moral voice.

Now to the greatest sadness of all. The sociologist Steven M. Cohen asked the following question in a series of surveys conducted among American Jews: "Do you care deeply about Israel as an important part of your Jewishness?" In 1983, 78 percent of those responding answered in the affirmative; in 1986, that figure dropped down to 63 percent because, according to Cohen, of a "heightened awareness of Israel's conflicts between left and right, religious and secular, Jew and Arab, rich and poor." To those 15 percent who have stopped caring, including some who may be in this congregation, my own unsolicited response: that when someone you love behaves in a way unacceptable to you, the appropriate response is not to pick up your marbles and walk away but to let the voice of your concern be heard, to join your voice to the chorus that is already there, to seek *d'rachim acherim* of how the free may live and the enslaved find hope, to struggle through it with concern, support and love, to make the moral voice strong again, loyally and with love.

And now to our beloved America, where we also have a moral problem.

America, which has been our golden land of opportunity, which welcomed us from the places and centuries of our suffering, but where suffering abounds on its own soil.

America, where the homeless camp out on doorsteps and the hungry scavenge in garbage cans.

America, where the nomination of a Supreme Court justice prods us to ask: What kind of America do we want?

America, where presidential candidates take undue liberties with other women and other people's speeches.

America, where baseball heroes scuff the ball to make it harder to hit and cork the bats to make them hit harder.

America, where college students are asked to prioritize their life goals and where, in 1970, 39 percent listed as a top goal being affluent, and in 1986, the number of those who more than anything else wanted to be affluent jumped to 73 percent, with altruism and social concern far down the list.

America, which takes pride in the people's right to dissent from popes and from presidents.

America, to which we Jews have our own message to deliver about how the free shall live and the enslaved find hope, about "what is right and what is good," beginning with ourselves. Because if all we have to show to our children and to ourselves is a full larder and the comforts of our comfortable life, if we do not seek out with our children all the ways to feed the hungry and shelter the homeless and confront those plagued by AIDS and confront the plague of the 73 percent whose only passion in life is to be rich, even at the expense of what is good and what is right, then we have torn up the message and we have lost our moral voice.

I have a dream, a Jewish American dream, spurred during these past two years as I have been able to be present on the front lines of the American Jewish community. We have a Conference of Presidents to serve as an advocate for the State of Israel. We have defense agencies to stand guard against anti-Semitism. We have the Synagogue Council of America, which is the umbrella for all the religious organizations of our country.

My dream, even though it means another Jewish organization, of which we have plenty, is a Foundation of Jewish Ethics, sponsored by the secular and religious leadership of this country, that would draw upon the finest scholarship and the most sensitive spiritual insights regarding the ethical issues that confront today's American. It would prepare papers and design seminars for corporate boardrooms and hospitals and courtrooms and classrooms and our homes and all other places in God's fragmented world where the moral lung power yearns for strength, beginning with ourselves.

We heard this morning the splintered, staccato notes of the shofar, those little pieces that get chipped away from our lives, from our world, from our souls, from our integrity. But then come these High Holy Days, when we pick up the pieces and try to patch them together. And then the *t'kiah g'dolah*—the one, long, sustained note of the shofar. Together again, but not without the seams that tell of the repair, the very seams that are the badge of our nobility, our power to pick up the pieces and put them back together.

We pray, O God, for power, with Your help. We pray, O God, for our moral voice with Your voice to restore the beginning of wholeness to our yearning world and our yearning selves.

Amen.

Rosh HaShanah 1987/5748

Beyond Auschwitz

After these High Holy Days some years ago, a member of the congregation reported that she had spoken to a relative from another community, only to discover that the rabbi of that distant synagogue and I had spoken on the identical topic during one of the services. My friend asked if perhaps there was some directive that was handed down from central headquarters that specified what the sermon should be for that year. I assured her that such was not the case but that if there was some particular issue that was high on the agenda of the entire Jewish community, it only made sense that on that New Year a large number of rabbis would speak about it.

Thus it could have been predicted already a month ago that the rabbis of the world would let their voices be heard during these High Holy Days on the subject of the convent at Auschwitz. It could have been predicted that they would have taken to task Cardinal Marcheski, for his refusal to move the convent despite his original agreement; and then Cardinal Glemp, for his scurrilous anti-Semitic tirade; and most of all the pope, for his refusal to intervene. For a month already, the fires of rabbinic indignation were being stoked, ready to blast forth on these High Holy Days.

And then last week, on September 19, the Vatican broke its silence and declared its recommendation that the convent be removed from Auschwitz. Whereupon Cardinal Glemp softened his tone, and Cardinal Marcheski announced his intention to abide by the original agreement and move the convent.

I have not consulted with my rabbinic colleagues, but I suspect what the prevailing opinion must be: that the least the pope could have done with his announcement was wait until after the Holy Days and let us rabbis do our thing.

Undaunted, I shall speak tonight about the Carmelite convent at Auschwitz, not only because old soldiers and new sermons never die but because the dynamics of that episode, however it has been resolved, speak directly and personally to our Jewish condition in the world on this Eve of the New Year.

Simply to review the background, some of which has not come into public notice: The convent, which is housed in a factory building that in World War II

151

was commandeered to store Zyklon B gas for use in the gas chambers, was actually established in 1984 for the ten Carmelite nuns who would pray there for the souls of Hitler's victims. No one objected until a year later, when a fund-raising concern in Belgium issued a brochure for the convent, in which not one mention was made of the mass killing of Jews there and in which veiled reference was made to the conversion of our "strayed brothers from many countries," which is usually a euphemism for conversion of the Jews. Soon thereafter, a twenty-three-foot wooden cross was erected next to the convent at the entrance to Auschwitz. The protest that then went forth from Jewish communities in Europe and around the world produced a meeting between Jewish and Catholic leaders in Geneva in 1987. An agreement was reached and signed by three cardinals, including Cardinal Marcheski, whereby two years hence, in February of 1989, at a location less than a mile away, an interfaith center for study and prayer would be erected, and the Carmelite convent with its ten nuns would be transferred to that site.

When February of 1989 went by with no visible progress, voices of concern were raised, and one group of American rabbis conducted a demonstration at the convent and climbed over the walls to speak to the nuns. They were then beaten by Polish workers and were evicted from the premises. As protests continued to flood in from many sectors of the Jewish community, Cardinal Marcheski announced that with so much ill will unleashed, all plans for the new center would be suspended, and the convent would stay where it was. Cardinal Glemp, the highest Catholic authority in Poland, then gave his speech with its warning to Jews not to intervene in the affairs of Poland and not to exploit their Jewish access to the media in order to champion their own cause against the position of the church.

Again the chorus of protest, but this time not only from Jewish voices but also from Catholic cardinals and bishops around the world. And it was in response to that swelling chorus that the pope decided to issue his public statement to recommend that the convent be moved.

What do we learn from the episode of the convent at Auschwitz? Mostly we learn about gaps of understanding on both sides. We Jews, in the overwhelming sense of our own Holocaust tragedy, sometimes fail to acknowledge that Christians were victims, too. One and a half million Poles were killed at Auschwitz (though some contend that the number was much less) for their resistance to the Nazis, and one purpose of the convent was to pray for their souls.

But from the other side, the Christian side, sometimes a far more massive gap of understanding, even a refusal to understand. In the extreme, there are those

Christians who insist that the Holocaust never happened, that it is but a fabrication by Jews to win world sympathy for the State of Israel. Or, like the brochure that started the tempest, Polish guides at the camp will sometimes omit any reference to Jews, and unless there is a specific request, their tour will not include the Jewish pavilion. Even at best, what many Christians fail to understand is the meaning of the Holocaust not only to Jews but in the annals of civilized history. Unlike the Poles, who were killed because they resisted the Nazis, the two million Jews who were killed there, and the four million elsewhere, were destroyed not because of anything they did but because of who they were. This is not to play the terrible numbers game of who had the most killed but to declare for purposes of historic truth, as Elie Wiesel wrote, that in truth, "all victims were not Jews," but also in truth, "all Jews were victims." Poland was chosen for the death camps because that's where the Jews were, three million once, three thousand now. Poland was chosen for the death camps because Hitler knew he could count on Poland's traditional anti-Semitism. He could predict that the populace would likely sit back and not rise up in protest against the fate of those Jews.

What some Christians, surely not all but some, fail to understand is why Jews are so distressed at the sight of that wooden cross at the entrance to the camp. For Catholics, it is a symbol of Christ's love; for Jews, it is the symbol of two thousand years of misery. And there in that place of ultimate misery, in that Auschwitz, the cross has no place. Leon Wieseltier wrote: "Auschwitz is the last place in the world for a shrine, Jewish or Christian. Auschwitz is the least holy place on earth."

What do we learn from the episode at the convent? That even with twenty years of dialogue between Jews and Catholics in the United States and Europe, one incident like this one could set off the old brushfire of anti-Semitism. During those months of tension this summer, anti-Semitic pamphlets were circulated in Cracow accusing the Jews of the economic woes of Poland. And Jews who visited the camps this summer were met with jeers and slurs from some of the local populace.

What do we learn from the episode of the convent? That had it not been for the dialogue of those past twenty years, had there not been those two decades of constant and conscientious effort to understand the Jewish side and the Catholic side—where each side was coming from—I am convinced that the brushfire that has now been put out would have escalated into a major conflagration. I am hard put to remember when so many archbishops and cardinals took public stands in opposition to their colleagues to insist that the convent be moved. And for one reason: to avoid offending Jewish sensitivity. It may be true that this brushfire was fed by the same old anti-Semitic kindling, but it is also true that those who came to put it out were a most ecumenical crew.

And what do we learn, we Jews, about ourselves from the episode of the convent? It makes us realize again, most of us if not all of us, that the Holocaust is always in our closet. It never goes away. Leonard Fein in his book *Where Are We?* quotes a passage from a Philip Roth novel in which the narrator tells how his ailing mother is asked by her neurologist to write her name on a piece of paper.

> *She took the piece of paper firmly in her hand, and instead of "Selma" she wrote the word "Holocaust"—perfectly spelled. This was in Miami Beach in 1970, inscribed by a woman whose writing otherwise consisted of recipes on index cards, several thousand thank-you notes, and a voluminous file of knitting instructions. But she had a tear in her head the size of a lemon and it seemed to have forced out everything except the one word it wouldn't dislodge. It must have been there all the time without our even knowing.*

The ghost is in our closet, and it comes out not so much when we are at work or at play, not so much in our personal lives, except, of course, for those who were there in the places of misery. But for the rest of us, whenever something happens on the world scene, when Israel was attacked in 1967, when Soviet Jews were persecuted, the ghost comes out of the closet, and we say, "Never again!" And we are moved to action.

Last year, I asked the confirmation class, whose members were born long after the Holocaust, to check off a series of items and the degree to which each of those items made them feel their Jewish identity. The items included the Torah, the Ten Commandments, Shabbat, the synagogue, the Passover seder, the State of Israel and the Holocaust. In the main, the two items that made them feel most Jewish were the Passover seder and the Holocaust. The seder because it was their Jewish family; the Holocaust because it was the Holocaust.

And that is what we learned about ourselves from the episode of the convent. That for many of us, like most members of the clan, the level of our Jewish feeling and the awareness of our Jewish identity and the intensity of our Jewish response are in direct ratio to the degree in which we feel threatened or persecuted. And anti-Semitism, in whatever guise, makes us feel more Jewish than anything.

A personal example: Two months ago, I was contacted by an official of an organization that reaches out to Jewish students. I was told that the organization allocates grants on college campuses to projects that deepen Jewish awareness and strive for greater understanding of Jewish values, and I was being asked to sign a fund-raising letter that would be sent to the Reform rabbis of the country. When the copy of the letter arrived for my approval and signature, I read as follows: "If you were on a college campus today, how would you respond to the barrage of anti-Semitic and anti-Zionist activity?" The entire rest of the letter was more of the same, and nowhere was there mention of learning more about Jewish values or sharing in Jewish observance or performing deeds of *tzedakah*. I called that official to say that perhaps I had misunderstood our original communication and that any colleague who knew me personally would be baffled by such a letter over my signature that equates Jewish identity only with anti-Semitism, and not with Jewish values or Jewish observance or Jewish learning or *tzedakah*.

"I agree with you," she said, "but when I raised the same question with the professional fund-raiser, he said that 'the only way you can get most Jews to give money, whatever the cause, is to wave the banner of anti-Semitism.'" And I did not sign the letter.

And thus my question for this New Year: Imperative as it is to defend our people against the assaults that are directed against us, how do we get Jews, ourselves, to realize that who we are is not only the Holocaust that was out to destroy us or anti-Semitism that is out to get us? We say to our children that they should have Jewish families and Jewish homes and Jewish children so that our Jewish people can survive. But should one of our kids happen to ask, as some have, "Why should the Jewish people survive?" then to answer only with the Holocaust or only with anti-Semitism is not enough of an answer. Harold Schulweis has written: "The Holocaust is our tragedy; it is not our rationale." Our rationale is the vision of what God's world should be and God's people should be, and that vision comes not from the ashes of Auschwitz but from the granite of Sinai. Our vision is of God's world where everyone can sit under his vine and his fig tree and walk the streets of his own city with no one to make him afraid, and that vision comes from Sinai. Our vision is of God's world where they will "beat their swords into plowshares and their spears into pruning hooks" and turn their money for armaments into cures for disease and food for the starving and shelter for the homeless, and that vision begins with Sinai.

And until that day comes and that vision is fulfilled, we are a people on the road, with the Book in our hand to keep exploring the vision. We are a people on the road, in the glow of Shabbat candles because their light makes us see the vision more clearly. A people on the road, doing acts of *tzedakah* and justice and caring because each of those acts makes the vision come true.

And until that day comes, we are back and forth on the road. Back to Auschwitz but then beyond Auschwitz to the granite and the God of Sinai. And then forward again to this night on our way to a New Year.

I conclude with another episode at Auschwitz, this one told by Elie Wiesel. It was the holiday of Simchat Torah in that place of misery. The gloom of that place was even darker because on this festival of joy, there was no joy, and on this day to dance around the Torah, there was no Torah.

An old man walked over to a young boy and he said to him, "Do you know the *Sh'ma?*" and the boy answered, "I know the *Sh'ma* and more than that." And the man said, "The *Sh'ma* is enough." And the man called to the rest, "Come, Jews, it is Simchat Torah, the time to dance around the Torah, to dance and to sing." And the old man lifted the boy as the Torah is lifted, and the Jews danced around the man and his Torah. They danced and sang and wept.

Beyond Auschwitz to the Torah of Sinai, and forward again to the youthful hope for tomorrow. And so may we, still on the road, with the blessings of the New Year.

Amen.

Rosh HaShanah 1989/5750

Israel

A Plea for Peace

From the prayer of Rabbi Nachman of Bratzlav, a nineteenth-century Chasidic rabbi: "Lord of the universe, Master of peace, make me worthy to be a true person of peace, a lover of peace, a true pursuer of peace, always with a complete heart."

It is a high Jewish compliment to be called a *rodeif shalom*, "one who pursues peace," because whoever deserves that compliment must first understand what shalom is: not simply the absence of strife, not simply a truce, but a state of being in which the pieces fit together in harmonious accord.

Whoever deserves that compliment of *rodeif shalom* actively pursues peace in his own life, not on the trail of some elusive bluebird that he knows he'll never catch, but coping with each day and the conflicts that each day brings, trying to resolve them, trying for some measure of shalom. When he feels shallow, it is shalom that will give him some depth. When he feels aimless, without direction or with too many directions, it is shalom that will put him on the road. When he feels fractured, in too many pieces, it is shalom that will put him together.

The *rodeif shalom* understands the dilemma of that man in the Chasidic story who had a problem finding his clothes in the morning. So much of a problem that one evening he made a great effort: He took paper and a pencil as he undressed and he wrote down exactly where he put everything. And it worked, because the next morning he read "cap," and it was exactly where the note said. And he read "pants," and there they were, and he put them on. And so it went until he was fully dressed. Then he said, "That's all very well, but now, where am I? Where in the world am I? Myself?"—which is the persistent question of anyone who pursues shalom within his own self.

Then he moves out into the world of other people. And in that world he becomes the living example of the words of a Talmudic rabbi of fifteen hundred years ago: "I am a creature of God, and my neighbor is also a creature of God. My work is in the city, and his work is in the field. I rise early to my work, and he rises early to his. As he cannot excel in my work, I cannot excel in his."

What the pursuer of peace does in the world of other people is not simply to tolerate their difference but to glory in them and in their work. He encounters other persons according to the persons that they are and not according to his pre-conceptions of what he might want them to be. What he pursues is not the counterfeit shalom of boring sameness but the authentic, exciting shalom of what Martin Buber once called "confirming each other's individuality."

And when it happens out in that world that the bond between him and another person, a bond that was once close and deserved to stay that way, but now, for some reason or another, is frayed or strained to the breaking point, the pursuer of peace responds to the summons of these Holy Days and does whatever is in his power to restore that bond, to repair that damage. With all the efforts and with all the preparations that go into these Holy Days, if, by the end of them, one grudge would be resolved, if a single bond could be restored because one has made the overture and the other has responded, then all the efforts for these High Holy Days would have been *l'sheim shamayim*—"for the sake of heaven."

And on this New Year, as the Jewish people come together in synagogues throughout the world, the fervent prayer of every *rodeif shalom* is: *Shalom Rav al Yisrael*, "May there be abundant peace upon the people of Israel."

As we pray that prayer this night, we give thanks for this year in which Menachem Begin and Anwar Sadat have walked the road of peace together.

But even as we pray that prayer, we are saddened and we are angered by the bloc of Third World nations who spew their rhetoric on the floor of the United Nations and who at this moment are plotting to strip Israel of its credentials, some of them the very nations to whom Israel gave help, financial and technological, in the infancy of their nationhood.

Even as we pray that prayer, we are saddened and we are angered by the almost total isolation of Israel by its erstwhile friends in Western Europe who have let it be known that Arab petrodollars and Arab oil are more binding than old friendships.

But what saddens us the most and angers us the most as we pray that prayer is the sequence of events in this, our own beloved country, and the baffling behavior of the president of the United States.

What was his intention a few months ago when he made a remark that the Palestinian struggle is to be equated with the Civil Rights Movement in the United States? What was President Carter's intention when Andrew Young resigned and some of the black leadership accused the American Jewish community of responsibility, and the president said nothing to correct that accusation but allowed his silence to confirm it, even though he knew very well that of the thirty-four Jewish organizations in the United States, only two had called for Young's resignation, and even though four weeks later, Secretary of State Vance made a public statement that the Jewish community was in no way responsible for Young's resignation, four weeks after Jimmy Carter's silence?

We do not know the reason for that silence. We do not know if Saudi Arabia was a factor, whether oil was a factor, whether some personal convictions of his own were a factor. We do not know if he intended by his silence to strain the relationship between Jew and black or if by his silence he intended to send some of the black community into the arms of the PLO, although leaders like Vernon Jordan warned the blacks against such foolish action. We do not know whether his intent was to boost the PLO constituency in the United States.

What we do know is that his silence produced every one of those results. What we do know is that the American Jewish community, or that part of it that supports the security and survival of Israel, was isolated and maneuvered into a moral corner on the moral issue of the Palestinians and their moral right to freedom and self-determination.

And yet, however much maneuvering over these past months, however much maneuvering over these past thirty years, during which Arab nations have politically exploited the plight of those Palestinian refugees and refused to give them refuge and indoctrinated them with hatred so they could wait for this moment in history to claim Palestine from Israel—with all of that political maneuvering and however effective it was, I would suggest for your consideration, if not necessarily for your acceptance, that the plight of the Palestinians is a moral issue from which no Israeli and no Jew can turn away. We who have known firsthand the plight of being homeless, we who have known firsthand the passionate wish to shape our own destiny on our own soil, we have no right, no moral right, to deny that same destiny to the Palestinians. The Jewish people cannot suspend the moral factor or else it stops being Jewish. If shalom is to be real, then the Jewish obligation is also real: to come to an understanding of the Arab mind and the Arab psyche according to the persons that *they* are and not according to the preconceptions of what we might want them to be, which is why this year's adult education program in our congregation is concerned with exploring the Arab mind and is so crucial to this moment in our people's history.

On our first trip to Israel in 1968, Priscilla and I had bought a piece of pottery from one of the refugees in Gaza. When the Israeli chambermaid in our hotel in Jerusalem saw it—and Israeli chambermaids are no less reticent than Israeli waiters—she went, "Pfft! Arabish!" and she spat, and she made me feel so guilty about my Jewish loyalty that I left the piece of pottery behind.

She was wrong, at least today she would be wrong, and Moshe Dayan is right when he insists that only by speaking to the Palestinians will we begin to understand them. His one condition is that anyone to whom he speaks cannot be an active participant in the PLO, even though that person may be a sympathizer with the PLO, because Dayan knows very well that he would have to look long and hard to find a Palestinian who is not a sympathizer with the PLO.

And if we believe in shalom and if, in the struggles of our own individual conscience, we arrive at the conviction that a particular policy of the State of Israel has set up a roadblock on the path to peace, then we have every right to express that conviction.

If someone believes, as I do, that while many of the West Bank settlements can be justified for purposes of security or that a settlement like Elon Moreh only serves to provoke Arabs with a Jewish presence, if we believe that Elon Moreh is wrong (as many Israelis believe and as members of the Supreme Court in Israel believe), then we are entitled as American Jews to make our voice heard. We claim that right not in order to interfere in the politics of the Israeli government but to take up the cause of three million of our people who are entitled to a respite of peace.

If we believe in shalom, we Jews must make it clear to the world that to us the aspiration of three million Palestinians to shape their destiny is indeed a moral issue. But we must make it equally clear to the world and especially clear to our fellow Americans (who may be the only ones who will listen) that the aspiration of three million Jews to shape *their* destiny is a moral issue of equal stature and not just the self-interested political strategy of the Begin government. We must make it clear that as long as the Palestinians, in asserting their right, deny that same right to three million Jews, as long as they support the PLO and its intention to destroy Israel and to terrorize civilians and to kill Arabs who support the Sadat-Begin accords, we must make it clear that as far as we Jews are concerned, the Palestinians have abrogated their moral claim. Abba Eban said rightly that the moral responsibility of Israel does not extend to its own suicide.

I asked a rabbi friend who lives in Israel and whose assessments are consistently objective whether at this moment the State of Israel could survive the existence of an independent Arab state. His answer was an unqualified and unequivocal "No."

What we have to make clear to the world at this juncture in history is that the burden of moral proof is not now on three million Israelis and those who support them but upon three million Palestinians and those who support them, to prove that they can live side by side before they can even think of living state by state.

What we have to make clear to our fellow Americans and to the silent president of the United States is that when we arrive at the frontal recognition of *two* moral issues and not one, then we shall have arrived at the threshold of peace.

In the words of Rabbi Nachman of Bratzlav: "Lord of the universe, Master of peace, make me worthy to be a true person of peace, a lover of peace, a true *rodeif shalom*, a pursuer of peace, always with a complete heart."

Amen.

Rosh HaShanah 1979/5740

The State of Israel: Jewish
Morality and Jewish Power

Rabbis are sometimes asked whether there is some central rabbinical agency that sends out an official list of topics to be discussed during that year's High Holy Days. The reason for the inquiry is that when members of one congregation ask members of another congregation what their rabbi talked about, the answers will often produce a striking similarity.

The answer to my inquirer's question is "No." We have no word from on high about this year's sermon topics. Instead, what rabbis do share is a question that we ask of ourselves: "What are the concerns on our people's minds? What are the concerns on our own minds?" And though the answers can be as diverse as the people who ask the questions, there are usually one or two themes each year that claim pervasive concern. And from synagogue to synagogue, they will become the subject for these High Holy Days.

This year you knew what it would be: The expedition into Lebanon that was ending when I began to write down this sermon, but even as of this moment is not yet ended; the dispersal of the PLO that seemed complete when I began to prepare this sermon, but as of this moment is not yet dispersed; the Reagan proposal rejected by Begin, deemed worthy of consideration by AIPAC (which is the chief lobbying group for Israel in the United States), endorsed by George Schultz, denounced by Al Haig, endorsed by Shimon Peres, who is then accused by William Safire of colluding with Reagan to topple the Begin government. Every day, all over the front page. Even if we weren't Jewish, we would probably be talking about it. And then juxtapose the findings of a recent survey that told us what we hardly needed a survey to tell us: that the vast majority of America's Jews are deeply concerned with Israel's security and Israel's future and that the opinions about what direction that future should take are broadly diverse. So with the first pages of the newspapers as they are and the American Jewish psyche as it is, the result is what one of my colleagues observed, "that we can't not talk about it." And the last time that same colleague and I made that same statement to each other was ten years ago on Rosh HaShanah, a few days after the athletes were

164

murdered at the Munich Olympics by the PLO—that we couldn't not talk about it.

As I tried to express this summer from Stockbridge, none of us claims secret wisdom. The most we can claim is a sharing of concern. And what I hope to share this morning is the struggling journey of my own concern and where that journey has taken me, with full awareness that you and your journey may be taking you to a different place, and with full awareness that where we are now may not be where we are six months from now or a year from now or tomorrow.

To set out the landscape of my own journey, I would share two experiences that date back to different visits to *Eretz Yisrael*.

One incident occurred in the home of a friend, now deceased, on a Shabbat afternoon. My friend was a sabra, either third or fourth generation, and in his own life and outlook he perpetuated the early Zionist dream. He was fiercely proud of the Jewish people on its own soil and in control of its own destiny. He was deeply immersed in Jewish culture and the arts, and he was even probing religious options (not too common in Israel) because, as he said, Israel needed a strengthening of its national vision, more than culture and history and the social framework could supply. And in the midst of our Shabbat discussion, my friend apologized for having to leave, but he was due at a neighborhood military defense meeting because no place in Israel, not even those beautiful hills outside of Jerusalem, were safe from the assaults of PLO terrorists.

After he left, his wife (who had come to Israel from South Africa twenty years earlier) asked me more with desperation than with expectation of an answer, "How long is it going to last, Jack? Will my children be fighting in wars, too, and their children? When can we start living normal lives like normal people?" Her children were in the room and said nothing, but I suspected that they, too, were waiting for an answer.

The second incident took place only a few years ago in the old city of Jerusalem in an Arab restaurant that I had visited on previous trips and remembered with pleasure. This time it was different. This time the wall was covered with a poster, newly hung, a life-size photograph of Yasser Arafat and a slogan printed in Arabic, Hebrew and English: "No man without a homeland." I looked over at the owner, whom I remembered from previous visits as cordial and pleased by his Jewish clientele. But this time I caught a glimpse of him looking toward me with hatred in his eyes, and I could not leave fast enough.

Those two episodes hardly begin to put together the jigsaw pieces of the Middle East puzzle. We would have to fit in the Soviet Union, the perpetual provocateur, stirring up crisis after crisis in place after place. We would have to fit in the

United States, the perpetual juggler, keeping Arab petrodollars and Israeli democracy and myriad other factors in the air simultaneously. We would have to work in the factionalism among the Arab countries, whose shared hatred of Israel is unable to overcome their own friction. Everything is part of the picture, but the view of it that I would share with you this morning is from that particular vantage point where my own journey has taken me, the view that focuses on my friend's question, "How long?" and focuses upon the hatred in an Arab's eyes.

This summer, when Israeli forces moved into Lebanon and proceeded beyond the twenty-five-mile zone to Beirut, a wave of confusion swept over the Jewish world. Was this episode necessary, this episode with its unprecedented number of civilian casualties, this episode initiated by Israel in which Israel's existence was not immediately at stake? Some of us were sick at heart and at stomach when we saw the pictures of Lebanese civilians with glazed eyes and the rubble of their homes behind them—the same sick feeling we had when we had read about the Arab teenagers who had been killed by Israeli police during demonstrations on the West Bank and about the other teenage demonstrators whose homes were then blown up by the Israeli police as warning to the rest of the community. My image of the Israeli soldier had always been of someone called from civilian pursuits to defend his country's life and blood, not a military official who shoots at teenagers and blows up houses.

I read and listen to the charges and accusations barraged at us from the capitals of the world and from the op-ed page of the newspapers, and some of them only rouse our anger, not at the accused but at the accusers. Like Arafat, who holes up his troops in apartment houses and the basement of schools so that civilians have to be killed if Israel is to achieve its announced goal of breaking the back of the PLO. Arafat, whose troops ravage the south of Lebanon and its civilians as if they were a conquered enemy. And Syria? Syria accuses Israel? Syria, whose military had slaughtered 10,000 or 15,000 of its own fellow Syrians in the city of Hama but barred the press and the photographers until the blood was cleaned and the corpses were removed from the streets? Iraq and Libya, who shoot dissenters on the spot? England, France, West Germany, Austria? Would they tolerate from across their borders the terrorist attacks that kill kibbutzniks and their children? Would they tolerate Maalot and Kiryat Shemonah and the casualty list dating from 1965 that reaches 1,400 dead and 6,000 wounded?

Who are our enemies who dare to judge us? But then, when the charges are made by our friends, including Israelis, including American Jews, including long-standing friends in Congress, and especially when we ourselves feel unsure of the ground on which we stand, when we ourselves ask, "What are my Jews doing?" then we are sick at heart and stomach.

And to that juncture does my journey take me, to the place where I must ask the question of myself: What are my Jews doing? Because I know that at the heart of this Judaism is its moral imperative for human justice and human compassion and human freedom. But I also know that for those past 2,000 years during which we have been the dust under the heel of the oppressor, we could announce that moral stance without condition, without reservation, because we were the oppressed ones. We advocated what someone called "the morality of powerlessness." But then we come to our own Land and to control of our own destiny, and then, as in our own lives when children grow up, morality and idealism and values confront the real world of power. And the Jewish people who had not known political power for 2,000 years now had to come to terms with its own newly won power, now had to grapple with the words in the Talmud that if someone comes to kill you, you are entitled to kill him first, assuming, of course, that you have the power. We always said that one of the differences between the Jew and the gentile through the Middle Ages was that the gentile hunted for sport but we didn't. To which someone responded: "But they had guns and you didn't. Now that you carry guns, will you become a hunting people? Now that you have power, what will be your morality?"

Part of the answer to that question came to light after the Lebanese expedition was well underway. There was not one known case of looting by an Israeli soldier, because the code of behavior that was handed to every soldier strictly defined the conduct appropriate to the Israeli Army and strictly prohibited looting and billeting in the houses of Lebanese civilians.

Rabbi Ira Youdovin, in a superb background report on Lebanon, tells how the Israeli Defense Force did everything within its power, even at risk to its own soldiers, to reduce the danger to the Lebanese citizens of Beirut. The very decision to lay siege to West Beirut instead of invading it included the moral consideration. After the damage, Israelis organized to provide food and clothing and medical attention for the Lebanese. And when someone cynically observed that they were only salving their guilty conscience, someone else responded: "Of course we have a guilty conscience! And rightly so, because that's what makes Jews different." Morality of power. A nation like other nations, but also a light unto the nations.

Should the Israeli Defense Force have advanced beyond the twenty-five miles? Did the gain justify the loss of stature and public support? In my own journey I cannot answer that question, in part because we have not yet seen tomorrow's newspaper. If the goal of destroying the terrorist PLO has been achieved and I can answer my friend in Jerusalem that her children and grandchildren will now be safer, perhaps even the accusers among our friends will soften their charge. But now, with Arafat's reception in Athens, and at Fez, and then, ghastly as it is to comprehend, by the pope of the Catholic Church, the power of the terrorist is far from shattered.

God willing, the dust in Lebanon will settle before long, but then there will still remain that owner of the Arab restaurant and the slogan "No man without a homeland."

In my own struggling journey, I have two responses to that slogan and to the demands of the Palestinians and to the West Bank.

My one response is to the Arab: that you cannot be permitted a homeland that will become the place from which you will destroy *our* homeland. You cannot have a homeland with Arafat at its helm and the PLO in its training headquarters. Speak morality all you want, speak freedom all you want. We have no moral obligation to provide for our own self-destruction.

And my second response is to my fellow Jews in the State of Israel, that we Jews, more than anyone else, know the hunger for freedom. We Jews, more than anyone else, sang the song of the poet:

> *By the passion of his spirit*
> *Shall his ancient bonds be shed.*
> *Let the soul be given freedom,*
> *Let the body have its bread!*

> —Saul Tchernichovsky

It makes no Jewish sense for the Jewish people to deny another people its freedom if we can guarantee our own safety. It makes no Jewish sense for Jews to blow up houses and to shoot at teenagers. It makes no Jewish sense for Jews to issue license plates of one color for Jews and of another color for Arabs, anymore than it makes Jewish sense for "colored" and "white" to have different bathrooms in the United States.

To this one Jew who stands before you, it makes no Jewish sense for the State of Israel to aspire to Mr. Begin's "greater Israel" with Judea and Samaria, with hundreds of thousands of Arabs either outnumbering the Israelis or being reduced to second-class citizens with different color license plates and censored newspapers. For this one Jew, it makes no Jewish sense for Jewish morality to surrender so completely to Jewish power. For this one Jew, Theodore Mann's assessment satisfies my good Jewish sense: that there is nothing un-Jewish or immoral in having to rule over hundreds of thousands of Arabs in the West Bank, but having to rule over them and wanting to rule over them are two entirely different things.

Thus would this one Jew not be so hasty to reject President Reagan's proposal without even discussing it. Without presuming here to analyze its specifics, it deserves our discussion and consideration. There was a parent in this congregation who once told me that each of her children accused her of being partial to the other, and thus was she reassured that she was being fair to both of them. Thus does Mr. Reagan's plan, or one like it, call for something better than outright rejection because the Palestinians will get a homeland, not with the PLO but in Jordan, and Israel will get recognition and a Palestinian neighbor, but not the PLO.

So to the Arabs we would say: "It is time to stop rejecting every proposal, including those in your own best interest. Your clock is running out." To Mr. Begin we say, "Stop saying 'No' so fast. Discuss with your friend and ally, the United States. For the sake of the Jewish people, you may have to give up Judea and Samaria. And until the Arabs will negotiate, you may have to rule over all those Arabs. But, Mr. Begin, please don't want to."

What we need and pray for in the New Year is anger to be defused. What we need is each side agreeing to accept not what it may want but what it can live with, not what is desirable but what is tolerable. What we need is an Arab leader's trip to Jerusalem, or Begin's trip to Amman. What we need and pray for is an answer to my friend's question, "How long?" What we need and pray for is that human eyes will be less filled with hate.

Amen.

Rosh HaShanah 1982/5743

Addendum on Israel and Beirut

When on the Saturday morning of Rosh HaShanah we were sharing those thoughts on Jewish power and Jewish morality, there was no inkling of what Sunday morning's newspapers would report about the massacres of Palestinians in Beirut.

And now a week later, a week flooded with pain and distress, a duo of truths is emerging, each day into sharper focus. First, that Minister of Defense Sharon, in allowing the Phalangists into camps, not only had to anticipate the savage outcome but, according to increasing number of reports, was apprised of the murders as they were happening, and they were allowed to keep on happening. If, indeed, the military command of the State of Israel was complicit in the murder of innocent men, women and children in those refugee camps, though not one drop of actual blood is on the hand of one Israeli soldier, then General Sharon's hands are soaked in blood, as are the hands of his soldiers, who like good soldiers followed their general's orders and kept their silence, as are the hands of those who tried to cover up the bloody hands so that they should not be examined.

And thus the first truth: that the military command of the State of Israel and those who supported its actions in the exercise of their people's power—if the charge is true—has abandoned its people's morality and has thus renounced its right to serve as leaders of the people.

And the second truth: that after Prime Minister Begin responded to any suggestion of Israeli wrongdoing with defensive self-righteousness, pressure for an investigation began to mount from President Reagan, from Israel's supporters in Congress, from American Jews, for whom Israel is the highest priority. But the truth was that no such pressure was needed to call the leadership of the State of Israel to moral accountability. Because that pressure, to its most powerful degree, came from the Jewish people in the State of Israel itself, and not only from the Labor government, which is in competition with Mr. Begin's coalition, and not only from *Shalom Achshav* (Peace Now), who have been the identifiable demonstrators for peace all along, but from a massive public outpouring, last night numbering perhaps 350,000, and with a chorus of outrage from the Israeli press, including those that usually support the Begin government. And they were all on

170

the same battle line, fighting for the Jewish soul, defending the very existence of Jewish morality against the invasion of Jewish power by their own leadership.

A Talmudic maxim: *Gam zu l'tovah,* "Even this may be for the good," a maxim reserved for tragic life experiences: that from all the damage and from all the hurt, some positive result may emerge.

So with this week's events in Beirut. Like those two Jewish travelers in the forest, each coming from a different direction and both hopelessly lost, each announcing to the other: "The way from which I have come is not the way; let us try to find our way out together."

So the Israelis and the Arabs: the Israelis, who know that when power abandons morality, there can only be the disgrace of a Beirut; and the Arabs, who know that when hatred is unleashed, there can only be the blood of a Beirut. So now Arabs and Israelis may be able to say to each other, "The way from which we have come, this is not the way." And then, even of these painful days in Beirut, it may be said, *Gam zu l'tovah.*

Yom Kippur 1982/5743

Anti-Semitism and Israel

My theme for this morning is anti-Semitism. I had intended to speak about it last Rosh HaShanah because, in the course of the year then ending, my file on the subject was bulging with material, with reports of bombs and swastikas, with analytical articles on causes and effects, with titles of new books, each offering its own reading of the thermometer complete with prognosis and diagnosis. Such was my intention last year, but with the unsettling events in the summer of 1982, last year's sermon time on Rosh HaShanah morning was preempted, albeit with some cynical certainty that the timeliness of the subject of anti-Semitism would not go away. And, indeed, a new file was started: "Anti-Semitism '82 to '83." And now, a year later, it, too, is pushing out at the sides. During one week in August: a synagogue bombed in Johannesburg, South Africa; a synagogue bombed in Baranquilla, Colombia; two synagogues and a rabbi's home set on fire in the suburban community of West Hartford, Connecticut. Between the covers of that file, the title of a new book, *None Is Too Many*, a documented exposé of how the Canadian government refused entrance to German-Jewish refugees before and during World War II. One of the writers tells how, in the late 1930s, an assemblage of Canadian college professors unanimously petitioned their government in Ottawa not to open its doors to German-Jewish intellectuals for fear that they might flood the universities in Canada. The only way a handful gained entrance was by listing themselves on the application form as Protestant.

In that same file, a plethora of material on anti-Semitism in the United States, which is our focus for this morning. One article by Earl Raab is entitled "Anti-Semitism in the '80s," in which the author reiterates the good news that has been announced over the past few years by practically all of the temperature takers and all of the poll takers: that pervasive anti-Semitism in the United States is at an all-time low. As much as swastikas on tombstones and fires in synagogues demand our urgent concern, as much as they deserve prosecution to the full extent of the law, they give no evidence, according to the analysts, of a frontal wave of an anti-Semitic tide. The evidence instead suggests individual acts of vandalism, often by unruly teenagers, in contrast perhaps to the rash of episodes in Europe that suggest a more coordinated effort by anti-Zionist, anti-Semitic forces in the Third

172

World. But in this country, essential as it may be to monitor hard-core anti-Semitic fringe groups like the neo-Nazis or the KKK or the so-called identity churches (which advocate gunning down all of the rabbis in America) with all of their spewing out of hatred, they mostly end up talking to each other. Not once in recent years has any candidate who campaigned on a platform of anti-Semitism received the endorsement of any major political party in his district.

To the contrary, the mainstream of America, beginning with the end of World War II, has moved farther and farther away from its old, derogatory image of the Jew: the Jew as dishonest; the Jew as unethical; the Jew as international conspirator. According to the polls, the number who still harbor those negative stereotypes is somewhere around 30 percent—hardly Utopia, but still a long way from the murky attitudes of the 1930s and '40s and even from the enlightened attitudes of the '50s and '60s. The barriers that once so massively blocked entrance into occupations and professions and academies of learning have slowly but progressively been lowered, albeit still with holdouts in the upper echelons of major banks and a cadre of major corporations, still in fenced-in neighborhoods, still in country clubs not yet in need of Jewish members to resolve their financial problems. But even with the holdouts, Rabbi Mark Tanenbaum expresses what may be the majority opinion: "We have made greater gains in the past twenty years than in the past two thousand years." Perhaps not that much, but close.

Let me share with you some of the data. Anti-Semitic attitudes are less prevalent in the age group below fifty-five than in the group over that age. Anti-Semitism is more prevalent in the South and Midwest than in the Northeast. Anti-Semitic attitudes decline as the socioeconomic level improves, with the exception of the highest socioeconomic level, where the downward trend of anti-Semitism takes a slightly upward tilt.

What are some of the factors that come into play? Surely the prosperity of the postwar years, because economic prosperity is the best weed killer of anti-Semitism and because those young men and women who are now in their thirties and forties grew up in a generation that knew not the Depression and knew not the radio talks of Father Coughlin. Surely a factor has been the confrontation by Christians, and especially the Christian Church, of the Holocaust, because that confrontation presented ghastly evidence of anti-Semitism let loose, unchallenged and unchecked. And surely there was the changing mood of America in the '60s, a move that helped topple that solitary image of white Anglo-Saxon Protestants and instead began to celebrate the rich diversity of the authentic American people. But of all the factors that the interviewers and the analysts explored, the one that ranked first in accounting for the decline in anti-Semitism was education. The higher the level of education with everything it teaches about diversity and democracy and civil liberties, the lower the level of anti-Semitism, except, of course, for the upward tilt among some of the well-to-do.

That's the good news: the lowest level of anti-Semitism in this country ever. The bad news is that so many Jews have such a hard time accepting and believing the good news. When it comes to the matter of Jewish well-being and anti-Semit-ism, we Jews often operate with what Earl Raab calls "a Jewish sense of forebod-ing." If things are good, who says that they're going to stay that way? And besides, who says they're that good? In one community after another, the inter-viewers found something of a pattern: that the Jewish assessment of anti-Semit-ism was usually higher than what the interviewers and the researchers themselves were able to ascertain. The definition of a Jewish telegram: "Letter follows. Start worrying." The Jewish sense of foreboding.

We know where it comes from: from the reasons of all those two thousand years; from what some of us have witnessed in our lifetime; from the world's will-ingness to let Jews die; from the world's indifference whether they die or not. It comes from a little saying our grandparents or great-grandparents learned in the ghetto at the same time they were learning about Torah and learning about Shab-bat: "If you scratch a gentile, you'll find an anti-Semite." And when our forebears left the ghetto, they sometimes left behind the Torah and the Shabbat, but they took that saying with them and put it in their knapsacks as they went out to find their way in the world. And some of them taught it diligently to their children.

Like some of you, I learned that saying when I was a child. And yet, what do you do with that saying when you walk up the road to Yad Vashem in Jerusalem, along that garden walk in honor of the righteous gentiles, each one of whom had risked his or her own life to save Jewish lives? How do you reconcile that little saying with the gentile people of Denmark who saved almost an entire Jewish community? How do you reconcile it with a pastor of Heidelberg who defied Nazi orders and gave food and clothing and comfort to Jews? Or with the Ger-man nuns who smuggled Jews across the border into Belgium, and on and on?

As one Jew, I do not believe that all gentiles are anti-Semitic, and even those who are are not all the same. On the one end of the spectrum are the hard core: the Jew haters, the Soviet Union. On the other end: the righteous gentiles and people like the late Senator Jackson, whose mother taught him that anti-Semit-ism was evil and who spent most of his professional life as an ally of Jewish causes.

Between those two poles are all the differences of degree, concerning which I would share with you the following personal experience. Just a year ago, soon after the High Holy Days, I received a call from a Christian clergyman. He told me that the adult education study group in his church had experienced deep distress over the tragedy of Lebanon and the massacres in the refugee camps. Some of the members of the group, he said, were experiencing in themselves some feelings of anti-Semitism, and then the minister added, "And I've been feeling a little bit the same way myself." He then asked if I would come to the church to share whatever thoughts I had with the group (which, incidentally, I had met on another occasion when we had talked about the Book of Psalms). I went and we talked about Lebanon: how we of the Jewish community were also anguished over the massacre and how there were differences of opinion in the Jewish community about the Israeli march into Beirut. I tried to set that discussion within the context of Israel's need for survival and Israel's need for security so that they could understand. Then I said, "Your minister has told me that these matters have churned up in you some anti-Semitic feelings, so let's talk about them." There was an embarrassed silence, whereupon I proceeded to tell them something about myself: how I had grown up in Cincinnati, which was very much in the Southern pattern on matters of discrimination against blacks, not KKK-style but the Southern style that blacks were inept and that blacks had their "place." And then, when I moved on to school and to college, I began to challenge that doctrine of my childhood, mostly because of my Jewish value system, and I could not let that old doctrine stand. I then joined the campaign in the late '40s in Cincinnati to desegregate restaurants and movie theaters and the Cincinnati Conservatory of Music. "But to this day," I told the Christian group, "all these years later, it sometimes happens that I am annoyed by someone's ineptitude, and if that person happens to be black, the old stereotype from my childhood leaps up and takes me by surprise. Despite all my commitment to human equality and my lifetime of activity on its behalf, the old ghosts jump out of the closet, and I recognize them for what they are, and then I send them off packing." Then I said to the church group: "This is what I suspect about many Christians I know, including, perhaps, some of you. For all these two thousand years, Christian children have been nurtured and later nurtured another generation on the negative image of a Jew: the stubborn outsider who would not believe in their God, who was even implicated in the death of their God. You, however, in your own lifetime, the more educated you have become and the more you have learned about the Holocaust and democracy and diversity, the more you yourselves have challenged and rejected that mean-spirited doctrine of your childhood. But every once in a while, I suspect, something happens with Jews, and the old ghost jumps out of the closet with its spirit of meanness, and that ghost upsets you enough that you were willing to invite a rabbi to help you drive away the ghost, to help you return back to the issue itself, whether it be the Middle East or anything else." And no one in that room disagreed.

We Jews make a mistake, I believe, when we lump all the versions of anti-Semitism into one pile. We do disservice not only to decent people, but we weaken our own effectiveness in combating the virus. If my assessment of most of the people in that church room was correct and if anyone had confronted them with the charge of being true anti-Semites, I believe they would have repudiated the charge with indignation, and they would have been correct. Most of them have learned their way out of the mind-sets of their childhood, but every once in a while, when the old mind-set is triggered, the ghost comes out of the closet. And when it does, I believe that an anti-Semitic remark or an anti-Semitic slur should not be ignored with the hope that it will go away, because I believe you can help a decent person or even a community in its struggle with the old ghosts. I believe you can communicate to a person or a community that its anti-Semitic slurs are at total odds with its own decent commitment to democracy and civil liberties and diversity.

There was a time during the crèche controversy when members of the Scarsdale clergy, Christian and Jewish, came together to discuss our respective roles. What some of the Christian clergy discovered in their own congregations is what began to emerge in the community and even in the high school: that some who felt strongly on the issue of the crèche were beginning to express that feeling not on the issue itself, not on the arguments of the issue, but with those old feelings of those old ghosts. If I heard my fellow clergy correctly, the ones who were most successful in handling the problem were the ones who called the anti-Semitic behavior for what it was and who then helped those persons understand how inappropriate it was and helped them in their struggle, which, I believe, in a community like ours, is one way to combat anti-Semitism.

And when it comes to the State of Israel, a Christian cannot be denied the right to criticize the actions or the policies of a nation-state without being labeled an anti-Semite. Only when that criticism or that discussion denies the State of Israel the right to its own existence in the family of nations has the criticism crossed the line. And then the anti-Semitism should be called what it is, which is one way to combat anti-Semitism.

And when it comes to ourselves, I believe that we Jews act irresponsibly when we enter the public domain only to press our own group interest, whether it be the State of Israel or the Soviet Jews or whatever. Not only do we thereby default on the Jewish mandate to make the world less hungry and less sick and less angry but, by holding back, we reject the opportunity of forging alliances with all the other groups in our country.

By holding back, we reject the opportunity of strengthening the social and economic soil against the weeds from the extreme right and the extreme left that are always ready to invade, always ready to target the Jews in their assaults on the democratic system, those very assaults that otherwise decent people may likely stand by and let happen. I am therefore among those people who support that decision of our Union of American Hebrew Congregations to join the march in Washington a few weeks ago, with the grave misgiving that it was scheduled for Shabbat. As it turned out, the presence of Jewish groups with all of the other minority groups, the forging of alliances between ourselves and some of them, was directly responsible for the aborted attempt of Third World sympathizers to use that march for anti-Israel propaganda, which is one way to combat anti-Semitism.

And when it comes to our children, as essential as it is for them to learn about the Holocaust, as essential as it is to instruct them about the ghostly antics of anti-Semitism, we should also give ear to the words of Rabbi Harold Schulweis: "The Holocaust is our tragedy, not our rationale." Our rationale is the covenant between God and the Jewish people to which our shofar called us this morning. We should take our children back beyond Auschwitz to Sinai. We should take our children forward beyond a system of life defense to a system of life value; beyond a sense of Jewish foreboding to a sense of Jewish commitment, and ultimately to the Shabbat and the Torah that some of our forebears left behind, which, in the final analysis, may be the best way of all to combat anti-Semitism.

Amen.

Rosh HaShanah 1983/5744

The Jewish Sense of
Family

Parent to Parent

The Torah understands the generation gap. It tells of a generation of slaves, born in Egypt, who then became the freemen of the desert.

It tells, too, of a plan, whereby the Jewish people would enter the Promised Land and establish a great society, founded on principles of the Torah, a society that would translate the ethical will of God into the daily lives of men.

But for reasons of good common sense, reports the Torah, this generation that had left Egypt, the men and women who had spent their entire lives in the transition from slavery to freedom, were not qualified for this adventurous, new task. Their vision was not fresh enough; their slave mentality still hung on. A new generation was called for, born free in the desert, with nothing to hold them back from the bright new land and the exciting new prospects that lay before them.

On Yom Kippur morning we read from the Torah of two generations, 3,300 years ago, that were worlds apart, and this Torah could have been written in our day, for our time, about our children and ourselves.

We, the parents, grew up in a world where military war was reckoned a logical instrument for resolving conflicts between nations, and we rallied around the banner of noble ideals. We could take up arms on the premise that a military war could make the world "safe for democracy."

But to most of our children, war is an instrument of unredeemed evil, and no war, except to defend life and limb on one's native soil, is ever justified. Our youth could cheer Israel but deplore Vietnam because, in their reckoning, the one was defensive, the other aggressive.

To us who are parents, the bomb, with all of its ominous repugnance, still marked the end of a war and gave victory to our allies and ourselves and brought our boys home. To our children, Hiroshima and Nagasaki mark the beginning of a new era in which man's value is cheapened and his survival is threatened. Psychiatrists who have treated young people report a pervasive concern about the bomb, even when it is not discussed openly. Today becomes everything because tomorrow may never come.

To us, in our world, the Negro was an unfortunate victim of social circumstances. Intellectually, we supported the proposition that all men are created

181

equal, whatever their race, creed or color. But somewhere in our childhood, we had acquired a repugnance to dark-skinned human beings, and to this day many a white liberal is more comfortable with a light-skinned Negro than one whose skin is pitch black. Women enjoy black dresses, men feel well groomed in black suits, but there's something about black skin....

I recall from my childhood that the son of the Negro janitor next door was always included in our baseball games until one day the landlord of our own building sent word that Frankie was no longer to play in our yard. I still picture him as he shamefully slunk home. A signal had come through to me that being Negro was somehow less acceptable than being white. I have sometimes thought of seeking out that boy, now a man, to ask for forgiveness, but I never knew his last name, which speaks volumes in itself.

And years later in the 1940s, when several of us were engaged in civil rights activities in Cincinnati, some of us who were white confided to our Negro colleagues that hardest of all was the effort to overcome our repugnance to dark-skinned human beings, to raise the level of our emotions to the level of our liberal intellect.

But most of our children are genuinely color-blind. They see skin color as they see color of hair or color of eyes. When our neighbor and my colleague Rabbi Maurice Davis was rabbi of a congregation in Lexington, Kentucky, many years ago, he was hosting a meeting in his home, and of the entire group, one man was Negro, and he was smoking a pipe. Rabbi Davis's son Jay, then four or five, now a student in college, was seated in his father's lap and shifted his glance around the entire room until he reached the Negro. And there he stopped in a fixed stare, not without embarrassment to those in the room, including his father. After what seemed an interminable silence, the boy blurted out: "Daddy, that man, he's smoking a pipe!"

They are a color-blind generation of children who cannot understand their parents' abhorrence even to discuss interracial dating, even when the Negro is Jewish.

And perhaps most basic of all, many of us grew up in a generation that called for initiative and hard work so that someday we might achieve at least a middle-class level of financial security for our families and education for our children. Many of us have achieved that level. We have sent our children to college, relatively free of financial burdens, to save them time and energy, only to discover that they are marshaling their leftover time and energy to attack the middle-class values of their parents. We may feel put upon when they take off on their own, far away from parents and from middle-class values, but they feel no compunction about calling home for a little extra cash, and the call is put through collect. Our children are the true plutocrats, to whom money is simply not a problem. Like a generation born slave and a generation born free, so different are the worlds of our children and ourselves. They are more outraged by slums than we are, and they even work in the midst of them. They care more about the children of Biafra than we do. They are more depressed about Vietnam and the bomb than we are. They are more indignant at political double-talk than we are. They were born free, and the assignment of the Promised Land is only for them. We try our utmost, but we are only dabbling. Only they are qualified to leave the desert and cross the Jordan. And if we tell them that, we will begin to bridge the gap.

But how were those children in the Sinai Desert to learn? Who would educate them to the demands of their new assignment? Who would be their teachers?

The answer was right there, in a Torah that understands the generation gap. The answer was in the two words *V'shinantam l'vanecha*—You, their parents, will teach them diligently to your children. You, the parents, will train the children for the very assignment that you are not qualified to carry out. You will lead your children to the River Jordan, to the border of the Promised Land.

In fairness to ourselves as parents—and even our children will not deny it—we did our job. To our credit, we taught them that war was hell, that a man's skin color should make no difference, that money isn't everything. To our children's credit, they took us seriously, sometimes more seriously that we had intended. (We sent them to college to acquire the best possible education, but we didn't expect them to restructure the entire university.) What we offered as intellectual propositions, they received as emotional directives. And what so many of us label "the generation gap" is not a gap between two sets of ideals but between two levels of acceptance of the same ideals, our intellectual level and their emotional level. And if we can say *that* to our sons and daughters, then we have helped to bridge the gap.

And in this mood of forthright exchange, we, their parents, might acknowledge two mistakes that we ourselves have perpetrated.

The first was a mistake of love, for we equated love with saying "yes" to our children's every wish. We never taught them how to wait. No child can be faulted for wanting what he wants when he wants it. We can only fault ourselves for always giving it to him.

I saw in the newspaper some years ago a full-page advertisement for December party clothes, for elegant velvet ball gowns to be worn on formal occasions. The price was $100, and the sizes were toddler 2 through 4. And I remembered from my youth that the first time a girl wore a formal was to the junior prom, and the girls eagerly awaited the occasion. And I could hear the new generation, a girl invited to the prom, to dress formal, and she would answer, "I wore one of those when I was three!"

We have raised a generation that never learned to wait, that want the Promised Land without crossing the Jordan. They are the instant generation: They want instant social change, instant hope, and as one of our own members remarked, "They want an instant Messiah."

Like anyone else, young people should strive for a sense of well-being, a clarity of perception about themselves and about life. But these are long-range goals and not instant experiences. They are achieved through many moments of self-searching and solitude, through much reading of philosophy, through much sharing with a beloved, and not by a few puffs on a marijuana cigarette. They are long-range goals, and once you've achieved them, they belong to you and do not require the maintenance dose of another cigarette.

Every human being seeks total sharing with a member of the opposite sex, and by Jewish definition, sexual intercourse is a joyful part of the sharing—a far cry from instant sex by two people biologically ready but emotionally not who have never been taught to wait. Robert Capon in his book *Bed and Board* writes: "If sexual relationships involve worthwhile and pleasurable discoveries, as they surely do, it's surely too bad to fumble one's way through them greedily in the back seat of some car when they could be savored and relished at leisure on a long winter evening—amid a pile of unpaid bills."

We should tell our children of our mistake and hope that they will correct it, and we should tell them we will not repeat it with their little brothers and sisters, and thus shall we bridge the gap between generations.

And our second mistake that concerns this place, this faith, this people:

Many of us grew up in a generation that looked upon the synagogue as a cozy place where Jews could be with other Jews, a kind of mutual defense pact against a world that was too often openly hostile. But our children, more secure and less suspicious, will reject any synagogue, any Judaism, however cozy, that does not address itself relevantly to the problems of the world.

Our mistake was this: that while we were teaching our children about war being hell and a man's skin color not making a difference and no man being an island, we neglected to identify our sources. We forgot to tell them that we were teaching them Judaism and that we learned it from our parents who were teaching us Judaism.

Our parents, many of them, were Jews by commitment and by knowledge. We, many of us, are Jews by momentum, and the momentum slows down from one generation to the next, and that was our mistake.

Our children watch us. They see us faithfully and religiously attend an open school night at public school and just as faithfully and religiously avoid an open school night at religious school because of something else to do or nothing else to do, and they draw their own conclusions.

Our mistake was our delusion that the momentum would continue without proof and without demonstration—and the momentum did not continue.

What would it mean to a child of ten or eleven to overhear his mother tell someone that they could not accept an invitation this Friday evening because that's the night they planned to go to services? What conclusions would that child draw, and what bridges could be built between the generations?

Last week at the Rosh HaShanah children's service, I told a story that was introduced by the question, "Who is important in your lives? Whom do you need?"

Hands were raised all over the sanctuary. I called upon one child who answered, "We need God." The other hands, however, remained up until one youngster said, "We need our parents." And practically all the hands in the room went down.

We are still their teachers, even when we admit our mistakes. We are still their teachers, and not only for the little ones, because the big ones watch and listen and draw their own conclusions.

We are still their teachers on the subject of life, their guides to the Promised Land of their tomorrow, as Moses pleads with us in this morning's Torah portion: "Therefore choose life, thou and thy seed; to love the Lord thy God, to hearken to His voice, for that is thy life and the length of thy days, that thou mayest dwell in the land that the Lord swore unto thy fathers, to Abraham, to Isaac and to Jacob to give them."

Amen.

Yom Kippur 1968/5729

Mixed Marriage

With this day, another week has come to an end. The days have flown by. The more we fill them, the faster they go. We race to the station, run to keep the next appointment, try to keep up with the ticking hands, but the day is soon gone and a new day is born.

The Jew, many thousands of years ago, made a protest against this tyranny of time and created the Shabbat, the one day, this day, when he could switch from man's time to God's time, from hectic human pace to one that is in no hurry because it has forever. The Shabbat was the one day when the Jew, if he chose, could catch his breath physically and spiritually. The world kept saying, "Hurry, you'll be late!" and the Jew answered, if he chose, "No, thank you. It is the Shabbat."

And with this day, another year comes to an end, and where did it fly? What happened to the books that never got read, the letter that never got written, the visit that never got made? What happened to the children growing up so fast that we hardly saw it happening? Where did the year go?

And the Jew, thousands of years ago, created Rosh HaShanah and Yom Kippur and the days in between, not only to catch his breath but to stop the world and get off and see what it looks like as it goes by, and to see what he looks like while he is standing there on the platform. Where has he come from? Where is he going? Where will next year take him? How far? Far from where? Where will all the flowers go?

It is the New Year, and on this morning and next week on *Kol Nidrei*, I shall ask you to share with me a view of that world and a view of ourselves. The subjects we shall approach are, in some respects, sensitive and delicate, and my hope is simply to open channels of discussion and dialogue that will continue into the months ahead.

This morning I turn to the question of mixed marriage, which ranks in the seriousness of its consequences with the more obvious problems of Soviet Jewry and the security of the State of Israel. For the day may come, God willing, when Russian Jews will find their way to freedom without being ransomed like captives, and the day may come, God willing, when Israel will arrive at some rapprochement with its Arab neighbors, but if the number of mixed marriages continues at its present rate of increase, then the strength of the Jewish people is as much in jeopardy as if Israel were to fall at the hands of the Arabs, God forbid, or as if 3 million Russian Jews were to be cut off from the mainstream Jewish community, God forbid.

First, a word of definition. A mixed marriage is a marriage between a Jew and a non-Jew who has not been converted to Judaism. Should such a conversion take place, it is not a mixed marriage, nor is it, as it is sometimes called, an intermarriage. It is simply a Jewish marriage between two Jews. According to Jewish tradition, a convert is no different Jewishly from one who was born a Jew.

The problem of mixed marriage is as old as the Bible, as new as America. In this country, the Spanish-Jewish community of the seventeenth and eighteenth centuries and the German-Jewish community of the nineteenth and twentieth centuries were in many respects strong and vigorous, and their contributions are woven into the fabric of American Jewish life, but nonetheless, their ranks were continually being depleted by the numbers who married out of the faith.

Had such a trend continued, the American Jewish community today would be as small in numbers and as weak in influence as the Jewish communities of European countries like Norway and Sweden are. What restored the strength was the influx of 2 million Jews from Eastern Europe between 1870 and 1914, who brought with them not only a strong sense of ethnic belonging intent upon group survival, but sheer numbers large enough to replenish a dwindling community. Some Jews continued to marry out, but when they did, the event was perceived more as a crisis for that family than as a serious threat to Jewish survival.

But today's serious problem, with perhaps more than 20 percent of Jews marrying out of the faith—and in cities like Los Angeles the figure may be 25 percent, some estimate 50 percent—our problem today is that there are no sources of supply to replenish our losses. For perhaps the first time in American Jewish history, the future of this community will be determined exclusively by those who are presently on the scene. For the first time, no one is waiting in the wings.

It has to be our problem because even though no one survey may be conclusive, all the surveys strongly suggest that the children of mixed marriages, in a majority of instances—one figure was 80 percent—are not raised as Jews.

It has to be our problem, all of ours, and words like "blame" and "fault" do not freely apply. The young people who are scoring 20 percent, and in Los Angeles 25 percent or perhaps even 50 percent, have not arrived at that juncture unaided and unabetted. From the day that our forebears set foot on the shores of New Amsterdam in 1654, they harbored the hope that doors of opportunity would be open to them regardless of their religious affiliation. We protested against restrictive quotas in schools and restrictive covenants in neighborhoods, and our motto was, "regardless of religious affiliation." And then it comes to pass that a Jewish son or daughter begins to date and perhaps to get serious and perhaps to contemplate marriage "regardless of religious affiliation."

Professor Leonard Fein once wrote that "the cost of freedom is freedom," and we are paying the cost. None of us who lives in an open society can declare himself exempt from its risks, and few would reject the open society even if he could be free of the risks. There may be a few who emigrate to Israel to reduce the risks. There may be some, though I don't know any, who join themselves to the Chasidim of Williamsburg and refuse to send their children to college. But for the rest of us, the risk is there: for our children and grandchildren the risk that they will be included in those statistics; the risk that the feeling of being Jewish and a part of a Jewish family will not be felt; the risk that the challenge of living as a Jew in a crazy world will go unchallenged, that the menorah will go unlit and the Torah will go unheld, that the *Kaddish* will go unsaid.

The risk is there in our new lifestyle, but we ourselves, many of us, increase the risk, unknowingly and unwittingly, because when it has come to mixed marriage, we have maintained a kind of strained silence. We have treated mixed marriage as though it were a dirty subject. With all of the articles in the press, with all of the debates among rabbis, with all of the discussions at dinner parties, at the crucial levels, where such open discussions could possibly reduce the risks, we have kept a strained and stubborn silence.

There is first the wall of silence between parents and their own children. No studies or surveys are needed to tell us that most Jewish parents, not all but most, look with disfavor upon the prospect of their children marrying out of the faith. Some will tell their children how they feel, but there are others who, for some reason, keep their feelings silently to themselves, at least as far as their children are concerned. Husbands will talk to wives and wives to husbands, but no one tells the children. Marshall Sklare, in his Lakeville Studies of twelve years ago, showed that the attitude of most parents was, How can I see to it that my child does not enter a mixed marriage? Twelve years later, in the same community, the prevailing parental attitude is, How can I accommodate myself, how can I handle my own feelings, if my child should marry out of the faith?

Such parents are caught on the horns of many dilemmas. They have accepted, as their children have accepted, the sacred proposition promulgated by our culture that happiness in marriage is to be equated with romantic love. And if parents want their children to be happy (and what parent does not?), how can they stand in the way of romantic love when it flowers into bloom, even if the beloved isn't Jewish?

What parents have failed to see, or failed to say, is that the sacred proposition may have defects of its own. It is one thing to say that romantic love is an essential ingredient to marital happiness. It is quite another to make the two synonymous. Romantic love by itself does not necessarily include the sharing of life experiences such as the religious experience. Romantic love does not necessarily include participation in a common commitment like the religious commitment. Romantic love does not by definition include that solid, mutual ground that somehow maintains their love when they don't feel romantic and sustains their happiness when they don't feel happy.

It is not to say that two people with different religious backgrounds cannot cope with their differences and establish a solid marriage. Some cope very well and establish very solid marriages. But some cope not so well, especially after they settle in and children are born and decisions must be made, some not nearly as well as they thought they would during the glorious days when they fell in love.

And we, the sometimes silent parents, who know of the distance between romantic love and genuine happiness, should teach that knowledge diligently to our children.

Some parents are caught in another dilemma that accounts for their silence. They are Jews the way some Jews are: They feel it more than they do it. The temple is there, but at a distance. Shabbat is there, but at a distance, with Rosh HaShanah and Yom Kippur and Pesach a little closer. And what troubles some parents is their own sense of embarrassment and vulnerability when they raise the subject of mixed marriage to their children and when they talk about the survival of the faith and their wish to have Jewish grandchildren.

What the parents fail to see is that their possible embarrassment could be less costly than their certain silence. In an informal survey among college students, among those who said that their parents strongly disapproved of mixed marriage, 6 percent said it was likely that they would marry out. Of those who thought that their parents were indifferent, 52 percent said it was likely they would marry out.

Children don't always do what we would want them to do, but they listen. They listen to what we say, and they listen to silence and sometimes construe it as indifference.

There is a time to keep silent and a time to speak, and this is the time for parents to break the silence, beginning when their children are young.

The second wall of silence sometimes stands between the two young people about to enter a mixed marriage. It sometimes happens that the non-Jewish partner has no specific religious affiliation. He or she may have been raised with one but no longer maintains ties with any church. If asked, if approached, he or she might be willing to explore conversion to Judaism and a Jewish marriage.

I do not look upon this as coercion, nor do I deny a minister the same right to seek conversion of a Jewish partner. The difference may well be that conversion to Judaism is not so much an embrace of a particular theology as it is an identification with a people, and the two people who marry then stand together on the common ground of that people.

But very often, when I broach the subject of conversion to a Jewish young man or woman, the answer is, "I would love it but wouldn't dare suggest it." And I wonder why and ask the young man of his fiancéé, "Why not? Maybe she is simply waiting to be asked." Or I ask the Jewish young woman why not and she will say, "On his own, he's not eager. I know that he would do it for me, just for me, just because he loves me and he would do it to make me happy." And I wonder and ask, "Why not? That's a very good reason, to identify himself with something that's precious to you, out of his love for you so that you will be standing on common ground and your children will know where they stand. Why not?"

There is a time to be silent and a time to speak, especially when the words are waiting to be spoken between two people who love each other.

And finally, there is the wall of silence that sometimes stands between congregation and rabbi on the subject of mixed marriage.

I am among those rabbis who do not officiate at mixed marriages. I see the role of rabbi as the representative of the Jewish tradition and believe I can legitimately assume that role only when the two people being married identify themselves and their marriage with that tradition. I feel that by participating in a mixed marriage, I, as a rabbi, would be giving public Jewish endorsement to an event that has built into it negative factors for Jewish survival.

Other rabbis take a different view. They maintain exactly the contrary: that to close the Jewish door on such a couple is to assure their alienation from Judaism and that the interests of Jewish survival are best served by acceding to their request and by sharing in their marriage.

Each of us can stand only where his conscience directs him, even though it entails the sadness of saying no to a young person you know very well and a family you know very well because you cannot share this special day in their lives. Like every commitment, this one necessarily carries its own measure of pain.

But what is not necessary, and what can only be destructive, is the wall of strained silence that sometimes springs up between congregant and rabbi. Because in the intense emotionalism of the entire matter, the rabbi's refusal is sometimes perceived as a negative judgment on the character of the non-Jewish partner, or it is sometimes perceived as a personal rejection of the Jewish partner. And what gets obscured in all the emotion is that the rabbi is not against anyone, he's for something—for the continuity of the Jewish people and the Jewish faith—and in his best judgment, this is the best way he can serve that continuity.

There is no reason for strained silence, for closed doors. There is only reason to sit and talk with the young couple about their relationship to each other, about the problems they will face, about their possible relationship to Judaism, about the prospects of raising their children as Jews. There is plenty to talk about, but not through a stone wall.

So I have a hope for this New Year, a hope for parents that they will speak to their children out of the deepest feelings of their own hearts, that they will not be afraid, that they will not abdicate their place in the continuity of the generations.

And I have a hope for children, for young people, for you who are prospective marriage partners, that you will value what the generations have preserved for you. Though it may sound inconceivable that anyone should even ask you to give up the one you dearly love, it is not inconceivable to decide in advance that the marriage you want for yourself is a Jewish marriage, and that you will always stand in the continuity of your people, that your marriage will be in the continuity, and that your children will become the living proof of that continuity.

My hope for you, the young people, is that you and your children and your children's children will take up the challenge of living as a Jew in a crazy world, that you and they will light the menorah, that you and they will hold the Torah, that you and they will recite the *Kaddish*, and that you and they together will be part of our Jewish continuity.

Amen.

Rosh HaShanah 1968/5729

The Jewish Sense of Family

The meeting that is recorded in this morning's Torah portion was called to order by Moses, who served as chairman and leader. The agenda consisted of only one item, an agreement to become partners, a people with its God. The terms were simple: You, the people, take His law; carry it with you wherever you go; learn it and live by it. And He, God, will be the sustaining force in your lives. You open yourselves up to Him, and He will become available to you. And the people voted in favor of the motion.

There has never been a congregational meeting quite like it, where the "yes" vote of those present was considered binding upon all future administrations, all future generations. Until this day, a Jew, by definition, is born into that partnership between his people and its God. He personally may decide to renege or defect, but he cannot change the definition. To be a Jew is to be a partner, to this very day.

Never has there been a congregational meeting like it. Three thousand years before woman suffrage, three thousand years before students even thought of asking for a voice in policy decisions. At this meeting three thousand years ago, *Tap'chem n'sheichem*—"the wives and the children"—were present, with a voice and with a vote. God's partners standing next to their human partners, their wives and their children. And the Hebrew word is *mishpachah*, which means "family."

I have the opportunity to speak with many young people who are considering conversion to Judaism. And I ask them what they already know about the faith that they are about to study and will ultimately embrace, and they invariably make some mention of the Jewish sense of family. With no aspersions on their own parents or siblings, they tell of having heard or read about or witnessed firsthand an unusual quality of closeness, which they are not quite able to describe but have already begun to admire.

And I try to tell them that in part we Jews had nothing to do with it: that when a Jew in a village of Eastern Europe was attacked by a mob of drunken peasants to shouts of "Christ killer"; or when a Jew in Italy in the sixteenth century was informed that the only trade open to him was the sale of secondhand goods, but because he had trouble obtaining used merchandise, he had to pay for new garments that he then had to slash with a knife so that they could qualify as secondhand; or when not so many years ago, a Jewish child in Germany would be made to stand before the class and suffer the taunts and jibes not only of his fellow students but of teachers; or when every man, woman and child had to walk the streets with the yellow Star of David sewn to their sleeves (the badge of shame, it was called), in the face of such a hostile and spiteful world, the only safe place, the one defense against inhumanity, the one place we could turn to and be sure of was our home and our family.

That was part of it, but the other part was of our doing. Let me quote a few lines from a poem by Henrich Heine called "Princess Sabbath," in which he likened the Jew to a dog under the witch's cane for six days at a time, but with the arrival of every seventh day, with the arrival of the Sabbath, "the dog," writes Heine,

> *Once more is human,*
> *And his father's halls he enters*
> *As a man, with man's emotions,*
> *Head and heart alike uplifted.*

That part was of our doing. We did not use our homes, our safe place, our families simply to huddle in fear or to nurse each other's wounds, but we used them to welcome the Sabbath, to sing the songs, to sit around the seder table and talk like men who were free and remind each other that we were God's partners, heads taller than the very ones who panted to crush us to the earth. We used our homes and our families to turn the badge of shame into an emblem of pride. And in those moments of strengthening one another, no human beings were ever more partners to each other.

But not only with Jews. From the dawn of humanity, marriage and family have served as this kind of mutual aid society. The husband trapped the animals and constructed the living quarters; the wife cared for the infants, tended the fire, prepared the food, minded the patch of garden; every child was another pair of helping hands. Everyone knew that if he did his job, the family would thrive. And everyone agreed that if enough families would thrive, the society would be strong, and from then until now, the ultimate test of any society is the stability of its individual families. With all of society's defense systems, its social welfare, its standards of education and production, the family is the litmus paper of that society.

It's all very practical and very utilitarian, so where does love come from? It comes, I believe, from a human fact: that man and woman, Adam by himself and Eve by herself, are lonely people, and they are drawn to each other physically and emotionally, and they form their partnership and commit themselves to each other and promise to work together, each doing his or her own job, and together they will confront the real world. And if and when they are blessed with children, the children will be assigned their tasks, and the parents will teach the children to live in the real world.

And so it goes from day to day, and in the course of many days, of partners working together, achieving together what neither could achieve alone, not without periods of shame and anger, not without arguments that we tell our children are discussions but that our children know are really arguments, but still standing next to each other and lying next to each other, after many days and many nights having come to love.

When Sholom Aleichem's Tevye asks his wife, "Do you love me?" and she regales him with all the domestic duties she has performed for all the years of their marriage, he suspects that she is evading the question, but she knows that she is answering it—that love, genuine love, is not the cause of marriage but the result of it. Two people who decide to stand at the altar are acting upon a premise, hopefully a well-considered premise, that after years of living and working together, of fighting and making up, of discovering that the other is not perfect, only then will they begin to trust each other—and trust is the stuff of which love is made.

But then I listen to young people, and they don't use the word "trust," they substitute the word "happiness," which they think is a synonym for love. And then I listen to the people they learned it from, to our generation, with its plethora of troubled marriages, its tidal wave of divorces, the grounds of their complaint being that one or the other or both are not happy.

And I must confess that I never quite understand what that means. I only know that marriage begins with a ceremony and the essence of that ceremony is a commitment, a promise to each other, and the purpose of that commitment is to tide them over all those times when the marriage would not be happy.

There is valid cause for divorce, and Judaism has always sanctioned it. But the deciding question is not "Are we happy?" but "Do we still trust each other? Are we still partners, unhappy right now, but still partners with each other?" And if the answers are in the affirmative, there is hope for love, even though for now it has gone into hiding.

If today's family is in trouble, it is because we of our generation, slightly intoxicated by the creature comforts that success made available, sent out the signal that this was what life and love were all about, this sensation of feeling good, of feeling high, of feeling happy.

If today's family is in trouble, it is because the second telegram never arrived: We never received the message, as Dr. Aaron Stern shared with us, that the purpose of life is not happiness but handling conflict, and if we're lucky, we can use our occasional moments of happiness as buffers against the conflict.

If today's family is in trouble and tomorrow's family is headed for trouble, the symptoms may be observed in those new kinds of arrangements among graduate students where they are not married but share bed and board as if they were. My concern here is not the morality of being together without benefit of clergy, but rather the attitudes they express about their own arrangement. They have avoided a ceremony not because it's just a ritual but because it does imply a commitment, which they are unwilling to make, since it complicates the freedom of either one to dissolve the arrangement. They define marriage and children as "dragging someone around." And most telling was the interviewer's observation that most of these couples were intensely earnest about themselves but minimally interested in anything outside of them.

If today's family is in trouble, it is because the experience of that Jewish family in the ghetto or wherever it was, that experience of not turning off the world but of together standing up to it, that experience has been lost in the happiness hunt. When a Jewish couple is about to be married, I tell them of the cup of wine, which is the world's joy, and the glass to be broken, which is the world's sadness; that marriage is for mature people who confront the world and do not push it away; that marriage is for mature people who are willing to make commitments and do all the unromantic things like earning a living and keeping a house in order.

Jewish marriage is what Jewish marriage has always been, partnered with God, and partnered with each other, to live in the world.

We should notify our children before it's too late, these very children whose parents have groomed them to the school of happiness and avoidance of conflict, who, when any commitment produces strain and discomfort, are the first to run.

We know of children who were assigned to classes in public school and the parent called to have the class changed and the school changed the class, for the child's sake.

We know of parents who allowed children to withdraw from religious school because they weren't "stimulated," for the child's sake.

And we know of very specific instances when the principal of a high school called parents to say that their child was involved with drugs, and the father's total response was, "I'll be down with my lawyer in the morning!"

That child will marry and he will be asked to make a commitment of which he will always be wary. He or she will be confronted with conflicts that he has always been taught to avoid, and he or she will answer that he will speak to the lawyer in the morning.

We should tell our children before it's too late that they should ignore the previous telegram, for this is Yom Kippur when a Jew acknowledges mistakes, even if they were mistakes of love. This is the day to do it, this day when a people made a decision to be partners of God, partners to each other, through wind and rain, with trust and love.

Amen.

Yom Kippur 1969/5730

A Message to Our Children

The announcement has ironically come during the week leading up to *Kol Nidrei*. In response to the terrorist demands of Arab guerillas and in the interests of Arab oil, the Austrian government has agreed to close down Schonau Castle, which has been serving as a transfer station for Jewish refugees on their way from the Soviet Union to the Land of Israel. Chancellor Kreiske, himself of Jewish descent, additionally added to his announcement that a limited number of individual Jews would still be allowed to pass through the country, in keeping with Austria's humanitarian tradition.

Aside from all of our other reactions of chagrin and concern, we could not help but respond to Dr. Kreiske's little addendum with our own painfully obvious question: How many refugees do you take in order to qualify as humanitarian, and where is the cutoff point at which humanitarianism must concede to political expediency and Arab oil?

It's the same old script with the Jew in his same old part. When Pharaoh in ancient Egypt refused the request to liberate his slaves because they were too valuable a commodity on the labor market, it was the Jew who played the slave part. When the kings and popes of the Middle Ages wanted a scapegoat to divert the hostility of the exploited masses away from themselves, it was the Jews who were given the scapegoat part. And when Hitler wanted not only a scapegoat for Germany's internal problems but an effigy to rock the moral, ethical system he so violently detested, it was six million Jews who got the part.

And whatever our individual theologies may be, whether we do or do not accept the traditional Jewish concept of the Chosen People, we cannot avoid the historic reality of all those instances in which morality collided with politics, or morality collided with expediency, or morality collided with savagery, and the Jew was stage front in the drama, whether he wanted to be there or not!

And in the midst of that same old script, and now with Schonau added to the plot sequence, we have walked into this sanctuary on this Yom Kippur Eve and have listened to the melody of *Kol Nidrei*. But what we heard is not what we might have expected, not a whimpering lament but a melody of poignant strength, touched with pain but unyieldingly strong. What we heard was not a dirge of woe but an invincible melody about the will to live and not to die.

The melody itself is only five hundred years old, but the truth of which it sings goes back to our beginnings, to Moses standing before the people as they are about to enter the Promised Land, in the words we shall read in tomorrow morning's Torah portion: "See, I have set before thee this day life and death; the blessing and the curse; therefore, choose life, that thou mayest live, thou and thy seed."

It was the most eloquent plea that Moses had ever made: If you will accept this assignment in the world and in history, if your lives will serve as proof of the one ethical God by the way you act and the way you react, then this people will live and not die. And even when the dark days come and you will fall victim to brute strength, this people will not succumb because brute strength will be no match for the power of your purpose and the power of your conviction. You will even take the reigns of suffering into your own hands and learn to cope. You'll take the bad days and the good days, and you'll shape them into a destiny that you will direct, a life-giving, hope-filled destiny of which *Kol Nidrei* always sings.

Moses gave us *Kol Nidrei* and we took it, but he gave it on one condition that was nonnegotiable, that it would also belong to our children and to our children's children because a destiny by definition can only be from generation to generation.

It is a Jewish axiom that when a Jewish child is born or when a child is adopted by Jewish parents, he or she is automatically enlisted in the Jewish generations beginning with Abraham and Sarah, and hardly has the little child seen the light of day then we pronounce a blessing as we give the child a name, and in the blessing we already chart out a life of study and good deeds and a good Jewish marriage, all of which mark him or her for the Jewish destiny.

Sometimes this particular Jewish axiom will come up for discussion, and someone young or not so young will sound a note of protest and argue that the mere accident of birth or adoption has no right to impose so much on this unsuspecting newborn, and we have to answer with the Jewish truth, mystical though it be, that the agreement is nonnegotiable, that if someone chooses to turn his back on his destiny, no one can hold him back, but the original agreement still stands, violated, but it still stands.

And from all that we've heard from our grandparents and read in the literature and saw in *Fiddler on the Roof,* Jewish families in the shtetl, from the beginning of Jewish time, consciously programmed their family's lives to give these children a sense of belonging to their destiny and their generations. The very warmth of the ritual and the very richness of the tradition gave the child this sense of being a descendant, and every time the door was opened for Elijah, who symbolized the hope of a far-off messianic day, the child was made to feel like an ancestor. And with grandparents often under the same roof or close by, the child had living proof of generations living together in their Jewish destiny.

And the reputation that still survives about Jewish family closeness and Jewish family warmth, equaled perhaps only by Chinese family life, this reputation derives, I would propose, not only from the pressures of the hostile world but from this extraordinary relationship of parent as the teacher of the child. Because in other respects, our families were no different from the families of other cultures: They cared for the physical needs of their young, they gave their children a feeling of belonging and intimacy, they transmitted cultural values. But the difference was in this one respect, the degree to which these Jewish parents were teachers with a special mission: to teach their children to grow up into people whose actions and reactions would attest to one ethical God; to teach their children of a destiny that glowed in the Shabbat candles and jangled in the *pushke*, the charity box in the kitchen; to gird them for the day when, God forbid, they would be locked inside Auschwitz or outside Schonau.

And with everything else that we liberal, enlightened twentieth-century Jews have traded away for the prizes of our open society, we have consciously clung to and claimed our Jewish sense of family, which is why we should give special heed to all the gloomy predictions about the breakdown of the family, the rising tide of divorce, the upward trend of nonmarital living arrangements, the dwarfing of the family circle with the dispersion of grandparents and relatives in many directions, and for those who are left in the family, the parents and the children, give special heed to a heightened atmosphere of isolation, often each child with his own room, each child with his own television, avoiding conflict by avoiding contact, except to work out or battle through whose turn it is for the family car, unless each one has his own.

The problems are real but the family still has enough functions to perform as a basic unit in our society that it will undoubtedly be around for a long time. With changes, of course. There will be more children with two sets of parents after their parents divorce and remarry other parents. There will be more acceptance and recognition of the one-parent family as a total family. There will be young couples living together who when they marry will appreciate their own marriage and family differently than if they had not married.

There will be changes, and the family may be different, but the family will survive. But there is one change that for everybody else is part of the package, but for

Jews it could mean the end of what is Jewish about the Jewish family. And in some families it is already on its way to happening: the Jewish parent no longer acting as the conscious teacher of the child on the subject of becoming a person who belongs to a destiny.

The mistake we sometimes made as liberal, enlightened, bewildered Jewish parents is that after ceding secular education to the public schools because they could do a better job, we kept giving and giving and gave religious education altogether to the synagogue, and sex education to the peer group, and education about the realities of life and death to the television set.

We gave away more than we had to and more than we had a right to because most of the time, nobody knows more about helping a child to become a person with a destiny than that child's own parent. Our problem was that we were sometimes so shaky in our own convictions and beliefs and are probably so oversold on the need of our children to make their own decisions and to make of their lives one big elective program that we stopped teaching them altogether about what it is to be linked to the past and directed to the future. There should be discussions with parents about how such a feeling might be conveyed to children. When we talk about simple rituals, parents will sometimes say that they can't light the Shabbat candles or put a mezuzah on the door because they don't believe in them, and we have to tell them the Jewish truth: that ritual is not something you believe in, it's something you do to link up with the Jewish past and the Jewish people, and you don't have to worry about feeling like a hypocrite because it's something you do to link up with the Jewish past and Jewish people.

And if we, as parents and teachers, are to teach our children what we're not sure of ourselves, we can at least teach them about our conflict and our ways of dealing with conflict, and that, too, will be a great lesson. Aaron Stern, the psychoanalyst, proposes that the real goal of life is not the happiness we tout to our children but the ability to handle conflict in life situations. We can teach our children how we, their parents, come into conflict with each other and that there are healthy and unhealthy ways to resolve the conflict.

We can teach our children about the conflict between the ideals of integrity and the realities of the marketplace and how we resolve the conflict, sometimes in ways that leave us less than proud.

We can teach our children of our conflict between the obligations to our business or profession and our obligations and love for our family, and of the conflict between watching a play-off baseball game and attending a Yom Kippur service at the temple on the most sacred day of the Jewish year.

We are the teachers of our children, and more than we ever suspected, they do listen. There are college students here tonight with their family on Yom Kippur, and there are college students away from here who have sought out a *Kol Nidrei* service, and four or five years ago, when we talked Judaism and family, we may have sworn they weren't listening.

And on the other side of the ledger, when parents of confirmands drop off the children or bring their tenth graders to Friday night services in fulfillment of their confirmation and drop them off and pick them up, or when children see parents change all plans to attend an open house at public school and stay away without hesitation or conflict from an open house at religious school, or should a parent choose the play-off over Yom Kippur—each time those children are listening and learning, even though the parent may have thought they weren't paying attention.

A survey of students asked who influenced them most in what they felt about their religion, and 84 percent said their fathers, 88 percent said their mothers, 30 percent said their rabbis, just so we should know who the real religious leaders are.

So on behalf of all of us enlightened, liberal and sometimes bewildered Jewish parents, I ask you to share with me, as the teachers of our own children, in this message, to be modified by each parent in his own way.

To you, our children, our next generation:

It was customary for Jewish parents, in addition to assigning their worldly goods, of which they had few, to leave for their children what is called an ethical will, in which the parent transmitted in writing what he hoped the child would learn, to be read by the child after the parent's death.

But since we believe that it is better for you to know now, and since there is no good reason to wait, please take up our words now.

We give you our hope that you will never be in want for material things, but that you will always want more than material things.

We give you our hope that you will confront the conflicts in your life not like one who is trapped by fate, but like one who is shaping a destiny.

We wish for you a Jewish life of study and good deeds.

We wish for you a Jewish family so that your children might take their place in the generations, so that you will teach them what it means to be a descendant and what it means to be an ancestor.

We wish for you that you will correct the mistakes of your parents, that you will mercifully attribute to them a lack of insight and a lack of wisdom, but never a lack of love.

We give to you with apology our feeble signals, with the hope that you will get the message.

We give to you, our children, our next generation, the melody of *Kol Nidrei* and the destiny to which you were born.

May God open your ears and your hearts, and ours, too.

Amen.

Yom Kippur 1973/5734

A Time for Renewal

James Reston, in formulating a list of issues that called for serious concern in our country's future, included the following: "How to deal with the squalor of our sexual and family life." His statement is a recognition that no society can be too much stronger than its individual components, and in our society, the central component is the nuclear family. It is what the Talmud recorded about the ripple effect of family life: that if the home is stable, there can be stability in the community; and if the community is stable, there can be stability in the nation, and then there is even hope for the world.

Especially did that formula hold true for us, the people of the covenant. For if we were to carry out our assignment of telling the world about the God of decency and compassion and justice, then we had to make room for those very qualities within the walls of our own homes. We had to try to achieve what in Hebrew is called *sh'lom bayit*—"the peace," the well-being, the harmony "of the home." If we were to proclaim God's ethical law to humanity, then in our own homes we had to do what the book *Life Is with People* singles out as the essential goal of Jewish family life, which is "to make children into people" (although the Yiddish is more expressive: "to make children into *menschen*"). It means that aside from arranging the music lessons and the tutoring for the SATs and the braces on the teeth, we help them to grow up as responsible, caring human beings so that on their own they will join the people of the covenant.

On this day of the New Year, as the shofar has waxed louder and louder, the renewal of our covenant with the God of history has to include the renewal of the Jewish family. Let me suggest what we should not do to confront the squalor of today's family life. We should not simply portray the idyllic picture of the traditional Jewish family: the father as moral authority; the mother as nurturer, the hub of emotional life, who, in the words of Irving Howe, would "draw a circle of safety in which her children could breathe"; grandparents very much on hand to dispense the wisdom of age; other relatives on hand to eat at the dinner table. Everybody's role was clearly defined, and all those roles were carefully orchestrated into the *sh'lom bayit*, the stability of the home.

It's a very tempting vignette, but we should resist the temptation. A man once came to me after he had visited with a Chasidic family in the community of Williamsburg in Brooklyn. He was describing the *sh'lom bayit* of that household, very much in accord with the traditional Jewish family, and he asked, half woefully, half critically, why Jewish families in our community have allowed such harmony to go by the way. He was not happy with my answer because I said to him: "You can have exactly that kind of family. All you have to do is move out of Westchester to the Chasidic community in Williamsburg, and if you like the country better, you can go to the Chasidic community in New Square, you can go to any community that has rigidly structured its own world, by choice, and has kept the rest of the world outside. But if the pattern of your life is to rush for the train while your children are rushing to school, and if you're all eating dinner at different times because you were held up at the office, and if on the weekends you're all in different directions to do your different things, and if you need a computer programmed with everyone's schedule to find an hour in the week when everyone will be at home at the same time, and if you want your children to attend an Ivy League school, if that's the lifestyle you've opted for, then you waste your time and your strength hankering after the *sh'lom bayit* that you sensed in Williamsburg. However, if you are asking how, within the context of where we are within *our* reality, how we can infuse some of that moral authority into our households, and how we can draw those circles of safety for our children, and how we can teach our children to be *menschen*, then indeed we have something to talk about."

The question that has to be asked today, not to be answered but to be explored, is how we are to move toward the renewal of our family life and how to achieve the *sh'lom* of our *bayit*.

Eleven years ago, I delivered a High Holy Day sermon on The Jewish Sense of Family, and I went back to it simply to discover what eleven years have wrought. Eleven years ago I referred to "new kinds of arrangements among graduate students where they are not married but share bed and board as if they were," and then I said: "My concern here is not the morality of being together without the benefit of clergy, but rather the attitudes they express about their own arrangement. They have avoided a ceremony not because it's just a ritual but because it does imply a commitment, which they are unwilling to make."

Now, eleven years later, that description is not totally accurate. There are still the risks in sharing bed and board for those who are not ready for such intimacy, especially for those who will get hurt when the arrangement dissolves. However, the difference between now and eleven years ago is what I learn from couples about to be married who have been living together anywhere from months to years and are totally open about it. What I often learn is that their living together is perceived by them not as an avoidance of the commitment of marriage but, on the contrary, as a testing ground to determine whether there should be a marriage. They are testing their living and loving from day to day to see whether they should make the decision for a lifetime.

There are some who legitimately question whether that test is a real test, but my speaking of it now is simply to suggest that the experience of marriage and family is much more within the framework of thinking today than it was eleven years ago. The attraction of what was then called "The New Morality," with the offer of fun and games, turned out to be more alluring than it was rewarding. A survey in *Time* magazine reported that the rate of marriage that had declined between 1972 and 1976 is again on the rise, and while the divorce rate is still climbing, so is the rate of remarriage. It seems that our young people are deciding to go back to good old-fashioned marriage, in some instances at least, and the decision is making everybody happy, especially parents and especially grandparents, and even the bride and groom themselves.

But sometimes what comes out in the course of that very decision, the decision to marry, raises questions that belong to this day of renewal. And here I acknowledge gratitude to many young couples in our congregation, some of them here today, because they have helped me in the exploration of these questions.

For example, a question arises about the very nature of the commitment that they are now presumably making permanent: to be concerned for each other; to be sensitive to each other; to be a team in the day-to-day experiences of their lives, which is all very beautiful and also very private, just between them. What it misses is something very Jewish: that when two people marry, besides being partners to each other, they now take their place as a new family, albeit of two people, but still as a new family with all the other families of the Jewish people and all the other families of Jewish society, or as one prospective bridegroom succinctly responded: "You mean now we're going public!"

No one denies, and you can only respect, the right of two people to be unto themselves and to treasure their time alone in their shared spheres of interest. No one denies, and you can only respect, the right of parents and children to be a unit unto themselves, as a strong family unit, and many families would welcome such unity. But when that unit becomes so exclusionary, when the door of that house opens only *in*, to get away from the world, and not *out*, to join the other families in that world to make that world better, when that family becomes so isolated and so insulated, as close and warm as it may be, it is missing what it takes to be a Jewish family. It has been invaded by privacy. It has succumbed to privatism, which is what happens when privacy takes over and becomes master of the house.

We cannot speak today of the renewal of family and marriage unless we confront that question of privatism, and not only between family and family but even between members of the same family. Prospective brides and grooms, and already married husbands and wives, will often speak of their need for private space in which each one can fulfill his or her own unique talents and potentials. What they are saying is different from the impossible question that people asked of their marriage in that sermon of eleven years ago, that no-win question, "Am I happy?" This question is more complex, less easily dismissed: "Do I have enough space for myself so that I can fulfill myself as a human being?"

It's more complex because the question is valid, because each of us has been created by God to pursue his or her own destiny in this world. And when two of those people marry, the Jewish marriage ceremony is saying to them that each one is entitled to be his or her own person, with his or her own destiny. But now, with this ceremony of marriage, there comes into being a common space in addition to each one's private space, and the success of this marriage will depend on how much time and effort they are willing to spend on that shared space, because it is on that common space that the differences get worked through. It's that common space that needs the sense of humor. It's that shared common space where Martin Buber's definition of love makes sense: that love is not simply the feeling of a wonderful emotion but the responsibility of an I for a Thou. And it is that common space that can sustain both of them when the private space gets shaky underfoot or when one or the other feels less than fulfilled.

If some of today's marriages are in trouble, it is because there has been such zeal for the private space, because privacy has succumbed to privatism, with the result that the common space has suffered from dire neglect. And when the neglect has turned to decay, then the marriage has ended, except for the formalities, which is why Judaism has always sanctioned divorce and why Judaism has insisted that a family where there has been a divorce is still a family. But sanction or not, every time two people are divorced, says the midrash, the altar sheds tears.

Sanction or not, there is always at least the hope that these two self-fulfilling individuals will come out of their privatistic corners and go to work on that common platform of their marriage. We all know of couples who click their champagne glasses on the twenty-fifth or the thirtieth or the fiftieth anniversary because instead of staying in their corners and licking their wounds, they went to work on that center platform and made it strong so that even on the days or nights when they did not feel close to each other, the platform would be strong enough to sustain both of them.

In that sermon of eleven years ago, there was no mention of the Women's Movement, which had then only begun but by now has exerted strong impact upon the home and the family. From time immemorial, at least in our culture, the husband-father was the provider, beginning as the hunter of game. From time immemorial, at least in our culture, the woman was the homemaker, the nurturer. It was a workable division of labor, each with his or her own job to do.

Where the woman got shortchanged was in civilization's advance. With the progress of technology and the expanding of horizons of knowledge, the man was able to choose from a wide range of options in accordance with his own unique talents and at the same time could fulfill his traditional role as provider. He could be a professional, he could be in business, he could be on the soil. For the woman, however, the most that the advance of technology could often do for her was to allow her to put the dishes in the dishwasher instead of washing them by hand or allow her to arrange the car pool instead of walking the children to school. Then came the Women's Movement to encourage her to pursue her talents and capabilities, even if it meant going outside the home and even if the need was not economic.

It all makes sense, and no man who is pursuing his talent at his job, even with its tedium and drudgery, can legitimately scoff at the desire of his wife to pursue her talent at her job or career, even with its tedium and drudgery. And there are untold numbers of couples, including many in this congregation, who have made it work, who have shared the fruits of self-fulfillment and have used them to enrich the platform in the middle.

But despite the validity and despite the record of success, there are still questions to explore.

A rabbi colleague told me that one day he was in his study after a Shabbat morning service where there had been a bar mitzvah ceremony. As he looked out of the window of his study into the parking lot, he noticed that all the cars had left for the reception, which was away from the temple. And then there was a knock at the door of his study, and he looked up, and there was the bar mitzvah boy of that morning. The child, almost in tears, said: "Would you believe it? They forgot me!"

Thus the questions, lest we forget about them, the ones we brought into this world, those questions that the traditional Jewish family never had to ask:

Whence the moral authority in the family?

Whence the circle of safety in which the children can breathe?

Whence the process of helping children to become *menschen* without pushing them into premature independence?

Whence the *sh'lom* of our *bayit*?

It may call for a redistribution of family roles and responsibilities.

It may call for some career postponement until children are grown.

It may mean limited commitments outside the home to allow time inside the home.

It may mean a wider range of volunteer activities that will call upon a wider range of talents and unique capabilities without the need of a paycheck to validate their uniqueness or to guarantee their fulfillment.

We do not know the answers, but what hopefully we shall decide on this day of renewal is not to surrender to self-centered privatism: that as partners with each other—husbands and wives, parents and children, families and families—we shall renew our covenant with each other and thus with the God of our lives.

Amen.

Rosh HaShanah 1980/5741

Ethical Wills

The custom emerged in the course of the Jewish centuries of writing ethical wills. Once a parent or grandparent had designated the bequest of material possessions, he or she would often proceed to this other kind of document. It put into words what that parent or grandparent considered to be of enough ethical and spiritual significance that it deserved to be transmitted to a future generation, sometimes even when the parent or grandparent was still alive.

These ethical wills served a dual purpose. First, they delivered a message that could impress itself on that future generation, the way Solomon was impressed by his father's charge to build a Temple in Jerusalem; or the way a father in the Middle Ages gently scolded his son for not reading the books on the shelves of their family library; or the way Rabbi Richard Israel, of blessed memory, a contemporary of mine, sitting in the fathers' waiting room of the hospital, wrote an ethical will to his soon-to-be-born child, that the child should be "happy, caring and Jewish"; or the way the mother who had emigrated to Israel bequeathed to her children "the fragrance of a Jerusalem morning."

Such were the messages that the children received. And then, the second purpose of those who composed them: to give themselves the opportunity to formulate their own convictions and priorities and values. In order to spell them out, they had to think them through.

And thus do I propose, as a New Year has begun and especially on this day of convictions and priorities and values, that we draw up in our own minds, perhaps eventually on paper, the ethical wills that we would transmit to our children and grandchildren. We shall have to proceed with caution in what we say or write because our own family members will be the first to call us up short should we try to get away with anything that rings less than true.

What do we include? What do we leave out? Where in our estimation should our future generation set their sights? What mountains should they climb? Which pursuits that have occupied our own lives would we commend to them and which would we just as well put to rest?

Thus, to our own ethical wills. For tonight's sample, I have selected three categories, not because they are the only ones—you might very well select others—but because in all of my years of interacting with Jews of all ages, these three—achievement, family and Jewishness—have been central to the message transmitted from one generation to another.

But first, a few questions. What should we tell our children and grandchildren about achievement, we who so often place such a high premium on setting high goals and attaining them? What shall we say when even those who have acquired a measure of success and achievement and rightly glory in them sometimes question how much these goals mean? It was the daughter of the author John Cheever who said that her father discovered the real meaning of success: that it doesn't make any difference.

What shall we say about success, those of us who have conscientiously struggled to distinguish between the trappings of success and the worthwhileness of what we do in our lives, and those of us who back off from the struggle?

What shall we say to our children and grandchildren about achievement, to the very ones I used to ask in confirmation class, "How many of you cheat in school?" They would raise their hands and answer my "Why?" with "Because everybody else does." And then I would ask, "Why does everybody else?" And they would reply, "To get a better grade," which translates into a better grade point average, which translates into a foot in the door of a preferred college. They're nice kids, and they cheat, and they achieve.

Where does the pressure come from? Rabbi Harold Schulweis tells of a powerful exchange with his own teen-age son. The father walked into the boy's room while the son was studying. The father put his arm around the son's shoulder, whereupon the son shrugged and backed away from the embrace. "Why did you do that?" asked his father. The son answered, "Because you only put your arm around me when I'm studying, never when I'm watching television." It could have happened to us.

In my own family, we always said to our children that it's what you learn and not the grades that are important. And one night there was a telephone call from our daughter at college. A paper had been returned, and our daughter's account was high with excitement. The professor had written responses to the contents, paragraph by paragraph, as though engaging in dialogue with the writer. And in the height of all this excitement, I could not restrain myself: "So what grade did you get?" So much for abiding principles.

What shall we tell our children and grandchildren when the message they receive sometimes from home, sometimes from school, sometimes from friends, sometimes from inside themselves is that what really counts are the grades and the in-groups and the winning of the current prize, whatever that prize is. My colleague Rabbi Jerome Davidson tells of a mother who came into his study to discuss her child, a lovely, decent young girl, who by all the usual criteria was not a winner. What brought tears to the mother's eyes was telling of her child's question: "Aren't there any prizes for just being nice?"

So what shall we tell our children and grandchildren about achievement?

And what do we say about family when we, especially we who are grandparents, often find ourselves on such unfamiliar terrain? What we knew as the so-called traditional family with father working and mother at home with the children applies to no more than seven percent of families in America today.

What do we say of family and marriage when 50 percent of marriages, maybe more, end in divorce? A young couple at whose marriage I was to officiate was sitting in my study. After reviewing the details of the ceremony, the prospective groom declared that he had a request to make: that in delivering the charge at their ceremony, I should not say that it was God who brought them together, because should they ever get a divorce, he did not want to feel guilty about sinning against God. To which I responded, "You're not even married yet, and you're talking about divorce!" The figure is 50 percent. But the good news is that 60 percent of younger divorced persons remarry within the next five years.

What shall we say to our adult children who, with their spouses, would sit in my study to discuss the pros and cons of having children? To which I would respond that they don't know what they're missing.

What shall we say to our adult children who, for whatever reason, do not marry? Are they not to find their own way to lead fulfilling and productive lives?

What do we say to those of our children who may be gay or lesbian? Are they not to experience the beauty and magic of love?

And what shall we say of grandparenting when in our own day miles of distance can come between the generations?

What then shall we say of family?

And then to Jewishness.

How do we as parents who have opened up the world to them, who have set before them this vast array of choices, this stunning panoply of options, how do we impress upon them that in this matter of their Jewishness, there should be no choice and no option? How do we as parents who may often come off as detached and casual about our own Jewish commitments, how do we let them know that we are serious about theirs, even as, down deep, we are serious about our own?

We are told that the intermarriage rate among Jews is 50 percent and many families in every congregation are included in that figure. What shall we say to them about Jewishness?

So with these questions in mind, I have prepared in barest outline a sample ethical will. If it will prompt you to compose your own, if it will encourage you to express to your children and grandchildren your own convictions and priorities and values, then this *Kol Nidrei* will have approached its purpose.

So to you, our dear children and grandchildren: No one goes to bed at night with full certainty of what the next day will bring. We, your parents and grandparents, have tried to sustain what life has brought to us, and the following have helped.

On the matter of achievement: As you set your goals and climb your mountains, may you never be spoiled by your success or shattered by your failures. Because in the very whirlwind of that success and in the very debris of that failure is still the wonderful person that you are—the child of your parents, the child of your God, endowed by your Creator with a sturdy spirit that neither success nor failure can take away from you if you do not surrender it. And if we, your parents, have sometimes overpressured you into tightly banded bundles of achievement, our intentions have been the best, if not always the wisest. The line is always thin between guiding and pushing, and without doubt, we have now and again overstepped it. But now a glorious opportunity lies before you: not to repeat our mistakes with your children. As you climb your mountains in your chosen careers and your chosen lifestyles, we offer you a standard of achievement that may be missing from your SAT manuals and your office promotions and your latest fashion style. It was formulated thousands of years ago, and now, with a few revisions, we give it to you: "It has been told to you, O human being, what the God of your life expects of you: to do justly, and to love mercy, and to walk unspoiled by success and unshattered by failure, to walk humbly and with dignity with your God and with your own sturdy spirit."

On the matter of family, our dear children and grandchildren: While some of us, especially your grandparents, hail from our own version of two-career families—the husband's career outside, the mother's career at home—some of you are choosing otherwise, with both careers outside. Your logic is unassailable: that all human beings, women and men, deserve the same right to exercise their own talents and climb their own mountains. And besides, you may need the money.

But know only this: that being married, if you are, is your third career. Thus does it need more than crammed-in time and leftover energy. It needs more than two people who will share bed and board but otherwise pursue their separate paths of fulfillment. It needs instead two people who will advance from their private places to be together in their common space, who, hand in hand, as someone has written, look up at the stars and down at the pile of unpaid bills. Your third career needs two people who rejoice in their gift of love and then in the newborn life that their love is able to nurture. That third human being (or however many more) is the highest career advancement any human being can achieve. Even when marriages fail, even when spouses die, parents and children can be there for each other. I once made the mistake of referring to divorce by the term "broken home" and someone rightly corrected me: "Our family is divided," she said, "it is not broken. Our home has never been so intact."

And should your own home ever be thus divided, and should anger and resentment keep the war going between you and your former spouse, make sure, make absolutely sure, whatever the occasion, whatever the circumstance, make sure that neither of you lets it happen or makes it happen that your own child ends up as the rope in tug-of-war, pulled from two sides, an innocent victim.

Should you remain single, seek out friends with whom to share the joys of life. Or should you claim yourself as gay or lesbian, seek out a partner with whom to share your love, and know that you have my blessing.

Seek out your grandparents wherever they are, because the better you know them, the more you will understand us. They will love you without qualification, and to their autumn years, you will bring brightly colored leaves.

And finally to Jewishness: We, your parents, are your Jewish history, and you are ours, and your children will be yours. That history laughs and weeps with the soul of the Jew, and so may you and your children.

That history is the sweet honey of the New Year and the bitter herb of Passover, and we know how to taste both, and so may you and your children.

Our history sets us always a little outside, always to ask of those on the inside, "Are you sure that you're right?" And so may you and your children.

That history goads us into the world to make it better—free from hatred, free from war, free from fear—and so may you and your children.

That history has blessed us with two precious gifts: the gift of our Torah and the gift of our *Eretz Yisrael*. Whatever it takes to get you to that holy place, go. Whatever it takes for your children to go, do it. And pray for peace and take up the banner of peace for that troubled land.

And should you be married to someone not of the Jewish faith, make sure that he or she is welcomed, warmly welcomed, into the loving circle of your extended Jewish family. And let your home be a Jewish home so that your children will take their place in that line of Jewish continuity from generation to generation.

And so we pass along to you our thoughts and our hopes. We pray that we will never be a burden to you. But if we are, everyone sometimes has to take a turn.

We pray for the health of your bodies and the strength of your spirits. May you be happy, loving and Jewish. May you know the fragrance of a Jerusalem morning. And may you live in a world that gives good grades for being nice.

To you, our children and grandchildren, whom we love and respect, may there be God's good blessings for this year and for all the years to come.

From your loving parents and grandparents.

Amen.

Yom Kippur 2004/5765

A People of Conscience

Why Is a Jew?

Generations of Jews have grown up with the question, What is a Jew? In our own growing-up years, the question was at times hotly debated, sometimes coldly analyzed, but rarely totally ignored. Like all young people, we were searching for our place on the human landscape, and in the course of that search, Jewish young people had some specific questions to ask: How did we as Jews fit into the collage of America? What was our connection with the then handful of pioneers who were already sowing the seeds of a Jewish homeland in Palestine? What were our doubts and reservations about the synagogue and Jewish observance?

None of these discussions ever coalesced into a single, universally accepted answer. Though we did not agree, we learned from each other. And we understood very well the declaration of the late Morris Adler, of blessed memory, who listed all the possible definitions of a Jew and finally proposed that "a Jew is someone who is always asking the question, What is a Jew?"

But of late, a new question is being asked, also by young men and women in their growing-up years. They are on college campuses, they are in the Peace Corps and Vista, they have followed the campaign trail of Eugene McCarthy, and they ask their new question: Why is a Jew? Many of them survived the grades of religious school training. Many of them sat patiently on the day of their bar mitzvah or the day of their confirmation while rabbis exhorted loyalty to the Jewish heritage, but they are not convinced. They do not minimize the contributions that Judaism has made to the ethics and culture of the world, but they feel the gift has already been made and there is no need to be Jewish to embrace ethics, even Jewish ethics, and there is no need to be Jewish to enjoy culture, even Jewish culture. The German Jewish philosopher Franz Rosenzweig, who wrote a century ago, could have been writing for today when he declared: "The new feature is that the wanderer no longer returns at dusk, allowing him to spend the night at home in an exclusive atmosphere of Jewish spirituality and learning. He finds his spiritual and intellectual home today outside the Jewish world."

Today's Jew has become more American. And America is more Jewish. And a generation is asking: Why a Jew? Why remain Jewish? They may even ask their parents, and their parents may try to answer: "You should be a Jew because that's what you are. That's what you were born." But the answer fails to bridge the gap. For when we in our generation asked what a Jew was, we were defining ourselves, we were clarifying our identity, in the world of men. But when a new generation asks why a Jew should be, they are rejecting that identity, choosing to join, unencumbered, the world of men, the universal human family. Their question is for real, and the answer must be for real, from the facts of life and the facts of the world.

The first fact of life is that the Jew himself is not always the arbiter of his own Jewish identity. Some years ago, in a former congregation, I was making my regular rounds at the regional hospital, and the procedure for all clergy was first to stop by the chaplain's office to consult the patient files, which were divided by religion, and then to visit any coreligionists from the clergyman's own community. I called on a man whose name I recognized and who I knew had married a non-Jew. I introduced myself, and the patient politely but firmly announced that he was no longer Jewish, that he had dissociated himself some three or four years previously. I wished him well, but by a freak of circumstance, another rabbi called on the same patient that afternoon, which produced a curt sign on his door: "Please, no chaplains are to visit this room."

I was sufficiently intrigued to ask the resident chaplain of the hospital how a self-avowed non-Jew was listed with the Jewish patients. The chaplain replied that it was always the nearest of kin who designated the religion of the patient, in this instance the man's non-Jewish wife. Nazi Germany made its own determination about who was and who was not a Jew, deciding that it would depend on the religion of the grandparents, even if the grandchild was a practicing Christian. And when First Secretary Wladyslaw Gomulka instigated the purge of Jews in Poland last year, he made no distinction between those Jews who were branded fifth columnists because they professed loyalty to Israel during the Six-Day War and those Jews who had all but left the Jewish fold, who had helped Gomulka into power and had served his government faithfully. All were purged.

And when Czechoslovakia's brief springtime of liberalism was abruptly halted by Russian tanks in the streets of Prague and Jew after Jew was deposed from public office, the Russian invader took little note which Jews attended synagogues and which lighted Shabbat candles. All were deposed. It is a fact of life, a crude and tragic fact of life, that the decision to be or not to be a Jew is not always of the Jew's own making. To which our younger generation responds: All the more reason that Judaism is expendable. Break down the barriers and Christians will no more badger Jews, and Jews will no more suspect Christians. Had those barriers crumbled centuries ago, would the soil of Europe be red with Jewish blood? Would six million have died?

Thus to the heart of the dilemma. No longer, What is a Jew? Not even, Why is a Jew? But a radical, postmodern question: Why particular religions at all? Why particular religious groupings that pit themselves against each other? Why not one individual, humanistic religion that will teach men to live as brothers and not as everything else but?

Because there is a second fact of life, a fact of man, that by his human make-up is incapable of belonging to an organization of three billion, that he needs tangible groups more personal than an amorphous mass of three billion. I quote from Louis Mumford: "[We need] the reassuring presence of a visible community, an intimate group that enfolds us with understanding and love, that becomes an object of our spontaneous loyalty and a point of inference for the entire human race."

Assume that the religions of the world, for the sake of a united humanity, would agree to will themselves out of existence. What groups would remain to evoke man's "spontaneous loyalty" and fix his "point of inference for the entire human race"? There would be the John Birch Society and there would be the militant Black Power group embittered by hatred for the white world. There would be the United Arab Republic and there would always be the Daughters of the American Revolution.

Why should Judaism survive? Why particular religions? Because of this third fact of life: that religions may be the only groupings in the world whose point of reference transcends their own survival and their own strength and extends to the survival and strength of the entire human family. As Eric Kahler has succinctly stated: "The substance of our Jewish particularity is our universality." For this particular Jewish tribe of the ages that emerged into history 3,500 years ago made a promise to the one ethical God when it entered into its covenant with Him: that we would be a light unto the nations, that we would open the blind eyes, that we would bring out the prisoners from the dungeon and them that sit in darkness out of the prison house.

And 3,500 years later, the members of this particular tribe who were purged in Poland and Czechoslovakia were almost to a man in the liberal movements of these causes, and Russia will not tolerate a tribe that insists that the oppressed go free.

And 3,500 years later, even with all the bigotry that lurks in Jewish hearts, we who are three percent of America still produced half of the young people who in 1964 went to Mississippi and risked their lives for the cause of Negro freedom.

We may protest the appointment of an anti-Semite like James Hatchett to responsible office at New York University, but we do not thereby disassociate ourselves from the Negro struggle.

Thirty-five hundred years later, we take note of the voting returns in a state like California, where two-thirds of the electorate *supported* Proposition 14, which was avowedly an anti-Negro constitutional amendment, while two-thirds of the Jewish population *opposed* Proposition 14, "to bring the prisoners out of the dungeon-house."

Thirty-five hundred years later, we observe that while 30 percent of American young people attend college, 80 percent of this particularistic Jewish tribe are on campus, and something like a quarter of the buyers of books in America are this three percent of the population—"to open the blind eyes" with the light of knowledge.

I cite the statistics not to say how great Jews are but how needed Jews are in that very kind of world that our young generation hopes for, a world that I refuse to entrust to John Birchers, and to militant black power, and to the Daughters of the American Revolution. I cite the statistics to suggest that with all the deficiencies in religious school education, with all of the poverty of Judaism in the Jewish home, something of the covenant has rubbed off on the very ones who ask the question, Why be a Jew? And if they remain Jews, they will transmit the covenant to their children, who will also ask, Why be a Jew?

And thus we return to the answer that parents give their children: "Why be a Jew? Because you were born a Jew, not to its nouveau riche vulgarity or its country club society or its synagogue trivia, which you are entitled to protest, but to its tears and its laughter, its music and its poetry, its covenant with God, its destiny in history, its mission to the world. Can you give that up without betraying a part of yourself?" "A person must not be born without a yesterday in his heart," goes the Yiddish proverb.

A beloved member of our family, of blessed memory, was crippled in the last years of her life. She insisted, however, that she walk down the aisle at her daughter's wedding without the cane, holding to the arm of her son. As she was about to take the first step, she whispered to her son, "Walk like a Rudin."

We live in a crippled world, and Rosh HaShanah breaks into that world with a message: Live like a Jew. Say with the words of Edward Fleg, who himself returned to his Judaism, "I am a Jew because for Israel, the world is not finished;

men will complete it. I am a Jew because for Israel, man is not yet created; we are creating him." Live like a Jew for the sake of God, for the promise of humanity and for the destiny to which you were born.

Amen.

Rosh HaShanah 1968/5729

Success and Failure

The first word is "success." It sparkles with brilliance and honor. It dwells in the tree-lined suburbs and well-appointed city apartments. It requires time and talent but is free from anxiety over tomorrow's bread. It respects learning and may even pursue it. It esteems culture and may even enjoy it.

A century of Americans have been reared on the success stories of Horatio Alger. Other authors succeeded him, but the plot did not change: The man at the bottom, despite overwhelming odds, climbs to the top. If he could make it by exercising the cardinal virtues of honesty and hard work, all the better. But if now and again he need walk the straight and narrow path between right and wrong, the goddess of success was lenient with those who worshiped her.

The second word is "failure." A report card marked in failing red, a rejection slip from college, the telephone that did not ring can overcast a young one's sky. The adult who finds himself dangerously close to the base of the ladder usually suffers alone because the only gesture that others extend to him is the one he wants the least—their pity. The play *Death of a Salesman* is the tragedy of Willy Loman, the pitiful failure.

A hundred years after Horatio Alger, it is the same language and the same cult. The successful one is acclaimed a credit to the human adventure; the failure has betrayed it. He is a traitor to life, a coward to go on living. I recall as a youngster in the '30s hearing of my parents' contemporaries who saw themselves as cowards to go on living because they had lost their money in the crash of '29. It was said of them: "They had lost *everything*," when all they had lost was their money. America is yet dominated by the cult of success.

And somewhere on the line between Horatio Alger and Willy Loman are all of us, and we come together in a synagogue on Yom Kippur Eve to hear the chant of *Kol Nidrei* and what it would speak to our hearts.

The episode is recounted of the Baal Shem Tov, the leader of the Chasidim in the eighteenth century, that in the midst of a business day, he sent word to all the merchants in town that they should gather in the square for a message of serious consequence. Anxious and apprehensive, not even taking time to lock the doors of their shops, they rushed to the town square. The Baal Shem Tov, standing on a wooden platform, signaled for silence. "I have summoned you this day for an announcement of supreme consequence: "There is a God in the world!"—and he walked from his platform and signaled them to return to their business.

"There is a God in the world," proclaims *Kol Nidrei*, in the whole world, in all of human experience. He is not the God of success and his adversary is not the demon of failure. He is the God of life, as much of the dark valleys as the high mountains, as much of the blasts of winter as the balm of summertime.

The first time a glass was broken at a Jewish wedding, reports the midrash, was not by the groom but by the groom's father, a rabbi. The guests were shocked into silence, and the old man turned to the young couple with a gentle warning: "You should only know that the air will not always ring with the sound of music. There will be days when the wine will spill and the glass will break into pieces. For your sake, for the sake of your marriage, for the sake of your lives, it is good that you should know this."

There is a time to weep and a time to laugh, a time to mourn and a time to dance. There is a time to fail and a time to succeed—because He is the God of life.

And His human creature is endowed with two natures, not simply good and evil, as some would have it, but first with *majestas*—"majesty"—with power over nature to till its soil, to extract its wealth, to uncover its secrets, to search to its outermost spheres, to rise to Promethean heights of human endeavor.

And second, He has bestowed upon man *dignitas*—"dignity"—the power to lose without the man being lost, the power to give up without being demolished, the power to stand against winter's blast and not be frozen: what David Riesman calls the "nerve of failure" and what Jacqueline Kennedy displayed when she walked behind the caisson draped in black.

The Hebrew word for faith is *emunah*, from *amen*, to be sure, to be strong against the winter's blast. "Yea, even though I walk through the valley of death, I shall fear no evil, for Thou art with me." There is a God in the world, says *Kol Nidrei*.

And on this day of days, He summons us to the bench of justice to state our case and to await the verdict in the familiar words: success or failure.

But the setting has changed. Not the crowded street or the marketplace or the cocktail party. And not the liberty to tamper with the evidence or make excuses on the grounds that everybody else is making his own excuse.

In here, white is white, black is black, and gray is gray. A bribe is not a gift but a bribe, and a payoff is not a goodwill gesture but a payoff. A specialist in business ethics has written: "At the moment we live in a world that has the cards stacked against the morally behaving man." In here, we face front to the unhampered truth of that world and to the question that cannot be avoided: How deeply can a man immerse himself in the jungle before he begins to lose both his majesty and his dignity? The Talmud rabbis were realists when they taught: When you observe the moral law, balance the material loss against the spiritual gain. When you break a moral law, balance the material gain against the spiritual loss.

Out there, a man takes pride in himself as a good provider for his family, but some men do not tell the whole truth: that they have outgrown the common success of a good provider, that they have become intrigued by the game itself—a race that has no finish line—that they have joined the cult of the goddess. Someone asked John D. Rockefeller: How much wealth does it take to satisfy a man? "Just a little more," he answered.

And then the evidence must be heard: Consider Tolstoy's farmer who was told that he would come into possession of as much land as he could encompass by foot in one day. He started out at dawn and did not stop until he had traveled three miles. The sun was high in the sky and hot on his back, but he drank from his flask and continued on the way. His aching body told him it was time to return, but the farther he went, the richer the land.

Finally, he made his way back, but he breathed heavily. He could see the crowd and hear them cheering him on. With all the strength he could muster, facing the crowd at the place he had started, he plunged forward and fell flat to the ground.

The crowd cheered and one of them said, "Rise up, strong man, you have won much land," but the dead man did not rise.

The crowd dug a grave for him, Tolstoy concludes, and from head to heels, it was only six feet long. But then, how much land does a man need?

What does a man give up in the big game? How much of himself to join the cult of the goddess? When the loss exceeds the gain, the success is a failure, and the melody is *Kol Nidrei*.

Out there, we involve ourselves in the welfare of our children, and devote ourselves to their best interests. We may sometimes screen their friends or gently guide them toward friendships we think will be good for them. We direct them toward colleges that will, we think, offer the best educational success.

But in here, in the austerity of a sanctuary, the question must be asked: For them or for ourselves? For their success or our own cult of the goddess? A few years ago, the Princeton University Admissions Office received a letter from an able freshman candidate asking them to turn him down and not to tell his parents about the letter because his parents had forced him to apply.

There was a time when it was in vogue to speak of a newborn child as a lump of clay to be molded and sculpted by attentive parents. As psychology has matured, we have altered the figure of speech: The glob of clay is now a seed that, given favorable conditions of warmth and care, will bloom into the flower that resides within.

It is the difference between a sculptor and a gardener, but whoever tries to make the difference seem obvious and self-evident has never had children of his own. Even if I do not always know the difference, I know there is a difference between failure and success because the melody is *Kol Nidrei.*

Some walk in here prepared for the worst. Yesterday some reasonable goal moved out of reach. Yesterday, in the world outside, I was a failure.

But here, the verdict must wait and the evidence be heard. In Alfred Sutro's play *A Maker of Men*, a bank clerk returns home after missing a promotion and says, "I see other men getting on. What have I done?"

His wife answers, "You have made a woman love you. You have given me respect and admiration, loyalty and devotion, everything a man can give his wife except luxury, and that I don't need. Still you call yourself a failure, you who within these walls are the greatest success."

Yesterday's failure, not so definitive in this courtroom.

Tomorrow the gates will close, and each man will chart his own road to success. I can only offer my own as a Jew, as a person: Success is the strength to fail. It is the moment of *emunah*, of strong faith, and the moment sometimes flies away to be rescued again.

Success is this day, standing as a beggar at God's door, asking forgiveness, seeking charity, re-creating myself. And that beggar is the richest man in the world.

Success is returning home and watching the children in their sleep, and asking the questions about their strength and their flowering and their success, the kind of success that Thoreau describes: "If the day and the night are such that you greet them with joy, and life is more elastic, more starry, more immortal, that is your success"—and the melody is *Kol Nidrei.*

Amen.

Yom Kippur 1973/5734

The Need to Speak of Sin

The journey begins tonight, the journey of these next ten days, by those of us who have wandered far and now are ready to come back home.

But there is one word without which the journey cannot begin, one word on which these next ten days depend. In Hebrew, it is called *cheit*, and in English, the word means "sin."

By Jewish definition, sin is a person missing the mark, his alienation from the moral center of his own being, from the moral center of the universe. Sin is indifference to our own moral capacities and to our own moral sensitivity.

The word is sin, and the problem of the ten-day journey that begins tonight is the word itself. Curiously, it is not a theologian but a psychiatrist, Karl Menninger, who pinpointed the problem in the title of his recent book, *Whatever Became of Sin?* Menninger asks the pertinent questions: "Doesn't anyone sin anymore? Doesn't anyone believe in sin?" The last time, states the author, that a president of the United States used the word "sin" was Dwight Eisenhower in 1953. But later, from his presidential perspective of a proud and confident people, he never used the word again. When a national magazine devoted its cover page in 1972 to what it called "the national disgrace" of spending $400 million to elect one of two leaders, the wording of the article never once included the word "sin."

Whatever did become of sin? And whatever did become of guilt? In part, what was once called sin has moved into the category of crime—the crime of theft, the crime of murder—and crime is a legal matter. In part, what was once called sin, like certain sexual deviations, has become recognized as symptomatic of emotional disorder, and pathology is a matter for doctors. And in part, what used to be called sin, including arrogance, greed and stinginess, remained in the churches and the synagogues, but like other things religious, no one paid much attention to them. At the bottom line, sin was for the sanctuary and guilt was for criminals who committed crimes and for neurotics who only thought they did, and the word "sin" was heard nowhere in the world. Rarely is it heard downtown, hardly ever at dinner parties, and even in our homes, scarcely is it uttered except perhaps

226

when the bounds of a diet are being overstepped and a piece of chocolate cake becomes a sin.

And the truth be told, even in the synagogue, even in its natural habitat, the word is used with discreet reticence. Like anyone who is in the field of communications, rabbis look for words that will push buttons to open up the channels of communication between themselves and their congregation. Sin, we suspect, is, for many people, not one of those words, and not only because in the world outside the word has become so empty but because in here, perhaps, the word may be too full and too real, too threatening. Because if it is truly for real, sin implies guilt, and guilt produces discomfort, and discomfort is not what many people want when they come to a sanctuary. They come here to feel better and not to feel worse, and they turn off the receiving instrument when the subject turns to sin.

And even more, the awareness of sin, by definition, is directed to the very moral center of my moral being, not to some peripheral quirk but to the most basic feelings of the person that I am. And yet, in our day-to-day lives, the lifestyle for which many of us have opted steers clear of that center. We play the games that people play, we jockey for position, we show and tell, we live as what Martin Buber calls "image persons," and we avoid the center of our beings. Only when life hits hard, for good or for ill, only when we stand at a graveside, or at a moment of true love, or at the crib of a newborn child, when we stand naked and defenseless against the truth of life, only then, perhaps, despite our "image selves," do we establish some contact with our true feelings. But even then, only for an instant, before we start playing the games again. It will often happen, in the discussion of a personal problem with someone, that the question that most often catches him or her short is the question, "But how do you feel about it?" Without that question and without the answer, there can be no talk of sin, no guilt, no atonement, no journey of these next ten days. Without that question and some answer to it, the word "sin" will have to stay cold in the prayer book.

But there is reason to believe that this Rosh HaShanah might be different. Life this year has hit us hard with blow after blow, beginning with the Yom Kippur War and its reawakening of concern for the survival and safety of the State of Israel, continuing with the darkening shadow of Watergate, which is still not dispelled, and then the lowering boom of economic uncertainty, which has not yet begun to lift. This is the year that was and, in many respects, should not have been. We are concerned for the present, for the future, for the quality of life, and that very concern has brought us closer to our own feelings, to the awareness of a center to our beings, and perhaps we are more ready this year to take the journey that begins with the word "sin."

This Rosh HaShanah may be different because for the first time in our lifetime, for the first time in the history of our country, a president has resigned. A leader of a people has betrayed the responsibility of his office. He retreated into his Oval Office and isolated himself from the people he had been elected to lead. He lied to us for the purposes of his own power and position; for the purpose of his own self-protection, he deceived us.

Some may call it a crime, which it was. Some may call it pathological, which it may have been. But mostly it was a sin, a *cheit*, a turning of the back on the moral God and on the moral fiber of the nation and the people. It was a turning of the back on his own moral self. We have seen up close what a sin is and what a sin can do. We have recognized, firsthand, how insightful the ancient rabbis were when they depicted sin as a visitor who at first comes for a brief stay but then, if you allow him even a night's lodging, will want to stay longer and eventually will become the master of the house.

The journey begins with a word, and each one of us begins with his own dossier of sins: all the ways we have turned against the moral God and our moral selves; all the little and big hurts we have inflicted upon our wives, our husbands, our children, our friends, ourselves; all the ways we have isolated ourselves in the "oval office."

A president of the United States was condemned by his own recorded words. The journey of these ten days begins with the playback of our own recorded words and our own recorded deeds of the past year. And who can stand up under such a barrage? Our spirits are bowed as we say, *Chatanu*, "We have sinned": not simply, "We have made mistakes," not simply, "We have committed errors," but *Chatanu*, "We have sinned."

And then we say, *Asham'nu*, "We are guilty."

Dr. Menninger tells of the strange character who stood in Chicago's Loop and every few minutes raised his finger accusingly at some passerby. "Guilty!" the man would cry, and the response of the accused was almost eerie. One man turned to his companion and said, "How did he know?"

And on the journey of Yom Kippur, we say, *Asham'nu*, "We are guilty": not the destructive guilt that lies buried in some corner of the psyche, not the neurotic guilt that rages far out of proportion to the sin, but good, healthy, regenerative, constructive guilt that moves a person to soothe the hurt and to change his way and to raise his bowed head and thus leads him to higher levels of moral responsibility.

And finally, t'shuvah, the "turning back": not to escape punishment, not because the fires of hell are burning, not even to remove a stain from one's soul, but because it is not right that a child should be far from his father, not right that a man or woman should be so removed from the center of his or her being.

We are told that a king's son was a distance of a hundred days' journey from his father. His friends said to him, "Return to your father." "I cannot," he answered. "It's too far." His father said to him, "Go as far as you are able, and I shall come the rest of the way to you."

We go as far as we are humanly able. We make the amends that can be made and bring with us the two words that have all but been banished from the language of the heart, the two words that children are sometimes forced to say by their parents, the two words that husbands and wives say to each other when they will not let the day end in anger. Bring with you the words "I'm sorry." Bring them with the broken fragments of your heart. And when the shofar will blow its final call at the end of Yom Kippur, we shall know that we are forgiven, that we have been pardoned. We shall know that we have come home to our moral God and our moral selves.

Only one condition: There can be no shortcuts on the journey. Just as those who have experienced the loss of a loved one must endure the pain of loneliness before moving on to the strength of new companionship, so there can be no forgiveness without the painful journey, without *Chatanu*, "We have sinned," and without *Asham'nu*, "We are guilty and we are sorry." No forgiveness without that journey, not even for a former president of the United States. It was a disservice to Richard M. Nixon that he was never allowed to say, *Chatati*, "I have sinned," and *Asham'ti*, "I am guilty," and that he will never feel the burden lifted from his own soul. For his own sake, he should have said it.

The journey begins tonight. It continues tomorrow morning and for these next ten days. May we say the words and feel the feelings, and may God give us strength for the homeward journey.

Amen.

Rosh HaShanah 1974/5735

The Plight of a Liberal

It was something of a stroke of genius that our ancestors assigned the blowing of the shofar such a central place in the experience of these High Holy Days.

There is something very Jewish about its earthy sound, the way it pierces through all of our layers of sophistication and stirs us on the level of our own visceral selves, just as these High Holy Days and the prayer book and the music all aim at our basic, essential visceral selves.

And there's something very Jewish about the way in which all of us take such obvious pride in the accomplishment of the shofar blower, including those who do not know him personally. The very fact that he could make such a sound come out of such a horn is proof that one person at least has met the challenge, and what are these High Holy Days about if not about challenge and our response?

And what is most Jewish about the shofar is the message that our ancestors attached to its various sounds. First, that there's a God in the world and in our lives, a Jewish conviction that continually runs the risk of being forgotten. And then, according to the prayer book, the shofar bids us and our children never to forget that we are of the stock of Abraham, that we inherit Abraham's promise to God that we would be God's deputies to the world, that we would show the world what it means to live as a community that is aware of a God that we did not create and conscious of a higher law that we ourselves did not legislate.

And finally, the prayer book announces *t'ki-ah g'dolah*, the "great blast," the promise and the plan for that great day in the future when all humanity, conscious of God and conscious of His law, will stand together at God's holy mountain.

The shofar says it all: There's a God and a people and a plan to improve the world, to bring it closer to that great and wonderful day.

And if I understand my fellow Jews correctly, I suspect that even those who have trouble hearing the first sound, who struggle with the Jewish conviction about God, who for their own reasons may even have rejected a belief in God—I suspect that they, too, hear and respond to the other sounds of the shofar. I suspect that they still have this sense of belonging to a community whose historic destiny it is to reach out with concern for the world and move history in the direction of that great and wonderful day. They may reject God, but they hold on to the people and the plan. They are those Jews whom Leonard Fein described when he said that they had a wonderful way of accepting the commands of the God in whom they do not believe.

With the God and with the people and with the plan, we brought our message to the world. And two thousand years ago, when Christianity tried to drown out the sound of our shofar with its own messianic plan, we refused. And about fourteen hundred years ago, when Mohammed tried to drown us out with his message and his plan, we refused. The shofar kept sounding, and the only times the sound was muffled was when we ourselves turned away from the world—the times when we were so beaten down, so threatened, so jeopardized in our own survival that we had to turn all of our attention inward to garner our own strength and mobilize our own defense against the threats and the jeopardy.

You could almost chart it on a graph. At those times in history when the Jewish people was relatively secure in the larger community, then we were out in the world with our master plan and with our voice of moral conscience. Then the overriding question was, "Is it good for humanity?" And at those moments when the clouds darkened over, when our sense of security was fragile, at those moments of jeopardy, then our overriding question was: "Is it good for the Jews?"

The remarkable fact was that even in the darkness, when the shofar was silenced to the outside world, we still sounded the *t'ki-ah g'dolah* in the synagogue because, in our heart of hearts, we knew that we would not resign from humanity, even though we were taking a leave of absence. In our heart of hearts, we knew that we could not abandon the plan permanently, though we were suspending it temporarily. Some day, when the climate would be more congenial, some day, we would come back.

And that day did come on these American shores, where the Jew felt at home more than he had felt in any place before. And nowhere as much as here did the Jew immerse himself in the affairs of society for *tikkun olam*, for "the improvement of the world." Nowhere did he make more contributions to the welfare of the community and involve himself in the process of social change. Nowhere else did the term "Jewish-Liberal" come off as one hyphenated word, even though there have been Jews who would not accept such a badge of identity (and the number has increased of late).

As one who still counts himself in the old ranks, I would share with you where at least one such Jewish-Liberal finds himself at the beginning of the Jewish year 5738.

He finds himself together with a lot of other people beset by the problem of definition. A recent issue of *Commentary* magazine was devoted exclusively to the question of who is a Liberal and who is a Conservative, and the opinion of several was that the lines between the two have become so blurred that even the words have lost their meaning. But as one who calls himself a Jewish-Liberal, I believe that the differences are very real.

A Liberal is different from a Conservative because the Conservative is intent upon keeping the system more or less intact even though that system may admittedly supply favoritism for some and deprivation for others. Whatever changes are in order should come slowly and gradually with a minimum of government participation. If the deprived are intent upon improving their lot, they should do so in the traditional manner of free competition in the open market, without the interference of the government, without government making up for their deprivation by infringing upon the rights and liberties of the rest of the population. Thus speaks the Conservative.

But the Liberal is also different from the Radical on his left because the Radical advocates the complete overhaul and sometimes the overthrow of the existing system. A Radical has no problem with simply taking away the privileges from the more or less favored and giving them to the more or less deprived.

The Liberal places himself between these two positions. He believes that the system should neither be kept intact nor does he favor its overthrow; rather he believes in locating those places in the system that have fostered inequity and in correcting that inequity. He does not agree with the Conservative that government should keep hands off, but he does believe that government's participation should be guided by concern for the rights and liberties of everyone, and not just those who have been deprived.

And because he is in the middle of those two positions, the Liberal is constantly weighing, balancing and struggling to discover on any given issue—whether it be the freedom of the press or abortion or capital punishment—where between these two fixed positions he can find a proper balance.

But if we go back twenty-five and thirty years to the early days of the Civil Rights Movement, Jewish-Liberals, including most of the national Jewish organizations, did not then feel the pull that the Liberal feels today. There was not yet on the scene a radical position to push us from the other side, and we knew exactly where we stood. We stood for *tikkun olam*, for the improvement of the world, for the removal of any restriction in our society that deprived any human being, solely on the basis of his skin color, of a job or an education or a place at the restaurant counter or a seat in the front of the bus. We agitated for change together with all other Liberals, black and white, and change did come, and the shofar rang out loudly and clearly.

But with the emergence of the Radical group within the black community in the 1960s, a new voice began to be heard, a voice that was often impatient and angry. It said that change was coming too slowly. It said that to remove long-standing restrictions was not enough, that ways had to be found to make it up to the black community for all those years of deprivation, that ways had to be found to bring them to a level where they could at least be in the running with the white community in the open market of free competition.

And it was here that the Liberal was confronted with his conflict. Because while he acknowledged that the members of the black community had been held back, if the only way to catch them up and to give them jobs or privileges was to take those jobs and privileges away from individual whites, if the only way to appease the black community in Ocean Hill—Brownsville was to replace white teachers with black teachers, then what happens to the principle of personal, indi-vidual liberty as it applies to those white teachers?

And for the Jewish-Liberal, the conflict was even more serious because the white teachers who happened to be holding those jobs in Ocean Hill—Browns-ville were Jews, and the community of Forest Hills that Mayor Lindsay chose as the site for a mammoth, low-income, largely black housing project was a Jewish community (with many Jewish-Liberals), raising the specter of street crime and mugging. And they understood what Mayor Rizzo of Philadelphia meant when he said that a Conservative is a Liberal who had been mugged the night before.

As a Liberal, he felt the usual conflict, but as a Jewish-Liberal, he felt a threat to his own self and his own fellow Jews, and he sensed that the clouds overhead were beginning to darken. Add to this the constant crisis and danger to the State of Israel that to the American Jew was yet another threat to survival. And add to this a new mood of ethnicity in America, with each group openly and avowedly pursuing its own self-interest. All of these came together, and from many quarters of the Jewish community—from Jewish newspapers, from pulpits, from intellec-tual journals, from national Jewish organizations—from many quarters came the warning that we had better concentrate on Jewish survival and not worry so much about the rest of the world. The time had come, they said, to concentrate on the question, "Is it good for the Jews?" And so we did, because for these past five years, the voice of Jewish liberalism has been silent and still.

And I suppose we could let it go at that were it not for that nagging shofar blast that pierces to our visceral selves on every Rosh HaShanah, reminding us that a temporary leave of absence should not become a permanent resignation from the ranks of humanity. There's still the God we know, there's still the people we know, but what about the plan?

And I suppose we could let it go at that if we were not about to be confronted, perhaps in these next weeks, with the most severe confrontation ever between the Jewish community and the black community. It involves the issue now before the Supreme Court concerning Allen Bakke, who was refused admission to the University of California Medical School because sixteen places out of one hundred were being held for minority students, even though their academic qualifications were inferior to those of Mr. Bakke. The position of the black community is that of the radicals of the sixties (though black moderates have joined the position): that groups that have been disadvantaged in the past are entitled to special consideration, to affirmative action; without such consideration, they could never compete successfully with the rest of the population.

Those on the other side argue that affirmative action may legitimately be applied to recruit black candidates, to provide programs that would help them qualify for admission, but the point at which admission itself is granted not according to the individual qualifications and merit of the applicant but on the basis of a certain number of places reserved for a particular group, at that point the so-called affirmative action program has become a quota system, which by any other name is still a quota system. And no one knows better than the Jew the curse of a quota system, because what then prevents any group from claiming a number of admissions according to its proportion of the general population? And the result for Jews, for example, would be 3 percent, not because the rest of the people are trying to keep Jews out, which was the case in the thirties, but because they're trying to get themselves in. A quota by any other name is still a quota.

It is a classic example of the Liberal conflict. On the one side, a group of Americans who have been deprived of their place in the sun and in college student bodies. And on the other side, the rights of individuals who, though not deprived as a group, may very well have struggled through their own individual deprivations so that they could line up before the door of that medical school or college faculty or whatever, only to have the door closed because of people who have been allowed to jump the line. It is the classic liberal conflict, not between good and evil but between two principles, both of which claim validity, between social equality and individual, personal liberty.

Which is why, in these next months, it is imperative for Jews and Jewish organizations that oppose the university's affirmative action program to take their position not only as Jews totally preoccupied with what's good for the Jews, but as liberals who struggle with the conflict and must eventually come out on one side or the other. If Jews oppose the university's affirmative action program (and I count myself in that number), it is not only because it keeps out Jews but because a quota system violates the American democratic principle of individual merit as the requirement for school admission or any other position.

But when we take that stand, if we believe our own liberalism, we should not stop with our opposition but should be pledging ourselves to *tikkun olam*—to the problem of soaring unemployment in the black community, to the curse of the urban ghetto, and to whatever else it will take to bring closer the day when young blacks who aspire to medical school will be able to make it in the way that everybody else does.

Nor do I believe that these Jewish-Liberals who, after their own struggle, come out on the other side and favor the university's admissions policy should be forced into silence for fear of being accused by the Jewish community of betrayal or treason to the Jewish cause. The voice that struggles with moral questions deserves to be heard on both sides of the issue, because when it comes to other issues on which our administration in Washington must take a position, such as the issue of the settlements on the West Bank, which the Arabs have tried to present as a strictly moral question with Jews as the immoral ones, we must be able to present our case not only as a group seeing to its own interests but as a group that, by its own record, is sensitive to moral questions and moral conflicts. And when we come with our own moral opposition to the PLO's strategy of destruction and our own moral demand for this United States to guarantee the security of free, democratic societies such as the State of Israel, we must bring with us not only a rhetoric of moral concern but a record of moral concern that by precedent recognizes the moral component of complex political and social questions, such as the admissions policy of the University of California.

The shofar we have stored on the shelf is getting dusty. The voice of conscience with which the Jew has tried to improve the world has been too quiet. And the world is waiting, with all its pains and all its hopes, the world is waiting outside our Jewish door for the sound of the shofar, for the God and the people and the plan, waiting for us to open the door.

Amen.

Rosh HaShanah 1977/5738

Religion and Politics

Some weeks ago, a seminar was conducted by the Synagogue Council of America on the theme "Judaism Confronts Modernity." According to the account in the press, the discussion soon turned to this season's topic of controversy: "Religion and Politics." Since a number of rabbis were present, they naturally discussed the question of whether such a theme was a proper topic during the observance of these High Holy Days. Some who argued in favor of it simply declared that the issue was so germane and had such implications for the Jewish community that for a rabbi not to talk about it would be to default on his responsibility to his congregation. Those who argued against it pleaded on behalf of the spiritual and introspective themes of these days into which a discussion of so controversial and so political a topic might only become an unwarranted intrusion.

I did not attend that meeting, but since a rabbi and the members of his or her congregation are entitled to be apprised of each others' thoughts and feelings on an entire range of subjects, and since one of the operating principles of this congregation has always been freedom of expression for the rabbis in the pulpit and freedom of expression for the congregation, be it in the temple bulletin or during Friday night *Oneg Shabbat* discussions or in personal conversation, I share my own sentiments on the question of religion and politics.

My answer actually begins twenty-two years ago when I was being interviewed for the position of rabbi at Westchester Reform Temple. One of the questions addressed to me during the interview was what sermon topics I had chosen for my previous High Holy Days in our congregation in New Jersey. When I responded that on Yom Kippur—and please remember, this was 1962—that I had discussed the issue of civil rights (which was the political hot potato of those years), the questioner asked me whether I considered such a topic appropriate to the spiritual ambience that Yom Kippur attempts to achieve. My answer then becomes the starting point for my sermon tonight, namely, that the issue of civil rights, with all of its complexities and all of its implications, rendered it one of the most spiritual topics I could imagine.

I do have a profound respect for the spiritual thrust of these days. They do take us to the gateway of our own souls. They are, in truth, for each of us individually a private journey to our uncertainties and disappointments, to our loneliness and our fragility. The journey of these days does take us to the utter truth of who and what we are as we stand in the presence of our God. And when the shofar sounds, it rings the clarion call of our hope: that with God's help, the fragility will be bolstered and our course will be set straight again. Thus is it called "The Season of Our Renewal."

As a Jew, like all of you, I have other business with God, however we conceive of God. This business is not private but public, not individual but corporate. For in that long ago day of history when we began our career as a people, the charter of our incorporation sent us out into the world of kings and their kingdoms with a divine blueprint for a moral and ethical society. So our question today does not inquire of the traditional Jewish position on religion and politics because that mandate has always taken us into the world of the governors and the governed. Our question today—and it is this question that has sparked the controversy—our question is: What is America's position, our country's position, on religion and politics? We ask that question with loving concern because this nation is the place where we as Jews, just like Protestants as Protestants and Catholics as Catholics and others as others, have all found a welcome place to be what we are.

Part of the problem in answering the question—and the cause of so much confusion on the issue—is, I would suggest, simply a matter of vocabulary. The word "religion" is an umbrella term. It refers not only to specific religions with their sectarian doctrines and their sectarian agendas but also to a more universal religious climate that is shared by most of those sectarian religions and that acknowledges a Divine Being and a divine moral law that make claim upon the social fabric of the human community. "Religion" is one word with two meanings—at least.

The word "politics" is also an umbrella term. To be sure, the word "politics" designates the arena of contest for positions of power in the conduct of government. But also, to be sure, the word "politics" designates the arena of debate and discussion on those public policies that have a moral impact upon the social fabric of the human community. Issues like freedom and equality and poverty and peace are political issues. The word "politics" has two meanings—at least.

It was to the great credit of the founders of this nation and those who followed them that they did not resort to umbrellas but understood the double meanings of both words. The spirit of universal religion was so much a part of them and their history that they could not conceive of the grand design of this nation without it. We would pursue our national destiny "under Divine Providence." We would be a nation, as George Washington stated in his farewell address, where morality cannot prevail "in exclusion of religious principles." Political issues and universal religion are a good mix.

But the founders of this nation also understood the other meanings of those words. They understood the meaning of sectarian religion. For just as they granted every sectarian group the freedom to establish its own community without government interference, so they let it be known that no specific religion had the right to seek special privilege that would give it an established position or official status in the political structure of government power. They knew only too well from their own history across the ocean how any established religion could wreak mischief and havoc upon the free spirit of this new nation. In the words of Henry Steele Commager: "They wanted peace and harmony in a society that was dangerously heterogeneous"; and so they established this line of separation, or as Jefferson called it, "a wall of separation," between the state and church. Thank God they did, because in America there has never been a religious war. Conflict, yes, but war, no. Political power and sectarian religion are a bad mix.

Thus our country's philosophy of politics and religion until this day: that every American is entitled to his own religious belief and is free to affiliate with a sectarian religious community of his choice, and that freedom includes the right not to believe and not to affiliate. In turn, each of those communities has the right to communicate its own teachings not only to the members of its own community but also in the public forum, especially when its own moral teachings relate to public issues and public policies. The Civil Rights Movement began in the religious communities of America. The anti-Vietnam War Movement began in the religious communities of America.

And if, on any given issue, different sectarian groups or groups that have nothing to do with religion have come to different positions on the same issue, then every one of them deserves a hearing in the public forum. It is the meaning of pluralism; it is the meaning of balance; it is the meaning of what jurist Leo Pfeffer calls "Creeds in Competition." It is, in my perception, the legitimate conjunction of religion and politics.

But when it happens that the balance is upset, when it happens that a sectarian group tries to inveigle its way into the political domain not simply with an issue that it considers essential but with its whole agenda, to have that agenda endorsed by political powers that be, then we have begun to cross the line. And when, conversely, an official in that political structure of government reciprocates the invitation, then the line has been overstepped. Then religion and politics have joined hands in the illegitimate conjunction of the two. It is that trespass that demands the separation of church and state, that calls for a wall. Most of the time it is a line rather than a wall. It is only when the line is overstepped that the spirit of America raises the wall.

If I understand the philosophy correctly, when Archbishop John O'Connor declared that he could not see how a Catholic in good conscience could vote for a candidate who supported abortion, I would suggest that he was not overstepping the line. If, in the conviction of the archbishop and his church, abortion constitutes a moral transgression that taints the society that allows it, then he has the perfect right to advocate his idea in the free marketplace of creedal ideas, just as every other religious group and nonreligious group has the right to deliver its message that the "right to choose" is of higher moral rank than any other consideration in the matter of abortion.

However, when a sectarian group like the Catholic Church then tries to bear down with the authority of the church upon persons in public political office, to pressure them to promote that doctrine, then religion has moved into the politics of power, and then we have begun to muddy the line.

The alarm mostly goes off when a sectarian group like the Moral Majority, with an agenda that embraces not only issues of public morality but theological doctrine, including its avowed intent to Christianize America—when that group, with its own political playing cards, seeks alliance with the person in the highest position of power in our nation, and when the person occupying that highest position of power responds favorably to such a liaison with a measure of courting of his own, then the line has been erased, the alarm goes off, and the people of America must raise the wall of separation. When my president joins hands with the Moral Majority, what happens to "creeds in competition" as one is selected over the other? What happens to the basic peace and harmony our founders intended if my president can brand me as sinful because I do not endorse prayer in the public schools, especially when my own opposition to that prayer is to avoid the very factionalism that my government is expected to prevent? What happens to my freedom of religious expression when my president embraces a creed that vows to Christianize this country? Who then will protect my rights to be a Jew? Who will protect the right of a Catholic or the right of a Protestant or the right of another? And if they need some evidence about the mischief caused when religion and government enter their illicit liaison, we can tell them about the State of Israel and what mischief the Orthodox Party has created. How do you redraw a line that is muddied? How do you reinforce a crumbling wall?

Do you know what I fear? I fear that the whole issue will quiet down, that it will continue to be deftly defused by able speech writers, and that the headlines will go away. What will not go away is the unflagging zeal of sectarian groups and their political allies in high positions of power to project sectarian doctrines into the bloodstream of American life with the imperious claim that they are upgrading the spiritual level of that life. The tragedy would be when some child in a classroom in America will listen to someone else's voluntary prayer that is alien to him, and that first child will say, "Maybe I don't belong here." The tragedy would be if we let it happen.

You know what else I fear? That our overwhelming concern for this illicit mixing of religion and politics may deflect us from its legitimate domain. When I read that most of America is on a high because we've never had it so good, and then, in the midst of our high:

I learn that 1 million Americans in 1983 dropped below the poverty line (an annual income of $10,178 for a family of four) and that the total number of Americans below that poverty line is 35.3 million...

I learn that as a result of our national budget and tax revision, householders who earned less than $10,000 suffered a loss of $270 and those earning $80,000 or more enjoyed an increase of $7,000...

I learn of patients discharged from mental institutions and sent into the community only to discover that the social services and health services that were to help them readjust to society had been cut off from that community...

I discover John Galbraith's statement that over the centuries, the fortunate "have managed to get the impoverished out of their thoughts and off their consciences"...

I read all of that and realize that while we're still on our high we need the rightful mixing of religion and politics.

When we read all of that, I know that we need, in communities like ours, the voice of the prophet Amos when he spoke 2,500 years ago:

> *You that lie upon beds of ivory,*
> *and stretch yourselves on your couches,*
> *and eat the lambs out of your flock,*
> *and strum upon your musical instruments,*
> *and drink wine in bowls,*
> *and anoint yourselves with ointments:*
> *But you are not grieved,*
> *you don't feel pain*
> *for the hurt of my people.*

When I read all of that, I know that we need the wisdom of that Talmudic rabbi in whose household there worked an impoverished maid. The rabbi's wife caught her pilfering some food and in outrage grabbed hold of the maid and pulled her out of the house to take her to court. As the two of them were on their way, the rabbi started after them. Whereupon his wife said, "No, you stay here. I don't need you to plead my case." To which the rabbi responded, "That's not why I'm going. I am going to plead her case."

That is our hope for the New Year: that this debate on religion and politics will stir us from our beds of ivory and that our voice will speak for those whose voice is not listened to.

This is our hope: to let our politics be inspired by our religion and not by our pocketbooks. Then, in truth, it will have been a fitting spiritual topic for these Holy Days, for this season of renewal.

When the shofar calls, may our fragility be bolstered and our course be set straight again.

O Lord, our God, renew us.

Amen.

Rosh HaShanah 1984/5745

Sacred Voting

Two hundred years ago, in 1788, the struggle was already underway. There were five thousand Jews on these shores, most of them the children and grandchildren of those who had fled the oppression of the Old World for the freedom of the New.

And here they were, after the Declaration of Independence, after the Revolution, at the very time of the Constitution. Here they were, many of them citizens of this new nation, with a citizen's right to practice his religion (which to the Jew was a blessing) and a citizen's right to pursue his economic interest (which to the Jew was a blessing). But not yet all of them with a citizen's right to hold public office or a citizen's right to vote, not yet a citizen first class. Because while any state that joined the Union after 1787 was required by act of Congress to grant full political equality to all of its citizens, the thirteen original states, by constitutional provision, were granted the right to make their own political decisions for their own citizens on the matter of political rights. So the struggle was on, state by state, with Madison and Jefferson and the Jews themselves in the front lines. The last holdout was the State of New Hampshire, which did not grant full political equality to its citizens until the year 1876.

So for those of you in our congregation whose forebears came to this country in the mid-1800s from Germany and Central Europe and Western Europe, the victory was well on its way. For those of you in this congregation whose forebears were in that flood tide of immigration from Eastern Europe at the end of the 1800s and the beginning of the 1900s, the victory was already total. Those forebears may have traveled steerage, they may have sweated in the sweatshops on the Lower East Side, but come Election Day, they were first class.

It was the promise come true. Now for the first time in centuries, the Jew had become the participant and not the victim of the ruling system. In the memoirs of some of those Jews on the Lower East Side, they write about the simple act of casting a ballot. Many of them would go to the election booths in suit and tie as though to the synagogue, as though this act were a blessing from God, as though the obligation to perform this act was a mitzvah, a sacred obligation in the voting booth, in the new Land of Promise.

I share this glimpse of our history and our civic pride because of something very upsetting that I recently learned, that calls for the attention of our own congregation: that of four million Jews who are eligible to vote on November 8, one million are not registered to vote. What until recent times was a figure of 90 percent of eligible Jewish voters who actually voted could now be 75 percent or even less (because it will include some of those already registered who will not vote).

That upsetting news calls especially for the attention of congregations like ours, because the largest group of unregistered Jewish voters is between the ages of eighteen and twenty-five, of which this congregation has a goodly number. And since our list of college students' names and addresses will not be compiled in time for the registration deadline of October 15, I turn to those students who are here—and we have to tell you the holiday is always better when you are here—to accept this plea. And I turn to the parents of those college students who are not here to urge them to assume their role as full-fledged American citizens and do their mitzvah as full-fledged Jews.

I have shared this glimpse into our history and our civic pride for still another reason: that however we individually will make our decisions on November 8, all these months of choosing a president and his party to be the leaders of our nation are a living example of what I tried to suggest last night: how the secular and the sacred can come into touch with each other in the every day of our own lives. Because beneath all those shells in the secular world of politics, beneath the hype of the nominating conventions, beneath the rhetoric of campaign speeches, beneath the posturing before the TV cameras, beneath some of those shells are sacred sparks that glow with value and meaning for us as Jews, as American Jews. And if we can find a way to release those sparks, they may even cast some light on our way through this journey of the High Holy Days and may even cast some light on our separate, individual journeys into the polling booth on November 8.

As example: Whenever there are issues in politics that affect Jewish security and Jewish well-being, we as Jews then move not only into the secular but into the domain of the sacred. "Thou shalt survive" is the eleventh Jewish commandment: between God (however we conceive of God) and us, from Abraham to us, from Sinai to us, from Auschwitz to us. What happens to us as *am kadosh*—as the "sacred people"—to help us or hurt us, what happens to the Land of Israel from its inside or its outside to help it or hurt it, to strengthen it or weaken it, is for us Jews not only a matter of secular politics but also a matter of sacred survival.

Therefore, when I say in my concern for Jewish well-being that I am concerned about Jesse Jackson's stance on Jewish issues and the influence that stance may have in the ranks of the Democratic Party, the Democrats tell me not to worry. They tell me that in fact Jackson did not become vice president, that in fact Jackson backed off from his insistence on a strong pro-Arab plank in the Democratic national platform.

They tell me not to worry, but I worry. As a Jew, I worry that a person with all of Jackson's social vision, which I applaud, and all of his influence in the black community in motivating the black voter, which I applaud, with all of this, he did nothing to combat the ugly anti-Semitic outbursts in his own home community of Chicago. As a Jew, I worry that Jesse Jackson is a friend of Israel's enemies. As a Jew with all those other Jews who have been allies of the black community, through all these decades, I worry that he does not see me in his social vision as a stripe in his Rainbow Coalition or as a patch in his social quilt. I worry about Jesse Jackson, with his influence in the ranks of the Democratic Party, that he may not be an enemy of anti-Semitism.

And then, when I say to the Republicans (and you knew that was coming) out of my concern for Jewish well-being that I am worried about the Christian Right and Pat Robertson and Jerry Falwell, not only in the ranks but in the power places of the Republican Party, they tell me not to worry because after all, Robertson and Falwell and the Christian Right are strong supporters of the State of Israel.

They tell me not to worry, and I worry. Because what Jew has not learned from the pages of our history that Jewish security and Jewish well-being in any society depend on the measure of pluralism in that society, the willingness of that society to accommodate diversity, the guarantees by that society to the minority that they will not be second-class citizens because they do not belong to the majority? I worry about the Christian Right because all of its preachments, which are given generous hearing in the power places of the political parties, those preachments are the exact opposite of a pluralistic and diverse America, the kind of America in which we Jews have always prospered and always thrived. I worry about the Christian Right in their vision of a Christian America that is Christian and only Christian, public school prayers and all.

The most recent example of my concern: How did the spokesmen for the Christian Right vent their outrage against the film *The Last Temptation of Christ?* The film was written by a Christian. It was directed by a Christian. But because it was produced by a company that had Jews in the executive suite, who is at fault for the blasphemy? We are. I have my own theory: that according to the Christian fundamentalist doctrine, whenever their Christ is attacked, whether on the ancient cross or on the Hollywood screen, we Jews are held responsible. Unless that movie is banned, they warn, the Jewish community will see a surge of anti-

Semitism. Unless that movie is banned, they threaten, the Christian Right may very well reconsider its friendly support of Israel. And for friends like that, there was no need to leave the Old World for the New. With influence in the government like that, what happens to the promise in the Land of Promise?

I know that Jewish leaders in both parties have voiced their concern for Jewish well-being. But too often, the complaint is lodged only against the other party. If all that Jewish Democrats can do is harp on the Republican Christian Right and not on the problem of Jesse Jackson, and if all that the Jewish Republicans can do is harp on Jesse Jackson and not on the Christian Right, then all they are both doing is playing their campaign games, their secular games. What they could do, what influential members of this congregation can do in the chambers of their own party, what we in the ranks can do is let our voice be heard, is take up the sacred cause of Jewish survival and lift the shell and let the spark glow.

Another intersection between secular and sacred. When November 8 is over—should it prove like Election Days gone by—the poll watchers will once again report their curious finding: that of all the religious and ethnic groups in America that have made their way up the economic ladder, there is only one group that votes not with its pocketbook but with its compassion, one group of haves that votes traditionally for the have-nots, one group that never forgets what it was like to be slaves in the land of Egypt. Whether we learned it at our parents' feet or at our Passover seder or in our religious school classrooms or in the sanctuaries of our synagogues, we Jews have this stubborn streak to make this world better and not just ourselves richer, to feed the hungry and not just stuff ourselves with the fat of the land. And every time a Jew votes on Election Day for the hungry and the homeless and the defenseless in God's world, the spark glows again. And this year again, God willing.

And on a totally personal level of this election campaign, one more spark, almost in prison under its shell, that will need our most vigorous effort to pry it loose.

Early in the campaign, an allegation was directed against one of the candidates that he had sought and had received psychiatric treatment. The candidate denied the allegation. His denial was corroborated, and the incident was over.

But then came a spate of articles and comments by observers of the Washington scene. They all said the same thing: that the mere fact of a political figure seeking psychiatric help was enough to destroy that person's political career. No one, they said, not the press and not the public, bothers to determine how serious the problem is or whether the problem will hamper that person's exercise of his official duties. Nobody bothers to consider that the public-at-large might be served better by a leader who has been helped to work through his personal problem than by one who must suffer silently with it. There is only one guiding principle, they said, in the words of a former presidential hopeful: "My advice to politicians from the third grade on is, Don't go near a psychiatrist. And if you do, don't let it be known; it's the kiss of death."

And thus our personal question for the sacred journey of these High Holy Days as we tug at the shell to pry it loose: How crazy can we get in our secular world? To be successful all of the time? To produce all of the time? To perform all of the time? And now, to be perfect, without flaw, without a problem?

I know sons and daughters in this congregation, some of them little and some of them already grown, who are still suffering because they have not yet climbed the impossible ladder of perfection that their parents set for them or they set for themselves. Rabbi Harold Schulweis wrote that there is a distinctive form of Jewish child abuse that is called "Being Disappointed": disappointed when their child doesn't get into the right school; disappointed in how the child dresses or how the child's hair looks; disappointed that their child isn't perfect, that they themselves are not perfect.

And these High Holy Days call out to us, plead with us, to pry that shell loose, to stand before the God of truth with the naked, sacred truth about ourselves: that as human beings and finite creatures, we are capable of being good but not of being perfect; that we are in the image of God but not God; that with all the virtue in being strong, we also have to make room for being weak without branding ourselves as weaklings. With all the virtue in achieving success, we have to make room now and again for failing, without branding ourselves as failures. With all the virtue in being right, we, as children of God, have to know that we have been entrusted with three of the most sacred words in the English language: "I was wrong." Because if we can't say that, why are we coming back next week for Yom Kippur?

Help us, O God, during the journey of these days to pry the shells loose. May the sparks glow with brightness. And may we be bearers of light:

for the sacred survival of our people;

for the sacred hope of Your humanity;

and for the sacred truth of our wonderful and imperfect children and our worthwhile and imperfect selves...

as we pray to you for the blessings of the New Year.

Amen.

Rosh HaShanah 1988/5749

I Am Seeking My Brothers

There is a scene in the Bible where Joseph, son of Jacob, is sent by his father to seek out his brothers in the field and then to bring word back to the father regarding their welfare. As Joseph begins his search, he is met by a stranger, who asks him: *Mah t'vakesh?* "What are you seeking?" And Joseph answers: *Et achai anochi m'vakesh*, "I am seeking my brothers."

It was with that same sense of purpose that Priscilla and I took leave at the beginning of last month for a two-week visit to the Union of South Africa. With four other rabbis and one other spouse, we went under the auspices of the World Union for Progressive Judaism, which many of you support, which is the umbrella organization for Reform congregations throughout the world. Our assignment was to visit and speak in various synagogues, to consult with the leaders and the members of the congregations and then, like Joseph, to bring back word. The second purpose, for all of us, was to learn as much as we could about the political unrest in that troubled land.

In many ways, the surroundings in which we found ourselves were little different from our own. The homes we visited and the lifestyle we observed could have been here in Westchester, with one noticeable difference: that most of the windows in those gracious suburban homes were barred, very decoratively, but they were still barred. And as you drove down the suburban streets, the lawns of those gracious homes were blocked from view because in front of every one of them was a high stone wall, wall after wall, a barricade of defense against whatever threat might lurk without, in that troubled country.

The entire Jewish community of South Africa numbers no more than 100,000, some say as few as 80,000, the majority of them of Lithuanian background. The number keeps dwindling because the number of those who leave the country keeps growing, especially among the younger generation from the twenties to the forties. Of the families we met during those two weeks, there was only one that had all of its young adult children still living in South Africa. One woman we met has one child living in Los Angeles and her other child in Sydney, Australia, at opposite ends of the world. The sons and daughters leave with the support and sometimes even at the urging of their parents because they can see

247

only a future that is gray with uncertainty, economically and politically. They leave because a nation in which segregation of blacks from whites is official policy is not a nation in which they want to live. They leave because they are unwilling to be conscripted into an army whose function it is to crush political dissent and to maintain the official system of racial apartheid. Most children leave, and most parents stay. As someone remarked, "We are becoming a country of mostly senior citizens." Parents stay behind because to leave means to start over in a strange place. To leave is to leave behind whatever capital they may have accumulated since by law they are not permitted to take it out of the country. To leave is to leave what has always been home and a lifestyle that they are unlikely to duplicate.

But some parents are leaving to go where their children and their grandchildren are because that's where they want to be. And some are still struggling with that decision. One of the most poignant evenings Priscilla and I spent was with a couple well into their sixties. One of their children is in Australia; the other is planning to go there. The family had lived in Rhodesia before and during the time it became Zimbabwe and thus came under black majority rule. And here they were in South Africa, with turmoil again in the offing. Here was the husband struggling to decide, and he shared with us the words that his wife had spoken to him that morning: "You have always been a person of decision. You have made your decisions, you have acted upon them, and even when they've turned out to be unwise, you have lived with them. Why is it, when it comes to this one—whether to stay or to leave—you are paralyzed by indecision?" And then he turned to us and said: "And my wife is absolutely right." And his eyes misted with his tears.

We were invited in Johannesburg to a meeting of the Jewish Board of Deputies, which is the South African counterpart of our Conference of Presidents of Major Jewish Organizations. We were inspired at that Johannesburg meeting by the high level of vigor in the Jewish community. Their Jewish youth movement is strong. Their participation in the Maccabiah sports events in Israel is a major community enterprise. Their financial support for Israel is the highest per capita of any Jewish community in the world.

And in another regard, an unhappy one, that meeting in Johannesburg could just as well have been in New York. Because there, as here, some of that Jewish vigor is dissipated by the rankling between Orthodox and Reform (except that there the Orthodox constitute 80 percent, the Reform 20 percent, with no Conservative Movement at all). Most of the laypeople I met, Orthodox (many of whom are not observant) and Reform, get along fine. The problem, I am embarrassed to admit, is among the rabbis. The problem in some communities is the doing of the Orthodox rabbis, who reject Reform Judaism as a legitimate Jewish expression. I was told of one prominent Orthodox rabbi who will not even appear on a public platform if a Reform rabbi is on the same platform. Oh, these Jews of ours!

But with strong Jewish pride, I bring back word to you that the Jewish community of South Africa, as an official body, through its Board of Deputies, has voiced its opposition and its protest against the nation's official policy of apartheid. (I would add that the leader of the Dutch Reformed Church, which is composed primarily of Afrikaners, who are the ruling political party, has urged his church body to take an official position against apartheid. Similarly, many citizens of British background have joined the Christian movements of protest.) With deep Jewish pride, I bring word to you that our synagogues and our sisterhoods in Johannesburg and Capetown and Durban and communities throughout the country are in the front lines of those who reach out to the black community. Their nursery schools enroll white children and black children. They provide programs of enrichment in black schools so that the boys and girls in those schools can rise above the low level of achievement that their otherwise inferior education imposes upon them. We spent time in those schools, including the special moment when a black teenager walked over to me and asked me what it was like to be a teacher in the United States. I tried to answer, and I asked her why she wanted to know. "Because," she said, "almost definitely, someday I am going to be a teacher!"

The crucial difference between their Jewish community and ours is the absence of their influence upon government policy. There is no Jewish influence in Pretoria, no Jewish lobby, as there is in Washington. There is no Jewish liaison to the president of South Africa, as there is in Washington. When the voice of the Jewish community speaks, it is listened to mostly by Jews. It is not heard by the party in power, which is the National Party, comprised mostly of the Afrikaners who are of Dutch origin, who themselves suffered under the British and who are now so zealous about maintaining their own power that they resist all external pressure, including that from the Jews and especially from the blacks.

We had gone to seek out our fellow Reform Jews, that 20 percent of the Jewish community. We had gone to seek out all our fellow Jews—Reform, Orthodox, Zionist—all of them. And all of them together are but 2 percent of the white community that numbers 5 million. And the white community of 5 million is but 14 percent of the total population of 35 million, which consists of 5 million whites, 28 million blacks and 2 million colored and Indian. A president of one of the congregations wistfully observed: "We Reform Jews are a minority within a minority within a minority." Add to that what one woman said to us after a Shabbat lunch: "We in South Africa are a pariah nation, but we Jews do the best we can. We pass resolutions, and we work for the blacks. We do the best we can." If you include her remarks in the calculation, then our Reform Jews in South Africa are a minority within a minority within a minority in a pariah nation. The word I bring back to you is the sadness of their isolation.

We loved the Jewish community of South Africa. We loved the warmth and the graciousness. We felt the vigor, and we felt the sadness of family separation and the sadness of isolation. And we felt the tension, the tension that is everywhere where Jews are, where everyone is.

And thus the second purpose of our journey: to see the troubled human landscape in that otherwise gloriously beautiful land.

The trouble, as universally perceived by whites and blacks, the root trouble is apartheid, established as official government policy in 1948 by the National Party, which is still the party in power. It was a policy that by successive legal statutes enforced strict separation of the races. No black could live in an area designated for whites, and all blacks who happened to live there were forced to leave in massive transfers of population euphemistically entitled "resettlement." Under the so-called Pass Laws, no black could even enter a white area without a special pass of permission. No black person could marry or have sexual relations with a white person. There were restaurants for blacks and restaurants for whites, hotels for blacks and hotels for whites, black beaches and white beaches, black schools and white schools, black public bathrooms and white public bathrooms. And as we ourselves realize from the dismal history of our own segregated South, the inferior facilities were considered good enough for the blacks. Apartheid, as someone said to us, is separate and unequal.

We talked about apartheid in the home of Helen Suzman, member of Parliament for thirty-six years, a Jew. For most of those years, from the beginning of her career, hers was the single prophetic voice against the evil and injustice of a system that she insisted would someday come back to haunt the nation, and it has. And now that her voice has been joined by a chorus, Helen Suzman bears the unofficial title of "Mother Africa."

In slight digression, I would share with you what happened on that unforgettable Sunday morning when we arrived promptly for our 10:30 appointment at her gracious suburban home, with bars on the windows. We were ushered into the lounge, where we waited until 10:35 and then 10:40—no Helen Suzman. Finally, at 10:45, we heard the outside door of the house open and close, and in walked Mother Africa with a cardboard box in her hand, and breathlessly she said, "There wasn't a biscuit in the house." Our intrepid leader had rushed to the bakery so that her guests could be fed. Mother Africa was also Jewish Mother Africa.

She told us that South Africa cannot survive apartheid. She told us of her lonely battle and of the continuing threats to her life by rabid segregationists. She told us of her visit to Nelson Mandela in prison and her plea to the Parliament that no resolution of the conflict can be on the horizon without including the Nelson Mandelas and the banned African National Congress and all the other voices of black protest. Her refrain was loud and clear: Apartheid is not only evil and unjust but will inflict a verdict of doom on that beautiful land and all of its people. Her words and her spirit on that memorable Sunday morning rang with the power of the Hebrew poet Saul Tchernichovsky:

> *By the passion of our spirit*
> *Shall our ancient bonds be shed.*
> *Let the soul be given freedom.*
> *Let the body have its bread.*

We also met with Afrikaners who are officials of the party and who also told us that apartheid is on its way out, by the decision of the very party that had devised it. One of them told us that a vital economy could not be sustained by the white population alone and that it made no sense for blacks who are needed for key positions in that economy to be barred from all of the other opportunities in the nation. He told us that the economy could not tolerate the billions of dollars that are spent each year on apartheid. He told us that were his own father, who had died ten years earlier, to return today, he would be astounded by the cataclysmic change. And he ticked off the list: how blacks and whites eat at the same restaurants, how they stay in the same hotels, how they swim on the same beaches, how the Pass Laws have been rescinded, how the intermarriage laws have been rescinded, how blacks move into certain white neighborhoods, against the law to be sure, but nobody enforces the law. While we were there, the press reported that 271 blacks had showed up at white hospitals for treatment, and they were treated. And in this week now ending, the city of Johannesburg made it legal for blacks and whites to use the same public transportation, which was not the case when we were there. With all of the concessions and all of the benefits, the official said, apartheid is on its way out. It just needs time.

The very next day, we had breakfast with a group of black business and professional men and women. I for one walked into that meeting with expectation that these were blacks who were making it up the economic ladder and had been co-opted by the white establishment. I expected to hear the party line. But what we heard instead was resentment and anger, polite and restrained, but anger. And no wonder, because in that room were black university graduates with specialized skills, and yet every one of them had to travel to Johannesburg that morning from their homes in the segregated black township of Soweto because they could not legally live in Johannesburg. And should one of them have accumulated enough capital to buy one of those elegant suburban homes, the only way he could do it was to have a white person buy it for him and then live there illegally.

We asked about the elections that were only a few weeks away, and to a person they said the elections were of no concern to them because by legal statute, no black in South Africa is permitted to vote in national elections. With all the campaign talk about the future of blacks in South Africa, the people around that breakfast table and their countrymen of black skin were the only ones who had no say in their own future. One woman said, "We're not interested in benefits. We're not interested in concessions. What we want is to vote. What we want is to participate in our own destiny. Time cannot wait for that. And until that happens, the soul is not yet free." And then I realized, Jew that I am, that the brothers and sisters I had come seeking in South Africa, besides being in the welcoming Jewish homes and welcoming synagogues, my brothers and sisters were here in that room, their skins black, their souls hurting, their voices choked with their simmering anger and with their cry for freedom.

The next day, we went to Soweto, the black community with two and a half million people, 60 percent under age sixteen. We did not travel on the usual route followed by the tour buses through the middle-class neighborhoods, but we went to the other Soweto. Forty people in three or four shacks in one yard, with one toilet and one garbage can and one water tap. We walked into a men's shelter, not for the homeless but for black men who were forced to leave their homeland far away to come to Johannesburg because there was no work in their homeland. And here they were, living six in a bare room, away from their families whom they would see only once or twice a year. I had come to South Africa to see my brothers and my sisters, and here they were, two and a half million in these hellholes and on these dusty and grimy streets.

We had come to South Africa with our own questions, and two weeks later we were leaving with more questions than when we came.

A question: When the day comes, God willing soon, that the voting booth will be open to blacks, will the black community, so long kept down and uneducated by their white rulers, be ready for the responsibility that awaits them?

If political power is determined by sheer numbers, is there the risk that South Africa will become a battleground of tribal rivalries and prey for a dictator's take-over as in some other African countries? Or, as Helen Suzman proposes, can some system of representation be devised by which whites and blacks share power, without either group dominating the other, but with both groups ruling together?

A question: Is the new president de Klerk serious about dismantling apartheid, or are the changes only cosmetic, what our black friends call Petty Apartheid, while Grand Apartheid, the real thing, will persist?

For an answer to that question, I asked an American diplomat about his sense of future prospects. I asked him, "In your opinion, is this government and its leadership demonic?" He thought a minute and said, "In my opinion, yes. The government and leadership of South Africa today are demonic."

Another question, the most persistent of those two weeks, a sermon unto itself (which I shall deliver some Friday night with discussion afterward), but now just the question:

While everyone agrees, white and black, that economic sanctions and boycotts and disinvestment have pushed the South African government toward the dismantling of apartheid, will further sanctions and boycotts speed up the process, or will further sanctions cripple the economy so fatally that the government and with it the structure of the country will collapse?

And then, as those who support sanctions hope (and the supporters include whites and blacks): Will, out of the shambles, come a new Africa?

Or, as those who oppose sanctions fear (and the opponents include both whites and blacks): Will, out of the shambles, come only the shambles? Is what is needed exactly the opposite: massive investment, to create more and more need for black skills and provide more and more money for black education, all of which will spell the finale of Grand Apartheid?

The most crucial question for South Africa, as one of our fellow Jews there worded it: Will there be enough goodwill in the black community and enough pragmatism in the white community to allow for a peaceful march on the road to freedom, or will that beautiful country be bathed in blood?

Our two weeks had come to an end, and we were on our way home. We had gone there to meet our brothers and sisters, and we had found them. We had gone there with our questions, and we came back with more of them. We took leave having made two promises: One to our fellow Jews, that we would do everything in our power to ease the pain of their isolation. And toward that end, I took the liberty of volunteering you, Westchester Reform Temple, as a partner congregation to the Reform Congregation of Durban to keep in touch, from our children to theirs, from our grown-ups to theirs, with small talk and big talk, with talk of friendship and concern, and most of all with connection.

The second promise we made was to our fellow black human beings: that as passionately as we could, we would make their cry for freedom be heard across the sea.

There was that one day, when we were being driven by one of our temple escorts from one place to another place in that beautiful land. I asked our driver whether apartheid bothered her on a daily basis in her lovely suburban home. She answered, "Terribly, to see how unfair and uncaring the white people of my country have been to the black people of my country." And when someone in our group asked, "Are you optimistic about the future?" she answered, "No, because the whites may be unwilling to share privilege and modify lifestyle."

My hope and prayer for this New Year is that she is wrong, that pragmatism and goodwill will win out over demonic fear and destructive contest for power. Because once again this morning did the shofar sound its urgent call:

> *By the passion of our spirit*
> *Shall our ancient bonds be shed.*
> *Let the soul be given freedom.*
> *Let the body have its bread.*

With God's help and blessing.
Amen.

Rosh HaShanah 1989/5750

Living Morally in a Complex World

The Possible Meaning of Entebbe

This past summer, I had the opportunity to read *The Final Days* by Woodward and Bernstein. It was gripping, suspenseful and depressing, and knowing how it would end in no way lessened the impact of the report.

Subsequently, I read a critical review by Max Lerner in which he commends the authors for their "investigative journalism." But then he maintains that such reporting (which he calls "hot history") is so close to the episode itself that it cannot yet qualify as a genuine record of history. The true record must wait until there is some sense of the deeper meaning of that episode against the larger backdrop of history, a meaning beyond what may have been the immediate impact or immediate response. And then we must wait again to see what consequences, if any, will grow out of that episode and its meaning. Who knows but that the nightmare of Watergate might not yet turn out to be a regenerative force in the history of our country and that the old Jewish slogan *Gam zu l'tovah*, "Even this is for the good," might not yet come to apply. It was said thousands of years ago in the Book of Ecclesiastes: "Better is the end of a matter than the beginning thereof," because in the end there is some sense of meaning and some evidence of consequences, and the Final Days are not yet at their end.

And during that same summer, another episode captured the attention of the world. At its beginning, it was disturbing but not so exceptional, because when the Air France jetliner on its way from Athens to Paris was commandeered by four terrorists, it was but one more in a long series of skyjackings that have become a standard technique of terrorist operations. But as we began to receive reports of the sequence of events, the skyjacking episode seemed to have some twists of its own. The destination was Entebbe Airport, Uganda, and the twist was that even though Uganda disclaimed any responsibility for or advance knowledge of or participation in the skyjacking, on the ground at Entebbe Airport, waiting for the arriving plane, were fellow terrorists. Armed Ugandan soldiers stood in two lines between which the hostages were ordered to walk from the airplane into the terminal, where they would be confined. And who was the self-appointed intermediary who would negotiate exchange of the hostages for fifty-three terrorists in five countries? Idi Amin, who had expressed public admiration for Adolf Hitler and had applauded the murder of the Israel athletes at the Munich Olympics three years ago.

The most frightening twist to the horrible episode came three days after the hostages were confined in the old terminal building. Announcement was made that the room had become too crowded and that some hostages would be assigned to another area. The "some," it turned out, were the Israelis plus any Jews who were not Israelis. The other passengers were soon dispatched to France, and concern deepened for those left behind. And in Israel, pressure mounted, especially from the families of the hostages, to accede to the demands of the terrorists.

The surprise came, of course, with the report on the morning of July 4 about the midnight flight of the night before: how three Israeli transports with their ground soldiers and paratroopers and motor vehicles had traveled the twenty-five-hundred-mile journey and had landed at Entebbe; how the terrorists and Ugandan soldiers were caught by surprise; and how, in the wake of gunfire and bewilderment at what was happening, the hostages heard those miraculous words in Hebrew, "It's okay, we're going home."

A personal note, with its own touch of pathos. We have a friend, an American, who was camping out with Israeli friends on one of the beaches in the Sinai on the night of July 3. Early in the morning on the fourth, they were awakened by the sound of an airplane flying low overhead, and then a second. They immediately suspected something unusual because this was no regular route for Israeli air transports. They turned on the radio (someone said of Israelis that they live from broadcast to broadcast), and when they heard the report of what had happened, they waited with anxious concern until the third plane flew over. And then on a beach in the Sinai, they danced and sang and laughed and rejoiced, until one Israeli broke into the jubilation with a worried question to our American friend, "Do you think your country will approve of what we did?" And they could not even celebrate their stunning victory without concern for the response of their only ally in the world.

Just as Max Lerner said about the final days of a president and Watergate: It is too soon to record the history of Entebbe. The final returns are not yet in. We are still in the stage of "investigative journalism," and all we can record are the episodes and the immediate response and the immediate impact, which, of course, was powerfully overwhelming. In Israel, a new wave of confidence swept over a nation that had been in the doldrums since the '73 war and that had been caught in the inflationary spiral and that had been increasingly abandoned and isolated by the rest of the world, which was selling itself for Arab petrodollars. But now, in Rabin's words, there had been a demonstration of the "latent power of this nation." Of course, there was mourning for the four casualties (in Israel, every death is felt personally by the whole nation.); of course, there was no glee because the enemy lay dead in the field, but still the mood was of a holiday, greeting each other on the street with *Chag samei-ach*, "Happy holiday," answering the telephone with *Mazal tov*, the Chasidim of an ultra-observant community breaking open a case of vodka and dancing in the streets, a bearded Jew hoisted on the shoulders of a young man and blowing the shofar. Israelis even stopped complaining about the latest tax, and when they learned that the decision to launch the rescue operation was a unanimous decision of the Cabinet, they knew that unanimity in anything in the State of Israel represents a minor miracle.

And Jews not only in Israel but worldwide responded in the way they do best when they want to do something: They sent money, and some contributions came from non-Jews. It was all spontaneous, and the only slight disappointment, I suspect, was that the episode took place in the summertime, when all of our UJA and Israel Bonds fund-raising apparatus is taking its annual rest. Think how much we could have raised if it had all happened last week or this week.

And from the non-Jewish world, a response of overwhelming admiration from individuals and from nations, including national leaders in black Africa, who publicly denounced Israel and privately praised it. Everyone loves a hero who has carried off a fearless exploit, and this was heroism at its bravest and most fearless, the kind that books get written about, the kind of spectacle that motion pictures get produced about.

I cannot prove it, but I suspect something else in that response of the world, something that may extend beyond journalistic reporting and touch on what yet may turn out to be the historic meaning of Entebbe, as follows:

In a world where the voice of justice and human decency has been stifled by brute power and oil power; in a world where self-styled revolutionaries have no qualms about terrorizing or killing innocent airplane travelers for the sake of their own revolutionary goals; in a world where the president of the UN Security Council for the month of September is the permanent representative of Libya, which is the leading training ground for terrorist activities; in a world where more Arabs are being killed by fellow Arabs in Lebanon than have been killed in all the wars with Israel; in a world where lurid petrodollars have seduced nations to lower themselves and individuals to prostitute themselves; in a world where, as the old Jewish proverb put it, "If God lived on earth, they'd break His windows, too!"—in such a world, this little nation carries off this impossible feat, and for that moment, at least, the topsy-turvy world is set aright, and for that moment, at

260 The Right Not To Remain Silent

least, the voice of God's justice and human decency breaks out of its imposed silence.

The historic meaning of that Saturday may be that a blow for freedom was struck for everyone in the world who cares about freedom and yet has bartered away some of his own. It was a declaration of independence from the cynicism that has come to tyrannize the story of humanity, that has made of the United Nations a mockery of the majority. It was a feeling that this is the way things are supposed to be rather than the way they've been. Into the snake pit had come a moment of sanity, as one member of Parliament remarked, "The Israeli action has done more for the role of law than the United Nations had done for twenty years," and this may be the meaning that history will ascribe to Entebbe.

But before history can record it truly, there still remains that other, the question of consequences, the question of whether this momentary spurt of justice will be roped off and isolated the way the Jews were in the airport, or whether the thrust of this moment will gain entry into the lives of nations and people.

In the United Nations, for example, will we see a serious effort to outlaw terrorism in the skies of the world despite the political ploys on the part of the Arab bloc countries to prevent it? Will we see a revival of self-respect by non-Arab nations as we witnessed for a fleeting moment when the Arab bloc tried to introduce a vote of censure for Israel's violation of Ugandan sovereignty and, in a rare display of non-acquiescence to Arab pressure, not enough support could be rounded up to bring the vote to the floor?

And, in the United States, will we as a nation commit ourselves to an effective law that will seek to prevent compliance with Arab pressure for boycotting Israel and anyone who deals with Israel, or will we as a nation opt for the style of our own U. S. Department of Commerce, which issued a memorandum suggesting ways to cooperate with the Arab boycott and still remain within the letter of our existing laws?

And when the election is over and the courtship of the Jewish vote is ended, will the president himself keep his promises about opposition to boycotts and about the commitment of the United States to the survival of Israel, or will he succumb to the pressure of the two hundred major United States corporations and twenty-five major commercial banks that are presently participating in the boycott? Senator Adlai Stevenson, one of the sponsors of the anti-boycott bill, set the matter forth in plain words: "This act may cost some business with Arab nations. If so, then it will be known that the sovereignty of the United States and its principles of decency and fair play are not for sale. It will be known, too, that the commitment of the United States to the survival of Israel is unequivocal and will not be sold for a barrel of oil."

There are those in the business world who will argue that such an approach is less than realistic, that it harbors serious economic risks, that America will lose in the bargain. But our fellow Americans in the business and banking world should know that such an approach is no less realistic and no less risky than a twenty-five-hundred-mile airplane ride into enemy territory to rescue hostages guarded by enemy troops, that what the Israelis lacked in realism, they compensated for in what one Israeli journalist called "the certainty of their moral position," which we Americans have been hungering for in our own country for a long time. And the certainty of that moral position produced a spirit of morale that we Americans haven't felt since the Second World War.

If the rescue at Entebbe inspires America and other nations to such moral certainty and such morale, then the consequences of that midnight ride will afford it a place in history. If what happened this summer continues to happen, then the moment of justice will be described in history not as a momentary spark that flashed in the darkness but as a flame that glowed brightly. And because of that Saturday night and Sunday morning, the Jewish people will have assumed its historic role:

> *A light unto the nations,*
> *To open the blind eyes,*
> *To bring out the prisoners from the dungeon,*
> *And them that sit in darkness*
> *Out of their prison house.*

Amen.

Rosh HaShanah 1976/5737

Lying and Other Moral Conflicts

Three separate episodes. The first as related in Joseph Borkin's frightening book on the *Crime and Punishment of I. G. Farben*. In the year 1933, I. G. Farben, Germany's most respected industrial establishment, signed a formal agreement with the new Third Reich whereby I. G. Farben would expand its facilities to produce synthetic oil and in return would receive a guaranteed payment of money. Four years later, in 1937, came the Nazi demand from the Third Reich that all Jews be removed from official positions in I. G. Farben, a demand with which the governing board readily complied. Five years later, in 1942, I G. Farben had already constructed a factory at Auschwitz so that it could make use of the concentration camp inmates as free labor. But then it decided that the operation was too inefficient and constructed its own concentration camp immediately adjacent to the factory. I. G. Farben then proceeded to work the inmates of the camp until they died and installed watchtowers and warning sirens and police dogs and gallows to remind their labor force of the consequence of disobedience.

The second episode, recounted in *The Economic War Against the Jews* by Walter Henry Nelson and Terence Prettie. In 1955, thirteen Arab League members and four Persian Gulf sheikdoms announced an Arab boycott against Israel and opened an office in Damascus. Twenty-one years later, in 1976, with the increasing power of the Arab petrodollar, the boycott blacklist had been extended to include not only firms in Israel but firms anywhere that had dealings with Israel. And then it was announced that any company that itself had no trade with Israel but did business with a company that did, that company would also be placed on the blacklist. It was all done by forms that had to be filled out, and any company that refused to fill out a form was immediately suspect and eligible for the list. One of the questions on the form was whether there were any Jewish directors on the board, Zionist or not. And an affirmative answer made that company eligible for the blacklist.

The way to stay off the list was, and continues to be, to declare oneself in complete compliance with the boycott. Another way, according to the book, is to pay a proper fee to an Arab intermediary, who then makes the proper arrangements to have the name removed from the blacklist. And yet another way to stay off the list is to have for sale a product that the Arab countries are otherwise unable to procure, and they will then close their eyes to the violation of their own boycott. By 1976, 90 percent of United States firms that received the questionnaire declared themselves in compliance. Fifteen hundred firms in the United States are on the blacklist.

And then the third episode, this one culminating on July 14 of this year, when Anatoly Shcharansky stood in a Moscow courtroom convicted of treason and was sentenced to three years in prison to be followed by ten years of hard labor in Siberia. Shcharansky's crime was his outspoken criticism of the Soviet government for its failure to provide its own citizens with the human rights that are guaranteed in the Helsinki Accords, including the right of any citizen to emigrate. Shcharansky's crime was simply his refusal to keep his mouth shut, not only to his fellow Russians but to Western newspaper correspondents. His crime, as he himself described it, was his refusal to cooperate with the Soviet government to destroy the emigration movement, even though the government had promised him that if he did, he could achieve his own freedom and would be reunited with his wife, Avital, who was already in Israel.

Before the judge announced the sentence on July 14, Shcharansky spoke these words in the Moscow courtroom: "For more than two thousand years, the Jewish people, my people, have been dispersed. But wherever they are, wherever Jews are found, every year they have repeated, 'Next year in Jerusalem.' Now, when I am farther than ever from my people, from Avital, facing many arduous years of imprisonment, I say, turning to my people, to my Avital, "Next year in Jerusalem."

And then Shcharansky concluded with these words: "Now I turn to you, the court, who were required to confirm a predetermined sentence: To you, I have nothing to say."

Three separate episodes, but what they bear in common is that each one poses its own moral conflict and dilemma. Not a dilemma for those at the top, not for Hitler or the Soviet high command or the masterminds of the Arab boycott. No dilemma for them because in their rise to power, they rid themselves of all moral baggage, and they are weighed down by no concern for the human rights of human beings.

The ones with the dilemma, the ones caught in the squeeze, at least in the beginning, were more likely those like the directors of I. G. Farben in 1937, who were no street hooligan anti-Semites but were respected citizens of the German nation. Because when that demand came from Hitler's office in 1937 to remove their own colleagues from official position, some of those German Christians must have had a moment's pause, a moment's moral conflict, which then they either resolved or evaded, because the Jews were removed. And then the directors of I. G. Farben had no more conflicts because by that very act, they had begun their own diabolic descent into the hell of Auschwitz.

The ones that get caught in the moral squeeze are some of those American businessmen, and I know some of them, respected members of their community, sometimes even active members of their churches. For some of them, there must have been a moment of conflict when the pen was poised and ready to sign one of those statements of their compliance that their own President Carter called "a profound moral issue that we should not shirk." There must have been for some of them that moment of uneasiness when they had to declare that their companies based in this land of the free and home of the brave were *Judenrein*, clean, laundered of all Jews. When they made that declaration, there must have been a struggling moment about their own freedom and their own bravery. Someone once told me that the moral criterion to which he subjects his own behavior on any given day is whether he would be willing to report it to his children at the dinner table that night. Would that businessman be able to pass that test?

And the other ones who may have been caught in the moral squeeze were those judges in the Moscow court. Despite the pressure from the high command, those judges were still lawyers, educated in their profession, knowledgeable about the rights of a defendant to call his own witnesses and to be allowed a fair hearing. And when those judges received their orders from the high command with the predetermined verdict and the predetermined sentence, could they not have experienced a moment of conflict? Did they tell it to their children?

Lionel Trilling once wrote that to have a conscience means not to run away. What each of these episodes has in common is its potential moment of conscience, and in each one of them it is the Jew who precipitates that moral moment.

We are not the only ones who test the world's morality, but we seem to do more than our share. Perhaps it's simply because we're in the minority and we're different, and our very presence is a moral test for the majority to see how well it can tolerate difference. Or perhaps it's because our entire existence is identified with the law, which was one of the main reasons that Hitler set out to destroy us.

Whatever the reason, whether it's God who has chosen us or we who have chosen ourselves or the Hitlers in this world who choose us, somehow we get chosen for the mission. Somehow we are the litmus paper upon which the moral courage or the moral cowardice of humanity is constantly being tested, and so often that paper turns out to be a cowardly yellow.

And for me, the powerful feeling of standing with the Torah on this day, for me the powerful feeling of listening to the shofar this morning is our statement to each other and to history that we are still here, we are still in business, jabbing at the conscience of mankind, still on a mission not yet accomplished, which will not be accomplished until the time of the Messiah.

And yet this one caution, as conveyed in the story told by Wesley Smith about the runner in ancient Greece whose mission was to carry the message from Marathon to the elders of Athens. He was almost dead with fatigue, but he kept running until he reached the city. And when he arrived, the elders of Athens were waiting, and they accosted him. "What is the message?" they asked. And the runner, who had survived the run all the way from Marathon to Athens, scratched his head and said, "The message? I've forgotten the message."

And that's how it sometimes is with us. As a Jewish people, we run the gauntlet of our mission, but as Jews, as individual Jews, we sometimes forget the message. We are a people that is the conscience to mankind, but with our own consciences, we're sometimes a little bit more relaxed and a little bit more casual.

It was before Rosh HaShanah that the rabbi was studying his ancient texts, inspired by the power of his people. And in the midst of his studying, a shoemaker came by the window. "Do you have anything to mend?" hawked the vendor, and the rabbi broke himself loose from his cosmic thoughts and he said, "Myself. I have myself to mend." So let me share with you, as we move toward the end of this service, one piece of our lives that might benefit from a little mending. Its state of disrepair is described in a new book by Sissela Bok, not a Jew, a book called *Lying: Moral Choice in Public and Private Life*. Her thesis echoes what the Talmud said thousands of years ago: "Jerusalem was destroyed because people stopped telling the truth." Her thesis is that as members of a society speak more and more in lies to each other, something must happen to that society, whether it's lawyers in the courtroom manipulating the truth to protect their clients, whether it's doctors lying to their patients even though their patients don't want to be lied to, or whether it's colleagues in a profession lying to each other, or parents and children, or husbands and wives lying to each other. Whoever is doing the lying, says Mrs. Bok, somebody's breaking the bond. Something of Jerusalem is being destroyed.

Some years ago, when we started our seventh-grade program with the weekend away, we discovered that we were receiving a rash of phone calls the Friday morning of the weekend to say that a child was sick and could not attend. We subsequently discovered that some of those children were not sick, that neither they nor their parents had ever intended them to go. But to avoid the consequences of not fulfilling the requirement, they had opted for this Friday morning strategy of lying.

And what Mrs. Bok is saying is that the parent who called on Friday morning, while concerned for the consequences for her child of not attending the weekend, ignored the possible consequences of the lying:

—that the child had now received sanction for a strategy that he could use on his own, even against the parent who had taught him how;

—or that the lie was being directed against the synagogue where the parent had enrolled the child so that the child might learn about Jewish ethics, like the Jewish ethics of truth;

—or that the lying, once discovered, had created such an atmosphere of distrust that even those whose children were really sick were now suspect, and the person who had been discovered to tell the lie now became forever suspect. "The penalty of the liar," says the Talmud, "is that he is not believed even when he tells the truth." Poor Jerusalem!

Most people lie sometimes, and some lies are white lies—a little exaggeration that doesn't hurt anybody. Some lies are harmless, out of genuine concern for the person being lied to, for example, "How do you like my new tie?" The Talmud says that we are permitted to say in the presence of the groom that the bride is beautiful and kind, even though she isn't, for the sake of peace in the world.

Some lies can be justified, contends Mrs. Bok, but far fewer than we think. We say "harmless," we say "white," we say "for someone else's benefit" when in reality they are only for us, for our benefit. Everyone who lied at Watergate pleaded that it was for someone else's benefit, but the American people and the courts failed to be convinced.

The best way to reverse the trend of lying, says Mrs. Bok and says the Talmud, is to call it for what it is and then to say, "What I am about to do is tell a lie," and then to ask the crucial question, "If this situation were reversed, would I want the lie I am about to tell to be told to me?"

And if we can answer that question about lying with all the honesty we can muster, there would yet be hope for Jerusalem.

Mark Twain once said: "When in doubt, tell the truth. It will confound your enemies and astound your friends."

So this message for the New Year, what Abraham Heschel calls "passion for the truth":

—for lawyers in the courtroom to respect the power of truth;

—for teachers in the classroom to see the truth of each child for what he is;

—for rabbis and their congregants to know before whom they stand;

—for businesspeople and their customers to deal with each other as human beings;

—for husbands and wives, and parents and children, and neighbor and neighbor, and friend and friend to respect each other enough to be honest.

This message for us who belong to a people still on its moral mission to the world, this message and this prayer: God, we pray for ourselves and our children that we may not forget the message.

Amen.

Rosh HaShanah 1978/5739

The Uses of Power

The decision was an agonizing one. Elie Wiesel had been invited to the White House to receive the Congressional Gold Medal of Achievement for his leadership as chairman of the U.S. Holocaust Memorial Council. The presentation was scheduled, by sheer coincidence, at the same time that protest was mounting over President Reagan's projected visit to the Bitburg Cemetery, with its graves of Nazi and SS soldiers. The president, trying to defend a decision that with more careful investigation would probably never have been made in the first place, had remarked on the day before the award ceremony that many of the German soldiers buried in the cemetery were as much victims as the Jewish inmates of the concentration camps. I happened to be present at a meeting of Jewish leaders in New York on the day that those remarks appeared in the press, and I can hardly describe to you the outrage that overran that room.

Wiesel, already in Washington, was being accosted from all sides: by certain Jewish leaders who urged him to boycott the award ceremony in protest and by other Jewish leaders who advised him to accept the award but to back off on Bitburg because the subject was so volatile.

Wiesel listened to everyone and then made his decision. He stood before the president of the United States and pleaded with him in a gentle voice "to do something else, to find another way. That place, Mr. President, is not your place. Your place is with the victims of the SS. The issue here is not politics, but good and evil, and we must not confuse them."

When Wiesel was asked what made him decide to speak as he did, he answered that our Jewish tradition commands us to speak "truth to power," even if that power be the presidency of the United States.

And with that answer was this sermon conceived. John Kenneth Galbraith has written that "not many people get through a conversation without some reference to power." So much of what happens to us and around us and in our world is perceived in terms of power, both when it is present and when it is not. Power*ful* and power*less.*

Even reading through a single issue of a daily newspaper: Iraq and Iran in the fifth year of their power struggle and their one million dead; the Middle East, a

268

cauldron of power, not only for Israelis and Arabs but between Arabs and Arabs, between Russia and the United States, between who knows who else; South Africa, the open, festering sores of apartheid, the power structure beginning to topple; South America, power versus power, from within and without.

Power, with all its ambiguities, all of its complexities, so resistant to simple analysis, so unresponsive to simple solution.

And the struggle for power, not only between nations but among human beings on the boards of their corporations, in the administrations of their hospitals and universities, even, heaven forfend, in some synagogues and churches, sometimes even in a marriage, sometimes even between parents and children, sometimes even between teachers and their pupils.

So devastating can be all the effects that even the sound of the word "power" becomes jarring. So much blood on so much soil, so much spouse abuse (including spouses in Jewish families, including spouses in traditional Jewish families), so much child abuse that even the reported figure of ten percent is considered below the actual. So much corruption in places of public trust. So frightening the power of the Moral Majority. Such power of the Soviet government to banish dissenters to prison or to psychiatric hospitals and have them injected with mind-crippling drugs. Such power of an earthquake to shatter life into rubble. Such power of disease to ravage the human body. All of it so menacing that the word broods like a dark shadow over the vocabulary of human existence.

In the spirit of this Yom Kippur, this Day of Returning to our authentic selves and our authentic lives and our authentic God, I ask you to go back with me to the authentic Jewish meaning of power, in ourselves and in our lives and with our God, all the way back to Adam and Eve, whom our ancestors, who wrote the Bible, depicted as the prototype of all human beings.

At the Bible's very beginning, before there's trouble, before there's a serpent, before there's corruption, Adam and Eve explore the strength of their bodies and the intelligence of their minds, and the passion of their feelings, and the sensitivity of their souls. As they begin to recognize how these capabilities can influence and direct the course of their lives (and later the lives of other people) and the events of their world, thus do they arrive at the awareness of their own power.

It begins that simply, that matter-of-factly. It begins neither as good nor evil but simply as the power to direct and to influence. Last spring, as we were preparing for the adult Bar/Bat Mitzvah service, I said to one of the class members who was to lead the congregation in the *Bar'chu*, "You take your hands and you signal the congregation to rise." And she said, "And they'll all stand up?" And I said, "They will." To which she responded, "Now that's what I call power!" which is the simplest meaning of power, before we have the chance to corrupt it and before we have the opportunity to ennoble it.

It means that besides the dark, corrupting shadow, there is the warm, ennobling light. Just as there is power to deprive, there is power to bestow. Besides the power to destroy, there is the power to preserve, and, in Elie Wiesel's words, even "the power to build on ruins." There is the power of the healer and the helper to heal and help. And the power of the one being healed and helped to share in the process. The power of parents and teachers to share knowledge and values with children, and the power of children to take their part in the sharing. There was the power of a Viktor Frankel, who wrote books on his ordeal in the concentration camps, the power to find meaning for life even in the midst of his suffering and thus to endure the suffering. The power to fail at something without branding oneself a failure. The power of one person to stand alone against the crowd. The power to make it through a hard day.

Following an automobile accident and surgery several years ago, I was told by the surgeon that I would be in permanent need of a cane, and thus was I introduced to a new world with its own shadows and lights of power. For example, I walk into a crowded subway car or a crowded bus in Manhattan. Sometimes there is a vacant seat marked "handicapped," and sometimes it's occupied and remains occupied by someone who may or may not be handicapped. More often than not, someone or more than one person will offer me a seat (which I do not take), and more often than not, the one who offers is an elderly person. The power to bestow.

Or sometimes we'll drive into a parking lot only to discover that the handicap spaces (which are closest to the entrance) are occupied by automobiles without handicap permits. More often than not they are luxury cars. The arrogance of power.

Or, for example, when we traveled to Boston with our daughter and had been told of a popular restaurant that accepted no reservations, I called in advance and learned that special accommodations were available for the handicapped. We arrived at the place in the rain and noted that the line stretched around the block (which, in truth, I suspect I could have managed). But instead, we walked to the front of the line, I on my powerful cane. As we were being led to our table in the crowded restaurant (the line outside still around the block), our daughter (whose permission I have obtained to tell this story) was totally embarrassed. When I tried to explain to her (the way President Reagan was trying to explain Bitburg) that my actions were justified because the restaurant had this policy, our daughter said, "Tell me one thing: If you weren't handicapped and you saw that line outside this restaurant, would you have waited until it was our turn to be served?" And I responded the only truthful way I could. We got up and left the restaurant. And thus was power called to account by truth.

In like manner, on this Day of Returning, do we arrive at the authentic Jewish meaning of power: that every power is a trust and that every human being in the exercise of his or her power is called to account, is held accountable by the Ultimate Power beyond our human selves, the power of justice and truth, whose name is God. In the words that have come through the generations to this day: "Know before whom you stand, before whom you are called to give account." Whoever knows that, my friends, is a believer.

For me, as a liberal Jew, truly to believe is not necessarily to believe in a God who divides Red Seas and works miraculous cures, but a God before whom we mortals stand to render account for the exercise of our own power.

Truly not to believe is to render account only to one's mortal self, or even one's mortal family, or even one's mortal nation, or even one's mortal ideology.

If we are truly believers, however subtle or complex the political turmoil in South Africa may be, any exercise of human power that deprives other human beings of lives and homes and freedom must be called to account to more than its own power.

And so in Russia and so in South America and in the United States and so in Israel, and so in our own homes and our own offices and our own schools and our own lives.

If we are truly believers, then that same call to accountability cannot be rendered mute in the places that are most private and most personal. How we put human beings down or lift them up; how we use the power of our personal material wealth whatever it may be; how, when we are requesting changes of tickets from one High Holy Day service to the other (in a procedure that is fair), we use either the power of cooperation or sometimes only the power of anger or arrogance; how we use the power to savor the blessings of our life and the power to sustain its betrayals.

On this Day of Returning, as we return to the authentic Jewish meaning of power, a comment about this prayer book. If the question were to be asked, Which of the prayers from this book has exerted the strongest influence on the rest of Jewish tradition? what would be the answer? Some, I suspect, might say, *Kol Nidrei*, because the power of that chant is so resonant in our Jewish souls. Some might answer, "The list of *Al Cheits*," for the sins that we have sinned against Thee, because that list of sins doesn't leave out anybody.

But none of those answers is correct. Because the only prayer that originated in the High Holy Days and only then was extended to the worship service of every day of the Jewish year is the *Aleinu*, which we call the "Adoration," and which includes the familiar words, "We bow in reverence before the King of Kings."

That translation, however, is inaccurate because *Melech Malchei HaM'lachim* means the "King of Kings of Kings," which brings us to the Jewish meaning of power:

That on this earth we are all kings and queens and princes and princesses in the personal places of our power, whether we corrupt it or ennoble it or both;

but that above practically all of us, other *m'lachim*, other powerful forces, that sometimes invade our lives and sometimes make us feel powerful;

and that above all of them is the ultimate *Melech* of truth and justice, before whom we stand and bow.

May God bless us with a true knowledge of our own powers.

May God give us courage to ennoble and not to corrupt.

May God give us the strength to stand before God and render an account of our powerful and powerless selves on this day and all the days of our lives.

Amen.

Yom Kippur 1985/5746

Beyond the Contract

Forty years ago this year, the death camps of Europe were liberated by the Allied soldiers. The terrible truth from behind those barbed wires was reported to an unbelieving world, and those who managed to hang on to life by a thread were then allowed the promise of a new life; and some of them are in this sanctuary this morning.

Forty years ago this year, World War II came to an end. And even as our nation and its allies mourned their dead, they celebrated their victory over the forces of darkness. Soldiers came marching home again, and some of them are in this sanctuary today.

Forty years ago this year, Hiroshima and Nagasaki, terrible and terrifying, a fear for the future, and the generation to whom that future was entrusted are all of us in this sanctuary today.

How then shall we label the year 1945? Was it a *shanah tovah*, "good year," or a *shanah ra-ah*, "bad year"? With its victory over darkness, was it a year of blessing? Or with the permanent shadow it cast onto the firmament, was it a year of foreboding? Or perhaps from that very commingling of forty years ago, might it be that the labels of good year and bad year apply more appropriately to bottles in the wine cellar than they do to the lives of human beings and the events of human history?

Isn't it true for us as we walk into the sanctuary this morning, as we turn the page from old to new? Jewish folklore tells us that everyone walks around with his or her own bundle, our own private mixtures of *mazel* and *tsures*, of blessings and burdens. Some of us are weighed down so heavily that we feel at a loss as to how to carry them, but we do because in that same heavy bundle are the blessings of good fortune that lighten it—the love of family, the support of friends, the strength from God. And even in those other bundles, so filled with good fortune and well-being and everything going right that they soar aloft, there is hardly a one without some stress or strain that tugs it downward, even a little. And for the rest of us, we're somewhere in the middle, the days that lift us up, the ones that drag us down. According to Jewish folklore and according to the wisdom that I learned from my mother, *aleha hashalom*, if all of us were to unpack our package and lay out the contents for all to see, and if we were then allowed to choose any package we want, most of us would pick up our own bundle again. Perhaps not all, but most.

And now to 5746 and the way it begins with these special days, with bundles opened for inspection, to get rid of some of the excess baggage, to add a new insight and new hope here and there. And then with the final call of the shofar on Yom Kippur, each of us to pick up our bundle and be on our way.

It is one such insight and hope that I would share with you from a compelling book entitled *Habits of the Heart,* written collaboratively by five authors: three sociologists, one philosopher and one theologian. The thesis of the book is that the traditions of the American people have changed radically through the centuries of our existence. The early settlers on this continent were influenced by what the authors call "the biblical tradition," which called upon each man or woman to create a community "in which the ethical and spiritual life could be lived." Then, with our emerging nationhood, came the second tradition, alongside the first. It was called "the publican tradition," in which educated citizens would serve the needs and purposes of the public community.

And then, according to the authors, came the third tradition, which dates back to Benjamin Franklin and proceeds through Walt Whitman and remains the prevailing tradition in America today. It is what the authors call the "tradition of individualism," with each individual attentive to his own needs, his own purposes, his own feelings. The presumption is that with each one pursuing his own self-interest and the self-interest of his family (perhaps but not necessarily), that with all of those collective self-interests, the good of the society will automatically result. The ultimate goal? Each one's self-fulfillment, so long as it causes no active harm to anybody else. And then, according to our most modern version of the theory, it will trickle down or trickle up or trickle sideways to bring benefit to the common weal of all society.

No matter all the times the theory of individualism doesn't work. No matter the countless ones who go without food and without homes because the trickle down doesn't trickle down far enough. No matter the ones with enough food and enough shelter who spend so many of their waking hours fulfilling themselves and yet cannot rid themselves of their own feelings of emptiness. No matter what, because according to the theory of individualism, the old questions, the old traditions: Is it ethical? Does it serve the purposes of the community? have given way to the new question: Does it make me feel fulfilled?

I came across this wonderful account in the newspaper of a twenty-five-year-old man who made a 1,500-mile trek through the Eastern states to interest college students in volunteering for public service. Now what a breath of fresh air that was. What a counterstatement to the "me generation." But in the very midst of that article was this quotation from the codirector of the project: "We want to stay away from the notion that students should be involved out of a sense of moral obligation. Rather, if we can convey to students that voluntarism can be enriching and fun, we'll stand a better chance of attracting more people to it." To which, I wanted to add, "But maybe not for long." But undeniably, that young man understands his customers.

The theory and tradition are all about individualism, and the best way to implement it, contend the authors of the book, is to negotiate "contracts," not with the wherefores and whereases of legal documents, but contracts nonetheless: to give for what we get, in the way people live their lives, day to day, person to person.

We see the contract in communities, communities like this one, where the unwritten contract reads like this: "I will pay my taxes, high as they are. I will even volunteer to be a class parent if my child is in the class. But you, the community, you, in turn, educate my children, pick up my garbage, control the traffic and noise on my street; and, above all else, you, the community, you protect the value of my property." What's missing from that contract is what used to be called "the spirit of community work" or "the public good." What results from contracts infused with that spirit is a shining cadre of those who volunteer their time and talent for no other reason than to strengthen that life of our community.

I am presently among those who are seeking some provision for senior housing in the Village of Scarsdale. We believe that the citizens of this village who have lived here through the years, by standards of simple decency, should not be forced to leave once they are no longer able to manage their former homes. It is our belief that the life of a community is enriched by the presence of many generations, including the senior ones. And yet, I am told, with all the ground swell of support we have received and hope to receive for our worthy cause, when the day comes with a specific proposal for a specific neighborhood, then we should get ready for the front of opposition that will come our way, for the reflex battle cry of "property values" and "congested traffic": "Don't put it on my street!" The tradition of individualism, and, above all, the unwritten contract.

Even when it comes to marriage. A survey reported that 96 percent of all Americans hold to the ideal of two people sharing life and love together. But when the question was asked whether most couples getting married should expect to spend the rest of their lives together, 60 percent of those same people said "No."

Because marriages, like so many other experiences, have become "the contract." Not like the old Jewish *ketubah*, which took care of financial matters, but this modern version covers all matters. Two people, each other's close friend, two people trust each other, two people support each other, two people respect each other's individuality—all that wonderful mutuality that inspires the 96 percent. But with all of it, there is that lurking concern that should one or another, for some period of time, falter in the friendship or disappoint the trust or fail to give support or step on the other's individuality, then the risk increases that the 96 percent may careen down to the 60 percent.

I speak of it today because we Jews are long-standing experts in the matter of contracts. The fact is that we made our appearance on the stage of history with a contract. It's called a *b'rit*, which, according to the Bible, was negotiated between ourselves and the God of history. The terms were direct and simple, if not always easy: I, the Lord, will be your God. I will protect you; I will assign you to be My messenger to the people of the earth. You, in turn, will obey My law and spread My message. And as in all contracts, if one party defaults, the contract will be nullified, and the relationship will be over, and the second party is released from its terms.

Which is exactly what happened. The Jewish people defaulted: They broke the law, exploited the poor and lusted after idols. The prophets then announced in the name of God that the contract was now terminated, that the people would no longer be protected, that the partnership was now dissolved.

But then there appeared on the scene another prophet. His name was Hosea, and the poignant power of his message has resounded through all the centuries, even to this sanctuary today. Hosea announced to the people that by the logic of the contract, the relationship between God and the people should now come to an end. But, said Hosea, I herewith announce that the love of God for His people is beyond logic and beyond contracts. The relationship is not ended, now or ever.

Centuries later, when one out of three Jews would be killed in the Holocaust, when, to many, it seemed that God Himself had broken the contract, the message of that prophet was still alive. As Eugene Borowitz has written, the Jewish people after the Holocaust had every reason to resign from history, to go on as individuals but to stop being Jewish. We had the right to terminate the contract. But instead, a State of Israel rose from the sand dunes, and instead, we and our children and our grandchildren are in this place today, because the bond between the people and its God was so strong that it was beyond logic and beyond the contract.

Listen to the way, to the metaphor by which Hosea announced his message:

> *When Israel was a child,*
> *then I loved him;*
> *and now he is grown up,*
> *and he has rebelled against me.*
> *But how can I give you up,*
> *O Ephraim?*

Hosea was a parent and started out like most parents with the usual contract, with the usual terms to which the child never actually agrees but is expected to comply.

According to the contract, the parents consent as follows: to feed, to clothe, to protect, to love, to guide, to educate, perhaps to send to camp, perhaps to the orthodontist. According to the contract, the parents consent that as their children gain in years, they will let them try their own wings, interfering in their lives and worrying about them no more than is absolutely necessary.

According to the contract, the children consent as follows: When we are young, we shall try to follow your direction. We shall try to please you and return your love. If we become the cause of problem and worry, we shall try to let you help us, even though we may falter at helping ourselves. And as we gain in years and try our wings, we shall try to balance our aspirations with your expectations. And because we love you, we shall try not to hurt you.

Thus the contract. But everyone can tell you of countless families in which children or sometimes parents renege on their promises. By the terms of the contract, the relationship should end, or at least the one should stop worrying about the other. But instead: "How can I give you up, O Ephraim?"

A disappointed parent went to the Baal Shem Tov and poured out her heart. "I did everything a parent could for a child, and now look what he's done: He has forsaken God's way and everything I tried to teach him. What shall I do about him?" And the Baal Shem answered: "Love him more."

Beyond the contract. So what I now say to young couples about to be married is that besides your trust for each other, there should be trust for the marriage. Besides your closeness to each other, there should be closeness to the marriage, because that second trust and that second closeness help tremendously on those inevitable days when, for whatever reason, you don't feel so close to each other or so trusting of each other, on those Mondays and Thursdays when, for whatever reason, the mutuality of your contract is having a hard time.

Not every marriage deserves to last, but a marriage has hardly a chance without that undergirding of trust and closeness beyond the usual contract of how they feel about each other or themselves. A marriage has hardly a chance when it is consumed by what one of the authors of the book calls "a relentless scanning of one's and the other's feelings: How do I feel today? How am I reacting today? Every day, am I fulfilled?"

Beyond the contract in the community where we live, beyond the alliance of private self-interests to the bond of public concern: *Al tifrosh min hatzibur*, "Do not separate yourself from the community."

Many years ago, on a confirmation weekend, we contrived a situation where a black family was contemplating a purchase of a home in the community. One of the confirmands was asked to take the part of a white homeowner who was being approached by his white neighbors to join with them to purchase the house in question so that it would become unavailable to the black family.

That had to be fifteen years ago, but I still remember the anguish in that boy's face as he was being pressured by his friends and his neighbors. And finally, he blurted out, "I can't do it, because it's wrong!"

And thus was it revealed to the authors of *Habits of the Heart*. Throughout their interviews, through the stream of all the usual language about self-fulfillment, and being responsible only to yourself, and rewarding experiences, people would sporadically come out with words like "obligation" and "commitment," "courage" and "right and wrong." The authors called it a "second language" because the people who spoke it were groping for the words, because the words didn't fit into their usual language of individualism.

But the words and their meaning were very much there, part of who those people were, part of who we are, part of our underground language waiting to surface. As Pablo Casals once wrote: "It takes courage for a man to listen to his own goodness and act on it."

Ten days from now, after the last call of the shofar, we will pack up our bundles and be on our way. Before we do, whatever these Holy Days may be, may there be this new insight and this new hope, this breakthrough into that second language.

Beyond language of self-interest to language of right and wrong.
Beyond individualism to relationship.
Beyond giving and getting to community.
Beyond the language of contract to the language of commitment and of love.
Amen.

Rosh HaShanah 1985/5746

The Meaning of Sacrifice

As we share this journey of the High Holy Days, our destination tomorrow morning, when we read the words of the Torah, will be Mount Moriah. It was the place where the father Abraham was summoned to that ultimate test: to sacrifice his own son, in truth his own self. And as the father arrives at that ultimate moment, God stops him short and directs him to the ram caught in the thicket, which Abraham proceeds to place upon the altar *tachat b'no,* "in place of his son."

However many times together we take that trip to Moriah, it never stops nagging with its questions: What kind of God is it that would make such a demand, even though in the end He retracts it? What kind of God would require of a parent to make an offering of his or her own child? Was it, as the philosopher Kierkegaard proposes, a moment when God put aside His own ethical nature? And what about Abraham, who earlier in the Torah had been willing to argue with God about God's intention to destroy the corrupt cities of Sodom and Gomorrah because, said Abraham, there might be a handful of righteous people living there? Why doesn't Abraham plead the cause of the innocent child who was his own son?

Sometimes I wonder, What if Abraham on the way up the mountain had simply said, "God, I can't go through with it. I can't give him up. And besides, what will it do to his mother?" (who is not even mentioned in our story). Had Abraham said that, had he refused, would his place in history have been forfeited? Would his name have been forgotten? Would that have marked the end of Jewish history hardly yet begun? Would we be here tonight? Thus our questions. And perhaps more of your own, besides.

Every once in a while when I go to that place, Moriah, I discover a possibility that I had never perceived before, a spark that is struck from the text as never before. Let me then share with you another perception of Mount Moriah.

What would have happened if Abraham had refused? The answer, I believe, is that God would have been willing to negotiate, just as he did with Sodom and Gomorrah. God would have settled, I believe, for what in Hebrew is called a *korban,* an "offering," of a goat or a bull or a bird or some grain, all of which, according to the Torah, is an acceptable sacrifice upon the altar before God as long as it

280

fulfills two requirements: that it has to be of choice quality and that it must be a precious possession. And not coincidentally, the altar to which those sacrifices would later be brought is the exact same Moriah that was to become the site of the Temple.

Thus do I suggest that Abraham did not have to say "Yes," to the sacrifice. In that same spirit, one rabbi in the midrash proposed the following radical possibility: that the *Akeidah* (the "Binding of Isaac" for the sacrifice) was not really God's command to begin with but rather Abraham's overconscientious zeal. It was only what Abraham thought God wanted, which is why God stops him short and why God never commands human sacrifice anyplace else in the Bible. A *korban* would have been good enough to begin with, if Abraham had only negotiated.

However we may interpret that story, the distinction is clear, except for those rare times that martyrs died for the sanctification of God's name. For us Jews, the meaning of sacrifice is not the surrender of self in the *Akeidah* or on the cross but the sharing of self, the giving of what we preciously have, our *korban*. We Jews do not have priests and monks and nuns who surrender their lives to God. But we are a people of priests who share what we have, of choice quality, on the altar of life in God's world. When that altar of Moriah was no more after the Temple was destroyed, what were the substitutes for the sacrifice? They were study and worship and repentance and good deeds, all of which call for our sharing, not our surrendering of who we are and what we have.

This, I believe, is what should be the meaning of sacrifice when we Jews use it in the lives of our families and ourselves. Surely we do not mean to withhold because that would be no sacrifice at all. What we do mean is to give of ourselves, but not to give away ourselves, a *korban* and not an *Akeidah*.

And yet, have we not seen the *Akeidah* of parents who give themselves away, needlessly, on the altar of their children's lives, when what would have been best for both the children and the parents would have been the sharing and not the surrendering? Have we not seen the *Akeidah* of children when it was their time to choose a college or a career, children who were then sacrificed on the altar of their parents' ambitions rather than on the solid ground of their own talents and possibilities? Have we not seen the *Akeidah* of otherwise intelligent and sensitive men and women like ourselves who surrender our total selves to the momentum of our careers, as noble as they may be, with too little left over to share in our own homes, in our own families, in our own communities?

Not the *Akeidah* but the *korban*, which comes from the Hebrew *korav*, which means "to draw near." A teacher shares with a pupil, a doctor with a patient, a friend with a friend, and each sharing becomes that sacrifice of drawing near. A husband gives to a wife and a wife to her husband, and they create a sacrificial marriage. Parents share with their children the best of their own wisdom and experience until, of course, the children may begin to get bored. They share material things with their children, enough but not too much, and they share—we share—with our children the values to live by, for which we parents must serve not merely as spokespersons but as models.

And so do we place our offering on the altar, hopeful that it will be accepted but never sure, hopeful that our children will also learn to sacrifice, not withholding and not surrendering but sharing who they are and what they have.

When this journey will come to an end ten days from now, many of us in this congregation who are able will share together in a Jewish act of sacrifice. We shall abstain from food and drink from sundown to sundown, and the act of our fasting will be our *korban*, our giving something of ourselves "to draw near" in the presence of our God. And when that fast ends a week from Monday night, we will leave this place for our homes and for the break fast that will await us. But during that same twenty-four hours, another fast will be taking place even as it is taking place these twenty-four hours and during each twenty-four hours of the ticking clock.

I speak of a fast that is not voluntary, the fast of one billion hungry people on this earth who fast, as Leonard Fein has written, "not out of faith, but out of famine." I speak of the fast that during each twenty-four hours of the ticking clock takes the lives of 42,000 children under age five who die of starvation. Our fasting will be a sacrifice; theirs is an abomination.

And that is why the project entitled MAZON, which is the Hebrew word for food, came into being. MAZON is the Jewish response to hunger. It allows all of the members of the Jewish community to provide resources that can be directed through existing projects to the hungry of this world, including Jews, of which there are some, and including non-Jews, whose numbers are countless.

And that is why on these High Holy Days, I am joining with Orthodox, Conservative and Reform rabbis throughout this country as I make this appeal: that every one of us will contribute to MAZON the cost of the food we shall not eat on Yom Kippur. Thus will this congregation, on the holiest day of the year, offer two sacrifices: our fast and our food.

In that same spirit, our temple's Board of Trustees has endorsed in principle the MAZON plan, which invites every family who celebrates a *simchah*, be it a wedding, bar mitzvah, bat mitzvah, birthday or anniversary, to calculate three percent of the cost of that celebration and send it as a contribution to MAZON for the hungry of the world. Someone estimated the figure of such expenditures on such celebrations in the American Jewish community to be between $500 and $800 million a year. Even at the lowest figure and even if only 20 percent of all who celebrate such *simchahs* participate, the result would be $3 million each year for food against starvation, for life against death.

What an ideal way to sacrifice, a *korban* of choice quality and precious possession, to take our most joyful joys and then to share them, three percent of them, on the altar of God's humanity, for the hungry of God's world.

Tomorrow is Moriah. Had Isaac died on that mountain, the Jewish people would have never wanted to sacrifice again. We would have never learned how to share because we already would have surrendered. Had Isaac died on that mountain, the Jewish people would never have made it through, because Yitzchak, Isaac, which means "laughter," would have been dead. And we, the Jewish people, would have been denied our laughter and our sense of humor, without which we could never make it through.

And thus do we bring our offering during our brief day on earth, rarely certain but never without hope. And thus do we pray on this Eve of the New Year: May the sacrifice we bring—the offering of parents for children and children for parents, the offering of husbands and wives for each other, the offering of the Jewish people and this congregation for the hungry of the world—may our offering, O God, be acceptable upon Your altar.

Amen.

Rosh HaShanah 1986/5747

Obstacles

A few years ago, after an occasion here at the temple, I was greeted by a young man who had grown up in our congregation but had been away for many years. He told me about his new family and about his career, and then he said. "And as far as my Jewishness is concerned, I want you to know that my bar mitzvah took."

The first goal of this sermon is a modest one: to ask you to explore with me what it might mean after today is over to be able to say, "This year, Yom Kippur took"; to be able to walk out of the sanctuary after the last call of the shofar not only to go home to eat but to be ready for Tuesday and for the world and whatever, with a newfound readiness because of a "Yom Kippur that took."

Actually, we're off to a very auspicious beginning if we are willing to take counsel from Woody Allen's assertion that "90 percent of making it through this life is simply showing up." For no one would ever contest the massive willingness of the Jewish people to show up on Yom Kippur, which is in itself a declaration of intent, maybe not 90 percent, but at least a beginning. For most of us, the very fact of our being here is our willingness to acknowledge that there is a personal meaning to the Yom Kippur words "sin," "repentance," "forgiveness." I do, however, recall a rabbinic student from many years ago who was also a philosophy major and who tried to argue that he had never sinned and that the word "sin" did not apply to him, and he lost the argument.

But most of us, I believe, would acknowledge the meaning of that word "sin" and its application to us, even though we may perceive the word differently. To some, sin is disobedience to a judging God who judges us; to others, it is a violation of a universal code of morals and ethics; to yet others, it is a defection from the standards of our own better selves or any combination of the above.

But as different as our perceptions might be, most of us would agree to the literal meaning of the word because in Hebrew it is *chatah*, which literally means "to miss the mark," "to miss the target," whatever the target may be. On the Day of Repentance, all of those misses are litter at our feet and obstacles on our way; and if Yom Kippur takes, then we will clean up the litter, and clear away the obstacles and get ready for Tuesday and for another year.

And so to the first modest goal of this sermon: that you will go with me through some steps that will allow Yom Kippur to take. The first step is suggested by an experience I had thirty-four years ago when I was first ordained a rabbi. I was serving a congregation in the South. My first High Holy Day sermon acclaimed the universal motif in Judaism: one God over all and one humanity in which all human beings are related to each other. Some people came over afterward to say how much the sermon had meant to them. A few weeks later, I brought to our congregational leaders a proposal that our synagogue sponsor in our sanctuary an Institute for the Clergy, to which we would invite all the ministers of the community. The first one to respond was one of those who had been among my well-wishers those weeks before. "It's a wonderful idea," he said, "but you must understand that the white ministers will have to sit on one side of the sanctuary and the black ministers on the other." "I don't understand," I replied. "Two weeks ago, when I said that all human beings were the children of God, you said it was wonderful." "It was," he said, "but you always have to watch out when you get specific!"

And that's the first step if Yom Kippur is to take. In the presence of our God and ourselves, to get specific: not just sin, which is a generality, not even categories of sin like stubbornness or selfishness or inconsiderateness or even xenophobia, because they are general categories. No generalities, because no one ever shed a tear of regret over a generality. Rather, all of those specific times when another human being got hurt and we were the ones who did the hurting; and those other times when the one who got hurt was ourselves, and we were the ones who did the hurting. All those specific times when we could have reached out but held back; and those other times when someone else reached out and we pulled away. All those specific times when we kept quiet and should have spoken up; and all those other times when we blurted out and should have kept quiet. All those specific times when we were too hard on everyone; and all those other times when we were too hard on ourselves. And all those specific times when we sat with each other in this sanctuary and said, "For the sin that we have sinned against Thee," and then, a little later, someone cut someone else off trying to get out of the parking lot a few minutes sooner. Big sins, little sins, but get specific.

And then the next step if Yom Kippur is to take: to make the decisions that will clean up the litter and clear away the obstacles, to decide, not easily perhaps, to seek out the one I have hurt and to make amends and ask forgiveness, which is according to good Jewish tradition; to decide, not easily perhaps, to settle a grudge that for too long has generated coldness and distance where once warmth and closeness were, which is according to good Jewish tradition. And then to decide, not easily, that when the usual opportunities present themselves to unleash our anger or explode our temper or make us act shabbily, we will remember Yom Kippur and say "No" and decide not to do it, which, according to Maimonides and to good Jewish tradition, is the true test of repentance, to say "No" and not to do it.

And then the third step as Yom Kippur will come to its end: to reach out beyond the limits of our own selves to each other, to our God, to all the shofar calls of history; to lift the load together; to be here together at *N'ilah*, tired and hungry and played out, but the load lifted, the spirits raised, the decisions made, because we are reaching out to our faith and each other, ready for Tuesday and for the world after a Yom Kippur that took.

Thus to the second modest goal of this sermon. It is based on a prediction: that when we go back on Tuesday, the roadways of the world will have no fewer obstacles than when we left them on Friday. There will be obstacles to safety in airports and on the streets and obstacles to agreement in Iceland, to peace in the Middle East, to resolution of conflict in South Africa and Central America, to human rights in the Soviet Union. And as Rabbi Zecher said last night, there will be obstacles to unity among Reform, Conservative and Orthodox. And on and on and on.

There is one prediction that rabbis can safely make: When we go back to our studies on Tuesday, even if Yom Kippur took, there will be plenty of obstacles in people's lives that were not cleared away on Yom Kippur. Sickness and the death of a loved one and the loss of a job and financial reverses and family problems are not necessarily the things we cause to happen and can therefore remove, but they are the things that happen to us. Fair or not, they are there. They are not our sins but our circumstances, yet as obstacles they are just as high.

And thus the second modest goal of this sermon is to consider this proposal: that if the steps worked for the obstacles that were there on Yom Kippur, then they are worth trying for these other days as well, that if the formula of Yom Kippur could take away our sins that were scarlet and make them white as snow, then it's worth a try on Tuesday and on the other days of our lives. Those who cope best, the true survivors of this world, are the ones who take that first Yom Kippur step and get specific, who make very specific distinctions between what is the way it is and what they can do something about, between what is beyond their control and what is possibly within it, between the impossibility of bringing the dead back to life and the possibility of reshaping one's own life.

Rabbi Morris Adler wrote of a man who had walked across the entire continent from Seattle to New York. At the finish line, a cadre of reporters was waiting to interview him. The first question was, "What was it that bothered you the most on your walk from one end of the continent to the other?" The expected response was some reference to the Rocky Mountains or the expanse of the desert or some crowded city. But this traveler mentioned none of those. The greatest obstacles he suffered, he said, were the pebbles in his own shoes.

Thus the question that the copers in this world make sure to ask of themselves: whether what's holding them back is actually the obstacles on the road or the pebbles in their own shoes, be it their own uncertainty or their own fear or their own self-delusions or their own self-pity. And then they make their decisions to go after the pebbles, one by one, and in order to do this, they are willing to reach out beyond themselves because they are willing to admit that they cannot always do it alone.

No one can ever make it sound easy. No one can ever play down the horrendous obstacles of sickness or death or family disintegration or even the obstacles of too much success. No one has the right to give grades on how poorly or well someone else confronts them. And yet, from all these years, I can tell you this: that there are some who are buffeted by the storms and are beaten down by them and only drag along and only get stuck in the way, and the question they hardly ever stop asking is, "Why did this happen to me?" But there are others, equally buffeted, who emerge not unscarred but also not sullied, whose questions are akin to the words of Rabbi Harold Kushner: "If this has happened to me, now what do I do and who is there to help me?"

However often I witness it, I never cease to marvel at the staying power of the human spirit. I see it in members of this congregation. I know that history will have to record the name of Anatoly Shcharansky because he showed us all how to do it, with a measure of courage perhaps beyond most of our own. He stood up to all the obstacles: nine years in prison, isolation cells four meters square, a quota of two letters a year that they allowed to come to him into the prison. But from the outset, Shcharansky made his decision: never to sink to the level of his own misfortunes. When the guards ordered him to walk in a straight line, he walked zigzag. When they put him in an isolation cell, he sang Hebrew songs at the top of his voice. When they made fun of him that the letters he was writing to protest the mistreatment of his fellow prisoners would never find their way out of the prison, he answered defiantly that even if the letters failed to save his fellow prisoners, they harbored the possibility of saving his own soul. On his last day as a prisoner, when he was brought to the bridge that would take him across to freedom, they confiscated his Book of Psalms, which had sustained him through all the years of his ordeal. In protest, he threw himself down in the snow and refused to walk another step until they returned the book, which they did.

After his release, when Shcharansky was asked how he had managed the ordeal of so many obstacles, he used the words "outside help." Even from behind the bars of the prison, he had reached out to the wife and the Jewish people, who were pleading his cause. He reached out, he said, to his Jewish faith and to his Book of Psalms. His courage may extend beyond mine and yours, but the questions he asked are the same that we can ask: "If this has happened to me, what do I decide to do now, and who is there to help me, and how do I reach out?"

The other day I was at the reception desk of White Plains Hospital. In the file of Jewish patients was a note attached to a patient's card that requested that a rabbi come to see the patient. I went to the room and introduced myself. The elderly lady told me that she had been very ill, on a very rocky road, but that the other day, somehow she sensed in herself the very specific need to say the *Sh'ma* with a rabbi. Whereupon she made the decision to do something about her need, and she left the request at the front desk. And there I was, and she and I reached out and clasped hands, and she said the *Sh'ma* by herself and then told me how much better she felt about the road ahead. I wished her good health and a good year and left the room. For her, the Yom Kippur formula had worked.

According to Jewish tradition, when a book of the Torah is completed, the words to be recited are, *Chazak, chazak, v'nit'chazek,* "Be strong, be strong, and let us strengthen each other." When this day will end, when the old book will be closed and the new one opened, may Yom Kippur take, on Tuesday and in our homes and in the world and in the temple parking lot.

As the new book is opened, may God strengthen us to be specific, even about the pebbles in our shoes.

May God strengthen us to make decisions and sometimes to walk zigzag.

May God strengthen us to reach out to God and to our faith and to each other.

As it is written: *Chazak, chazak, v'nit'chazek.*

Amen.

Yom Kippur 1986/5747

Jewish Names in Public Scandals

As the preacher once said, "Before I begin, I'd like to say something." I would like to say that the Jewish prayer of *Shehecheyanu* is reserved for occasions that are new and special. We said *Shehecheyanu* once tonight to welcome the New Year, and we are also together for the first time in our newly enlarged sanctuary. I can look out to the last row and it is not as far away as I feared from the architect's plans. And since the public-address system, which finished being installed this afternoon, works and since we are here in burgeoning numbers to welcome the celebration of our temple's anniversary and our Jewish faith and our Jewish selves, I ask you to join me and say the words again, *Baruch Atah Adonai Eloheinu Melech ha-olam shehecheyanu v'ki-ymanu v'higi-anu laz'man hazeh.* "Blessed art Thou, O Lord our God, Sovereign of the universe, who has kept us alive and has sustained us and has brought us to this day. Amen."

And now I begin. This message for the New Year of 5748 began last January at the New Year of 1987. The front pages were ablaze with the scandals that were ravaging City Hall and were rampaging on Wall Street.

The names of the accused—Mannes, Friedman, Levine, Boesky, Siegel, and most of the rest—could have been a page from the membership roster of a synagogue. According to the press reports, some of the illegal deals were negotiated at UJA dinners, and one such deal was made even in a Jewish home on Friday night, before the host and his guests sat down at the Shabbat table.

And then the report that a yeshivah on the East Side of New York, founded by a renowned Talmudic scholar, was indicted for illegally laundering money for local stores in exchange for a contribution to the yeshivah, which, they said, needed money badly.

And then a rabbi and his son-in-law were indicted for cheating the government of more than $100 million in taxes since 1979.

And then, and then, and then…Jewish name after Jewish name, Jew after Jew, Jewish scandal after Jewish scandal. Scoundrel after scoundrel.

So it was on the first Friday night in January that I delivered a sermon entitled "Jewish Names in Public Scandals." Since the numbers in attendance on that first Friday night of the secular New Year were somewhat fewer than those who attend on the Jewish New Year, some of those present suggested that I adapt the sermon for these High Holy Days.

From January until now, as the net has spread to Mario Biaggi and Meade Esposito and Francis X. Smith, the suspect list has turned more ecumenical. When the net closed in on fifty-eight highway superintendents and purchasing directors, who were offered a total of 106 bribes of which 105 were accepted (the one being refused because the amount was too small), there was hardly a Jewish name among them, perhaps for the reason that Jewish young people rarely grow up to become highway superintendents or purchasing directors.

Exclusive or not, we have more than our share, and we recently added Meyerson and Ohrenstein. And if we subscribe to the Jewish principle that *Kol Yisrael areivim zeh la-zeh*, "All Jews are responsible to and for one another"; if we subscribe to the Jewish teaching that when one man bores a hole in the floor of a boat, even if it's under his seat, the whole boat gets swamped; if we accept the Jewish thesis that the conduct of every Jew implicates the destiny of the entire Jewish community, then we cannot say that it's their business and they are lone practitioners. If we as a Jewish community respond with pride to the number of Nobel laureate Jews, we cannot refuse to respond to the number of crooks who are Jews.

What used to be a response to the scandals (and still is on the part of some) was an uneasy fear that the front-page stories might spark a rage of anti-Semitism. But by now, the Jewish community in America, or at least in New York, is secure enough and sophisticated enough to understand that Jewish misconduct hardly ever causes anti-Semitism but only fuels the fire of those who are already anti-Semitic to begin with. Another response from some Jews: that with so many Jews in New York City and therefore so many in city government, and with so many Jews in finance (the number is guessed at somewhere around 60 percent), and since Jews are as human as anyone one else, if there are going to be scandals in City Hall or on Wall Street, then the names are bound to be Jewish. The fact is that the media have played down the Jewish factor in the corruption scandals, which, according to the thinking of predisposed anti-Semites, is simply due to the predominant Jewish influence in the media.

Whatever the reason, in the midst of the corruption crisis, the Jews, we Jews, did not have to run for shelter. Nor were public rallies organized to fend off the threat of anti-Semitic attack as we may have done with Father Coughlin in the 1930s.

What many Jews experienced was not so much a feeling of being threatened but much more a feeling of being embarrassed. What they feared was not a pogrom by their enemies but the cocktail party talk by their non-Jewish associates, even their non-Jewish friends, when they were not around: "smart Jews," "money grubbers," the Jew as Shylock.

And although I cannot document it, I detect yet another ingredient in that Jewish feeling of embarrassment. Not so much what others have to say about us but what we have to say about ourselves. What we have to say is that America has been good for us Jews, as it has been for others—a golden land of opportunity; and that opportunity has been defined by us, as it has been defined by others, not only in political but in economic terms. Ivan Boesky and Stanley Friedman are so typical of so many Jews in America, including those who did not break the law, whose parents, by dint of hard work and creative opportunity, started their climb up the ladder of the American dream. And their children did no more than follow them on the upward climb.

Then there are Dennis Levine and his young disciples in their mid-20s, also typical of many young Jews, including those who did not break the law, who are children of parents who have already made it, and the children are out to make more and faster and riskier. I am still hard put to understand why Mark Siegel, who earned $2 million in 1985, had to resort to illegal activity for another seven hundred thousand? Why when they make one million or five million do they have to make more?—except for the sake of making it, except for the fact that the only way they define success is financial success, except for playing "the game," in the words of the poet, "with a passionate intensity," except for the sake of over-dreaming the dream. Why does he go for more? In the words of an eleventh-century Jewish philosopher, Bachya ibn Pakuda, "He is like fire, which blows more fiercely the more wood is added to it."

Those wonderfully talented young people, described by adjectives that would make any Jewish parent proud: motivated, bright, conscientious. Or, as they were described in a *New York Times* caption: "Young, Eager, Indicted." How the mighty have fallen!

But in all fairness, to be regarded as a successful Jew in America, requires more than just making it. I remember my reaction as a young rabbi at a fund-raising dinner thirty-five years ago when someone announced his gift for that year would be $1 million. Ivan Boesky was munificently generous in his support of Jewish and civic causes: the UJA, and the New York City Ballet, and the Jewish Theological Seminary, whose library bore his name and which, at his request, has been removed. By the general consensus of the Jewish community, making it is sanctioned by sharing it, as any guest of honor at an industry UJA dinner will tell you.

What was rarely asked in the Jewish community, not even in the synagogues, was the means by which one made it. What was rarely discussed was how Jewish ethics and Jewish values relate to economic gain and professional advancement and institutional power, including the institution of the synagogue. What was not discussed is how Jewish tradition relates economic gain to the boundaries that divide the straight from the crooked; how it addressed the questions of fraudulent conduct toward customers and competitors; how it addressed questions as specific as the use of inside information to gain advantage over a competitor; how it addressed the question of ill-gotten gain in public office.

But rarely were such questions asked in the American Jewish community: not until that barrage of Jewish names. And then they became a goad to our own embarrassment, not because of what others say about us but what we have to say about ourselves. A. M. Rosenthal wrote in *The New York Times*: "It's not that Jews are more ethical than others; it's that they think they ought to be."

Thus our question for the beginning of a New Year, of a new page in the Book of Life. We want to know, even in this renaissance of Jewish identity and Jewish activity that abounds across America, what has happened to the voice of Jewish morality by which God commands us? What has happened to the voice of Jewish conscience by which God nags at us? What has happened to the morality and this conscience, which are supposed to be the underpinnings of Jewishness? We want to know why so many people cheat—so many Jewish adults, so many Jewish kids. We want to understand how some of us can get so caught up in the race for whatever we're racing after that everything else is allowed to fall by the way, sometimes even our own marriages, sometimes even our own integrity, sometimes even the success that we have labored so hard to achieve.

What we want to know is what has happened to the moral vitality of the Jewish community that was once willing to struggle, issue by issue, not only for the sake of each one's individual integrity but for the collective integrity of the Jewish people and its eternal mandate to bring God's ethical word to a floundering world. How do we do that with a "passionate intensity"?

As this New Year begins, we ask the questions, and the questions are asked of us. As the Holy Days proceed, we shall attempt some answers. I shall deal tomorrow morning with the Waldheim affair and its moral implications for the Jewish community. On Yom Kippur, I shall attempt, or presume to attempt, a Jewish ethical perspective into our own personal lives. And Rabbi Zecher will address the ethical issue of surrogacy, including Baby M.

Awesome questions for these Days of Awe. Sacred questions for a people who, from its beginning, banded together to carry its sacred dwelling, its sacred burden, from place to place in the desert.

Urgent questions because we are at risk, we and our children, of losing our way in the desert. We are in need, we and our children, of finding our way back, which in Hebrew is called *t'shuvah.*

The questions are pressing because in the teaching of our tradition, the Gates will close at the end of Yom Kippur, ten days from now. Time is a factor. The time to change is now, not in some indefinite future, but now before the Gates close.

The questions are holy because there is always that one question that God asked of Adam in the Garden and has been asking ever since:

O man, O woman,

Where art thou?

Amen.

Rosh HaShanah 1987/5748

Personal Jewish Morality

It was one of the most impressive Jewish gatherings in all of our history. As our Torah reading tomorrow will describe it, the meeting took place in the open desert. The attendance numbered upward of a half million people, and somehow they managed it without double services, without a public-address system, even without a separate session for the children. Indeed, everyone was there, including, said Moses, the generations not yet born, including all the generations that would take their place eventually in Jewish space and Jewish time, as on this night.

Moses stands before the people and confirms the agreement, the covenant. He reminds the people of the conditions: that if they, the people, will live their lives according to the law of God, then they will continue to qualify as the people of God and bring God's message to the rest of the world. And as often as we say it and in as many ways as we try to say it, it never ceases to astound that thirty-two centuries later, we come together at this time, in this space, and attest to the fact that we listened to Moses, more or less, and kept the covenant, more or less, and we still have the message, more or less.

Some say that what has kept us alive has been the external pressure of anti-Semitism. I cannot accept that thesis. Because without an internal counterpressure to keep the covenant and keep the message, there would have been no reason and no will to exist. We survived because we did not crumple under the universal human question, Why is this happening to us? Instead, we stood tall with our specifically Jewish question, How are we going to get through this one? We survived because when we hit a dead end, we dug out a new road and built a new Temple and a new Jerusalem in whatever place in the world we happened to be, without ever forgetting the old one. We survived because we still wanted to have a *b'ris* for our children and say *Kaddish* for our parents, because we believed that the Torah was worth saving for another generation, and yet another and another. We survived because we claimed a code of morality that was more powerful than those who were overpowering us, and we even believed our own claim. We survived because we were willing to be different, more or less, and to stand on our own mountaintop, more or less. We survived even when 6 million did not because their Jewish deaths as Jews cried out to our Jewish lives—to live as Jews in Israel, in America, in the world. And even in this, our land of freedom where Jews are free, free even not to live Jewishly, there has been no rush to the exit doors. We have kept the ranks, more or less, and if my conversations with young people in our own congregation, many of whom are here tonight, are any indication, the ranks will still be kept, hopefully more rather than less. And they will bring their own children into the covenant and, God willing, their children's children.

We survived to tell the tale because, together with all the other reasons, I would call to your attention a detail of grammar in tomorrow's Torah portion. Moses begins his discourse with *Atem nit'savim*, "You stand this day, all of you, before the Lord your God." The Hebrew word for "you" is in the plural. But before the discourse is finished, Moses has switched to *atah*, "you" in the singular: "You, each Jew, I have set before you this day life and good and death and evil, for I command you this day to love the Lord, to walk in His way and keep His Commandments, laws and teachings, that you may live and increase...."

We have survived, and we are here tonight in this time and place because of that unsubtle message that the covenant was contracted with every Jew individually, that no Jew ever has to ask "for whom the bell tolls" because he or she knows very well that it is tolling for him or her. No Jew—rabbi or congregant—can ever confront the issues of Jewish morality that we have been trying to confront during these Holy Days without that first moral question from God to the first humans on earth: "Adam, Eve, where are you?" And if, like them, we have been hiding in the garden, Yom Kippur is the day to come out of hiding. It is the day for the generations to stand together, side by side, each member of each generation, to confront the question, the moral question, "Where are you?"

If we are of the older generation, however we choose to define that term, how much of our youthful idealism have we had to surrender? And how much did we give up without a fight?

And those of the youthful generation, you who are on the threshold of your grown-up world, you have been taught the moral precepts of your parents: How much will you test them on your own? How will you ask your own moral questions?

And you, our young children, still well on this side of the threshold, too young for the world but old enough to think, you have received all kinds of moral signals, some from your parents, some from your friends, some from your teachers, some from your temple. But, as Dr. Robert Coles, the child psychiatrist, has asked, "How will you figure out which ones you consider important and which ones you are prepared to ignore?"

My own attempt, during the rest of these minutes, will be to offer some Jewish tools for confronting these questions. I shall attempt some Jewish advice for living an ethical life. As I have told you before, I am mindful of the risks involved, as one child wrote in an essay about Socrates: "Socrates was someone who lived in Athens and went around giving people advice. They poisoned him." It shouldn't happen in Scarsdale.

And now for the advice, suited to recent days.

To those in public office who betray the public trust, the Sages said, "The greater the person, the more powerful the inclination to do wrong."

For the Jim Bakkers of this world, Rabbi Elazar HaKappur said, "Envy, sensuality and unbridled ambition destroy a person's life."

For the inside traders who knowingly violate the law, the midrash says, "The first question to be directed to the soul at the moment of final judgment will be, 'Have you been honest in your business dealings?'"

And for all the rest of us, Ben Zoma said, "Who is the rich man? He who rejoices in his lot."

But with all the specific advice with which our tradition is full—for doctors, for lawyers, for people in business, for teachers, for parents—my attempt tonight is to go beyond the specifics, or more accurately beneath them, to discover some general Jewish principles that can guide us, each one individually, on our own ethical way, in our own personal way, in our own ethical lives. Such a principle was presented some two thousand years ago by Rabbi Akiva based on a verse from Leviticus: "You shall love your neighbor as yourself." Or as Rabbi Hillel formulated, "What is hateful to you, do not do to your neighbor."

I reported several years ago on a book about lying by Carol Tarvis, and her position corresponds to Rabbi Akiva's principle. Tarvis said, "This lie, that I am about to tell, if the roles were reversed, would I want this lie told to me?" And according to our own answers to the question, we then proceed. Or, "With the course of action I am about to follow with my parents, would I, in a similar situation, be willing to have my child take that course of action with me?" And then we answer and proceed accordingly. Or, "The patient with whom I, the doctor, am about to discuss his condition, if I were the patient, how would I want it discussed with me?" And so with lawyers and clients, and teachers and students, and rabbis and congregants, and husbands and wives. Rabbi Akiva's Jewish version of human empathy is a guiding principle of human ethical behavior.

But then came another rabbi, my favorite, Rabbi Ben Azzai, who announced a principle that was considered by the Sages even greater than Akiva's. From the fifth chapter of the Book of Genesis, these words: "This is the book of the generations of Adam. When God created the human being, God created the human being in the likeness of God, male and female created He them." How is it a greater principle? By tracing all of humanity to a single Adam and a single Eve, Ben Azzai extended the embrace of ethical responsibility beyond neighbor to neighbor, beyond friend to friend, beyond citizen to citizen, now to all human beings in the world. Amazing! Two thousand years before mass communication, before television pictures of distended bellies and sunken eyes and starving people in Ethiopia, Rabbi Ben Azzai discovered in the Torah the fundamental principle that each of us, individually, is responsible to all those other people.

How a greater principle? Because that single verse in the Bible teaches yet more, including the Jewish truth that men and women were created equal. It teaches that the *tzelem Elohim*, "likeness of God," in us, by which we were created, is our human capacity to do justly, even as God is just, although we may not be sure where the path of justice lies. Our *tzelem Elohim* is our human power for compassion, even as God is compassionate, although we're not always sure of the best way to show our compassion. At the center of our being, in the likeness of our moral God, at the very center, is our moral self, with the power to think in terms of right and wrong, even if we're not always sure of the difference, with freedom to make moral choices, even if we're not always sure of our choice. But when we are sure and the choice is clear and that thing we are about to do next we know is wrong, then the *tzelem Elohim* at the center of our being gives us moral power to say "No" and not to do it. As a member of our congregation has wisely said: Even if there is a shadow of moral doubt, then it is also in our power to say "No" and not to do it, lest we chip away at the center of our moral being. Thus Ben Azzai's twofold principle for every Jew to lead an ethical life: Our connection to the human beings of the world whether we know them or not; and our connection to our moral selves whether they have been hiding or not.

And if the members of this congregation, including myself, are willing to accept that guiding principle not simply as a rabbi's sermon from the bimah but as a principle on which they will stake their lives, then those people who are desperately chasing after the train to catch it before it leaves without knowing where it is going, those people will then stop chasing. They will, as someone said, "stop rolling grenades under their own tent flaps." I know people who, if they accept that guiding principle, won't have to keep proving how much they're worth and how successful they can be because they will look now into the mirror of their own souls and see how valuable they are to begin with, *b'tzelem Elohim*—"in the image of God."

And if we, as parents, could transmit that guiding principle to our children, then we would pay as much attention to their ethical training as to their academic training because, as Walker Percy wrote, "You can get all As and still flunk life." We would share with them our own ethical dilemmas and our own process in trying to resolve them. We would share with them even when the moral solutions are not at hand, and we would let them know that even we are not exempt from the struggle.

If we would accept the guiding principle of *b'tzelem Elohim*, then the members of this congregation, in all of our positions of influence, would be ready to take our message beyond this place to that morally endangered species of the world. Because the danger in the world is not that cheaters are cheating, because cheaters have always cheated. The danger in the world is that the rest of us are beginning to receive a message, a message that is morally cynical, a message that what people are doing is alright, which it isn't; and that it doesn't matter, which it does; and that everybody's doing it, which they aren't.

Because then comes Yom Kippur to call us out of our moral hiding places, out of our trick-playing consciences, out of our moral cynicism. Then comes Yom Kippur, when we know before whom we stand, because for most of us, writes Leonard Fein, "we may not take God literally but we do take God seriously." We need God to monitor our souls. We need the moral God to return to our moral selves, to take up our moral compass. We need the holy God to return to our own holy selves.

The Jewish term for a moral model is a tzaddik. And those of you who have traveled to Israel, to Yad Vashem, have seen the Garden for the tzaddikim, the righteous gentiles who risked everything, including life, to save Jews from the Nazis. A survey was conducted among two hundred such tzaddikim, and it delineated three traits that characterized most of them. The first was that each of them had a parent or parents who had served as a model of moral conduct. The second was that the tzaddikim tended to be more doers than talkers: They believed they could make a difference in the world, even by caring for one human being. And the third was that they felt a little different from other people, somewhat isolated, on their own mountaintop.

What greater prayer for ourselves and our children: to have a moral model and to be one; not to talk as much as to do; and to make a difference, to stand on our own mountaintop, more or less.

It is written that we mortals are blessed because we are created *b'tzelem Elohim*, "in God's image." Especially blessed are we when we realize that we are so created, mortal and moral, with a sure compass to guide us on the way.

Amen.

Yom Kippur 1987/5748

Living with Ambiguity

Even before I was a rabbi, the story in this morning's Torah portion bothered me. I don't recall how old I was when I first heard that God called to Abraham to offer his son Isaac on the altar of sacrifice. But whenever it was, the discomfort began then and has never gone away.

The nagging question: How could this God who is supposed to be ethical administer a loyalty test that amounted to an act of murder, with the father as the perpetrator and the son as the victim?

And on Abraham's part, why didn't Abraham argue with God? If Abraham could take on God to defend the morally corrupt cities of Sodom and Gomorrah from God's punishment, why didn't he take on God to save this innocent child who was his own son?

What I have never proposed, however, in all the Rosh HaShanahs we have grappled with the *Akeidah*, is that we would be better off without it. What I have never suggested is that Reform Judaism should have discarded it, which easily could have been done because Jewish tradition designates this story for the second day of the holiday, which Reform Judaism did let go, and the *Akeidah* could have gone with it. But that encounter with God and a father and a son and an altar of sacrifice is so compelling and sparks so many questions on so many levels of human experience and of human struggle that we actually transferred the *Akeidah* from day two of Rosh HaShanah to day one, so that as Reform Jews we could keep grappling with it year by year.

And so today, I would share with you some of my own personal struggles during my years as a rabbi, and in doing so come back to the *Akeidah*, because in that story, I believe, there is a particular kind of struggle that none of us can ever escape. Because this time it's not the struggle between the power of good and the power of evil, even though we could talk about plenty of those struggles. And it's not the struggle between the power of temptation and the power to resist temptation, and we could tell our share of those. This time, the struggle is between something that is good and worthwhile and something that is good and worthwhile: loyalty to your God and concern for your child. Good and good, good versus good, and the struggle to make the choice.

We are all Abraham on the mountain. And if I could rewrite the Bible, Sarah would have been put right up there with him. Because no one escapes the struggle. The first time, for example, a teenage child of ours wants to spend the day in the city without the protecting presence of parents. And there it is: the good concern for the child's safety and the good need for the fledgling to take leave of the nest. And there is the struggle to choose.

Or, as many of us forge ahead in the careers for which we have been trained, for which we have talent and in which we may already claim some good success, there is also the good of our family. Our children still in the nest and their need to hold a loving hand as they explore their universe. Their need for a loving presence to be there to listen to what happened in school that day. I see it all the time: career and family, good and good. And the struggle is not for women only.

On so many moral issues that have confronted our society during my years as a rabbi, many decent people have taken a firm and absolute stand, convinced which is the side of right. But I must confess that on some of those very issues, I am not and have not been always so sure, not so absolutely convinced which side is right. Instead, my struggle between good and good.

Just as one example, on an issue like capital punishment. I acknowledge all the arguments, including the religious arguments, against capital punishment: that life is sacred and the state has no right to violate that sanctity; that the state can make mistakes and execute the wrong person; that capital punishment has never been proven to deter capital crimes. All good reasons.

But I also cannot dismiss a reason on the other side—for me, a religious reason: that the stability of God's world and humanity requires a balanced scale of justice for which all of us are accountable. And when one human being destroys the life of another, that balance is radically upset, and the only way to restore it may be to call the murderer to account with his life. Life for life. Not tribal vengeance, but justice in God's world. Perhaps.

So I live with that ambiguity, with the good arguments on both sides. And yet I have taken my stand with those who oppose capital punishment. Not because I am sure it is absolutely wrong but because, with all the other reasons, I know that if capital punishment should become the law of the land, it would become, in our imperfect world, the law mostly for the poor. They would be the ones to pay that final, irreversible price, and not all the others who could afford to find the ways and the means to avoid it. And then justice would be undone in God's world.

And that, I believe, is how we live with ambiguity. We examine the good on each side. And then, with the best of our knowledge and our values and our insights into our tradition, with the best of our understanding of ourselves and what our hearts tell us, we decide which good is best. And then we take our position, and we move into action, and we raise the banner of the cause as committed advocates. As committed advocates, but not as blind zealots who refuse to see any possible rightness on the other side. The zealot is sure that God is on his side. The rest of us, as Abraham Lincoln once said, hope and pray that we are on God's side, that we have come up with the right answer. Because ultimately, I believe, on every moral issue there is one best, right answer, one that is right with the one ethical God. The only problem is that we don't know what it is. So in the affairs of our world and in our personal lives, we do the best we can. And because of that possible rightness on the other side, we will at times try our best to accommodate. And we are willing at times to compromise because there could be rightness on the other side.

During these twenty-eight years of partnership between a congregation and a rabbi, between you and me, we have had our issues of good and good. I mention but one of them as current as a report in this week's newspaper.

When I was ordained a rabbi in 1952, the factor of mixed marriage between a Jew and someone not Jewish by birth or by conversion was not very high on the agenda of the Jewish community. The percentage of Jews who married someone not born Jewish was negligible, somewhere around five percent in the early 1950s. Since most of those marriages involved a conversion to Judaism and since conversion makes it a Jewish marriage, I don't remember even asking myself whether I would or would not officiate at a marriage where no such conversion had taken place because, like practically all of my colleagues, my assumption was that I would not. My assumption, my unchallenged assumption, was that when I participated at a wedding, I was the representative of the Jewish people and the Jewish religion, and for me to stand there authentically, both parties had to be Jewish. When that was not the case, it was the place for a nonsectarian justice of the peace, but not for me.

By the time I stood here for the first time in 1962, the five percent figure had risen to 15 percent, with conversion to Judaism still the rule of the day, with approximately 80 percent converting, becoming Jews-by-choice. And the assumption, by my colleagues and myself, that we would officiate only at Jewish marriages continued unchallenged. For me then, there was only one right side, and I was on it.

From 1962 until now, with everything else that has emerged from a society that is ever more open, the number of Jews who marry someone not born Jewish (in the word used by sociologist Gary Tobin) has "skyrocketed" from 15 percent to something that may be between 40 and 50 percent. And the number of conversions in those marriages (in Tobin's word) has "plummeted" from 80 percent to somewhere between 20 and 25 percent.

The result? The staggering increase of mixed marriage between a Jew and someone not Jewish, either by birth or by conversion, at the time of the marriage.

The result? That in congregations like ours, in Reform and Conservative congregations alike, an ever-mounting number of young men and women who went through religious school, through bar/bat mitzvah, through confirmation are now entering into mixed marriage to become life partners with the person they love, the person who is dearest in the world to them.

The result? Ever since the numbers began to skyrocket, for rabbis like myself and my colleagues, the assumption that once went unchallenged has now been called to the witness stand.

The challenge now comes from parents because, say some of them, it is their child's marriage and it should be their rabbi who blesses the marriage. And the rabbi's refusal, they say, is perceived as rejecting and not welcoming the person their child loves and, therefore, rejecting the child himself or herself. That rejection, they argue, may push the couple away from the Jewish fold altogether.

Or, the challenge comes from the young person himself or herself who professes a strong feeling of Jewish identity and declares the intention to continue that identity through children yet unborn. Should not a rabbi stand with that Jew under the chuppah? A good argument.

And for sure, the old assumption has been reassessed by rabbis, too. No rabbi likes to be the cause of anyone's pain. And surely, it is not comfortable to be the target of someone's anger. The pain is for us, too. When we have been close to a family and a child through the years, nothing could give greater joy than to stand with that child now grown up and with the person that child loves at the altar of marriage. The pain is for us, too. And the struggle is for us, too. And some Reform rabbis, according to the report 35 to 40 percent, have, under certain conditions, such as the promise to raise the children Jewish, changed their position, and they will conduct a mixed marriage. Sometimes it is because they have been pressured to do so by their congregation. And sometimes it is because they themselves have moved to a different place in their own thinking.

So as rabbi to the congregation, I would share with you the course of my own struggle. I believe that a rabbi by definition bears a commitment to his or her congregation, and we do the best we can to fulfill that commitment. But there is a second commitment that belongs to a rabbi. Because on the day we are ordained and the hands of blessing are placed on our heads, we become the caretakers of the Jewish people and of its covenant with God, for which the shofar blew this morning. To be a rabbi is to do everything within our human power to preserve the people and the covenant from one generation to the next.

Most of the time, these two commitments go hand in hand: at every bar/bat mitzvah, in every Bible class, at every child naming. Most of the time, we are, simultaneously, rabbis to the congregation and rabbis to the covenant. But there are other times, as when we are asked to officiate at a mixed marriage, when we must decide whether the two commitments are at odds and which one we must choose.

I have read the literature and I know from my own experience that in almost every instance of marriage between a Jew and someone not born Jewish, when there has been a conversion, the children of that Jewish marriage have been raised as Jews. When no conversion has taken place, the most recent figure is that only 28 percent of those families were raising their children as Jews, and many of that 28 percent are in this sanctuary this morning and give strength to our people. But in the other 72 percent, there is no Jewish people and there is no Jewish covenant in the lives of those children, whether or not their parents were married by a rabbi and whether or not they had once expressed the intention to raise their children otherwise.

And thus my struggle, and thus my decision: that as a rabbi, I can share the sacred event of Jewish marriage only between a man and woman both of whom are committed to the people and the covenant. I can stand there only as a representative of the Jewish faith. It's not being against anyone; it's not rejecting anyone. It's being for something—for the hope that our grandchildren will be Jewish and that the covenant will continue from generation to generation. I am saddened by the few who may feel pushed away because that was never my intent. I am heartened by all the rest who know where their rabbi stands and may even be influenced by that knowledge.

But there is still the rightness on the other side, the young person's feelings of Jewish connection to a tradition or a rabbi. And so I welcome every opportunity to meet with the couple in a mixed marriage to wish them well and to welcome them to the temple. I promise them and keep my promise that there will be no pressure, and whatever they seek of Jewish content for their home or family or whatever else they want to talk about, as a rabbi I am there to help. When I share with them my own struggle and my reasons for not officiating, I have discovered almost without exception that the young people understand, which sometimes the parents do not. A parent once said to me, "If it were a board member's child, I bet you would officiate." It was the most abusive insult I have ever received as a rabbi.

And thus have the years taught me that the road we travel can sometimes be dimly marked. And there are all those times when there are two roads, two good roads. And like Jacob in the Bible, we take on the struggle and we decide which road, and sometimes we feel the pain that goes with our decision. Like Jacob in the Bible, sometimes we walk away limping.

In the issues of our world and the issues of our lives, we make the decision and we hope that we are right. We admit that we are not 100 percent sure because only God knows. And once we admit that, we are allowed to be human and even to make mistakes. Once we admit that, there are no guarantees and we can never get arrogant.

I conclude with an experience of this summer. We spent an hour in Vermont with a potter whose name is Malcolm Wright. As we were admiring his work, he invited us to see the kiln in which the clay was fired. He told us how he begins each piece by shaping the clay, always with an eye to the final product after it has been finished in the kiln. He told us how, after the shaped pieces are set in the kiln, the fire is fed with thirty to forty sticks every five minutes for a period of ten hours. Such care! And after the fire dies down and cools, the finished product is brought forth.

And then the potter said, "Sometimes I shape a piece and set it in the kiln and say to myself: 'When this one comes out, it will be extraordinary.' And then the time comes to take it out, and I look at it, and it's just so-so. And there are other times when I am barely satisfied with what my hands have shaped, and I set it in the kiln, and it comes out extraordinary! Because once I have done my job and let go of it, it takes on a life of its own. And there are no guarantees."

And thus have the years taught me: As we live our lives from day to day, as we raise our families, as we raise our banners and decide which road to take, we do the best we can, and there are no guarantees. And we hope and pray that we are right.

And for the year that is new, even as we pray for health and strength and peace, so do we pray for the works of our hands, of our minds, of our souls, of our hearts as we shape our lives from day to day.

For the year that is new, we pray a prayer that is old:

O God, strengthen the work of our hands.
Yea, the work of our hands and our lives.
Make them strong and bless them.

Amen.

Rosh HaShanah 1990/5751

The Right Not to Remain Silent

I begin with the first of two perennial questions about human nature: What is there in the complexity of human nature that allows one group of human beings to take on the responsibility of murdering 10 million other human beings, including the 6 million of our own? What is there in the darkness of the human soul that can explain the massive pileup of children's shoes that we first saw in Auschwitz and again at the Holocaust Memorial Museum in Washington?

And for those who watched the recent program on PBS about the U.S. role during the Holocaust years, what was there in the soul of Assistant Secretary of State Breckenridge Long that made him responsible for directing that memo to all the consulates in occupied countries to "postpone, postpone, postpone" the granting of visas, keeping Jews from traveling to these shores and sending them instead on a journey to death?

And after all the rational explanations—how the Nazis made a political decision to use Jews as scapegoats for the disgrace of the German defeat in WWI, how ordinary Germans were co-opted into the Nazi regime and swiftly followed their orders, how even in the U.S. the soil of anti-Semitism in the 1930s spread to the ranks of the State Department, including Breckenridge Long—after all the explanations, there is still, inexplicably, that streak of evil that can infest the human soul, that can make the captain who lived next to Schindler's factory kill at random, that can make the soldiers laugh when their victims cry out in pain, a streak of evil that can be so obsessive that Hitler and his high command diverted much-needed manpower and supplies from their own war effort to make sure that the ovens at Auschwitz would keep burning and that every Jew would be exterminated.

Thus a message from the Holocaust: Evil, even unexplained evil, is real. The enemies of the ethical God walk this earth, and they heap up piles of children's shoes.

And a second message from a second group of non-Jews in Germany and occupied Europe during the dark years—this group not overtly anti-Semitic and not guilty of breaking Jewish windows, burning synagogues, or spitting on Jews in the street. Some of them even felt sympathy for the suffering victims. But while they themselves would never have inflicted suffering, they did nothing to relieve it either. Whenever they were asked to hide Jews from the Nazi dragnet, they refused: It was not their business. They could not get involved. They could not take the risk. Peaerl and Samuel Oliner in their book *The Altruistic Personality, Rescuers of Jews in Nazi Germany* refer to those people as the bystanders, and there were untold millions of them, and many Christian churches, and the government of the U.S. Elie Weisel calls it the "Sin of Silence" because the bystanders claim their right to be silent and to keep their distance and even give their reasons, political and otherwise, which is exactly what the world is doing about Bosnia while ethnic cleansing proceeds—exactly what happens when otherwise good people stand by and do nothing.

But then there is the third group, because in that same five years during which the Nazis murdered the 6 million and the non-Jewish millions stood by, there was this third group numbering between 50,000 and 500,000, non-Jews who risked their lives and spent their money to shelter and rescue Jews from their hunters. Granted they were only a fraction of the total population, but still our question: What is there in the makeup of those human beings who lived geographically in the Kingdom of Evil that prompted them not only to stay clear of the evil but actually to resist it by protecting its victims?

Just as there were Jews who resisted the evil when the Warsaw Ghetto fighters fought their valiant battle or when concentration camp inmates struggled to preserve their own human dignity against every diabolic strategy to destroy that dignity, so these non-Jews at risk of death hid Jews in their homes, fed them, cared for them, smuggled them to hoped-for safety, and thus did they resist the evil.

What was it that impelled Oskar Schindler to do what he did, and Raoul Wallenberg, who may have saved as many as 100,000 Hungarian Jews? And all those for whom the trees are planted in the garden of the righteous gentiles, many of whom are embarrassed by all the attention, who simply answer that "it was the ordinary thing to do."

So our question for this Service of Responsibility: What made them do it while the bystanders stood by?

After interviewing hundreds of rescuers and bystanders as well as Jews who were rescued, Pearl and Samuel Oliner answer the question thus: The essential difference between the two groups was that the rescuers, to a much higher degree than the bystanders, emphasized the ethical values they learned from their parents, who served as their ethical model. They spoke of what they learned about fairness, which included fairness to self and fairness to others, and what they learned about caring, which meant reaching out to others who had less than their fair share. The bystanders, on the other hand, spoke of parents who taught them primarily about self-interest and making a material success of themselves.

But even when the bystanders spoke of the ethical values they learned from their parents—and the bystanders saw themselves as ethical people—the circle of those to whom they felt ethically obligated was more limited, including only family, friends and colleagues, while the circle of the rescuers expanded outward even to human beings whom they did not know, even to Jews.

As one rescuer said, "I saw the Nazis shooting people in the street, and I could not sit there doing nothing"—while the bystander stood by.

Said another rescuer, "Nobody was going to touch these children. I would have killed for them"—while the bystander stood by.

But with all of that, there is one difference between the rescuers and the bystanders that the authors of the book do not report. It is what we have talked about together many times in this sanctuary and in Bible class and in confirmation class (and I look with pleasure at all the confirmands who are here). Because what we said through all these years is that the God of life keeps calling to us all the time, not only in the risk-filled time of the Holocaust but in all those other times when God's other children are lonely or sick or hungry or embattled. And again ours is the choice: to be silent and stand by or to claim our right not to be silent and to respond the way the prophet did: "Here am I. Send me."

Can we think of all the times when we heard the call, and the surge of sympathy stirred within us, and we intended to perform an act of caring rescue—to perform the mitzvah—but then we got busy with other things, and we never made the call or wrote the note or wrote out the check? And thus do we, sometimes, even with our good intentions, become the bystanders and not the rescuers. Between the intention and the deed lies a decision that may or may not come.

But more important, what made the rescuers during the Holocaust truly rescuers was that fewer than three percent of them performed only a single act of rescue, while well over 50 percent continued their rescue work anywhere from two to five years. One Polish family harbored eighty Jews during the course of the war. What began as a spontaneous mitzvah they decided to make a mission. And one of the indelible memories of my years in this temple is when the Social Action Committee took in, under its own auspices and at its own expense, a Vietnamese family, and no sooner did they succeed in settling that family, then they came back to the board and said, "We're ready for another family." And so now with the Soviet refugee families. And that is how a mitzvah becomes a mission. That is how a rescuer declares that he or she can make a difference in the world, even at the risk of occasional failure. Behind a mitzvah and behind a mission always comes a decision.

In memory of those who lie in nameless graves and in tribute to those who have stood against the tyrant and eased the pain of the victims, both inside the barbed wire and beyond it, and with trust in ourselves and our children and our children's children to whom You, O God, are always calling:

May You strengthen us to move from good intention to good deed and from good deed to the righteous mission of making this shabby world better. May we decide to live as rescuers.

Strengthen us, O God, to respond to our covenant with You, in the teeming streets of the city, on the field of bloody battle, or within the walls of this blessed congregation.

When You call to us, O God of life, as You do every day, may we know how to answer: *Hineini*, "Here am I. Send me."

Amen.

Service of Responsibility 1994/5754

The Book of Life

Remembering

Remembering a loved one is for moments that are personal and intimate. And yet this service to honor the memory of parents and loved ones who were once preciously in our midst but whose place is now empty takes place in a sanctuary with a full congregation. So personal and so intimate, yet given over to a public gathering.

A newspaper item last year reported two casualties in Vietnam, two young men of nineteen whose families lived a block from each other in the Bronx. One of the mothers said: "I don't know the other woman, but I plan to pay her a visit. We shall have much to say to each other."

The reason for reciting *Yizkor* in a sanctuary, a public gathering, is that we have much to say to each other.

We are here to tell each other, for whatever it's worth, that whoever has loved and lost is not the only one who has loved and lost. Empty and desolate though the valley of the shadow may seem, it is the most traveled road in all the world. It bears the footprints of every human being who bears some private grief in a lonely corner of his heart.

It is said that a man visited a physician in Naples. He complained of a deep feeling of sadness that would not leave him. The physician said: "My advice to you, sir, is to visit the theater where the great Carlini is playing. Every day he convulses the crowds with his laughter. My advice to you, sir, is go and see Carlini." The patient burst into tears and cried, "But you see, Doctor, I am Carlini."

The bereaved who have witnessed the tragic moments when death and life stood starkly face-to-face are the largest company in the world, and we have much to say to each other, much for victims of grief to share with newcomers to grief, to say that there is a turning point where the path winds upward out of the valley back to life and back to laughter and back to beauty. Someone said to me, "For some time after my mother died, whenever I remembered an incident we shared, I would cry. Now I smile."

We are here together to share the blessing of memory. Our family visited a house this summer. Its former owner had died. The house was high on a hill, and all around it, the original owner had planted hedges and around the hedges a stone wall and around the stone wall a wall of shrubbery.

I never knew the man, only that he lived alone, only that he had fenced himself off from the world and its people. I can only surmise that when he died, no one mourned, no one grieved, no one cried out, "Why did this happen to me?"

There are street urchins in Saigon who shine the shoes of GIs. They live in the streets and do not know who their parents are. When their parents die, no one mourns, no one grieves, no child remembers.

We are here to say to each other that the time of parting was sad and grievous and mournful because there were the good times that had gone before. There was the ache of loneliness only because there had been the joy of companionship. There were good reasons to cry, which soon became the reasons to smile.

In the fashionable quarter of London, there is another house, the mansion of the Rothschilds. People who walked by would see that one of the cornices was unfinished. They would ask in puzzlement: Could not the richest man in England afford to finish that cornice, or was it shabby neglect? But then the answer was given: Lord Rothschild was an observant Jew who, according to Orthodox tradition, had to leave some part of his house unfinished, a testimony to the world that the man who lives there is only a pilgrim on earth. "This is not Lord Rothschild's house. It is his inn, his hotel, where he spends some time on his journey to eternity."

Our beloved have left the inn for their homeward journey, for eternity with their God. And we remain behind to finish the corner of their house, to complete the tasks they began with all they taught us, with the gifts of memory, with all the reasons to smile.

May we furnish their house with hands of love even as we build our own, which someday we shall leave unfinished.

Amen.

Yizkor 1966/5727

Precious Gifts

The day will soon be over. The gates will soon close. We have journeyed from evening almost to evening, from *Kol Nidrei* almost to *N'ilah*.

The journey has been tiring. The hours of self-searching are draining; the human spirit grows weary. We already look forward to the last moments of the day when the shofar will sound with its final call and we shall be restored by a sense of wholeness. We shall be at peace with our God and ourselves, with a sense of genuine, personal shalom.

But first these moments with the memories of our loved ones, to help us say what in many respects we already know, that the journey from *Kol Nidrei* to *N'ilah* could not be complete without turning to them. They are very much a part of us, even as they were in the daytime of their lives. They give to us now, even as they did then. They are part of the wholeness, part of the shalom.

I once met a lady soon after she, her husband and child arrived in this country from Hungary as part of that group that emigrated after the uprising of 1956. She recalled how she had grown up in a remote village in the mountains. Somehow her mother had a knowledge of English, which she imparted to her daughter, and once, when she was still a child, her mother had said to her: "We have no wealth to give to you. All we can give you is knowledge."

And then the lady recalled her arrival in America only a few months before. And what had been for all the other immigrants the staggering obstacle of a strange language was for her no problem. And then she added: "My mother never realized what a great gift it was."

Our beloved, when they walked with us on earth, never realized how precious the gifts were, nor did we. What may have been a passing remark is now remembered and now inscribed forever in the book of our memory. It may have been a parent's commentary on life or people; it may have been a beloved's words of love; it may have been a child's innocent poem. Each one of them has become a rare and precious gift.

Perhaps we did not realize the full value of the gifts at the time our loved ones died. All we knew then was that someone precious had been snatched away. All we knew, perhaps, was the darkness and confusion of wandering aimlessly in the night.

It is to the credit of Judaism and to the rabbis of those ancient days that they were so sensitive to this human experience of grief. Not only did they turn to God to find strength in their weakness, but knowing that such strength might be hard to come by, they charted a journey through the roads of ritual and custom that might help the bereaved find his way out of the dark valley so that he could view his gifts in their full beauty.

The journey begins with a stark and realistic recognition: that death is entitled to grief, total grief. Philosophically, we can declare that death is part of life, but humanly, we know that death means separation, and separation means loss, and loss means grief. Even though the person who dies has been blessed with an abundance of years and we are comforted by the fact that he lived a full life, we are still grieved by the fact that his place is empty. And when someone dies in the springtime of his life, the sense of loss is compounded by the sense of tragedy. The unlived years are the hardest to cope with.

And at such moments, Judaism says to the mourner: "You are entitled to your grief, to your tears, to your anger. You are entitled to weep for your beloved and for yourself." And at such moments, Judaism gives good advice to well-meaning friends in the words of an ancient mishnah: "Do not attempt to console your neighbor while his dead still lies before him."

Then came the shivah, the days immediately following the funeral, when as much as possible of the daily routine was suspended so that the mourner could be given full opportunity to experience his own sadness. Friends came to call, to share his grief, to talk about the deceased, and the friends who arrived were the first gentle reminder that there was still a world outside, that life as usual was still there.

Then came the sh'loshim, the three weeks after the shivah, when the mourner gradually returned, with some exceptions, to the routine of life; the work had to get done.

And then the next months to finish the year—in some traditions it was eleven months—and it was then that the journey of mourning and grief was brought to its end; and at that juncture the road sign had but one word pointing forward: l'chayim, "to life."

Someone who had suffered her own loss wisely suggested the reason for the year as the end of the grief experience, because during that time the mourner would have passed through every one of those special occasions where the sense of loss would bear down especially hard—a birthday, an anniversary, a family seder, the High Holy Days, Chanukah, Thanksgiving—each one its own ordeal, each one a painful reminder of the empty seat, but also each one letting the mourner know that he can get through it, and perhaps the next one will be less painful.

So Judaism charted its own journey of grief. It hoped for the day, as the journey ended or even before, when the mourner would wake up some morning and look at the sunlight and know that he had turned the corner of his own grief; that with God's help and his own effort he had freed himself from the dark shadow of his tragedy; that now, in the broad sunlight, every little memory is no longer a ghost but a beautiful gift to be cherished and warmed by. And now, blessed and enriched with his new gift, he is ready for the world and for life and for people who have been patiently waiting for him.

Elie Wiesel writes of a visit to his native village of Sighet, where there were practically no Jews left:

> I met a Jew, one of the rare survivors, and we walked through the cemetery of Sighet.
> "To be a Jew," I asked, "what does that mean to you? Does it mean turning your heart into a cemetery?"
> "No," my companion said. "The heart of man is a sanctuary, and the dead, by definition, have no right to be there. To be a Jew is to fill the sanctuary with light, without betraying the cemetery."

And this is what the Jewish journey means, this is what *Yizkor* means: to do honor to our beloved dead by filling our hearts with the light of their lives and not the darkness of their death, with gifts and not with ghosts, with peace and not with pain.

The journey of Yom Kippur is almost over. Our beloved have traveled their own journey to God's eternal home. They are with us even now on our journey for life and for peace.

Amen.

Yizkor 1972/5733

The Mystery of Death

The subject of death, which at one time was an appropriate theme for poems and *Yizkor* sermons and private thoughts, has now become a matter for discussion and analysis in the public forum. As many as two or three full-length books are being published each week on the subject of death and dying. Panels of doctors and psychiatrists and clergymen and laymen abound with debates on the complex questions of euthanasia and the treatment of the dying patient.

"Death with dignity" has become a watchword. I recall a session being conducted by the directress of a home for the terminally ill in England. She showed a picture of an elderly woman, propped in the arms of a nurse, drinking a cup of tea, and the directress told us that the picture was taken on what turned out to be the last day of the patient's life; and then she added that despite all of the advantages of intravenous feeding, a dying person is entitled to tea out of a cup. "Death with dignity" implies that a dying person is still a human being and is entitled to be treated like one.

And yet, with all the discussions and the books and the openness, the day will never come when death will be deprived of its mystery, anymore than birth and life themselves, regardless of all our knowledge, are denuded of their mystery. We who have confronted death firsthand can attest to the mystery, and we who have lost someone we love, can testify that all the knowledge and all the discussions, as helpful as they may be, do not take away the pain and do not remove the grief, and the words of Job, who had lost so much, his words of mystery and pain, are still the words we recite at every funeral:

> *Adonai natan, Adonai lakach.*
> *Y'hi sheim Adonai m'vorach.*

> The Lord hath given, the Lord
> hath taken away. Blessed be
> the name of the Lord.

We listen to these words, to the mystery and the pain, and who of us in some wishful moment has not wished that the words would simply say: "The Lord hath given."

These words, in the imagery created by Felix Salten, convey something of that wish:

> *The leaves were falling from the great oak at the meadow's edge. They were falling from all the trees. One branch of the oak reached high above the others and stretched far out over the meadow. Two leaves clung to its very tip.*
>
> *"It isn't the way it used to be," said one leaf to the other.*
>
> *"No," the other leaf answered. "So many of us have fallen off tonight, we're almost the only ones left on our branch."*
>
> *"You never know who's going to go next," said the first leaf. "Even when it was warm and the sun shone, a storm or a cloudburst would come sometimes, and many leaves were torn off, though they were still young. You never know who's going to go next."*
>
> *"The sun seldom shines now," sighed the second leaf, "and when it does, it gives no warmth. We must have warmth again."*
>
> *"Can it be true," said the first leaf, "can it really be true that others come to take our places when we're gone and after them still others, and more and more?"*
>
> *"It is really true," whispered the second leaf. "We can't even begin to imagine it; it's beyond our powers."*
>
> *"It makes me very sad," added the first leaf.*
>
> *They were silent a while. Then the first leaf said quietly to herself, "Why must we fall?"*
>
> *The second leaf asked, "What happens to us when we have fallen?"*
>
> *"We sink down..."*
>
> *"What is under us?"*
>
> *The first leaf answered, "I don't know. Some say one thing, some another, but nobody knows."*
>
> *The second leaf asked, "Do we feel anything? Do we know anything about ourselves when we're down there?"*
>
> *The first leaf answered, "Who knows? Not one of all those down there has ever come back to tell us about it."*
>
> *They were silent again. Then the first leaf said tenderly to the other, "Don't worry so much about it. You're trembling."*
>
> *"That's nothing," the second leaf answered. "I tremble at the least thing now. I don't feel so sure of my hold as I used to."*
>
> *"Let's not talk anymore about such things," said the first leaf.*
>
> *The other replied, "No, we'll let be. But what else shall we talk about?" She was silent and went on after a little while, "Which of us will go first?"*
>
> *"There's still plenty of time to worry about that," the other leaf assured her. "Let's remember how beautiful it was, how wonderful, when the sun came out and*

shone so warmly that we thought we'd burst with life. Do you remember? And the morning dew, and the mild and splendid nights...."

"Now the nights are dreadful," the second leaf complained, "and there is no end to them."

"We shouldn't complain," said the first leaf gently. "We've outlived many, many others."

"Have I changed much?" asked the second leaf shyly but determinedly.

"Not in the least," the first leaf assured her. "You only think so because I've gotten to be so yellow and ugly. But it's different in your case."

"You're fooling me," the second leaf said.

"No, really," the first leaf exclaimed eagerly, "believe me, you're as lovely as the day you were born. Here and there may be a little yellow spot, but it's hardly noticeable and only makes you handsomer, believe me."

"Thanks," whispered the second leaf, quite touched. "I don't believe you, not altogether, but I thank you because you're so kind. You've always been so good to me. I'm just beginning to understand how kind you are."

"Hush," said the other leaf and kept silent herself for she was too troubled to talk anymore.

Then they were both silent. Hours passed. A moist wind blew, cold and hostile, through the treetops.

"Ah, now," said the second leaf, "I...

Then her voice broke off. She was torn from her place and spun down.

Winter had come.

—from *Bambi*

It is what we read in a passage from the prayer book: "We loose our hold upon life when our time is come, as the leaf falls from the bough when its day is done." A book that is started is a book to be finished. A journey that is begun is a journey to be ended, when the time comes. The late Stewart Alsop, in his beautiful and sensitive book, *Stay of Execution: A Type of Memoir*, writes these words: "A dying man needs to die as a sleeping man needs to sleep, and there comes a time when it is wrong as well as useless to resist." The Lord who giveth must also taketh away, when the time comes.

They were good gifts that God gave us when our beloved walked on earth: There was love and laughter and beauty; there were human strengths and human weaknesses; there were human virtues and human failings. Our beloved were not perfect because they were human, and what God gave to us were good human gifts.

And then, in some dark moment, the gift was taken away, and it all seemed so ridiculously canceled out. But somehow, after the nighttime of grief, a shaft of light began to break through, and we began, slowly we began, to grasp a new truth: that the person was gone, but somehow through some great mercy, the love and laughter and beauty were stored in our memory as precious human gifts. A problem arises and eventually we are able to say: He or she would have handled it this way, and we are not shattered with grief by the thought of it. Or we encounter a moment of special beauty or deep tenderness and we are able to say: He or she would have enjoyed it, and we are not shattered by grief—touched by sadness perhaps, but not shattered by grief. And we ourselves are able to say: The Lord gives, the Lord takes, but He leaves something for us to remember and live by.

But with all the acceptance and all of the understanding, the one leaf still asks of the other, Why some so young? Why was my beloved taken away in the springtime of his life?

What is not known cannot be answered. But what is hoped and what is trusted are something of an answer. And this is our hope and our trust: that when God takes, He not only takes away from us, but He takes back unto Himself, to His care and His peacefulness and His eternity. I share with you the words of Elisabeth Kubler-Ross, who has devoted her career to the care of the dying: "Before I started working with dying patients, I did not believe in life after death. I now do believe in a life after death without the shadow of a doubt."

The Lord hath given, the Lord hath taken back unto Himself, and with all the strength and hope we can muster, we bless the name of the Lord.

Amen.

Yizkor 1974/5735

To Weep, to Be Silent, to Sing

With the final call of the shofar, the Gates that opened before us last evening will close, and we who have made this journey of the spirit will return to the world. But first, these few moments with the memory of our beloved, gone from the world but surely not from our lives and surely not from the private places of our hearts. They are moments not for sadness but for strength, not only for what we have lost but for what they left behind that not even death could take away.

We speak then of life, all of life, including the reality of death. To us Jews, death is very real, incomprehensible perhaps, and mysterious perhaps, but very real, and who knows its reality better than we? Someone once said that neither the sun nor death can be looked at steadily, the one so bright, the other so dark, and who knows better than we?

Jacob, we are told in the Bible, struggled with the angel of darkness through a long and trying night. The ordeal exhausted his strength and drained his spirit, but he did not surrender. With the light of morning, it was the dark angel who retreated, and he even gave a blessing to Jacob before he took leave.

Who knows better than we who have lost someone we loved the ordeal of that long and trying night—the numbness, the anger, the weary traveler on his lonely way? For some, the darkness may not have come until later, after the shock wore off and the realization settled in, after the people stopped coming, after we were alone in the night.

It is the universal struggle of grief, but in almost twenty-five years as a rabbi, I have known hardly anyone who hasn't made it; hardly anyone who would not or could not break loose from the grip of death and loss; hardly anyone who ended up spending all his days pathetically in a valley of shadows with more anger than love and more agony than peace.

Because for most of us, there came a time, perhaps when we least expected it, that somehow we knew that morning had broken through the darkness and the long night was over. We were on our way out of the valley, and like Jacob in the Bible, we had not surrendered.

Where did the strength come from? In part it came from the voices of the living, our families and friends, who let us know that they needed us, that we couldn't stay away too long, and simply to respond to their needs and their call, we had to break loose from the grip of our grief. There is nothing more strengthening than members of a family who need each other.

Where did our strength come from? In part from the very ones who left us in our lonely way—from their very love, the treasure of shared moments, their wisdom, their zest for life, their unlived years.

And from where did our strength come if not from Him who gives life and takes it away, who is my Shepherd, who leads me beside still waters, who restores my soul to the land of the living?

With such strength, we left the dark valley for the sunlit day, and even now and again, when shadowy moments return, they linger for only a little while and for only a few tears, and then they go away, and thus we know that we have survived the struggle.

But somehow we do even more than survive. I have been in houses of mourning where there visited someone who had suffered just such a loss, and from that someone came more consolation than from all the rest of our well-intentioned but feeble efforts. He had been through it himself, he knew, his sensitivity shone through because, like Jacob in the Bible, the ordeal of that dark night had left him with a blessing that now he could share.

There are three ways to mourn, said the Baal Shem Tov. The first is to weep, and in the depths of the valley, we did our share of weeping. A fifteen-year-old in our congregation, Jean Kaufman, wrote the following when a friend died:

Today I cried one thousand tears
For someone who'd never see them.
And then I cried one thousand more
Because I knew it did no good.

We have done our share of weeping.

The second way to mourn, said the Baal Shem Tov, is to be silent, to sense the mystery and not to say a word, to miss someone very much and wish that he or she would be there, just as we did on our way out of the dark valley.

To weep, to be silent, and then the third way: to sing a hymn of praise to life that still abounds in sights and sounds and vivid colors in the brightness of sunlight, with the valley now below us and now behind us. We sing the songs of our beloved, we aspire to their qualities of spirit, we take up their unfinished tasks and their unlived years.

The Gates will soon close, and this is what the journey means and what *Yizkor* means: to fill our lives with the brightness of memory and not the darkness of death, with songs and not with sadness, with blessings and not with pain.

We are like Joshua, who must proceed on his way without his beloved Moses. And the words were spoken to Joshua: *Chazak v'ematz*, "Be strong and of good courage."

The same words come to us from the memory of those we loved and send us onward in our own journey: *Chazak v'ematz*, "Be strong and of good courage."

Amen.

Yizkor 1976/5737

Memory and Melody

The day is almost over, the day on which a Jew stands before his God with the totality of his being: not mind alone, not feelings alone, but the person that he is.

And then, almost at day's end, this service of *Yizkor* to remind us of what we already know: that who we are and what we are are bound up in some mysterious and wonderful way with the very ones whom we now remember.

For me, this service of *Yizkor* began on a Sunday afternoon this summer at the Tanglewood Music Festival with a performance of Mahler's Ninth Symphony conducted by Leonard Bernstein. It was the last symphony that Mahler completed before his death in 1910. One of his biographers suggests that the symphony may have been a requiem for his own daughter, who had died not long before, and for his own brothers and sisters, who had been long since dead.

It may thus have been for Mahler a very personal *Yizkor*. But for anyone who has ever listened to it, it can become for that person an encounter with living and dying and loving and remembering; at least it did for me. From its melodies and its rhythms, there came joy and weeping. There was childhood, and there was nature. There was dazzling springtime and leaves trying on colors, and there was bleak winter. There were moments of exaltation and moments of groping to break out of emptiness. There was the longing for life and the insistence of death. There was finally the lingering farewell of the cello and fragments of a melody and then total silence and peace.

The critic's review that appeared in our local Berkshire newspaper stated that the challenge of Mahler's Ninth lies in making the pieces fit together and that Bernstein rose to that challenge. And then the writer added, "Bernstein picked out every detail, every inner voice and line and gave each its due importance."

And thus on a Sunday afternoon this summer did I think of today and did this service of *Yizkor* begin. Everyone who has loved and lost becomes a trustee of those lines once written, once lived, once shared, and later remembered. There are some of us who live constantly with their memories. But for others of us, suddenly a shared moment flashes into our consciousness as though from nowhere, but we know it was there all the time in our own safekeeping. We ourselves say something or see something in our children, and we ourselves are surprised at how well the lines have been remembered.

And thus this service of *Yizkor*, when we become the conductors. We put the pieces of memory together; we listen to what they wrote in the lines and what they wrote between the lines, each line its own statement of the person they were or else would have been had there only been more time; we listen to the saying of yes to life, to the surrendering to the no of death, to the why of grief, to the silence.

We put the lines together, and we take them with us for our own journey of the spirit on Yom Kippur. And those memories, fitted together, become a source of strength and of beauty and of understanding as we proceed on our own journey before the closing of the Gates.

From where we sat at Tanglewood, we could watch Leonard Bernstein's face, and there were tears on his cheeks. He was saying *Kaddish* without words; he was delivering a eulogy without a name.

For the dead of our people who lie in unmarked graves, we have no names, and for them we say *Kaddish*. But for our own beloved, we do have the names. In fact, said the rabbis in the midrash, there are three names that belong to each person: the name given to him at birth, the name by which others call him, and the name he creates for himself. It is that third name that we take with us on this journey of the spirit, its life and love still with us. Even when the cello has played its part, even with the total silence, there is still the memory and the melody that make the world still sing.

Amen.

Yizkor 1979/5740

Mind the Light

There was a window near King David's bed that opened to the north. Each night, the king would hang his harp opposite the window. The chill north wind would blow, and from the breeze through the window, the harp would play of itself, a melody of sadness and of uncommon beauty.

In this hour of our remembering, we who have loved and lost, we for whom the harp has played its melody, we can tell each other that we never altogether forget the sadness of a place left empty. Each death is a story unfinished—sometimes cut short too soon in the telling, sometimes dragged out too long in the dying, and yet each story is unfinished: Words that may never have been spoken; good-byes that may never have been said.

We rabbis during the course of the years stand beside many gravesides. Too many. We recite the prayers and try to weave together some words of farewell. We try to bring solace. But no rabbi I know would dare even make the attempt to silence the sad melody borne by the chill wind. Death is what it is. Death is final, and the story is unfinished, and we speak the words at the graveside, and yet we have nothing to say. Nothing except *Yis'gadal, v'yis'kadash, sh'mei rabbah*.

At each year's service of remembering, the same words are uttered again, but not the same. Because somehow with the healing balm of time, the melody that plays on the harp strings now sings also with the uncommon beauty of memory: shared years and shared love.

The following account was written by an elderly widow who was the keeper of a small lighthouse in New York harbor between Manhattan Island and Staten Island.

I was a young girl living at Sandy Hook, New Jersey, when I first met my husband. He was keeper of the Sandy Hook Light and took me there as his bride. I was happy there, for the lighthouse was on land and I could have a garden and raise flowers. Then one day we were transferred here, to Robbins Reef. As soon as we arrived, I said to my husband, "I can't stay here. The sight of water wherever I look makes me too lonesome. I won't unpack." But somehow all the trunks and boxes got unpacked.

327

Four years later, my husband caught cold while tending the light. The cold turned to pneumonia, and they took him to the infirmary on Staten Island.

I stayed behind to tend the light. A few nights later, I saw a rowboat coming through the darkness. Something told me the message it was bringing. The man in the boat said, "We're sorry, Mrs. Walker, but your husband's worse." "You mean he's dead," I answered, and there was no reply.

We buried my husband on a hillside on Staten Island. Every morning when the sun comes up, I stand at a porthole and look across the water toward his grave. Sometimes the hill is green, sometimes it is brown, sometimes it is white with snow. But it always brings a message from him, something I heard him say more often than anything else. Just three words: "Mind the light."

It is that message that our beloved, *alahem hashalom*, left for us—every parent for the children, every husband for his wife, every wife for her husband, even a child taken too soon for a parent: Mind the light. Take up the unfinished chapters. Care for the living. Live. Laugh again. Love again. In the words of Ernest Hemingway, "Discover and write the truest sentences you know, and mind the light!"

A rabbi officiated at the funeral of a young husband and father. The rabbi had known the deceased only casually, but all his friends had conveyed to the rabbi the wonderful qualities of the man: his humor, his gentle warmth, his powers of perception.

A year later, the rabbi was officiating at the unveiling. He was pleased that the family was so well on its way. The wife and mother, for no other reason than that she was a proud mother, showed the rabbi the report card that her son had received in school. The comments by the teacher were practically word for word what the friends had said about the father a year before, remarking on his humor, his warmth, his powers of perception. For all those years of life, the parent had shared the gift with the child, and now the child, very much his own person, was his father's son.

The mystery that was so silent by the graveside begins now to hum its own melody as we write the words on the unfinished pages with the truest sentences we know—the truth we heard from them as we mind their light that even now shines upon our way.

We were once saddened by the death and still gladdened by the life. Now and forever.

Yis'gadal, v'yis'kadash, sh'mei rabbah. The wind blows through the window, and the harp strings play.

Amen.

Yizkor 1984/5745

At the End of the Day

Soon after Priscilla and I arrived in South Africa this summer, someone used familiar words in a context that was unfamiliar to us, and at first, I did not understand. The person was discussing some issue or other, and then he said, "And at the end of the day, I would like to know that I have taken my stand on the side of the right." And then when I heard someone else say those same words in a similar vein, I came to understand what they mean: when all is said and done, in the final analysis, when the verdict comes in, on the bottom line, or, as they say, "at the end of the day."

When a person dies and a rabbi is asked to officiate at the funeral, the rabbi usually arranges to meet with the family in advance, with as many members of the family as possible, not only to discuss the arrangements but to talk about the eulogy. I ask everyone to share memories, to recall anecdotes, to tell how they personally were affected by the one they loved. What I usually hear first are the virtues: the love for family, the zest for life, sometimes about a flair for style, a commitment to causes, a gift of humor. And when someone recalls something funny that was so true to the spirit of the person that everyone laughs, that laughter no less than their tears is the most tender tribute of all.

And then I say, "But no one is perfect. Everyone has human failings." And then I say, "You know I will be discreet in writing the eulogy, but your sharing of those feelings will help me to derive a sense of the total person." And most of the time, the honesty of the responses is moving and touching.

So now I have a new phrase to entitle those family sessions and family sharing. Because what they say then, when a person has died, is the verdict of a life. What they say then, in truth, is in those words "at the end of the day."

In this service of remembering, what each of us has to say in the silence of our heart is a chronicle of treasured moments etched in memory and in love, moments when their hearts pulsed in rhythm with ours, when their laughter rang in chorus with ours, when their gentle hands guided us on our way. All of those moments are bundled in blessing, even as their failings seem to fade with the passing of time. And those blessings are with us still, at the end of the day. And such a day never ends.

This summer, a member of our congregation suffered the loss of his father (and I tell you this with that congregant's consent). We were away, and I called the house and spoke to the daughter-in-law of the man who had died. She told me that on a Thursday evening, he had traveled from Long Beach to Far Rockaway for a card game with his friends. He had just won a hand, and then he slumped over. And his life came to an end. And the daughter-in-law said, "How nice to die with a winning hand!"

Wouldn't we all settle for that? But we frail mortals are not always so blessed. Sometimes death strikes in the middle of the day, a melody half-sung, a poem half-written, the hand not yet played out. And we seek strength from God and each other and, God willing, at the end of the day, we find the strength.

For all the rest of us and our loved ones, how nice to die with a winning hand, because then the daughter-in-law told me how one of his fellow card players had come to pay a call during the shivah. He walked over to the son in mourning and put out on the table the three and a half dollars that were the father's winnings at the game. And the son urged the friend to take the money for some good cause.

Wouldn't we all settle for that? That whatever we may achieve during this brief day on earth, at the end of the day, there would be those whom we loved who would feel blessed by our achievements, our winnings, our love, our laughter, our zest for life, our commitment to good causes.

The end of this day will soon be here, and the Gates will soon close. May our beloved have journeyed to the peace of their eternal home. They are, in the words of our prayer book, "like the stars by day, not seen by mortal eyes." Yet they shine on always in the days of our years, always in the peace of their eternal home, at the end of the day.

Amen.

Yizkor 1989/5750

The Lonely Climb

In the episode in the Torah, Moses comes down from the mountain with the commandments in hand, sees his people dancing around the calf of gold, and is so distressed that he smashes the tablets to the ground.

Although there is no actual death, the episode is dominated by the mood of grief because now Moses has lost the people he loves. His spirit is drained. Around him are only the shattered pieces. And then, according to the story, God calls to Moses to go back up the mountain. He has no choice but to make the lonely climb.

So for us who share this hour of *Yizkor*. Each of us in his or her own way has lived through the shattering time. Life sparkled with beauty and then came death. Life lilted with laughter and then came death. Life was blessed with love and then came death. And then each of us—at one time or another, some even now, the tears not yet dry—had to make the lonely climb.

Friends helped and family helped more than we can ever thank them. But with all they did to keep us from being alone, they could not keep us from being lonely. As much as they tried, as much as we tried, there were no shortcuts on the uphill journey. We had to learn for ourselves the emptiness of days and the loneliness of nights without the one we loved. We had to learn for ourselves what someone wrote about a friend who had died: "It is not at floodlit moments we miss him most but in killing time when he could have livened it."

Then, in the course of the lonely climb, we came to discover that moments come and moments go when we are released, ever so briefly, from the prison of our own grieving, when we feel strong enough to make it on our own through a day and a night. We look around and we see those who still need us, who still need our love and our hand, and their need is strength for us.

And then in the course of the lonely climb, there comes a time that we never thought possible when the pieces were first shattered and the wounds were painfully fresh. There comes a time when we discover that remembering the ones we love can move us beyond the pain of missing them. What they gave to us in their lifetime—the laughter, the beauty, the love—can reach beyond their deathtime to stay with us, not as ghosts but as a blessed melody in our lives.

I once shared with you an experience of many years ago when we were attending a concert at Tanglewood. Isaac Stern was playing Mendelssohn's Violin Concerto, and the melody sang with uncommon beauty. Suddenly, without warning, the skies darkened and the heavens broke loose. A strange sight as the man guided the bow over the strings as though without a sound, a pantomime, because all we could hear was the thunder. And then suddenly, the thunder still rumbling, above that rumbling, we could hear the magic melody of the violin.

And that's what comes to all of us eventually in our lonely climb up the mountain: a magic moment when we begin to hear the melody above the storm, when the remembering of the beauty and the laughter does not cause the pain but begins to soothe it. It's at that moment that we have neared the mountain's peak, as close as anyone can get because no one ever climbs all the way. Some of you here now are still on your upward climb. And the rest of us who have neared the peak can turn to you and give you reason for hope and reason for strength. Because we made it up this far and because we have good reason to thank God for our own hope and our own strength.

And that, I believe, is one meaning of faith: to know that the melody is playing even when we may not hear it; to know that our beloved are safe even if they are beyond our sight; to know that God is God even if beyond our understanding. It may not be the ultimate answer to the mystery of life and death. But it may be the best one we have.

May we listen to the melody. May it become a blessing in our lives, for beauty, for laughter, for love, for life.

Amen.

Yizkor 1990/5751

National Leadership

Installation As CCAR President

When Priscilla and I first went to Westfield, New Jersey, almost thirty years ago, we were young then, and the friends we made were not only people of our own age, but among our closest friends were those in their sixties and seventies. And thus did we make very early in our lives a discovery about the rabbinate: that we crossed the generations, that we are ageless—whether young or old—and I count this as one of the blessings of being a rabbi. This is my feeling tonight as I accept the *kavod* that you bestow on me and upon my fellow officers. My journey to this moment and this place is in the company of the generations, *l'dor vador*. And I would like to tell you something about them.

First, the generation younger than I am. You see, being of the middle generation has certain advantages: We are old enough to feel experienced, and we are young enough to still think we may be immortal. I spent two wonderful weeks in Cincinnati a few years ago, at the College, and some of those men and women are here at this conference now as rabbis. But especially do I speak concerning that generation of my associates and interns through the years. They have always challenged me with their new ideas. They have always helped me to test my old ones. They have kept me young. And in these changing worlds that whirl around us, I am like that man in the cartoon who was sitting at a bar with a friend, and turning to his friend, he said, "Somehow, every time I get to where it's at, it is already someplace else." And my younger generation helped to keep me young.

L'dor vador. Because there is our own generation. I marvel at what bonds must have been forged in our student days that they have withstood the passage of time and the distance of miles. And the blessings of these conventions with all our efforts of good programming is of the highest value: It is to give embraces and kisses and handshakes and to talk as though no time has passed since the last time we met.

And the blessing of the *kallot*, as we have seen them around the country, is to help us forge new bonds with new friends, because this is what I have discovered as a rabbi: We share our coded signals that no one else understands. We are human beings with the calling of a rabbi. And to me, it makes precious little difference whether the *Kadosh Baruch Hu* initiated the call or we did. We are human beings with a calling, and one of the reasons we are drawn to each other is that I am not sure that anyone else other than a rabbi or a rabbi's family understands that combination of being a human being with a calling.

And then the *dor avoteinu v'imoteinu*: those who have gone before us. I was fourteen-years-old when my rabbi James G. Heller, *alav hashalom*, of the Isaac M. Wise Temple (where Samuel Wohl, Amiel Wohl's father, *alav hashalom*, was also a rabbi) said to me, "Jack, have you ever thought of being a rabbi?" And I said "Yes." Then he began teaching me Weingreen's *Grammar*, week after week. And then I began to teach under the direction of Ceil Singer. I mention her by name because I want you to know that she was part of my journey. Not only mine, but a lot of rabbis in this room tonight learned from her that *talmud Torah k'neged kulam* and that you were teaching not only a Jewish subject but a Jewish child.

I wish some of you colleagues had known Sam Cook in the days when he was director of NFTY. He was part of my journey because he guided the whole generation of so-called youth rabbis to hold our vision of a Jewish future. Many of the young people under his wing are in this place tonight or are now rabbis in Israel. But there was one rabbi in that old generation who was my closest companion in the journey to this place and this moment. His name, as you already heard, was Jacob Philip Rudin, *alav hashalom*. He was my closest teacher, my closest rabbi, my closest friend. From him came my greatest gift, his daughter, Priscilla, to be my wife. I learned from him not only to love the tradition but that each *pasuk* was a rock from which to strike the spark. He loved not only humanity but human beings, one by one, which is sometimes hard to do. He loved not only the Jewish people but also Jews, which is sometimes not easy to do. He was a lover of beauty, majestic and simple beauty, but especially the beauty of language. Each word was a jewel, and he set the jewels into a crown that the rest of us call sermons. He was passionate about everything—about his people and his God and about this Conference, which he served as president thirty years ago. Just as I take the gavel from you, Gunther, I take it also from Jacob Rudin and from all those who served as my illustrious predecessors. Jack's wife is here, and his son is here, and his daughter-in-law is here, as is his daughter and two of his grandchildren. And he is at my side.

And thus my second line of *dorot*: my family. I would not be here without Priscilla. I do not want to be anywhere without Priscilla. When I heard Alex Capron's story the other day about the man who was dying, I recalled that in the past eight years, when I had meningitis, when I was hit by an automobile, and when I had heart surgery, each time Priscilla was at my side. And I recalled Alex

Capron's last line, "You may be bad luck to me, sweetheart." Then there are our children. A lot of ego stuff can get in the way of being a rabbi. So how do you stay human? You do it when you have three kids, who, after a sermon, when everyone is saying Good Shabbes or Good Yom Tov, are saying eight, or nine, or five, or three, which is their rating of the sermon on a scale of one to ten. There have even been times when I have looked out into the congregation at one of my children, and I see either thumbs-up or thumbs-down. Jonathan arrived at 6 P.M. tonight from Washington, where he is a lawyer who defends the accused who are too indigent to hire lawyers of their own. David is studying to be a rabbi, now in his third year at Hebrew Union College. Our daughter, Elsie, could not be here because she is drama director at Camp Swig, and this was the first day of the drama group. She had to be on the job at Camp Swig—after all I have done for Reform Judaism.

Thus do I stand before you, my colleagues and my family, awed by the responsibility and touched by the honor.

L'dor vador. You are my generations: you, my rabbis; you, my family; and also my congregation. All of you are taking on the responsibility and the honor with me.

L'dor vador. And from the depths of my being, I answer, Hallelujah.

1985/5746

President's Message, 1986

Having served as president of our Conference for a year, I can identify with Avraham Avinu when God spoke to him in Bethel: "Raise your eyes and look out from where you are, to the north and the south and the east and the west." Having spent this year not only in looking but also in traveling into all of those directions, I can share Abraham's exalted sense of wonderment at the vast array of challenges and opportunities that lay before him.

The essential distinction, of course, is that Abraham was the *av*, the pioneer in our covenantal adventure, whereas each successive president of the Conference is a *ben* (someday a *bat*). Each of us begins with a *yerushah*, an inheritance from all those who have gone before, from the leaders and members of this Conference in its almost 100 years of history. Their names and visions and controversies are recorded between the blue covers of those books that line the shelves of our libraries.

Another difference: Abraham, unlike the president of this Conference, stood there *l'vado*, all by himself—no fellow officers, no executive board, no committees, no network of regions, no office staff at 21 E. 40th; no Sara Siegel to be every rabbi's Jewish mother; no Elliot Stevens to tend to every day's details; no Stanley Dreyfus to worry about everybody's career; no cadre of supportive colleagues in every one of those compass points to infuse the *eretz* with life and energy.

And especially was Abraham *l'vado* because he did not have our Yosef at his side or on his back. Joe Glaser's entire life is a vision, which he is convinced is realizable, of a community of rabbis who care about God, Torah, Israel and each other. Joe Glaser understands, as much as or more than any of us, that the built-in risk of any organization of 1,437 rabbis is that it might become a *guf* without a *neshamah*, a body minus its soul. Our best insurance against that risk is Joe Glaser's own Jewish soul. May God continue to bless us with him.

Abraham had Sarah, and Priscilla and I have each other and our three children. She sustains me in whatever direction I raise my eyes. The simple fact that our marriage has withstood not only thirty years of preparing High Holy Day sermons but also the birth pangs of this President's Message is eloquent testimony to the strength of the Jewish family.

With so much help and so much support, the luxury I enjoy as president of our Conference is being spared the details of day to day and being able to lift my eyes to the landscape. What I would share with you this evening are some perceptions along the way.

One such perception, widely but not universally shared within our Conference, is the desirability of *achdut*, of strengthening bonds of unity among the denominations of the Jewish religious community. That goal, shared with other denominations, was responsible for bringing together, into several periodic meetings, the president of the Rabbinical Assembly, the president of the Rabbinical Council of America, and myself. The three of us operated on a simple premise: that *ahavat Yisrael* must take precedence over *sinat chinam*—over divisive, unwarranted hatred—and that the conversations among the three of us were one way to validate that premise and to establish that priority of *ahavat Yisrael*. The three of us likewise agreed that thorny issues should not be skirted but that all energy should be expended to keep them from tearing us apart.

A case in point: The Resolution on Patrilineality that was approved by our Conference in 1983 continues to elicit strong negative reactions within both the Orthodox and Conservative communities. From both communities has come a call to rescind it.

The following has been something of my response. When the Patrilineality Resolution was debated on the floor of our Conference in 1983, my own hearing of the debate was that no one in our Conference was calling into question the practice of patrilineality, which had become acceptable procedure for half a century. For all of that time, most of our colleagues had been persuaded by the good sense of welcoming as Jews, without an official conversion, those children of Jewish fathers and non-Jewish mothers who were raised and educated as Jews. The rationale, from a Reform stance, was self-evident: to be inclusive rather than exclusive, to strengthen the Jewish people and not to weaken it.

What was debated on the floor of the Conference in 1983, therefore, was not the long-standing de facto practice of patrilineality but whether that practice should now become an official de jure position of this Conference. The floor debate predicted vehement reactions from the Orthodox community, but the prevailing argument contended that the Orthodox would reject our conversions under any circumstances.

Perhaps what was not anticipated during that debate was the intensity of negative reaction not only from the Orthodox community but from the majority of the Conservative rabbis. They, who on so many issues consider themselves our allies, feel painfully alienated from us on this one. From the leadership of the

Rabbinical Assembly has come a call to rescind patrilineality. At its recent convention, the Rabbinical Assembly voted to establish sanctions that may be imposed upon their own members who follow the practice of patrilineality. I would add that some of our own Reform colleagues, reacting to the vehement response especially from the Conservative community, have questioned the wisdom of the 1983 resolution and have suggested the possibility of some form of reassessment.

Thus my response: We are saddened by the pain, but any consideration of rescinding the Resolution on Patrilineality is entirely beyond the realm of possibility. Aside from all other considerations, the reason is inherently logical: that even those Reform rabbis who question the wisdom of the resolution would be unwilling to abrogate the accepted practice of fifty years, and any retraction of the principle at this juncture would logically require a repudiation of the practice.

My proposal, therefore, is that all of us—Orthodox, Conservative and Reform—consider the approach that has served the three presidents so well during this past year: that when the difference between positions is perceived as so major as to be irreconcilable, then the task at hand is how to walk around the differences rather than to resolve them. In the face of such issues, what we tried to avoid was rhetoric; what we tried was to be pragmatic.

And so with patrilineality. We should be done with rhetoric such as "The Coming Cataclysm." We should be done with talk of two Jewish peoples in the year 2000. Instead, we should simply state that Reform Judaism stands the ground of its own principle that designates the offspring of mixed marriages as Jews, with stipulated conditions that do not require formal conversion, halachic or otherwise.

But by the same approach, if the Orthodox or even the Conservative decide to investigate the genealogy of a prospective bride or groom at whose marriage they are officiating and such investigation discloses that the person in question is Jewish according to Reform patrilineality but not according to traditional halachah, then I for one can find no quarrel with their requirement of halachic conversion. Meanwhile, however, I have reminded my traditional colleagues of an alternative approach also espoused by Jewish tradition, which is, not to ask the question. Who can fathom how many suspected *mamzerim* (before there was a Reform Judaism) lived their lives without penalty in the midst of the Jewish community because no one asked the question?

A footnote to my Orthodox colleagues: While I for one have no quarrel with your requirement in America, in Israel or wherever, what is not your right, or, more accurately, what the government of the State of Israel has no right to allow, is for the Orthodox demand for its own conversion to become the law of the land of the State of Israel, which belongs to the entire Jewish people and not only to its Orthodox contingent.

To my Conservative colleagues, this footnoted response—not a rebuttal but a response: Do not dismiss the possibility that ten or twenty years from now, you, too, may seriously consider the adoption of the Patrilineal position. If you do, you will be responding, on your own, to the same realities of social change that we have because your members are entering into mixed marriages in the same number that ours are. You will then turn, perhaps, to that same "patrilineal thread" in our tradition and accept, perhaps grudgingly, what you now staunchly oppose, and you will do it, just as we did, for the sake of Jewish strength and Jewish survival.

But the principle still remains. The refusal by the Orthodox to accept as Jews either our converts or our patrilineal offspring bears the same logic according to their principles of religious truth as the ordination of women and patrilineality bear logic in ours. Any attempt to reconcile these principles may only make the battle worse. The serious risk of a proposed National Beit Din that would attempt to adjudicate for all segments of the Jewish community is just this: that with all good intent, it may seek to reconcile what is essentially irreconcilable and might only make the battle worse.

I recognize that within our ranks, as in the ranks of Orthodox and Conservative, are those who contend that every concession becomes a surrender and that we do disservice to our Movement when we constantly back off from the field of battle. They contend further that the heated conflict between Pharisees and Saducees, between Maimonists and anti-Maimonists and between Chasidim and Mitnagdim, far from impoverishing the texture of our history served only to sharpen its contrasts and to rescue it from blandness. And, they allege, should our self-assertive determination produce two Jewish peoples by the year 2000, we can be assured that by the year 2100, like the Chasidim and the Mitnagdim, we shall be back together again.

To all of which I can only respond, *Ish b'cho-ach*, each one according to his own temperament. I align myself with those who prefer the road to peace, however rocky, trying our best to walk around the rocks and on occasion to remove them. I am confident that even though the Orthodox have withdrawn from the Chaplaincy Commission because of the endorsement of a woman rabbi, we shall work around this one, too. I align myself with those who accept tension as a given; but by that very tension, they are moved toward a more precise definition of themselves rather than toward an attack on the other. I take my stand and urge you to do the same, along with those who are convinced that the road to peace is paved not only with ideology but also with pragmatism, that the Jewish people have enough battles on enough fronts that it makes precious little sense to wage an internal one.

I therefore call upon all of our colleagues not already engaged in this particular pursuit of peace to seek out in their own communities those within the Conservative and Orthodox and Reconstructionist communities who might qualify as *rod'fei shalom*, pursuers of peace, and to begin the process of dialogue. What our colleague Irving Greenberg is fostering in the lay community is what we should foster in the rabbinic community. Our efforts should not presume to bring on the Messiah, with all disputes settled, but should at least remind and reassure all of us that the plea for *shalom rav al Yisrael* is directed not only to the Holy One but to us, all of us, who are His people Israel.

A second place on the landscape:

These past few years we have witnessed, throughout our entire Reform Movement, revived interest in the matter of personal spirituality. In no small measure did the impetus derive from our own Mohonk gathering, which, according to all reports, was a numinous experience in spiritual self-discovery. Those few days together, under the guidance of Jerome Malino, regenerated an essential Jewish truth all but lost to the Jewish agenda of our own time: that the human soul "thirsts for the living God"; that the human spirit, sometimes shattered, sometimes frightened, sometimes jubilant, sometimes confused, sometimes tired—that this center of our being, so fragile and so noble, gropes beyond itself toward the Center of all being.

What our colleagues discovered during that experience was that when we are able to help each other and ourselves break through our own wall of spiritual silence, then we feel emboldened to take on the massive silence of all those who call us, in theory at least, their "spiritual leaders." What a difference it could make! We all have in our congregations candidates for such a spiritual quest. I speak not of those for whom such an adventure would become yet another scheduled hour of self-improvement aerobics, nor of those for whom such a quest would be just another plunge into narcissistic self-absorption, nor of those who would see themselves as a spiritual elite above all those others who have not yet "seen the light." Rather, I speak of those whose spiritual encounter would direct them from inward to outward: those whose lives in the world, and whose moral decisions in the world, and whose behavior toward other human beings and the environment of the world would be consciously and continually directed by their own consciousness that there is a God in the world.

It would mean that besides secular Jews and ethnic Jews and philanthropic Jews and organizational Jews, we would also have spiritual Jews whose lives in the world and in our congregations would express their own spiritual awareness of the One before whom they stand.

What a difference it could make among our Jews, not only in their worship, their study, and their personal behavior but even in a domain like social action. We are so blessed with the vigor and the vision of our Religious Action Center and our Commission on Social Action and our Conference Committee on Justice and Peace and our own little cadres of social *actioniks* within our congregations. But on the level of the grass roots, if we were to sound out most of our congregants on their commitment to feed the hungry and bolster the poor and clean up the environment and avert the nuclear doomsday, we would be met, I suspect, with varying degrees of resounding silence.

The usual explanations are familiar to us: about the dominant mood of our culture that is directed to self and not to others, about limited supplies of Jewish energies better spent on Jewish causes, about the alleged incongruity of political issues on the agenda of temple board meetings.

We know the explanations. My appeal to you is that not one of them and not all of them together can justify this surrender at our grass roots of our Jewish commitment to *tikkun olam*, to the moral improvement of our world.

What has been all but lost in our congregations, including mine, is the soul-stirring call of our Reform forebears to sally forth as God's ethical messengers to the world. Those early Reformers gave back a voice to the prophets and shone a light on that old prophetic vision of a society embraced by compassion and justice. If we fault those Reform forebears for turning away too much from the mitzvot of our tradition and our ritual and our peoplehood, then we also would be faulted if we made the mistake in reverse: if in our own justified zeal for rediscovering and reinstating the mitzvot of tradition and ritual and peoplehood, we were to turn away from the mitzvah of our God-given ethical mission to the world, and if we were to allow the fire of that moral passion to cool.

The time has come for the grass roots of the Reform Jewish community to recover from its prophetic laryngitis, again to stoke those moral fires. As one example, I have a fantasy that, like Joe Glaser's visions, I hope is realizable: that on the eve of *Kol Nidrei*, when so many of our congregants are sensitive to the language of the spirit, all Reform rabbis will read from the bimah a manifesto on a subject like world hunger.

And thus to the final place on the landscape, which is this place and this time and this community of rabbis that is called by the name Central Conference of American Rabbis.

Well over a decade ago, this community of rabbis struggled with a problem also related to the issue of mixed marriage. This time it was the role of the Reform rabbi as officiant of such marriages.

The problem was resolved in the resolution of 1973 that read as follows:

> The Central Conference of American Rabbis, recalling its stand adopted in 1909 "that mixed marriage is contrary to the Jewish tradition and should be discouraged," now declares its opposition to participation by its members in any ceremony that solemnizes a mixed marriage.

The resolution was then amended to include the following:

> The Central Conference of American Rabbis recognizes that historically its members have held and continue to hold divergent interpretations of Jewish tradition.

Many of us who were present at that time recall the tenor of the discussions that preceded the final formulation and approval of the resolution. They were riddled with pain and with adversarial turmoil. And yet our common resolve was not to allow the issue to tear us apart. We had too much at stake together in our fellowship and our shared visions and our personal loyalty to the Conference to sacrifice all of them on the altar of this issue. Thus did we arrive at the amended resolution, a compromise, and from then until now we have been able to live with the compromise.

What, then, revived the issue and projected it into a climate of controversy?

If my perception is correct, the issue reemerged not because rabbis were contesting or contending with rabbis but for a collateral reason: In more than a few congregations, the lay leadership was imposing pressure upon their rabbis to officiate at mixed marriages. Similarly, in the process of rabbinic placement, some congregations would not even interview a candidate who officiates only at marriages between two Jews.

The statement of November 1984 entitled "Reform Rabbis Anti Mixed Marriage," with a group of rabbis, including myself, as signatories, had one specific intention: to respond to and to protest against this inappropriate imposition of pressure. The purpose of the document was to reaffirm that rabbis who officiate only at marriages between Jews are acting according to the official mandate of this Conference. The document then proceeded to validate that mandate from the mainstream tradition of the Jewish centuries.

The purpose of the document, therefore, was to offer support to those rabbis who were following the official Conference position and who were being pressured by their congregations not to. It was never intended to attack those who hold to "the divergent view," even though, upon rereading the question-and-answer section of the document, I could see how it was perceived otherwise.

Then began the volleys back and forth. Then came the testimonies by recognized scholars back and forth. And in the course of the volleying, some of us were shocked into a rude awakening of the preposterousness of the situation. Why are we rabbis fighting with each other? Why are we firing our upset at each other when it should be directed at those who are the cause of the problem?

I can tell you from my travels around the country that, with rare exception, no one in our Conference is eager to wage battle or polarize the Conference over this issue. While our colleagues want to preserve respect for their own positions, arrived at on the basis of conscience, they are not interested in re-debating the issue. They want it cooled, they want it sealed, they want it concluded.

Thirteen years ago, we rabbis solved our problem. Now the time has come for certain congregations to come to terms with their problem of conduct unbecoming a congregation, of denying to their rabbi the right of his or her own spiritual decision, his or her own spiritual independence.

What is at stake here, I believe, is not only rabbinical independence but the integrity of our Reform Movement. Thus my proposal: that this Conference call upon the Union of American Hebrew Congregations to assume its rightful responsibility through whatever mechanism it deems best to urge its member congregations not to pressure rabbis and not to discriminate against rabbinical candidates because of their refusal to officiate at mixed marriages or their insistence upon following the dictates of their own conscience. If that directive can be delivered and if that directive can be received and acted upon, then even this controversy will have been *l'sheim shamayim, sofah l'hit'kayeim,* "in the name of heaven, and in the end will lead to a positive result."

Centuries after Abraham, his descendants again looked to the landscape. Some were discouraged because of the overwhelming obstacle that blocked the way, that made them feel like helpless grasshoppers. But Joshua and Caleb were our ancestors of hope, and Caleb spoke the words that underlie my message tonight: *Ki yachol nuchal,* "For we shall surely overcome."

Kein y'hi ratzon.

1986/5747

President's Message, 1987

Last year on this occasion, I associated with that early moment in our people's history when Abraham beheld the terrain of a new land spread out before him "to the north and the south and the east and the west." This year, I connect with that moment, later and more seasoned in our people's history, when they constructed the first *Mikdash* in the desert, with its specific dimensions for north and south and east and west, toward its points on the compass and its place in the cosmos. My opportunity this past year has been to move at times from the outer court into the inner court of our people's sanctuaries and even to witness at times an offering upon the altar.

As example: Last year, we spoke of the process of dialogue that had become ongoing among the presidents and executive vice presidents of three national rabbinical organizations. That dialogue resulted in the Statement of Unity, signed by the three presidents and sent to some 3,800 rabbis in 2,500 synagogues for reading from the bimah on Shabbat HaGadol. As you may recall, the statement differentiated between the "Covenant of Fate," where we are able to stand together on matters of common Jewish destiny, and the "Covenant of Faith," where, by self-definition, we are divided on matters of theology and ideology.

For some rabbis, especially in the right wing of the Orthodox, the statement was an act of sabotage by their own colleague, and for that reason, among others, do I pay him public tribute for his courage. From some of our own Reform colleagues, in addition to expressions of support, come laments that the statement was too weak, a whisper, a non-statement. Some newspaper reporters were disappointed that we did not delve more into the issues of patrilineality and divorce and conversion, which would have provided a more titillating story for the reading public. I responded that the very intent of the statement was to correct a distorted public impression that all the denominations do is fight with each other. And thus the statement became, hopefully, a corrective, and thus a modest contribution to Jewish unity.

All of this is without the pride of sponsorship. It is, however, with the conviction, stronger now than a year ago, that the more consciously and purposefully we create mechanisms for Jewish unity, even with the irreconcilable differences, the more hope there will be for that unity to blossom into life. And yet another step: Plans are underway for an academic conference, to be jointly sponsored by our three national rabbinic organizations, on the subject of "Jewish Responses to Moral Public Issues." This twenty-four-hour conference, primarily for rabbis but with a session for the local community as well, will be held on the campus of George Washington University in December. There may yet come the day, in our own lifetime, when the forces of moderation in all the denominations will allow even the slightest movement, even on some of the matters of faith that now divide us. If that bothers some of you, I can tell you from the dialogues of these past two years that between the two poles of surrender and victory, there is a considerable range for pragmatic compromise: compromise with integrity to each one's own belief, compromise for the sake of a larger good, compromise *l'sheim shamayim*, the kind of compromise that courses through our people's history but that we have only begun to explore in our own time.

Last year at this time, I made mention of the pressure being exerted by congregations upon our rabbinic colleagues in the matter of officiation at mixed marriages. I shared the conviction that this issue, far from being cause for contention within the CCAR, was instead a reason for the UAHC to assume its own rightful responsibility and to address its member congregations regarding this sensitive and critical matter. Joe Glaser and I presented the proposal at a meeting within the inner court of our Reform Movement attended by the leadership of the three institutions. I am pleased to report a unanimous response of support and that, henceforth, a letter, over the signatures of the president and the board chairman of the UAHC, will be sent to all congregations that request placement. It will urge them in the strongest terms possible not to allow the matter of officiation to become the determining factor in the choice of their rabbinic candidate. We proceed, of course, under no delusion that the letter will work magic, but it will establish an official standard that until now has been absent.

Thus the more I have moved around within the inner court and over the total terrain of our Reform Movement, the more I am convinced of the need for such standards: for our congregations, for our rabbis, for our Reform Jews and for our Reform institutions themselves. The best hope for those standards to come to life is for our three parent institutions to join forces for that very purpose. Even with each institution's own priorities, understandably, even with the fortifying of each one's own institutional strength, understandably, even with the occasional tugs of competition, understandably, even with the principle of autonomy for congregations and for individual Reform Jews, the impatient hope of this Movement awaits our three parent institutions and their constituencies to take strong stands and to set their minds concertedly on those shared agenda items, which redound to the dynamism and vitality of this Movement.

I cite for now one example. Already familiar to many of you is the shrinking pool of qualified candidates for the rabbinate. It is obviously not only the College's problem because the rabbinic leadership of this Movement is the entire Movement's problem. Particularly is it our problem as rabbis because most candidates now come from Reform backgrounds, and 50 percent of those candidates attribute their choice to the influence and example of their own rabbis, even when their own rabbis did not single them out individually.

I have a hypothesis to explain, in part, the diminution of rabbinic candidates. The hypothesis is lacking in scientific research, but I share it anyway. With all of the various motivations that brought us into the rabbinate, foremost among them was not financial. And yet, the rabbinate did promise a modicum of security for our families and ourselves. By contrast, the homes in which many of today's potential candidates have grown up have already positioned them at such a level of security, and often beyond; and those very young people, still in their twenties, get caught up in today's torrent toward financial gain, and trips to every place in the world, and dinner out more than once a week. When some of those couples come to me to get married and I gain some inkling of their combined income, I want to retire and let them support me. A nephew of ours is graduating from undergraduate school and, with his computer skills, will receive exactly the same salary as this year's ordinees, with their five years of graduate study—the same salary that causes some of our UAHC congregations that have to pay it to moan and groan. A recent survey of almost 300,000 entering college students reported that 73 percent listed "being well off financially" as a top goal, and it reported that altruism and social concern showed a marked decline. The *summum bonum* of academic pursuit in our day has become the MBA, and MBAs do not opt for the rabbinate.

The conclusion of my hypothesis: that we who are here can no longer allow our role in rabbinic recruitment simply to be limited to our incidental influence, if indeed it has been thus limited. We have to do some shoulder tapping, to single out those young men and women who are spiritually sensitive and intellectually adept and morally concerned, and then share with them our own rabbinic journey and explore with them the possible glory of their own, and then direct them to the College—Institute and to all the programs that have been designed to continue the process. I cannot accept the premise that the latter-day poor showing by rabbis in the matter of recruitment is simply our own dissatisfaction with our own careers. For some it may be so, but for the rest of us, it is simply the need to shift from passive to active, to become part of an effort by our entire Movement to solve the problem and to fulfill the injunction of *har'beh tal'midim*, to raise up "many disciples," even if we choose them one at a time.

This past year provided entrée, somewhat, into the labyrinthine inner court of *Eretz Yisrael*. I have been there twice during these past months: once in November for the glorious dedication of the HUC-JIR Education Center and the youth hostel of the World Union and once in March for the Mission of the President's Conference. Like many of you, each time I go to that place, the more I become exasperated and the more I fall in love. When the leadership of Israel conducts itself in a manner of which some of us may disapprove, I contend that such disapproval should not serve to cool our ardor but to strengthen it, and not only within ourselves but within our congregations, where any signs of "cooling off" should mobilize us into action. We have every right to criticize Israel in the recent Pollard debacle because the Israel we love behaved shabbily in its partnership with the America we love, but not because we fear being suspect of greater loyalty to the blue and white than to the red, white and blue.

Each of these visits to Israel has pointed up even more the vacuum that the voice of our liberal, spiritual Jewish faith is sorely needed to fill. And thus the role that we on this side of the ocean are called upon to play: We are the "enablers," through our support of ARZA, of the Jerusalem campus of the College, of the World Union and its youth hostel, of the Reform kibbutzim and the Leo Baeck School and the synagogues and MARAM and the Israeli lay movement (and any others that should have been included in this list and the omission of which is bound to get me into trouble).

We are the enablers who allow it to happen, but the doers who make it happen are in Israel itself, our Reform *chaverim* and *chaverot*. A peak experience of these two years was a day last November when I met first with the lay leaders of the Israeli Movement and then with our rabbinic colleagues in MARAM. What moved me most was the poignant combination of their despair and their hope. The odds against which they must struggle, their failure to receive public recognition, their condemnation by the Orthodox establishment, their battle to maintain a standard of living for themselves and their families—all of these combined into no small reason for despair. But then there were embers of their hope, fired each time that a dozen Israelis in a neighborhood were willing to come together to explore Jewish values; each time by the opportunity to engage children and young people who never before have heard such a Jewish voice; each time by the determination of our colleagues to see the challenge through. The glow of that hope sent me back with the commitment we have presumed to make on your behalf. I repeat it now in the presence of Tovia Ben Chorin, president of MARAM: that we will strengthen every possible bond between colleagues here and colleagues there. However we may strengthen your hand, many times more do you strengthen ours. We admire you and pray with you: *Uma-aseh yadeinu kon'neihu*, "The work of our hands, with yours, establish Thou it."

And now to another inner court, this one most directly connected to our own *chevrah* in this place at this time. Just as *Eretz Yisrael* is portrayed as a nation of presidents (which is no easy handful), the CCAR is a congregation of rabbis (which is no easy handful). All of us, with our families, are the members. The officers and board members and committees are the leadership. The regions are the *chavurot*, and I, as president, and soon Gene Lipman, as president, are no different from your presidents back home. We have ideas of our own. We offer ourselves to the fullest extent of our ability. Yet we are truthfully aware that the most telling connection with this congregation of rabbis is with its rabbi, Joe Glaser, the one who is in the trenches full-time, the one at the center of whose life this congregation is. He understands its strengths and its lacunae. He is its staunch defender and its severe critic. My admiration for him is not only for his dogged concern for every member of this Conference; not only for his appreciation of the key roles that are played by Stanley Dreyfus and Elliot Stevens and Sara Siegel and the rest of the staff, whom all of us admire; not only for his wily sense of humor; not only for his humane concern for American Indians and California grape workers; not only for his conscientious self-control in not trying to impose his personal Israeli politics on the rest of us. Above all of these, my admiration for Joe Glaser derives from the sheer stamina, from the very expenditure of emotional energy to begin all over again every two years with a new president. Just think of it: Plaut, Stern and Lipman in six years' time. If the Torah had not ordained a *Shabbaton* for the seventh year, the CCAR would have had to invent one. Every new president charges into office with his, and someday her, new and revolutionary ideas, most of which are not new and not revolutionary. But our Rabbi Joe is unfailingly responsive and patient even when he does not agree and even when patience might well be wearing thin. He encourages us in whatever direction we wish to lead this Conference that will redound to its strength and well-being. Thus does every president of this Conference pay tribute to Joe Glaser, not because he is expected to but because he wants to, as I pay tribute now with thanks and love for two of the most exciting and fulfilling years of my rabbinic life.

One difference, however, between the congregation here and the ones back home: When testimonials are tendered to rabbis back there, the congregation has naturally borne witness on its own to the role of the rabbi's spouse in the life and career of their leader. In this congregation, however, because it spans the borders of a continent and because so much communication is by phone and by mail, the power of Agathe Glaser's presence is not always automatically apparent. But Priscilla and I can tell you, as members of the same community to which the Glasers belong and even of the same congregation, that no tribute to Joe Glaser is complete without Agathe. She is our rabbi's loving admirer and honest critic. She is his wise counselor. She is sometimes even his temperature and temper control. She is the nurturer of her family and friends. And in her own right, she is a creative artist and powerful and eloquent teller of true life stories, as our own congregation in Scarsdale discovered a week ago when she read from her autobiography about the infamous Night of Broken Glass, Germany, 1938. To you, dear Agathe, from all of us: *Kol hakavod!*

Something else happens in congregations back home, but only rarely in this *k'hilah* of ours. So get ready. The only times, to my knowledge, that the CCAR has ever promoted a major fund-raising effort has been for the relief and subvention of needy colleagues and their families, and last year for the assistance of our Israel colleagues. Your response on both occasions was heartwarming. Tonight we are about to launch the Centennial Fund Campaign of the Central Conference of American Rabbis. In two years, we shall celebrate our 100th Anniversary, and in the course of that century, we have taken a place of respected permanence in American Jewish life and even beyond, and surely in the community of Reform Judaism. We have created its prayer book; we have innovated programs of study and worship; we have strengthened and supported the rabbinic leadership of its communities.

The CCAR is here to stay. Thus the time has come when the income from dues and publications no longer suffices to implement the vast array of possibilities, whether in liturgy or career guidance or rabbinic outreach, that could enlarge the scope and influence of this Conference (which perhaps someday will occupy a living space that we shall claim as our very own). The time has come, perhaps the first time, when we can turn for supportive strength not only to ourselves and to each other but to the members of our congregations, who themselves have been the beneficiaries of these past 100 years, as they will be for the years to come. What more fitting way for them to pay honor to their own rabbis than to support this congregation of rabbis, this Conference, to which their rabbis belong and whose destiny they share? So get ready.

And now I come to the *in'yan*, the essence of my message (or, as Gene Lipman suggested, to my second speech): to the subject of the rabbinate itself. Perhaps you, my colleagues, whatever the number of your years in this Conference, have noted that no president has completed his term without addressing the theme of the rabbinate. I used to think that it was a tradition, but now I realize that it is simply a temptation utterly beyond resistance.

As I speak to the theme of the rabbinate, I shall speak of relationships. Martin Buber has sensitized me to the truth that "all real living is meeting," that all life, genuine life, including ours as rabbis, is lived in relationships: with our families, with other human beings, with the radiance of our tradition, with nature's song of beauty, with the world's cry for justice, with all of the emanations of the Holy One in our cosmos. As we stand before the Holy One, nothing *kadosh* can be alien to us. And yet the span of our days and years is simply too brief and our temperaments too different to allow prime time and place for every relationship. Some among us are primarily scholars and relate to the text. Some among us tend primarily to the human needs and silent pain of our flock. Some of us primarily sally forth against the shabbiness in God's imperfect world.

In one way or another, we all try to do it all, but in truth, we relate primarily to our own favored interests, and with the rest we do the best that we can, and we learn from each other. And then we teach, because the primacy that all of us share is that we are all teachers: on the bimah and off, in the classroom and out, what we say from speech to speech, and how we live from day to day.

In that same spirit of relationships, then, these thoughts about the rabbinate must include mention of some with whom my own being a rabbi is related and who thus become germane to this message.

I acknowledge with gratitude all of my colleagues who have spoken at conferences and who have written in our *Journal*, and all those of every generation with whom I have engaged in endless discussions on this very subject.

In a sense, I have little to say that is substantially new, but the more I read and the more I interact with colleagues, the more convinced I am that each of us, as the person that she or he is, has a new rabbinic story to tell, and for each of us, the personal relationships are part of our story.

Like all of you, I acknowledge my relationship with forebears who exerted strong influence in my rabbinic life, and what they have taught me is part of this message. Jacob Philip Rudin, *zichrono livrachah*, was my loving and beloved father-in-law. Aside from everything else, he taught me about being a rabbi, and he impressed upon me the power of the Word as it speaks forth from the bimah. However heavily the writing and delivering of sermons may weigh upon some of us, remembering Jack Rudin's teaching does not allow me to shed the burden, even with all of the appealing alternatives we have created to replace it. The alternatives are in addition to and not instead of the sermon, with its inimitable power to provoke the human mind and to lift the human spirit.

As I speak of the rabbinate, I acknowledge my gratitude to all of the young colleagues with whom I have interacted and worked throughout the years. If these observations tonight strike their target, they will reflect an ever-growing awareness that among our diverse perceptions of who and what a rabbi should be, the factor of generational difference is major and deserves our ongoing attention and discussion. Especially have I learned about such generational difference from my own remarkable colleague Deborah Zecher, my rabbinic associate. I welcome this opportunity, in the presence of colleagues, to express to her my love and gratitude not only for holding the rabbinic fort back home during these past two years but also for serving as a rabbinic model for her generation of rabbis, surely for our congregation in Scarsdale, and surely for me.

As I speak of relationships within my own rabbinate, it can never be without Priscilla and our three children, Jonathan, David and Elsie, who are the stays of my life. Priscilla is the keenest observer of the rabbinate I know, being the daughter of a rabbi, the wife of a rabbi, and in two years hence the mother of a rabbi. By her own declaration, the role she enjoys the most is the last of the three. The same is true for most, if not all, of us: that who and what we are as rabbis is linked in no small measure to who and what we are as husbands and wives, as the parents of our children, even as the children of our parents.

Now to the bottom line of rabbinic relationships: the rabbi and the congregation. By now we are all well aware that only half of our almost 1,500 CCAR members serve in synagogue positions. Even taking into account that of the remainder several hundred are retirees (some of whom still render some form of synagogue service), there remains that considerable number of our colleagues who serve in non-synagogue posts: as faculty of our HUC-JIR, as administrative leaders in our Reform Movement, as Hillel directors, as chaplains, as officials in Jewish communal organizations, as academics in universities, and whatever else I have left out. Even though my remarks will be directed primarily to the rabbi and the synagogue-congregation, I ask you to consider that each of those other constituencies is potentially a congregation, insofar as the rabbi in that place perceives himself or herself in the role of rabbi. It is the difference between the rabbinic faculty member who simply teaches the text to the class and the rabbinic faculty member who teaches that same text as a rabbi in relationship with the congregation of that class.

Regarding the synagogue-congregation, I shall not belabor the obvious to which most of us are firsthand observers: that the congregations that we serve and lead in the 1980s are comprised of such a multiplicity and diversity of smaller constituencies, each with its own agenda and its own needs, that our rabbinic serving and our rabbinic leading are radically different from even fifteen or twenty years ago. Aside from young singles and middle-age singles and widowed and divorced singles and senior citizens and *chavurot* and the intermarried and the converted, aside from all of those, fifteen or twenty years ago, we were not organizing the schedules for our children in the religious school around the alternate weekends that they must spend with their divorced parent who lives out of the house. Fifteen or twenty years ago, when young people came to us to be married, they were not so interested in the contents of the ceremony because for many of them the ceremony was simply their rite of passage on the way to the wedding bed. Now, having shared that bed for some period of time, they have begun to concentrate on the spiritual significance of the wedding ceremony; they even want to know what the Hebrew means. Fifteen or twenty years ago, we did not spend nearly as much time counseling or even trying to make contacts for fifty- or fifty-five- or sixty-year-old men who suddenly found themselves forced out of the positions in which they had spent most of their adult lifetime. For a comprehensive and personal profile of our changing constituencies, I commend to your reading the fine paper presented by our colleague Ros Gold during the 1985 convention.

I also commend to your reading a book by Calvin Goldscheider entitled *Jewish Continuity and Change*. It offers valuable insights into these very changes within our communities to which our synagogues can respond or which they can neglect. In his study of the greater Boston community (and his findings might well echo within many of our own communities), Goldscheider discovered that of the Jewish population in the age bracket of twenties and thirties, over three-quarters have resided in the communities of their current residence less than three years and therefore are most likely without family ties or communal roots. Of that same population, approximately 90 percent have moved at least once in that last decade as contrasted with those over age sixty, more than half of whom have lived in the same neighborhood for over twenty years.

Goldscheider further contends that despite all the gloomy predictions about weakening Jewish commitment through assimilation and intermarriage, the research findings suggest the exact opposite. This population of young Jews, however transient and however mobile, are consciously seeking some form of Jewish expression that will respond to the sense of Jewishness that they already feel, including their own awareness of Jewish values; including their own desire for Jewish family experience; including their own need for a network of Jewish friends. If the synagogue is not a place that is ready to respond to those needs, they will seek other places that are.

I can testify firsthand about the gain to the synagogue when we are the ones who do respond. Ever since we instituted in our synagogue a Parenting Center to which new parents come with their new infants, not only do they share experiences under the guidance of professionals but they also meet with the rabbis to explore the possibilities of creating a Jewish home and a Jewish family life. Thus does the interaction begin at the beginning and not when the children are ready for religious school or when they have reached the deadline for bar or bat mitzvah eligibility. A new constituency has thus been added to the larger congregational family, and the total congregation is transformed. Thus with synagogue nursery schools, thus with synagogue day schools, thus with all of those creative experiments that are not gimmicks but are creative attempts to respond to social change, which, I submit, have always been a factor in our own survival and have always been our offering upon the altar, and have always kept Judaism alive and have kept rabbis young.

Yet one more constituency that belongs to the changing synagogue of the '80s. Their names are on our membership rosters, they pay dues, and they seem, at first glance, simply to belong to that massive Jewish assembly who come together for the High Holy Days and rarely in between. A harder look, however, reveals a distinct difference between this particular constituency and their fellow absentees. These Jews stay away from the synagogue not because their level of Jewish commitment is low but because their Jewish energies and their Jewish loyalties, indeed the high level of their Jewish commitment, are pointed in another direction: to the sacred places of our federations, and our UJAs and our defense and communal agencies. These "sacred places" are perceptively described by Jonathan Woocher in his book *Sacred Survival: The Civil Religion of American Jews.* Woocher depicts the structure of civil religion thus:

A sophisticated political system, with hundreds of local and national organizations operating through a complex network of linkages to raise and expand hundreds of millions of dollars to carry out the "public" business of American Jewry. This public business includes support for Israel, maintenance of social welfare and educational programs for American Jews, and opposition to anti-Semitism.

The appeal of civil religion is its strong assertiveness of the value of Jewish peoplehood and pride in Jewish identity, values that the synagogue likewise upholds. Its attitude toward denominational religion is described by Woocher as one of "benevolent neutrality." Surely it seeks synagogue support in its fund-raising campaigns, to which we hopefully respond. It even appoints rabbis to its boards and calls them up from their seats at the far end of the dais to invoke or bless, but rarely are the religious institutions and their leadership included in the top level of decision making, with exceptions, of course. This prerogative belongs to the leaders of civil religion, some of them our best and our brightest, some of them only rich, but all of them committed to the articles of their sacred faith, which excludes the Divine, except for invocations and benedictions. According to civil religion, the oneness of the Jewish people is more compelling than the oneness of God. And because of the ascendant power of civil religion, states Woocher, the role of the synagogue and the rabbinate—the life of study, prayer and ritual observance—is no longer primary in Jewish life.

What shall we do about it in the synagogue of the '80s? What we should not do is surrender so passively. Our concerted attempt, I submit, should be to seek out from within our congregations some of those same very best and those same very brightest, not to pirate them away from the shrines of their civil religion but to fill in the gaps that their civil religion does not presume or pretend to fill. What is missing in those other shrines is a regard for personal human concerns and personal human behavior. What is missing in civil religion is encounter with the Transcendent and search for the Divine. What is missing in civil religion is exactly what the religious communities of Judaism and their rabbis have to offer and have to teach. And I and others can tell that once we seek out that constituency, some of those very civil religionists are not only receptive to the offering but take it back with them to their other sanctuary.

What we should not do in the synagogue of the '80s is take a backseat simply because the backdoor is open for us. Because there are still all those other Jews who, in Woocher's words, are seeking in Judaism not a public cause but a guidepost and rationale for their daily lives. Can Judaism provide a spiritual focus, a moral compass, a transcendental purpose in immediate and personal terms? Can it enrich their family lives, restore a sense of personal worth, help them cope with success and failure?

Valid questions for the synagogues of the '80s. Answers? Still on the way.

And now to the rabbi's side of the rabbi-congregation relationship. I purposely shun the oft-discussed question of whether the rabbinate is a "profession" or a "calling." The question is unhelpful because we are, of course, both. We belong to a profession that requires specific training and skills for which our College—Institute should supply the resources and for which our Conference should provide the reinforcement. We are professionals who are entitled to contracts with specific vacation time and maternity leave and all the rest. I admire and cherish those among us, usually of our senior generation, who never entered into contracts because the mutual trust and respect between them and their lay leadership produced an agreeable result. I also know, however, that some of those results were less than agreeable and were accepted by the rabbi with disappointed and disillusioned silence. I also know that with the usual exceptions, those were the "good old days," B.C.—before corporations, before the corporate mentality invaded the temple boardroom and the thinking of some of its lay leadership.

The rabbinate is in fact a profession and in truth a calling, a calling to respond to all of those trenchant questions that Jonathan Woocher has set before us. Can we, as teachers of Torah, offer to those who are willing to learn "a spiritual force," a moral compass, a transcendental purpose, a sense of their personal worth? Can we help them release their own bottled-up spiritual energy? Can we persuade them to live their lives in awareness of the One before whom all of us stand?

My answer to these questions, after thirty-five years in this Conference, is that every rabbi I know has stood before some kind of thornbush. Every rabbi I know has responded to some kind of calling, and that calling is at the soul of that rabbi's life. Every rabbi I know has his or her sacred stories to tell.

We touch lives and we teach Jews even more than we ourselves may realize: not only when the *b'nei uv'not mitzvah* stand with us in front of the ark but during the preparation time when they are sure they can never do it, and we give them the assurance that they can; not only in the moments of *kiddushin* under the chuppah but when we ask them in the pre-marriage discussion why they want to be married, and sometimes for the first time they confront the holiness of that question; not only when we say *Kaddish* at the graveside or give the eulogy at the funeral but when we talk to the family in advance, and one by one they weave a sacred story of love and of life.

We teach and we touch not only the faithful who are there from Shabbat to Shabbat or from class to class, but those who are there in crisis, and not only the crises of their personal lives but also of their world: Sabra and Shatila; Jewish names in public scandals; the Friday afternoon on which Jack Kennedy was killed that became the Friday night when our synagogues were thronged. They came for "transcendental purpose," for "moral compass," to be taught and be touched and be held.

But the rabbinate, too, has changed. I, for example, as a member of the now senior generation, used to accept the thesis that being a rabbi implied an almost total availability and accessibility. I used to believe that whatever the need being expressed by any person or any cause, the rabbi should be there to respond to it.

Similarly, in those old days, did our wives have a calling, which was to mind the home front and to care for the children and often to fulfill the role of two parents, sometimes with an uneasy explanation and justification for their father's absence. Even when we did the best we could as rabbi, husband and parent, whatever success we achieved was because our wives accepted their calling, allowing us to pursue ours. And when we failed, it was simply because two such callings were too much for only two people to handle.

For no small number of our colleagues, especially in the young generation, those were indeed the "old days" but not necessarily the good ones. Now with two careers in a family, each one a "calling" in its own right, what happens is that hearth and home and children become, both for husband and wife, a second calling, as divine a calling as there can be.

All of this is not without struggle, not without conflicts, but also not without trying to resolve them, sometimes even successfully. What we have come to understand, together with our younger generation of rabbis and with the invaluable guidance of our Spouse Support Group under Priscilla Poller, are the multiple meanings of the word "trade-off." We have come to confront the challenge of living a Jewish life in our own families when the parent-rabbi is off somewhere being rabbi for other families and when *al achat kama v'chama*, both spouses are rabbis or rabbi and cantor. We have come to protect our personal time, but, hopefully, not with such rigidity that a genuine cry for help goes unheeded.

What some of us have come to discover, especially, is that the personal-human part of us and the rabbi-model part of us need not engage in such constant and stressful combat. Being a rabbi need not deprive us of the enjoyment of an off-color story, but it does require some *sechel* about whom we repeat it to. Being a rabbi does not deny us a small measure of envy of some of the opportunities that our congregants can financially afford, but it does caution us against escalating a little envy into a big resentment. Being a rabbi does not preclude us from being assertive even when it comes to our own interests and to the well-being of our families, but it does caution us that our anger can weaken our assertive claim rather than strengthen it. Being a rabbi does not exempt us from our struggle with the *yetzer hara*, but it does remind us, in the wisdom of Rabbi Shelomo, the Chasid, that the worst damage the *yetzer hara* can do is make us forget that we are *b'nei uv'not HaMelech*, "children of the Holy One"—make us forget that we stand before the One and before the congregation that calls us Rabbi.

Human beings that we are, rabbis that we are, every time we stand before our own thornbush, something happens by the time we walk away. None of us remains the same after we officiate at the funeral of a suicide or of a child, or when the one who lies before us was our friend. None of us remains the same when we stand under the chuppah with brides and grooms whom we knew when they were children or, above all, when they are our own children, *im yir'tzeh HaShem*. None of us stays the same after we have given a really good sermon or a really bad one. Never the same, as our marriage blossoms with one at our side to give us strength and love and to tell us the truth about our sermons. No rabbi remains the same after our first child is born, which is precisely the time we cease to be experts on children. No rabbi remains the same after the first trip to Israel or the second or the tenth, or whenever we breathe the air of a Jerusalem morning.

So here we are: these human rabbis with a profession and a calling. And here they are: these changing congregations with many good people, many caring Jews. Some of them in need, some in search.

Why then, aside from those loving, trusting relationships between some congregations and their rabbis, why in those other relationships so much conflict and so much strain? The fault, sometimes, is not "in our stars," not even in our congregations, but in ourselves, when even we rabbis succumb to the *yetzer* and forget that we are *b'nei uv'not HaMelech*. The need sometimes is to hone our own rabbinic professional skills. How to communicate a message is a skill that does not demean the message. How to proceed in contractual agreement can be a skill that avoids painful confrontation. Resolving disputes can be a skill, whether or not the rabbi is one of the disputants.

Sometimes a rabbi is in inner turmoil, connected to but not necessarily caused by the functions of a rabbi. Sometimes all of us harbor inappropriate expectations of attentiveness and gratitude and validation from members of our congregations and only become embittered when they are not forthcoming. Sometimes, as Rollo May reports from his experience as a psychoanalyst, clergy lay claim to "the divine right to be taken care of" and then suffer pain when that right is not granted.

My hope for our Conference, in addition to the valuable career counseling provided by Jerome Malino and the hotline staffed by Jason Edelstein, is that it provides a network of opportunities and resources that will respond to the personal and professional needs of our colleagues. Pain can be avoided, sometimes. Confrontation can be headed off, sometimes.

Why the strain and conflicts? Sometimes, I believe, because of a gaping void on the other side: in the education and understanding on the part of our congregational leadership about their relationship to rabbis. How does the leadership of a congregation shift gears from the moment when they decide who will be their new rabbi to all of the subsequent moments when that same person (whose destiny they have just determined) now becomes their leader, their teacher, and sometimes even their critic, hopefully their loving critic? How do they then shift back again at contract time when the destiny of their leader and their critic is again in their hands? How does the leadership of a congregation respond to the new corporate mentality that prepares questionnaires to be distributed to the entire congregation for the evaluation of its rabbi? How should a congregation be guided to a *cheshbon* of its own moral accountability when it considers disengaging the rabbi who has served for twenty or twenty-five years? How do we motivate congregational leaders who have carefully listed the rabbi's responsibilities to the congregation to ask of that same rabbi, "And what do you expect of us?"

Ultimately, how do we construct a model, a realistic model, for rabbi-congregation relationships where mutual expectations are Jewishly appropriate and graced with integrity?

At the heart of the matter is an experience that was a low point during my two years in office. Joe Glaser and I were attending a meeting of the UAHC Executive Board. I do not even recall the issue, but at some point in the discussion, in which Joe and I had participated, someone made reference to "you rabbis" as opposed to "we congregants"; "you, the CCAR" (the rabbis' union) as opposed to "the lay leadership" (the corporate management).

At the heart of the matter is a perception of an adversarial attitude, whether by rabbis or by congregations or by both. At the heart of the matter is this "bad seed" that can infect the morale and morality of our Movement. At the heart of the matter is the painful need for the leadership of our three institutions to position this matter at the top of their shared agenda (and I include the College because it is sometimes there that the adversarial seed is planted). At the heart of the matter is the imperative for congregations and rabbis to acknowledge that an adversarial climate is the failure of the relationship and not inherent to it, that rabbis and congregations are *shutafim*, partners, in transforming their building and themselves into what their title often claims them to be: a *k'hilah k'doshah*. For all of us, may it come to pass in our day.

I conclude on a personal note. If I were to select the two experiences in my life that have made me feel most fulfilled, most authentic, most validated as a rabbi, number two would be these past two years, not only because they have brought me into so many inner courts of Jewish life but because they have brought me to so many of you, who have helped me expand the bounds of my own experience. These two years have shown me the enormity of what this Conference and this Movement have achieved and the enormity of what awaits. It has connected me

364   The Right Not To Remain Silent

to all the generations of rabbis in this Conference, and I thank you, my colleagues, for all the ways in which you have taught me and touched me.

The number one authenticating experience happened some fifteen or twenty years ago. It was an ordinary day in my study (which for all of us is never that ordinary). There was a telephone call from a young man who identified himself from Great Neck days when I was assistant to Jack Rudin and served as youth director in the congregation. The man was now in his late twenties and was calling to ask if I would officiate at his wedding. Why? Because, he said, when he was a teenager, everyone, including his family, had given up on him academically and personally. As his rabbi, I was the only one who had communicated to him a sense of his personal worth. Everyone else had only confronted him with his *yetzer hara*, but it took a rabbi to remind him that he was still a child of the Holy One.

Thus do all of us, even with our doubts and our conflicts and our struggles, come together in this place with our own sacred stories that dub us "Rabbi."

Thus do we stand at the thorny bush and take from it the flame, unconsumed, through the desert, to the altar of the sanctuary.

Not yet at the Holy of Holies. But closer and closer.

1987/5748

Milestones

Caring

Many years ago, I was attending a dinner where the speaker of the evening, aside from being renowned for his extensive accomplishments, was also renowned for the extensive length of his speeches. The program chairman of the evening, discreetly but firmly, had informed the speaker of a specific time limit. When his time came, the speaker stood up and said, "Dear Friends, before I begin, I'd like to say something," which he then proceeded to do.

And so on this particular Rosh HaShanah, at the beginning of this particular year, before I begin, I'd like to say something. Tonight marks the beginning of our twenty-fifth year as a congregation. And in this sanctuary tonight there are some who have worshiped on Rosh HaShanah, as part of this congregation, for all or almost all of those twenty-five years. And even though I hope they have come to terms with the growth and the change that have taken place over the years, I suspect they must still feel a bit of nostalgia for those "old days," when the congregation was very small and very intimate.

The rest of us, however many or few the years of our belonging, including some of you who may be here tonight for the very first time, have discovered or hopefully will discover that the strength of a bond need not be dependent on the number of years. In no time at all, a synagogue can become a second home.

The feeling tonight is not unlike that of a couple I knew who were celebrating their twenty-fifth wedding anniversary. And one of the couple said to me, "Now that we've made it this far, it really feels that we're married." So now that we've made it this far, twenty-five years, it really feels that we're a congregation, and that calls for a blessing: *Baruch Atah Adonai Eloheinu Melech ha-olam shehechey-anu v'kiy'manu v'higi-anu laz'man hazeh.* Blessed art Thou, O Lord our God, King of the universe, who has kept us alive and sustained us and brought us to this day.

And now, having said that, we're ready to begin. We begin at the beginning, with Abraham, our first Jewish ancestor. We shall meet him in tomorrow's Torah portion when he responds to God's command to take his son up Mount Moriah and there to offer him as a sacrifice. According to those who wrote that story in the Bible, the purpose of the command was to test Abraham, to see whether he would give up the life of his child to prove his loyalty to his God. And if he could pass that test, then he would qualify as God's representative on earth. Then he would become the leader of the people who would carry this new, revolutionary idea of one ethical God to the rest of the world.

Brilliant minds and sensitive spirits have wrestled with that passage, which we shall read tomorrow morning. Mostly their intent has been to find some mode of interpretation that would play down the severity of that demand. But their attempts fail because the writers of that story said exactly what they wanted to say: that God was testing Abraham, and even though at the last minute the command was rescinded, it was Abraham's willingness to take the test that made him pass it and that qualified him as the beginner of the Jewish beginnings.

I count myself among the admirers of Abraham. I love the way he was willing to pull up his roots, to mark out new directions, to climb the craggy hills of Jerusalem; and when he does that, I and many others like me can walk right alongside him. But then when he takes his son up Mount Moriah for that ultimate test, at that moment we may stand in awe of him but cannot walk alongside him. We may be moved by the poignancy of that moment, but we cannot identify with it. Give up a child to pass a test? We'd rather fail. But Abraham passed it, and thank God it was he and not we. For most of us, Mount Moriah is too high to climb.

But ten days from now, when the High Holy Days are about to end, we shall bear witness to another journey. In the haftarah portion of Yom Kippur afternoon, God will call to Jonah to leave his place and go to Nineveh, there to warn the people of their impending doom. Not only does Jonah bear little love for Nineveh, but the very expectation that he should give his time, his energy, his self for such a public cause is to him an invasion of his privacy, and he resents it. Instead of traveling to Nineveh, he boards a ship to Tarshish, which is in exactly the opposite direction. He reverses the direction from the world of people and the world of humanity and moves to the world of his own single, private self.

We see Jonah on his way to Tarshish all the time. Young couples will come into the rabbi's study to discuss their forthcoming marriage, and sometimes they will say that what they prize the most in their relationship is their respect for each other's privacy. And my reaction is, "That's very nice, but does it have to win first prize?" Does it have to supersede Martin Buber's definition of love, which is "the responsibility of an I for a Thou"? Does it have to supersede the caring of one human being for another?

We see it sometimes even in the synagogue. You may recall what happened on Pesach a year and a half ago. The chairperson called for parents to help with the seder in the religious school. She made one hundred calls before thirty people would agree to help. Of the thirty who agreed, eight did not show and gave no explanation and made no call. One mother arrived late, after her own child's seder was over and there were three remaining that needed helping hands. But since her own child's seder was over, she turned around and went home. Another mother was called and asked if she would make *charoset*, to which she answered, "No, I won't, because my child doesn't like *charoset*."

We see it all the time. We see it in our children, even when they aren't such children anymore. The report from college campuses, from our grown-up children, is almost zero interest in social causes and the affairs of the world. Everything is the individual. Everything must be personal. Everybody is so busy finding himself that he can't find anyone else. Everybody is on the ship to Tarshish.

I have seen it even on this pulpit. It will sometimes happen that a thirteen-year-old boy or girl will stand where I stand right now on the day of his or her bar or bat mitzvah. We try our best to make that ceremony personal for the child and the family. But we never let it be overlooked that the ceremony is intentionally held in the synagogue because the synagogue is a public place and intentionally during a worship service because a service is a public Jewish occasion. And for good reason: because the intent of that ceremony is to escort that child across the threshold from his own childish, self-centered, privatistic world into the world of the public community. But sometimes, when I seek from the parents the assurance that this son of the commandment or this daughter of the commandment will fulfill the mandate of public community study by continuing in the religious school, I am then told that they are leaving that decision to the child, which is usually a clue that the child is resisting and will probably decide in the negative. And unintentionally, what they are doing is taking this public experience and totally privatizing it. What they are doing, not intentionally, is taking their own child who could have been on his way to Nineveh and putting him instead on the ship to Tarshish, and they are paying his fare and giving him their blessing.

We don't do it intentionally, but we Jewish parents sometimes want our children to feel so loved and so worthwhile and so special that we sometimes forget to send the second half of the telegram: that other children and other adults are also special, also deserving of love, also full of worth, and that message could encourage our children to reach out of their own little privatistic worlds and be on their way to Nineveh.

We don't do it intentionally, but in attempting to cultivate in our children a backbone of independence, a reservoir of self-reliance in the best tradition of Judaism and of Ralph Waldo Emerson and of America, what we sometimes forget is to send the second half of the telegram: that people also need each other and depend on each other in what Peter Mann calls "a web of reciprocity." And when those very children sense the responsibility of an I for a Thou, they could be on their way to Nineveh instead of being crowded with all those other private selves on the ship to Tarshish.

When the prophet Jonah went to Tarshish, comments the midrash, he tried to get a discount, but they wouldn't give it to him. He had to pay full fare. And so with our modern-day Jonahs, the passage to Tarshish is not cheap. It is reported in one survey of college students that as the level of absorption with self rises higher and higher, the capacity for human caring sinks lower and lower. And Herbert Hendin, who conducted that survey, writes as follows: "For both sexes in society, caring deeply for anyone is becoming synonymous with losing." There's plenty of sex but little of intimacy. The way to be is cool, detached, private, protected from the risk of getting hurt when people come too close.

The price we may be paying for our trip to Tarshish is the human capacity for caring, which, according to some psychologists, is an inborn capacity that can dry up from day-to-day neglect.

The price we may be paying for denying to ourselves and our children that wonderful experience of doing something for someone may be the crumbling of the web of reciprocity to such a degree that, no longer caring and no longer cared for, we could end up as isolated human beings, as lonely and isolated as Jonah was when he ended up in the belly of the whale. And with Jonah's lament, we might then cry out against the cold, impersonal world, unaware that it was our own privatism and our own self-isolation that put us there in the first place.

But when the moment came that Jonah the Prophet could acknowledge what he had done to himself, it was at that moment that he and all the modern-day Jonahs could reverse their direction and begin their journey to Nineveh and discover the world again and people again and thus become caring human beings again:

—the kind of caring that all of us know, more or less, when a parent listens to a child after he's had a hard day, but also when the child listens to the parents, because parents have hard days, too;

—the kind of caring that a teacher feels for the children in his class, not only with regard to what they learn about the subject (which redounds to the credit of the teacher) but what they learn about life (which redounds to the future of the child);

—the kind of caring that doctors can feel for their patients, that rabbis can feel for their congregants, that congregants can feel for each other.

What we mean by caring is husbands and wives taking time out from finding themselves in order to find each other. What we mean by caring is how friends try to sense what gives each other pain and what gives each other joy. What we mean by caring is what Martin Buber said when a young man came to ask him a question and Buber was so involved in his own reflection that he simply answered the question and ended the discussion. A week later, the boy died, possibly by his own hand, and then Buber said, "I made the mistake of answering only the question the boy asked. I failed to deal with the questions he did not ask."

May it be for all of us a year of such caring for the members of our families, for our friends, for the human creatures of God's world and a year of responding to the questions asked and the questions unasked.

May it be a year when all of us who could not pass Abraham's test will know that at least we can go with Jonah, when those of us who could not make it up the mountain of Moriah will at least turn toward Nineveh, away from Tarshish toward Nineveh.

Amen.

Rosh HaShanah 1977/5738

Twenty-Five Years

On a personal note: As our president Rosemary Berdon said last evening, the first Rosh HaShanah that I stood on the bimah of this congregation was twenty-five years ago today. Some of you who were here then are here now, and I thank God for your persistence. Some of you here now had not yet been born or were still in the years of childhood, and to you the year 1962 might very well fall into the period of prehistoric time, before the home computer, before the space shuttle, before the Giants moved to New Jersey. Some of you twenty-five years ago were perhaps in other places, perhaps in other synagogues. But as you well know, when a Jew joins a congregation, its entire life story, including that of its rabbis and its cantor, instantly becomes yours.

I found the sermon I preached on that first Rosh HaShanah in 1962. It discussed the issues, then being hotly debated in our country, of whether spiritual values should be taught in the public school and whether public prayers should be recited in the classroom—exactly the same issues that are being hotly debated today. Nothing changes. But everything changes because into the arena of that debate have now today come the political forces of the Moral Majority and the Religious Right, who proclaim their campaign to Christianize America. And that changes everything.

Twenty-five years ago, the technological revolution was already in full force. Soon, thereafter, Alvin Toffler wrote his book called *Future Shock*, which I discussed in a Yom Kippur sermon, sharing with the congregation some of the startling, incredible-sounding possibilities that lay in store for us. One of them was the opportunity for a woman to have a fertilized frozen embryo implanted in her uterus, which she would then carry for nine months until giving birth as though the child had been conceived in her own body. And now, less than two decades after Toffler wrote his book, that procedure is being conducted in Australia and, before too long, will be possible in the United States.

Technologically, most rabbis I know would never consider composing a sermon on anything other than a word processor or personal computer, while I, the truth be told, still cling to the yellow lined paper, anachronistically. I am comforted somewhat by the published data that those who are most comfortable with the computer are in the age bracket under fifty-five and that those under thirty-two would not consider working without one. Priscilla and I were in a retail establishment and the person behind the desk was unable to determine the next step on the computer to process the transaction. She turned to a fellow worker in her twenties who then continued the process but was then herself stymied, whereupon she turned to the stock boy, who was fifteen or sixteen, and he solved the problem. The future, technologically, belongs to the young. And the truth be told, sometimes after listening to a telephone recorded message on weather conditions or a movie schedule, I will still say "thank you" to the recording, anachronistically.

Twenty-five years ago, the Civil Rights Movement was beginning to come into its own. In 1964, I went to Mississippi to see for myself and then reported to the congregation on Rosh HaShanah what many of us considered to be an essential Jewish issue because it concerned the destiny of God's children on this earth. Some members of our congregation did not agree with my assessment of its Jewish significance.

The '60s were a time of soul-stirring social change, when young people on college campuses and in the streets refused to accept anything at face value. Simply because black people in the South had always sat in the back of the bus did not mean that it had to be that way. Simply because the president of the United States decided that it was in the best national interest to send troops to a far-off place called Vietnam to fight in a no-win war did not mean that it had to be.

Everything in the '60s was fair game for challenge: the president, the administration of universities, social traditions. And everything was fair game for experiment: dress style, sex, drugs, religion, whatever. One couple in those days came to me in advance of their marriage. In the course of our discussion, the prospective groom asked about the significance of the custom of breaking the glass in order to determine whether they wanted to include the custom in their own wedding ceremony. After I offered the appropriate explanations, he apparently was satisfied because he turned to his future bride and said, "That settles it. I will wear shoes for the wedding!"

That was the '60s. Then we drifted into the '70s. I say we drifted into the '70s because we left behind much of the social crusading and were left with this universal and high-powered campaign that everyone should "do his and her own thing." And we were barraged with all the slogans that went with it: "If it feels good, do it" and "I want it and I want it now." The key word in those days was "relevant." Everything had to relate to everybody individually, no matter whether it related to someone else or to society-at-large or to the sweep of human history. No matter, because it had to be relevant to me.

The bane of the '70s was boredom because boredom was not instantly gratifying, not fulfilling, did not give pleasure. And when people would say that their children had complained of a boring day at school or at home or, God forbid, in religious school, my answer would be, "Isn't that wonderful! Because now your child knows that he can tolerate an occasional day or hour of boredom and not be undone by it." But parents did not always accept my response because that was the '70s, the *me* generation and the *now* generation, the generation that looked more into mirrors than through windows, that wanted the Promised Land without the effort of crossing the Jordan. One social critic described it as the most narcissistic decade this nation has ever known. Another depicted its foundation as a "floating sea of values."

And now the '80s. And if my reading is correct, we of the '80s are like that man in the old Jewish story who was walking through the forest and met another man who said that he was lost, to which the first man replied, "I can tell you one thing: Don't take the road that I'm on because I'm lost, too!" Whereupon the two joined forces to seek their way out of the dark forest together.

That, I believe, is where we are in the middle of the '80s, with a gnawing awareness that the roads we have been taking for all these years have only gotten us lost; that the premium we placed on feeling good and not being bored is somehow related to the plague of drug abuse that has infested our society—from the private offices of corporate executives, to the streets of Harlem, to the schools of Scarsdale, even down through the grades of the junior high—that our easy mandate of the '70s to "do your own thing" is somehow related to the thousands of young people who have been enticed into mind-numbing cults because for some of our youth "doing your own thing" can be the loneliest thing in the world; that the easing of social strictures in a generation of "me first" and the "fast track to success" is somehow related to doctors who practice without licenses and judges who accept bribes and public officials who wallow in corruption and high school students who cheat on the SATs and college students who participate in prostitution rings. And in response to all of it, a public reaction that is less and less shocked and more and more cynical.

Like those two people in the forest, what many of us are beginning to feel is a crying need to find our way out, to do battle for the souls of our society and the souls of our children and the souls of ourselves.

And thus do we come to a place like this, you and I, for the past twenty-five years, this congregation for thirty-five years, the Jewish people for thirty-two hundred years. Because it is this place, this faith and this people that have always strengthened us to do battle; because through all the changes and all the technologies and all the floating seas of values, we're here, with our children, and someday our children's children, to tell the tale. We're here, still to do battle for humanity when it shoots itself in the foot, still to do battle in the name of the God of humanity, in spite of ourselves.

We who know that we're lost now need that strength to communicate to you, our children, that there is no disgrace now and again in being bored; that you don't always have to have a better time than you're having, which is the reason that kids give for taking drugs; that if you are willing to accept the everyday woes that come into every human life, you will appreciate all the more the beautiful feeling of everyday highs without the need of a puff or a sniff.

We who know that we are lost in the forest, we need that strength to communicate to ourselves, as parents, that if we simply shower our children with things—or in the words of one of our own children, "Why do you give me needs I don't have?"—then we are not helping them. And if we give them too much simply because they want it, simply because they're asking for it or because their friends have it, if we say "Yes" too much, we may never teach them how to say "No" to themselves, when, for their own sake, no would be better than yes.

I can give an example. It sometimes happens that a thirteen year old, having distinguished himself or herself on the day of his or her bar or bat mitzvah, now wants out because sleeping or doing something else on Sunday morning is more fun than religious school—a line of reasoning for which a thirteen year old can hardly be faulted. But when parents accede to that request, when they allow that child to remove himself or herself from the very place that can help strengthen that child against the onslaught of the drug culture or a cheating culture or a high-powered sex culture, the very place that can keep that child from drowning in the floating sea of values, when that parent says "Yes" to that child's request, the parent, I believe, is depriving that child much more by saying "Yes" than by saying "No."

What needs reviewing is our Jewish formula that has sustained us for twenty-five years, for thirty-five years, for thirty-two hundred years: that in whatever place we live, we always make sure to take one Jewish step away from that place so that we can assess it critically from the outside. Even when they let us in and let us take part in it, we never let ourselves be completely co-opted by it. We always keep one foot on that place in the world and the other foot at the mountain of Sinai. When the people in our world place ask whether something will work technologically, we ask from Sinai whether it is right ethically. When the people in our world place play games with the truth, we answer from Sinai that there is a God of truth. When the people and the nations of our world place play games with the life of humanity, we answer from Sinai that there is a God in the world before whom all men and nations must stand to give account. And when the people in the world forget the past and ignore the future, then we answer from this place, "*l'dor vador*"—We are from generation to generation.

And finally, on a personal note of twenty-five years. In the year 1954, my father-in-law, Jacob Rudin, of blessed memory, stood in his pulpit for his twenty-fifth Rosh HaShanah as rabbi in Great Neck. He said that after a quarter of a century, a rabbi no longer believes that he will change the world or bring it closer to holiness. Rather, he is willing to settle for one corner of the world, even one person, maybe even himself.

Thus my Jewish hope for these past twenty-five years, the one sermon I have tried to deliver: that we are all blessed with our families and our homes and our gifts of mind and heart and spirit; that we belong to a precious people that bids all of us in our changing worlds and our changing lives to use our gifts in order to bring that world one step closer to holiness, or at least one corner of the world, or at least one person, maybe even only ourselves.

My father-in-law, on that occasion, told this story that I tell now because, like you, I have been blessed for all these years. A rabbi in Eastern Europe received a gift from America for his yeshivah. He went all around his little village showing everyone not the gift, which was substantial, but the letter itself and pointing to the closing words. "Look," he kept saying. "See how my friend in America signs himself, 'Very truly yours.'"

As for the twenty-fifth year, we join with each other to find the way as we wish each other a year of health and strength and love and peace, a year of God's blessing, with a touch of holiness. I remain…

Very truly yours,
Rabbi Jack Stern

Rosh HaShanah 1986/5747

What My Teachers Have Taught Me

Twenty-eight years ago tonight, I stood on the bimah of Westchester Reform Temple for the first time. I still remember the sensation of butterflies swarming and storming in my stomach. I had always known that Rosh HaShanah was the Day of Judgment, but this one was different, because on this one the judgment was not only on high but down here in that sea of faces out in front of me.

I remember yet another sensation on the first Rosh HaShanah. Because when any of us rabbis is asked during the interviewing process why we would consider leaving one congregation for another, the answer is almost commonplace: "Because I'm excited by the challenge." But the commonplace is often true, and the challenge is exciting.

And the excitement for me twenty-eight years ago focused on a particular challenge. I had grown up in the Reform Movement. I had chosen to become a Reform rabbi because I was convinced that here was a way for modern Jews to be authentically Jewish in their modern world, a way to conduct their lives by Jewish values not only in the synagogue but at home and in the community and in the office, downtown. Here in Reform Judaism, for me, was a way of understanding our tradition and values that could send us back to enhance the quality of our lives in all those little corners of our world.

And when I stood here twenty-eight years ago, having met the leadership of this congregation, I was excited by the hope that Westchester Reform Temple was a fertile field for my particular challenge and that the congregation and I could till that field together.

Now, twenty-eight years later, as I stand on the bimah for my last Rosh HaShanah, still with the butterflies, it is with my prayer of thanks for all the ways in which that hope has been fulfilled.

There are now seven Reform rabbis who have come from the families of this congregation. There are also two Orthodox rabbis who have sought out yet another path to their Jewish fulfillment. From our congregation have come one professional Reform Jewish educator, one temple administrator and two professionals in the national body of our Reform Movement. And there are all those who as lay volunteers stand in the front ranks of Jewish leadership in our community and in our country.

Here in this place tonight, I can look into the congregation and I can see some of those who had grown up in Reform Judaism and then discovered through these three decades, not always easily, that a basic tenet of Reform is its capacity to change, to re-form, not capriciously but thoughtfully, and we shall speak of some of those changes on Yom Kippur, when I share my vision of the future of this congregation. But for now, your willingness over the years to share in that process of change has been the fulfillment of a rabbi's hope and a source of a rabbi's strength.

In this place tonight, I can look out into the congregation and see some of those who through the years joined Westchester Reform Temple for whatever reason, sometimes for the reason they thought: that Reform Judaism was the easy Jewish way, the least demanding, the path of Jewish convenience. But what some of those very people have discovered over the years is that instead of one easy path, there is an array of compelling paths: whether a path into the sanctuary for Jewish prayers they can understand, or a path into the classrooms for Jewish knowledge they can understand, or a path into the social hall to foster a sense of Jewish community and human connectiveness that every human being can understand. Understanding is the key, and from understanding comes commitment. And the number of committed Jews in this Reform congregation is the fulfillment of a rabbi's hope and a source of a rabbi's strength. And for some of the rest of you who are here tonight, I like the phrase of the Jewish philosopher Franz Rosenzweig: "not yet," not yet committed.

There was another level of my excitement twenty-eight years ago, and that was excitement tinged with uncertainty. Because it was not only I who was coming to a new place and a new life but my entire family: Priscilla and our two young children, with Elsie not yet on the scene. We were coming from a friendly place and a friendly temple to this new place and our new temple, and it took very little time in this very welcoming community for that uncertainty to go away.

Twenty-eight years later, I can declare to you that no rabbi could be more richly blessed by a family than I have been, by those of my family who surround me and those who are no longer walking this earth. No rabbi ever had a family that understood better that to be a rabbi was not only to do a job but to live a life and that then was willing to share in that life.

The blessing is Priscilla, and Priscilla is Priscilla, which is why our life has never been boring. She wins the prize for the sheer number of rabbinic connections: daughter of a rabbi, wife of a rabbi, mother of a rabbi, and, now, mother-in-law of a rabbi. Priscilla is wife, mother, friend, and all the time she is Priscilla. When our son David was asked to address the Reform rabbinate in 1980 on the subject of the rabbi's family, he said, and I quote my son: "When my father is running around catering to others, it is my mother who takes care of the family, organizing, disciplining, explaining. She must comfort the mourner who calls on the phone when the rabbi is out of town, and she must be a secretary to all those congregants who call at midday and strangely proclaim, 'I didn't want to bother him at the office.'"

The blessing is our children, who came to understand with Priscilla's help how their father could sometimes be pulled in two directions, from the rabbi side and from the father side. There had to be times when they resented the rabbi side, but there were all those other times when they consoled me by standing next to me while I was being the rabbi. Our lawyer son, Jonathan, helps me with my logic, and not infrequently has a sermon been revised between the early service and the late service because Jonathan comes into my study and helps his father patch up some flaws in logic. Our rabbi son, David, now with his rabbi wife, Nancy, at his side, David and his father have talked family talk and rabbi talk for a long time, and both subjects with equal ease and with equal laughter.

And our daughter, Elsie. Elsie recently observed that the pattern of attendance at worship services being what it is, the assumption by many may be that these High Holy Day sermons will be my farewell to the congregation, even though I do not retire until next June 30. Therefore, suggested Elsie, I should announce tonight that my farewell message would be on some regular Friday night during the year, the date not to be announced in advance, and if you want to hear it—*Shabbat shalom*!

The blessings, the challenge, the hope, the butterflies. But what I could not anticipate twenty-eight years ago were all the doors of opportunity still undisclosed through which I would someday walk and which would enhance the landscape of my life.

Mine was the opportunity, as some of you will recall, to travel through Mississippi in 1964 at the peak of the Civil Rights struggle and to witness the human spirit striving to be free: to speak to that nine-year-old black boy who had written an essay, a copy of which he gave to me, from which I quote: "I want to become a psychiatrist. As a psychiatrist, I can help my fellowmen to get their fair right and dealing in life."

And there has been for me the opportunity to work hand in hand with other rabbis—Reform, Conservative, Orthodox, Reconstructionist—to learn firsthand how embracing unity can only strengthen Jewish destiny and how backbiting can only grind it down.

There was the opportunity to learn from Elie Wiesel "how truth can speak to power."

There was the opportunity, the grim opportunity, to stand at Auschwitz and to walk the road at Birkenau, from the place where the trains stopped to the place where the gas jets were turned on, and to know that I would never be the same again.

There was the opportunity to discover my second Jewish home in the Land of Israel: to marvel at the green places of its desert and the sparkling stones of its Jerusalem; to embrace the staunch spirit of its people; at times to be a loving critic of its leaders; and always, always to be a supporter of its noble cause, of its right to life and of its place in the sun of history.

There was the opportunity so many times of seeing history turn itself around: to see Russian Jews so long captive in their own land embark upon their great exodus, including the one hundred and fifty thousand who will come to Israel this year. And to see, wonder of wonders, enemies turn to allies, because if there could be Sadat and Begin together and if there could be Gorbachev and Bush together, there may yet be hope for the peoples of the Middle East together. In the words of the Yiddish proverb: "If you live long enough, you live to see everything." We should only live long enough.

All of those rich opportunities, and the richest one of all, what Rabbi Judah said in the Talmud: "Much have I learned from my teachers, more from my colleagues, and from my students the most."

From you, the members of this congregation, from those of longest standing to the ones for the first time here tonight, from you I have learned the most.

Because in my thirty-eight years as a rabbi and twenty-eight years with you, I have learned that a rabbi's life is never boring. Frustrating, sometimes; wearing, sometimes; annoying, sometimes; but never boring. Time plays funny tricks on a rabbi, but it never drags.

In my twenty-eight years here and my thirty-eight years as a rabbi, I have never stopped learning about the human condition. I have stood under the chuppah with brides and grooms and parents at their side, and I have learned that there are moments in human life when the thought of everything else—including caterers and flowers and table arrangements—gives way because in the loving eyes of those two people, the blessing of God descends into the world.

And with many of you, I have stood at the graveside and I have learned that in moments of life's mystery and death's mystery, a rabbi can say the prayers, but in truth there is nothing to say. I have learned from you that grief shatters, but sooner or later we are able to pick up the shattered pieces and put life together again, not as it was before but together nonetheless. I have learned that the grief of a parent losing a child is like no other grief in the world and that the scar of a Holocaust survivor is like no other scar in the world.

I have learned from you, as I learned from myself, that beyond all the other successes for which we may strive, the surpassing success is the Jewish one, *sh'lom bayit*—the well-being of our households, the togetherness of our families: husband and wife, parents and children, grandparents and grandchildren, sisters and brothers, the whole *mishpachah*. And like all other careers that need time and care and attention, this career of family needs no less: time to work through tensions and differences lest they assume the power of the destroyer. And on this road to family success, I have learned from you and from myself about the redeeming power of a sense of humor and the saving power of a good laugh.

Even when a marriage fails and the family divides, I have learned from some of you that there can still be *sh'lom bayit* in both parts of a divided family.

But I have also learned from some of you, sadly, from people who once loved but love no more, how feelings of anger and betrayal and vindictiveness can turn into weapons to hurt. I have even been witness to children pulled and pushed from both sides, parents hurting their own children: child abuse, family-style.

I have learned from you the miracle of *t'shuvah*, of reconciliation, between spouses, between parents and children, between members of a large family, between friends. I once preached a sermon on the destructive power of a grudge between two people, once close but no more, and how one of those people could die and the other would be left only with an empty grudge, and how these High Holy Days call for *t'shuvah* between human beings who bear grudges.

A week after Yom Kippur that year, a member of the congregation came to me and said that my sermon had moved her to call a relative from whom she had been alienated and estranged and that her telephone call was the first step in mending the grudge. By my own reckoning, that was one of the most successful sermons I have ever preached.

I have learned from you that there are givers and takers in this world and that the givers give not only of what they have but of who they are. And the takers are always on the take, always demanding, always one way, their way, and some of them even take handicapped parking spaces because it puts them close to the entrance, especially on a rainy day.

And above all, what you have taught me and what the years have taught me and what life keeps teaching me is the power of the human spirit, the God-given power to do the *t'shuvah*, to make the turn of which these Holy Days speak: from taking to more giving, from grief to more sunlight, from grudges to more forgiveness, from tearing life down and tearing ourselves down to crowning life with glory and honor.

After twenty-eight years, and this is not my farewell sermon, what prayer shall I speak on this sacred day of prayer?

The Chasidim tell of the simple peasant who stood before the ark.

"Lord of the universe," he said, "I am a simple man. Oh, how I wish I had the words to fashion beautiful prayers to give You thanks.

"So listen to me, God, as I recite the letters of the alphabet. Because You know how I feel. You take the letters, God, and You shape the words of thanks to You that are in my heart."

And the peasant recited, "*Alef, bet, gimel, daled...*"

And so I ask You, "What words, O God, can I speak for the blessings of my life?" So I simply set my blessings before You:

—the love of my family and how it has sustained me;

—the Torah of my people and how it has lighted my way;

—the partnership with this congregation and how it has taught me with love to be a rabbi;

—and Your blessing of life itself, O God, who has kept me alive and sustained me and brought me to this day.

I set these blessings before You, and now You, O God, You put them together into a hymn of my thanksgiving that will be acceptable before You, my Rock and my Redeemer.

Alef, bet, gimel, daled...
Amen.

Rosh HaShanah 1990/5751

To the Next Rabbi

Many years ago—as I related from this bimah several years ago—after a wedding ceremony at which I officiated, one of the guests, a young man in his mid-thirties, came up to me and identified himself as someone whose family had once belonged to the temple years ago, before they had moved away. I remembered him very well, and we talked about his years in religious school, his bar mitzvah and his confirmation. He told me that he was now married with children of his own and was actively involved in a synagogue of his own. And then he added wistfully, "And what I want you to know, Rabbi, is that my bar mitzvah took."

Tonight, at the end of *N'ilah*, with the last blast of the shofar, the Gates will close, and we will be on our way into a new year. And the highest compliment that could be paid to these hours we have shared—beyond what the music was like or the sermons or the words of the prayer book were like—the highest compliment would be that the High Holy Days took: that now some grudge would be mended; that now our shortcomings have been more honestly confronted and our blessings more generously appreciated; that now some healing has come to the pain of loss, some strength to the fear of loss of a beloved, a friend or a job. If all of that happens or if some of that happens, if we leave here tonight with new confidence, new direction, new hope, then we shall know with certainty that this year the High Holy Days took.

On this, my final Yom Kippur as rabbi of the congregation (and this is not my farewell sermon), I would share with you some of my own hopes and thoughts for the future of Westchester Reform Temple.

Like every such futuristic gaze, it cannot be contemplated without a glimpse into our past and our present. It cannot exclude the determination thirty-seven years ago of that handful of families to establish a congregation of their own, to come to worship together, to give their children a Jewish education, to mark the Jewish rites of passage of their lives. It cannot exclude those thirty-seven years from then until now, and it cannot exclude all of you whom those years have brought into our synagogue community. It cannot exclude how, through those years, that original, small collective of families has grown into an established religious institution in the community-at-large and in the larger community of Reform Judaism and in the world community of the Jewish people.

And through all those thirty-seven years, with all the diversity of needs and all the branching out of programs, the persistent challenge to the leadership of this congregation, to the lay and professional leadership, has been to keep the climate of feeling from ever getting cold, to keep this place personal, to encourage everyone to take his or her own personal place. I have a clue that tells me when that has happened. Because when someone makes reference to "my temple" (and I love to hear the children in our school say, "so-and-so goes to my temple"), or when a congregant speaks to me or to some other congregant and says, "our temple," then I know that our efforts have borne fruit. But when some congregant says to me, "your temple," I know, sadly, that he or she is officially a congregant but not yet personally.

So, grateful for the past, mindful of the present, I turn to the future with this letter addressed to the rabbi who will be my successor, whoever he or she may be.

Dear Colleague:

When you were asked during your interview why you would want to leave your present congregation and come to this one, you probably answered, as we all do, "because of the challenge." I can now promise you that in this place there will be no shortage of challenges. In fact, I have a few left over that you might be willing to take on, in your own way, of course, with your own style and with your own special touch.

For example, a challenge that first confronted me twenty-eight years ago and that I recently shared with the congregation: It happened in 1962, soon after our first High Holy Days. We were at a gathering in someone's home where a group of congregants had been brought together to meet the new rabbi and his wife. As we sat around the circle, we all told something about ourselves and our backgrounds, and as this one woman finished her statement, she added, "My husband and I want you to know, Rabbi, how much we enjoyed the High Holy Day services this year. And we're looking forward to next September, when we can come back to the temple again."

That lady has long since moved away, but when you, my colleague, look out into the congregation on your first High Holy Days a year from now, you will see a fair number of her counterparts.

I know a lot of them very well, and I can tell you that they are not alienated from their Jewishness or else they wouldn't be here. It's just that in their scheme of things, in their style of life, the Jewish cause and the Jewish covenant that are so paramount to some of us simply are not at the top of their list—not even serious contenders.

When a Gallup poll was investigating religious attitudes in America, one of the questions was, How important is religion in your life? According to the results, 55 percent of all Americans said that religion is very important. The number of Jews to whom religion is very important was 30 percent.

I know a lot of that other 70 percent very well, my colleague. And I know that many of them would be quick to tell you that even though they may not be synagogue goers, they feel their Jewish identity very strongly. They feel connected to their Jewish history and are proud of their Jewish heritage. And they are telling the absolute truth.

Because in truth, when it comes to what they do, their careers are what they do. Their museums and ballet and theater and opera are what they do. Their tennis and golf are what they do. But for some of them, when it comes to their Jewishness, it's something they only feel and not what they do, except perhaps when they do Pesach with their families or when they do Chanukah with their kids, and except perhaps for the High Holy Days, which they look forward to doing next September. In the words of Eugene Borowitz: "They are content to live as Americans with a little Jewishness thrown in (as long as it isn't disruptive)."

And there is your challenge, my colleague: to help them move from what they truly feel to what they are truly capable of doing; to put some of those incredible talents they have to Jewish work (and it doesn't have to be just in the synagogue); to put their Jewish values and their Jewish ethics into their secular American lives, even if at times it means disrupting those lives.

And what a challenge! To help them seek out the spiritual needs that many of them do not even know they have, except perhaps in a hospital bed, or at a graveside, or in a foxhole, except perhaps under a chuppah or on the bimah when they hand the Torah through the generations to the bar or bat mitzvah child or grandchild. Those moments are truly spiritual, but then the moment passes.

To you, my colleague, I give all those other challenges that await you in this congregation:

—the challenge of making new members feel welcome and old members feel wanted;

—the challenge of making the synagogue a Jewish home for everyone: for families and for singles; for Jews who were raised Orthodox, Conservative, Reform or none-of-the-above; for those who are Jews by birth or Jews by conversion or neither of those and yet, with their Jewish spouses, have chosen Judaism as the religion of their home and the religion of their family, and this is their synagogue home;

—the challenge, on many a Friday night, to welcome the person standing alone at the *Oneg Shabbat*, awkwardly jiggling the coffee cup because no one walks over to extend a hand of welcome;

—the challenge of children in families of this congregation who have been taught very young how to thrive in their close circle of friends but have never been taught how to open the circle and let some in from the outside;

—the challenge of persuading parents that the bar and bat mitzvah of their children is a rite of passage to the next stage of their Jewish learning about the ethics and values of their tradition and is *not* a path to the nearest exit door of the religious school for a quick getaway. It is the challenge of persuading parents that the decision whether to proceed to confirmation is not a decision for a thirteen year old but for responsible Jewish parents who assume their parental role responsibly. It is the challenge of persuading parents that they are at least equal partners with the synagogue in the Jewish upbringing of their children. A family resigned from our temple because, the mother said, "There were too many things that went on in the classroom when the teacher should have been concentrating on the ritual observances that our family does not do and will not do at home." I said to her, "We can only be your Jewish partners. We cannot be your Jewish surrogates." And she resigned.

A mountain of challenges, my colleague, and you'll have to take your time. But what I can promise you is that you will not face those challenges alone. Because this congregation has come to realize, I hope, that what we rabbis need are not disciples to sit at our feet but allies who will stand at our side, who will make the rocky climb with us, who will care about each other just as we care about them, who will comfort each other just as we try to comfort them.

So for each challenge in the pile, I promise you a cadre of allies. Some cadres are too small but a cadre nonetheless, who will climb with you:

—a cadre of students who will sit and study every Shabbat morning to make the Torah come to life;

—a cadre of parents for whom the Jewish upbringing of their children calls for standards that are higher rather than lower, that will move from feeling to doing;

—a cadre in this sanctuary on a regular Shabbat who have discovered, in Abraham Heschel's words, "a palace of time," in which the goal is not to own but to be, not to have but to share, not to control but to give;

—a cadre of those who are *Ohavei Yisrael*, whose own passionate commitment to the Land and the people of Israel, to its right to be and thrive and rescue lives, is on the way to becoming the shared commitment of this entire congregation;

—a cadre of allies who want to make God's world better and God's humanity better, who have brought refugees from Vietnam and immigrants from the Soviet Union to this community and have given them a second chance in their lives, who have brought Jewish poor from the boroughs of New York into this synagogue and made them feel as if it were their second home. And here now, even as I read this letter, there is an ever-growing cadre in this congregation who will contribute to MAZON for the millions of people who are hungry and starving. An ever-growing number will write out a check in the amount of money that the food that they did not eat on this fast of Yom Kippur would have cost.

And I leave for you, proudly, a cadre of lay leadership for whom the highest Jewish value is ethical integrity. I attended a meeting at which a particular issue had to be resolved, and the choice was between a businesslike decision that was well within the bounds of the law and a truly ethical decision that went beyond the legal requirements. They opted for the ethical decision and it cost the temple some extra money, and the stature of the temple soared heavenward.

And, finally, I leave for you a congregation that in the spirit of Reform Judaism is always open to change, that over the years has witnessed a change in the prayer book, a change in the amount of Hebrew, a change in the nature of the music. Each new group of officers and trustees, each cantor, each assistant rabbi, each rabbinic intern has opened a door to change. And as you, my colleague, will open doors of your own, I promise you that the congregation will listen. And I promise you that they will discuss and discuss and discuss. And once a decision has been reached, I promise you, in the loftiest spirit of our tradition, that not everyone will agree to the change.

You should also know, my colleague, that there is one change about which some of your future congregants are a bit shaky, especially those who have been connected to the temple for a long time. Because when there has been only one senior rabbi for all these years, the prospect of a new one whom they don't yet know can be an ominous one. A few of them have even mentioned that when I retire, they might resign and not belong to a temple.

And I want you, my successor, to know, how I have answered them—something like this: "I understand your shakiness, but I can assure you that whoever is chosen as rabbi will deserve to be the rabbi of this congregation. I understand your unsettled feeling, but if you allow that feeling to push you away and sever your ties with the temple, then what I have labored for all these years will have been branded a failure. Because if all I have succeeded in doing is forge a bond between you and me and not between you and the synagogue and everything that this synagogue represents from generation to generation, then I have not done the job I set out to do twenty-eight years ago. But I like to think that I have and that all of you, all the generations, will stay exactly where you are with your arms open.

And since some of them have even said to me that my being their friend has transcended my being their rabbi, I wanted them to know that there is no better way to express that friendship than by being there for you as allies at your side. Because, after all, you're going to be my rabbi, and they'd better be good to my rabbi!

If that happens, God willing, someday I will be able to go up to you, the new rabbi, and to this congregation and say what that young man said to me at the wedding: that my twenty-eight years at Westchester Reform Temple took. Because there they are still learning, still discovering, still caring, and their arms are open.

May God grant strength to you as you will soon take up the unfinished task, even as God has strengthened me.

May those who will now call you their rabbi walk with you and climb with you closer to their God and their people and their humanity, and closer to each other.

And may you, my colleague, in your way, with your style, with your own special touch, find as much challenge and fulfillment in your years as I have in mine.

With love and blessing,

I remain,

Your colleague and your new congregant.

Amen.

Yom Kippur 1990/5751

Spiritual Aging

When I was in kindergarten or first grade, I remember coming home after the first day of school and telling my parents that I had a very pretty teacher, and also that she was old. I was five, and I'm sure that my teacher must have been no more than twenty-five.

I am now seventy-three, and when I speak of someone as old, it is usually a person in his or her nineties. And I'm sure that when I'm eighty, God willing, "old" will be someone over one hundred—always that necessary buffer.

So I believe I speak on behalf of my own general age-group when I say that "old" is what we are not yet. Getting older, yes, but not old. Old is a condition, fixed in one place. Getting older is a process, moving right along. Old is a cesspool, whereas getting older is a flowing river. And I know some people in their nineties, God bless them, who are still getting older.

Much of our experience regarding the aging process is about the onset of limitations, some physical, some cerebral, and about how we are able to respond to them creatively. I shall focus my remarks on yet another aspect of growing older with its own creative possibilities. Specifically, I would call your attention to the spiritual dimension of growing older. My premise derives from an incident reported by Rabbi Harold Kushner. One of Agatha Christie's husbands was an archaeologist. A reporter asked the renowned mystery writer, "Miss Christie, what is it like to be married to an archaeologist?" to which she responded, "It's wonderful. The older I get, the more interested he is in me."

Thus my premise for this morning: that the older we get, the more spiritually interesting and interested we are capable of becoming.

But before anything else, we should revisit that word "spiritual." The closest we come to it in the Bible is a familiar word, *kadosh*, usually translated as "holy, sacred, nonphysical." But in its original meaning, *kadosh* is to be separate, unique, other than the ordinary. God, however differently each of us may conceive of God, is *Kadosh*—Other, with a capital O.

And according to our Jewish teaching, each of us is endowed with this *kadosh* capacity, which allows us to connect in one way or another with that *Kadosh* Other, with the capital O. In the words of Rabbi Lawrence Kushner, "the self of

389

the I with the Self of the universe," which is what we mean by "spiritual." When we feel weak or diminished or lonely, we can reach out to that *Kadosh* Other for strength and support and healing. Or when we are blessed with some good fortune, some gift in life, we can reach out and say, "Thank you, God, that in Your world such good things can happen."

Some psychologists use the term "spiritual instinct," inborn, and part of what convinces them of its existence is the prevalence of spiritual feelings among young children, before they have been exposed to any religious instruction or indoctrination. In the words of Robert Coles, professor of psychiatry at Harvard Medical School, "These children were revealing an unusual capacity to strive for connection beyond themselves in knowing what their inner world is all about," or to use our Jewish vocabulary, to know what this spiritual *Kadosh* connection is all about.

But then what happens? The children grow into adolescents, and with hormones getting busy and everything else going on in their lives, spiritual matters are not at the top of their list. And then they become adults, and more and more, matters of the inner life give way to matters of the outer one—to careers, to the needs of their families, to making things work and getting things done. When children have to be given breakfast and sent off or taken to school, there is little time to ponder what life is all about. And there is scant attention to the wonderful mystery of our days and years on this earth when the mystery at hand is how to get the bills paid and still have a positive balance at the end of the month. I am convinced that one reason for the current wave of spirituality among some of those very men and women in their young and middle years is that they have begun to ask what else there is and want to find their way back to that inner *kadosh* world.

And eventually come the autumn years, and those old responsibilities that once ruled our lives are behind us, somewhat. The children are on their own, somewhat. The clock is no longer such a tyrant, somewhat. And there is time left over for other things, including *kadosh* things.

And if we are in relatively good health, which most elders are, even though the machinery of our bodies may be slowing down, even though our memory for names may not be what it used to be, even though our physical energy may be springing leaks, our spiritual energy is affected not at all. To the exact contrary: It may be more ready than ever to be fired up because now, with time and a slower pace on our side, we are ready for what Zalman Schachter-Shalomi calls "Spiritual Eldering," being open to the mysteries we never confronted before, open to questions we never asked before, open to insights we never probed before.

Consider the following contrast. Many years ago, I was walking in downtown White Plains, New York, and in front of me was a mother with her child. The child had stopped, entranced by a caterpillar inching its way along the side of a leaf. The mother was annoyed and told him to stop dawdling because she had so much to do. And she yanked that child away from his *kadosh* moment of spiritual wonderment at God's world.

Now, contrast that with the following essay written by a child in the third grade. It is entitled "What Is a Grandmother?" and I quote it in part.

> A grandmother is a lady who has no little children of her own. She likes other people's. A grandfather is a man grandmother.
> Grandmothers don't have to do anything except be there. When they take us for walks, they slow down past things like pretty flowers and caterpillars. They never say "hurry up."
> Grandmothers don't have to be smart, they only have to answer questions like "Why isn't God married?" and "How come dogs chase cats?" When they read to us, they don't skip lines or mind if we ask for the same story over again.
> Everyone should try to have a grandmother, especially if you don't have a TV, because they are the only grownups who have time.

So, with time on our side, how do we cultivate the art of Spiritual Eldering? And I would propose an answer that comes from an episode we read from the Torah portion of just a month ago.

Jacob is fleeing from his brother, Esau. He lies down to sleep with a rock as his pillow and then has this strange dream: He sees a ladder standing on the ground with its top reaching to the heavens and angels climbing up and down. Jacob awakens from his dream and exclaims, "Surely God was in this place and I did not know it."

Thus, the itinerary for our own Spiritual Eldering, up and down that ladder.

Up there, when we think the heartwarming thoughts about those who have graced our lives and still do either in person or in memory, about all the good times when life smiled on us and God's world was good to us.

And then to come down here and to give something back in return, down here to make good things happen in God's world and in the lives of God's children, to give back some of our time and some of our expertise and some of our money. And if we need examples, it is reported that the most generous givers to philanthropic causes tend to be from those aged sixty-five to seventy-four. If we need an example, then it comes from this population of elders who continually provide a major pool of volunteer service *l'taken et ha-olam*, "to make the world better," whether as aides in a hospital or as surrogate grandparents in classrooms or as advisers to start-up businesspeople or a myriad of other possibilities.

And if down here there are parents to be taken care of, as someone said, it is not role reversal and it is not the children now becoming the parents, it is simply the children giving back to the parents who gave so much to them, down here at the bottom of the ladder.

And again up there, in solitary moments, like spiritual seekers whatever their age, when we seek a rudder in the storm of illness or financial distress or the grief of a loss or the pain of loneliness, and then to some down here, in our own synagogues, in a service of healing or a support group for grieving to find strength from each other, or in a class of Torah to find strength from the wisdom of a text, or in a Shabbat service to find shalom of heart and soul. Down here at the bottom of the *kadosh* ladder, no longer suffering from the pain of self-imposed isolation but reaching out to give strength and gain strength. Down here, making it through a rough day.

And up there, in solitude, to ponder the mysteries and meaning of life and death, including our own life and our own death. Because we who have spent a lifetime affirming life and preserving life, now that the autumn has come, we know that winter is in the offing and that our day on earth will come to an end. So we try to fit together all the pieces of our lifetime, what someone called "A Life Review": how some of what we did made a difference and how some of what we failed to do could have made a difference but we didn't know it at the time. We include in our life review the values and the truths we have come to prize the most, and when we do that, we have, in the words of the Psalmist, "gotten us a heart of wisdom."

And then we carry that wisdom down the ladder, and hopefully we do what many Jews through the generations have done: We compose an ethical will as a message for our children and grandchildren that will outlive our own wintertime. We write about life and love and disappointment and courage and completeness and Jewishness. It may be in the form of a letter or a recording on tape or simply in words spoken and thoughts expressed on an ordinary day. In whatever form, it will fulfill a major Jewish mitzvah: "You shall teach them diligently to your children."

But even more than that, when we were up there putting the pieces together, now and again we encountered a broken piece not yet fixed, a family member or a once-good friend, once close and caring but for whatever reason, not anymore.

And then we come down the ladder with our broken pieces and we go about fixing what deserves to be fixed. We engage in the serious spiritual business of settling our grudges, of seeking forgiveness and granting it, of tending to what someone called "our unfinished business," and we don't wait for Yom Kippur.

I read about a nurse who had spent twenty years working at a hospice facility. She reported that the most important lesson she learned about terminally ill patients is that there is an "easy death" and a "hard death." When people die hard, they struggle. When they die easy, it all happens peacefully, sometimes because their unfinished business has been completed.

And then she said, "All of us have unfinished business. You have it, and I have it, and most patients have it. It is impossible to die in peace unless the unfinished business is put to rest." To which we can add from the wisdom of our own tradition that no one need wait until the deathbed to finish it.

And thus the way toward our own Spiritual Eldering:

Up there, to utter the silent thank you's for the blessings of our lives and then down here to give something back that will bring blessing into other lives;

Up there to seek strength and down here to share strength;

Up there to review our lives and down here to transmit our wisdom and to fix the broken pieces and not wait.

And yet one more ingredient to that *kadosh* ladder for up there and down here. Mary Pipher has written a book entitled *Another Country: Navigating the Emotional Terrain of Our Elders*. During the course of her research she interviewed a man who had been married sixty-three years and asked him to what he attributed the longevity and stability of his marriage. He responded, "It's very simple. Every morning when I get up, I look in the mirror and I say, "You're not such a prize, either." With all those other ingredients, a sense of humor about life and the world and people, and mostly about ourselves. Whoever surrenders that is no longer aging but just old.

I conclude with a quote from Abraham Joshua Heschel. He made this statement not about aging but about Shabbat. But of everything I have ever read, nothing comes as close to a description of Spiritual Aging as his words about Shabbat, which he calls "a palace in time." Heschel writes, "There is a realm of time where the goal is not to have but to be, not to own but to share, not to subdue but to be in accord."

And so, for those in their autumn years, there are all those doors up there and down here into the palace of time. And once we enter them, *unlike* Jacob in the Torah, we shall be able to say, "God is in this very place, and I know it very well." Amen.

Emeritus Shabbat 1999/5759

Trying to Be a Mensch

Every human being can designate markers along the path of his or her own character development. These are mine.

Limping Along

When I was five years old, a life-threatening infection in my right hip necessitated three successive surgeries. The procedures left me with a right leg that was shorter than the left and limited mobility of the right hip. When I eventually returned to school, my right leg was casted from foot to hip, and a wheelchair was my mode of transportation. After a year had passed, I could stand and walk on my own but with a noticeable limp. Since baseball had been a special passion of mine, my friends allowed me to wield the bat, and whenever I succeeded in hitting the ball, a team member would run the bases in my stead.

The experience of that illness and its aftermath have had a defining influence on my character development. Even though the ordeal had to be traumatic for my parents (they had already endured the loss of two young children and I was close to being number three), they managed to treat me not as essentially handicapped or disabled but as a normal kid. I learned from them the power of constructive nurturing. Through all the years since, whenever I come into contact with someone who is disabled, I try, not always with total success, to relate to that person as a normal human being who simply happens to have a handicap.

During successive surgeries, I received extraordinary kindness and support from my doctors and nurses. Consequently, at the age of ten, I decided to become a doctor and provide to others the same nurturing support that had been extended to me. But some years later, when I was assigned to dissect a starfish in a high school zoology class, my hand trembled so uncontrollably that then and there, I decided to seek an alternative outlet for my nurturing aspirations. And that's how I later determined to become a rabbi. As no stranger to the experience of pain, I could, perhaps, reach out to other human beings in their own times of physical or emotional distress.

Constructive Nurturing

As the years passed, my entrance into the domain of the handicapped enabled me to witness human behavior not generally encountered or acknowledged, like that of the bus passengers who offered me their seats and the pedestrians who raised their hands to hold up traffic when lights changed too quickly for me to make my way safely across the street. Whenever I find myself in New York City, the day offers yet more testimony of human caring. But then, of course, there is the underside, especially when handicapped parking spaces are usurped by nonhandicapped drivers—human nature degraded.

The experience of that childhood illness must have proven to me the vigor of my own survival instincts. Whether from nature (the genes that I inherited) or from nurture (all the love and support I received) or from both, the survival instinct of that five year old stood by me for whatever else my life might have in store.

Slinking Home

I grew up in Cincinnati, gateway to the South, where "Negroes" were perceived as inept and inferior and were to be kept "in their place." Nonetheless, our backyard handball game always included Frankie, the black son of the janitor from the house next door. During one of our games, a tenant in our building called out from the window of her apartment: "I just spoke to the landlord (unfortunately, my own grandfather), and he said that Frankie should go home, and he can't play in our yard anymore." To this day, I visualize Frankie, humiliated, slinking from our yard to his. I must have felt my own share of disgrace because years later, as a student at Hebrew Union College, I joined with my classmate Michael Robinson and others in sit-ins at restaurants that refused to serve blacks. We also participated in protest marches at the Cincinnati Conservatory of Music, which soon thereafter admitted blacks into its student body. And in the early years of my rabbinate, I addressed the local Rotary Club during Brotherhood Week. In the course of my remarks, I pointed to the fact that there were no blacks at the luncheon. How, I asked, is it possible to speak on the theme of brotherhood when they excluded human brothers who were not born with white skin? Several Rotarians stormed out of the room. Some rabbis I know are invigorated by such confrontations, but I am not one of them. It is not in my nature. Yet there have been many times in my life when there was no alternative but to take a stand, and at such times, I could not remain sitting down.

Still, all these years later, if I am annoyed by someone's ineptitude and if that person happens to be African American, the old stereotype springs up and takes me by surprise. Despite all my commitment to human equality and to a lifetime of acting on its behalf, the ghosts still have a way of jumping out of the closet. What I do then is call them what they are and send them off packing—because I still remember Frankie.

A Day in Court

When I was in my teens, an uncle of mine who served as a judge in Family Court in Cincinnati invited me to attend and observe a session. That day, a teenager was standing before the judge on the charge of stealing. "What do you have to say for yourself?" my uncle asked him. The young man replied, "I did it, Judge. I know I've got the punishment coming. So just put me in jail. "At that moment, the boy's mother stood up and berated her son: "You just can't stand there and say that you did it and should be put in jail—because then they'll let you out of jail, you'll do it again, and you'll go to jail again. That's not why I clean houses every day from morning until night and hold so many jobs, not so you can stand there and say, 'I did it and put me in jail' and then get out and do it again. You're going to shape up and account to me."

I have never forgotten that woman who called her son to account for setting his moral bar so low. I have tried to apply her message of moral responsibility and accountability to my own life and rabbinate. That has meant telling congregations that they are responsible for conducting their affairs on the highest ethical level in the way they deal with staff, in the compassion they extend to their members, and in the conduct of their financial affairs. Congregational laypeople and rabbis fulfill their own ethical responsibilities not only by avoiding the big pitfalls (cheating, exploiting, stealing) but also by minding the smaller potholes (causing embarrassment to another human being, not heeding a call for help, not listening with their total selves). I consider myself a fairly ethical person, but whenever I trip into some of those potholes, I hear the voice of that mother calling her son to account.

The Accusing Finger

Criticism hurts, whether concerning something I did or did not do or regarding something I said or should have said. From early on, Priscilla—my loving wife and, when necessary, my loving critic—helped me sort out the merits of an indictment. Was I fair in what I said or what I did? Did I take into account what the other person might have been feeling? And based on those helpful questions,

I was able to keep my mind open and to evaluate the accusation that had been leveled at me. Even when the harshness of the criticism might have been deemed unjustified, I was still able to look for a kernel of validity and, if I found one, to redirect myself accordingly. What I have striven for is a degree of humility, not self-effacement but self-honesty. As I have learned from the midrash, a person should have two pieces of paper, one in each pocket. One of the papers reads, "I am created in the image of God," and the other reads, "I am but a particle of dust." It is for us to determine which piece of paper to take out in response to a particular time and situation.

Filling the Glass

Last November, I was scheduled for surgery (the hip again). Having proceeded through all of the presurgical testing, I was lying on the gurney in a surgical gown, all ready for the operating room, when one of the medical personnel noticed a sore on the back of my thigh. The surgeon then announced that he could not perform the operation for fear of infection. I was devastated. "What do I do now?" I asked him. "You get dressed and go home, and we'll reschedule." After recovering from the shock, I asked myself the same question: "What do I do now?" I answered my question: "I'll reschedule for three weeks from today, which means that I will be able to celebrate Thanksgiving with my family."

It goes back to the vigor of my survival instinct that was an outcome of my childhood illness. I learned early on to make the best of what starts out as not so good. It's not just the human power of positive thinking but the power of positive acting. It's not so much seeing the glass half full instead of half empty but looking for a way to refill the glass that circumstances have emptied. Some glasses, however, can never be refilled. When my wife died, the glass was shattered altogether. But by now there is yet another glass filled with memories, with family, with friends, with life, even as that first one still lies in broken pieces. It's the attempt to make the sun shine even on a dreary day. It's the energy to search out the redeeming qualities in people from whom we would otherwise keep our distance. The highest compliment I ever received as a rabbi was, "You make us think we are better than we are, and that makes us try to be better."

A Work in Progress

When it comes to character development, I'm still learning. Not long ago, on a day when I was experiencing much physical discomfort and feeling discouraged, I had to call the office of an organization I serve as a board member that finds affordable housing for the homeless. The woman who answered the phone said,

"How are you doing, Jack?" "Oh, I'm still on crutches," I replied, with a real kvetch in my voice. She responded, "Good for you!" I felt viscerally annoyed at her response but said nothing. After I finished the call, I recalled that the woman I had been talking to is permanently confined to a wheelchair. From her vantage point, "Good for you!" is a loud cheer for someone who is able to walk on crutches. I had placed before me my own stumbling block—feeling sorry for myself—and as a result, I had totally misconstrued the encounter. Suffice it to say that character is not simply a list of attributes to be enumerated but, for each of us, a work in progress. Essential to the task is a sense of humor—the ability and the willingness to laugh at people, at life, and mostly at ourselves.

At the End of the Day

I'm eighty years old and still trying to live by the earthy Jewish advice that rises to the power of a command: Try to be a mensch.

Spring 2006/5766

978-0-595-39461-6
0-595-39461-2

Printed in the United States
52937LVS00003B/22